Springer Series in Design and Innovation

Volume 34

Springer Series in Design and Innovation (SSDI) publishes books on innovation and the latest developments in the fields of Product Design, Interior Design and Communication Design, with particular emphasis on technological and formal innovation, and on the application of digital technologies and new materials. The series explores all aspects of design, e.g. Human-Centered Design/User Experience, Service Design, and Design Thinking, which provide transversal and innovative approaches oriented on the involvement of people throughout the design development process. In addition, it covers emerging areas of research that may represent essential opportunities for economic and social development.

In fields ranging from the humanities to engineering and architecture, design is increasingly being recognized as a key means of bringing ideas to the market by transforming them into user-friendly and appealing products or services. Moreover, it provides a variety of methodologies, tools and techniques that can be used at different stages of the innovation process to enhance the value of new products and services.

The series' scope includes monographs, professional books, advanced textbooks, selected contributions from specialized conferences and workshops, and outstanding Ph.D. theses.

The volumes of the series are single-blind peer-reviewed.

Keywords: Product and System Innovation; Product design; Interior design; Communication Design; Human-Centered Design/User Experience; Service Design; Design Thinking; Digital Innovation; Innovation of Materials.

How to submit proposals

Proposals must include: title, keywords, presentation (max 10,000 characters), table of contents, chapter abstracts, editors'/authors' CV.

In case of proceedings, chairmen/editors are requested to submit the link to conference website (incl. relevant information such as committee members, topics, key dates, keynote speakers, information about the reviewing process, etc.), and approx. number of papers.

Proposals must be sent to: series editor Prof. Francesca Tosi (francesca.tosi@unifi.it) and/or publishing editor Mr. Pierpaolo Riva (pierpaolo.riva@springer.com).

Daniel Raposo · João Neves · Ricardo Silva
Editors

Perspectives on Design III

Research, Education and Practice

Springer

Editors
Daniel Raposo
School of Applied Arts
Polytechnic Institute of Castelo Branco
Castelo Branco, Portugal

João Neves
School of Applied Arts
Polytechnic Institute of Castelo Branco
Castelo Branco, Portugal

Ricardo Silva
School of Applied Arts
Polytechnic Institute of Castelo Branco
Castelo Branco, Portugal

ISSN 2661-8184 ISSN 2661-8192 (electronic)
Springer Series in Design and Innovation
ISBN 978-3-031-43515-7 ISBN 978-3-031-43516-4 (eBook)
https://doi.org/10.1007/978-3-031-43516-4

This Springer imprint is published by the registered company Springer Nature Switzerland AG
The registered company address is: Gewerbestrasse 11, 6330 Cham, Switzerland

Paper in this product is recyclable.

Preface

The purpose of design is the conception of artefacts with value and utility for human beings, which have the potential to facilitate the use, understanding, communication, access, comfort, and safety of the user.

By excluding the human factor in the design project, we turn objects into a mere formal exercise that does not achieve design status. Design exists for people and design artefacts make sense in a social context. In these times where exclusivity, equality and sustainability are proclaimed, social design emerges as an innovative way of designing where people are put first and thus, refer that design goes far beyond the aesthetics of the product.

As a discipline and project activity, design combines multiple factors, including ethical, logical-functional and aesthetic, operational requirements, production, and economic constraints, determined by the context, compatible with the needs, aspirations, and lifestyles of the addressees. Design implies the identification of data, and its analysis and synthesis are essential to generate information and knowledge, allowing informed decisions to be made throughout the design process. Through an analytical action of the respective data, it is possible to identify patterns, trends, and gaps, as well as to better understand the needs and behaviours of stakeholders and users in a competitive context, as well as to evaluate the interest, performance, and impact of design proposals.

From the author's perspective, design should be the result of an enlightened view of the problem in a context, constituting itself as a creative manifestation that aims to express ideas and concepts and fulfil a useful function for people, considering a cultural context, time, and market.

On the other hand, from the perspective of product production, design plays a fundamental role in the optimization and efficiency of processes, both in saving resources, reducing waste, environmental impact, and improving energy efficiency, namely through the circularity of the production cycle, all of which ends up referring us to the current trend of sustainable design.

Considering merely the object, design ensures the utility of things, optimizing the form and performance of artefacts for human factors (physical, visual, symbolic, and emotional) and in a sustainable way in the social, environmental, and economic dimensions.

From a design perspective, artefacts are interfaces that mediate the communication or performance of useful functions to people in a context of use, in a complexity of relationships between the individual and the product (including at the end of the product's life). The design object fulfils aesthetic, cultural, symbolic, and functional functions in full combination.

Thus, in design aesthetics plays one role from the various requirements for the good performance of artefacts and design is the way to give shape to these same objects, considering that man is at the centre of design activity.

In recent decades, design and design thinking have been highlighted for their strategic contribution in the development and active implementation, reality, it is possible to affirm that it is the catalyzing strategy for innovation, regeneration processes, and improvement action in research, teaching, business, government, or social contexts.

Research and innovation processes in design have gained importance in both academia and industry, seeking to respond to social problems, especially in complex frameworks or even contributing to advances in the technological field.

Future Design consist in co-creating artefacts for future scenarios, which are defined based on information about stakeholders, key resources, signals, trends, drivers, and forecasts. Therefore, Future Design aligns current needs with future values.

If we take as a reference the 17 Sustainable Development Goals defined by UN for the year 2030, we get the clear notion that design research can actively and significantly contribute to addressing the most pressing global challenges, such as poverty, hunger, inequality, climate change, and quality education, just to highlight a few. Within this scenario, we observe how Design also holds a strong social component, where it plays an important role in making the world more inclusive.

Taking all these factors into account, the book we are now publishing is a good example of the alignment of design research with UNESCO's 2030 Sustainable Development Goals, as can be seen in two sections:

I. Communication Design and Design Education as a Catalyst for Change
II. Fashion Design and Product Design for Sustainability and Collaboration

The chapters of the first section seek to deepen knowledge on the contribution of co-design methodologies to new models of governance that are more open and participatory, models of cooperation and development integrating the perspective of stakeholders. In the same section we find articles that inquire about the multidisciplinary and integrative character of design, as well as about models of design teaching, considering interaction, social expectations, and environmental problems.

The second section presents a set of chapters that explore the role of imagination in design, the challenges brought by trends for fashion design practice in the post-industrial era, the relationships between fashion design education and sustainability, the Circular Economy, Upcycling technique, and the study of Prospective Ergonomic. Finally, the contribution of furniture design in the creation of more collaborative and sharing scenarios, as well as intersections between design research, the business sector, music, and performing arts.

The chapters presented are the result of an invitation made by the Steering Committee to the authors who best demonstrated their research skills with the best papers presented at the 8th EIMAD—International Meeting of Research in Music, Arts and Design, 2022, Portugal. Nevertheless, new, and relevant contents are presented, new perspectives on design research, its teaching and professional practice.

Although we recommend reading this book in its entirety, it allows reading centred on themes and by chapter.

Castelo Branco, Portugal

Daniel Raposo
João Neves
Ricardo Silva

Contents

Fashion Design and Product Design for Sustainability and Collaboration

Communication Design and Design Education as a Catalyst for Change

Youth Participation in Local Governance: Co-designing in the Democracy Reloading Initiative

Olga Glumac, Anne Grønsund, Laura Van de Vyver, Ellen De Grauwe, Filipa Pereira, Amal Hamich, and Laszlo Foldi

Abstract This paper investigates co-design methodologies aimed at enhancing local democracy practices through stakeholder engagement and direct cooperation between children and/or young people and municipal workers. The authors introduce their approaches to implementing the Democracy Reloading framework in their respective regional/national practices. Democracy Reloading, launched in 2015 as an initiative between Erasmus+ Youth and European Solidarity Corps National Agencies, is a comprehensive programme that identifies 24 essential competencies for effectively involving young people in decision-making within municipalities. The authors emphasise the significance of capacity building and mentorship for fostering long-term intergenerational collaboration, highlighting key findings from their co-design practices in Belgium, Norway, and Portugal. The paper underscores the collaborative efforts of Erasmus+ Youth National Agencies, practitioners, and experts, aiming to contribute to structural changes in local governance. The co-design approach aims to ensure setting up the foundations of the necessary changes

O. Glumac (✉)
LoCY—Lab of Collaborative Youth, Figueira da Foz, Portugal
e-mail: olga.glumac@gmail.com

A. Grønsund
Lindesnes Municipality, Norway
e-mail: anne.gronsund@lindesnes.kommune.no

L. Van de Vyver
East Flanders, Belgium

E. De Grauwe
Bataljong, Antwerp, Belgium
e-mail: ellen.degrauwe@bataljong.be

F. Pereira
Braga, Portugal

A. Hamich · L. Foldi
BIJ—Bureau International Jeunesse, Bruxelles, Belgium
e-mail: amal.hamich@cfwb.be

L. Foldi
e-mail: laszlo.foldi@cfwb.be

D. Raposo et al. (eds.), *Perspectives on Design III*, Springer Series in Design and Innovation 34, https://doi.org/10.1007/978-3-031-43516-4_1

in a systematic way. By exploring this topic, the paper sheds light on the relevance of this initiative for social innovation at the European and national scales.

Keywords Youth participation · Local governance · Co-design · Democracy Reloading

1 Introduction

This paper describes and analyses the approaches to the co-designing and operationalisation of collaborative frameworks and new democratic practices through intergenerational partnerships at the municipal level. They upvote the knowledge that already exists on the application of co-design in active youth citizenship [1], for democracy [2] and social innovation [3]. The authors start from problem framing to defining a roadmap for social innovation through systematic change [4]. They describe attempts to embed co-design capability within social systems to improve their functionality towards youth participation in local governance.

The establishment of norms for youth participation and the alignment of expectations between young people and adults in families, schools, neighbourhoods, and cities are pivotal factors being addressed. Schools have the potential to serve as effective gateways to citizenship by actively promoting the development of citizen-driven competencies and ensuring young individuals have the freedom to exercise their rights. However, expanding civic participation beyond schools to the neighbourhood and municipal level often remains limited to youth councils [5], participatory budgeting initiatives [6] and youth-led projects within youth associations. The need to institutionalise youth participation [7] and establish youth-friendly environments in municipalities remains. With it, young individuals may feel more welcomed and valued in democratic processes. This includes providing accessible physical spaces, utilising digital platforms, and implementing policies that enable the engagement of diverse youth populations in the long-term. Inclusivity empowers young people to contribute their unique perspectives, breaking down barriers and promoting a sense of belonging and ownership.

Efforts to strengthen democracy through local youth participation align with the Sustainable Development Goals (SDGs) defined by UNESCO 2030. SDG 4, focused on Quality Education, underscores the importance of education for sustainable development and the promotion of global citizenship. All relevant stakeholders such as policymakers, municipal workers, professors, other professionals in the youth field, students and young people in general with the requisite knowledge and skills contribute to the establishment of a more balanced democratic society. Moreover, youth participation in democracy can support SDG 16, which centres on Peace, Justice, and Strong Institutions. This goal aims to foster peaceful and inclusive societies, ensure universal access to justice, and build effective and accountable institutions at all levels. Young people engaged in democratic processes help cultivate transparency, responsiveness, diversification of ideas and solutions and participatory governance, which can enhance the realisation of SDG 16.

The New European Bauhaus initiative, launched by the European Commission in 2020, seeks to integrate sustainability, aesthetics, and inclusivity in the design and creation of urban spaces. While not directly correlated, the principles of inclusivity and participation embedded in the New European Bauhaus initiative align with the concept of involving young people in shaping their communities and engaging them in decision-making processes. Both initiatives share common objectives of fostering inclusivity, sustainability, and active citizenship, albeit employing distinct approaches.

Youth empowerment represents a complex challenge, and the authors critically examine existing barriers that hinder progress. In some cases, these barriers include the lack of, (i) diversification of engagement formats when it comes to youth citizenship; (ii) long-term or day-to-day practices promoted to youth; and (iii) and the effective involvement of local authorities and decision-makers (schools, other relevant institutions) in supporting and amplifying youth voices. The authors consider that youth citizenship is achieved when young individuals are ready to express their opinions and critically reflect on the actions that have an impact on their lives (e.g. conditions at school to eat healthy meals, propose reading materials, recommend how public space should be used, etc.); while people in intermediary or decision-making positions take those opinions on board, continuing discussion with young people and jointly finding the solutions. With the democratisation of processes through the participatory design movement, there have already been advancements when children and young people co-design educational programmes [8], policies [9] and other matters of their concern [10]. In some cases, the children and young people are trained designers while in others they are in-training through collaborative projects that foster youth participation. There is no distinction in ownership and social responsibility between a trained young designer and a young designer in training [11]. These approaches can be influenced through evidence-based policymaking when investigating and demonstrating the positive impact of youth on the development of local communities and their competencies in local governance [12].

The practice of citizenship can only work if integrated systematically into all pores of education and community life so that it becomes natural for young people, and other relevant stakeholders, to practise it every day in interactions in schools and local communities. In addition, there is an increasing recognition of the capacity-building needs of local policymakers and municipal workers responsible for developing effective strategies, action plans, engagement formats, and practices to achieve meaningful outcomes in civic youth participation. While there has been a lot of work already performed in the capacity-building of youth and youth workers, for the past decade, the focus has included the capacity-building of municipalities and their employees. The efforts are driven by international, regional, national and local policies, strategic partnerships, and initiatives funded through mechanisms like the Erasmus+ Youth programme, available to the European Union and associated countries.

One such example is the Democracy Reloading initiative [13] introduced and commented on in the subsequent sections. The authors of this chapter are composed of municipal workers, trainers and researchers who were selected by their National Agencies for Erasmus+ and underwent long-term training of trainers for Democracy Reloading from June 2022 until April 2023. They joined to reflect on and share their co-design in democracy practices in Norway, Belgium and Portugal. To provide evidence-based insights, the authors employ, test and validate the programmatic co-design methodologies proposed in Democracy Reloading and describe their attempts to leverage social innovation and systemic change to elucidate the participatory processes, results, and outcomes of implemented and assessed activities. The methodology and approach will be shared with the Democracy Reloading network and national agencies for replication in other European contexts.

2 Democracy Reloading Approach

2.1 Background

Democracy Reloading was launched in 2015 as a collaborative programme initiated by 10 Erasmus+ Youth and European Solidarity Corps National Agencies to improve the effectiveness of young people's involvement in local governance and decision-making processes through engagement of municipalities, youth, experts and researchers (see Fig. 1).

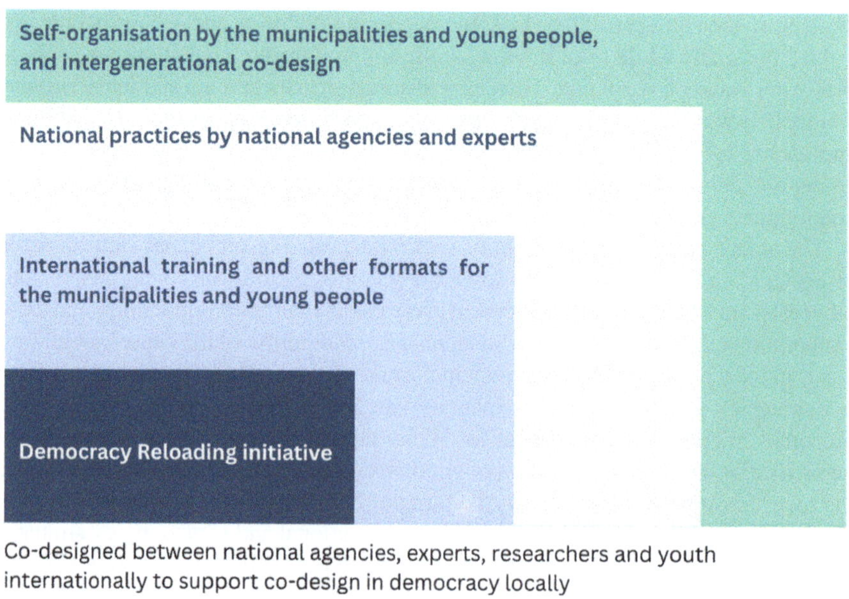

Fig. 1 Democracy reloading co-design framework

The partnership has designed a specific participatory methodology based on long-term research and experience in this topic. 24 competencies essential to create conditions, capacities and structures that can reach the aim of local governance with youth were co-designed.

These competencies were incorporated into a Reference Framework (see Fig. 2), encompassing attitudes, values, knowledge, and skills required for the development of a supportive environment within municipalities, including youth empowerment for municipal decision-making, development of strategies and structures to support youth in municipal decision-making and management of such practices and impact assessment. It thus supports youth representatives at the local, regional, and national levels while recognising young people's rights to participate and self-organise.

In addition, the partnership developed a Toolkit (see Fig. 3) to accompany each competence with various resources that aid in understanding theories and concepts, exploring related practices and success stories, and enhancing implementation skills. The Toolkit is aligned with the European Youth Strategy 2019–2027 [14], which actively engages young people, youth organisations, and other youth work organisers in policies that impact young people's lives at all levels. The municipalities and others interested in the Reference Framework and Toolkit are invited to do an online self-assessment and identify their gaps according to the Reference Framework and prioritise these in their capacity-building.

The initiative proceeded with the dissemination and exploitation of the Reference Framework and Toolkit by developing launch events, webinars, international training courses, stakeholder meetings, study visits and other knowledge-transfer events to

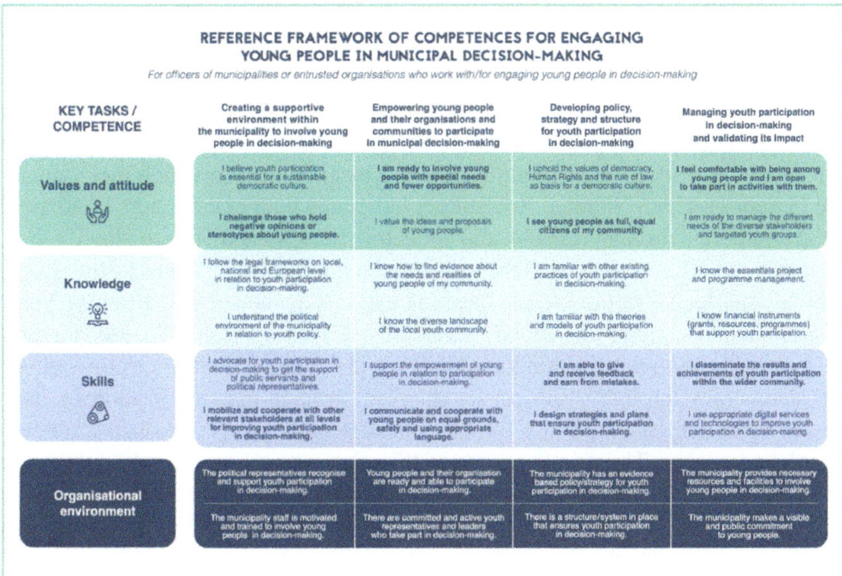

Fig. 2 Democracy reloading reference framework

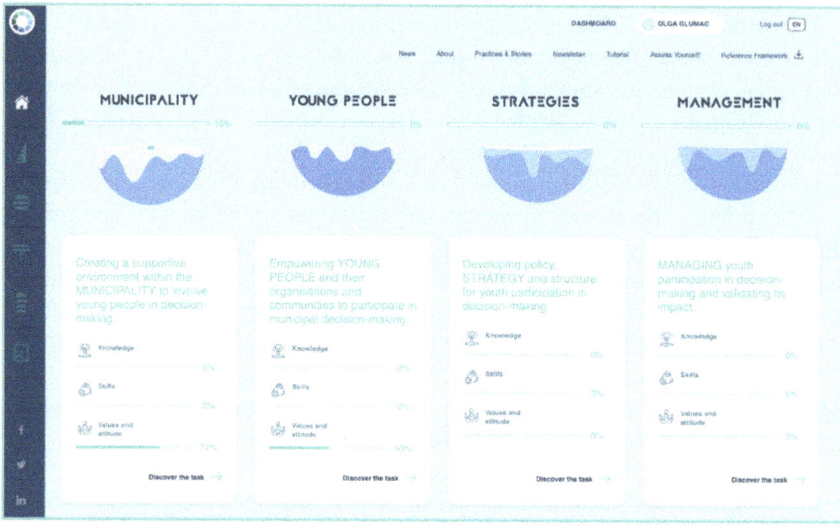

Fig. 3 Democracy reloading toolkit

bolster the scalability at the European scale. Also, a pool of experts has been created to foster continuous support and mentorship of the municipalities interested to pursue this path.

2.2 *Methodology*

Democracy Reloading is a long-lasting initiative (2015–2027) that has thus far mapped and defined the required competencies necessary to achieve organisational change in the work of municipalities and the local context in which they operate. The Erasmus+ Youth National Agencies collaborated with practitioners and experts in the youth field through research and collective learning activities to identify these competencies. The production of the toolkit and platform was managed by the Bureau International Jeunesse, the French-speaking national agency of the Erasmus+ Youth programme in Belgium. The Toolkit is a step-by-step dynamic user-focused learning platform with up-to-date information, theories, practices, and resources for "reloading" democracy through youth participation in decision-making. It adopts a user-centred approach based on non-formal education methods [15] to stimulate self-organised learning. The primary users of this platform are municipal workers, yet it can be utilised by consultants, youth workers, researchers and other experts with interest in youth. Among municipal workers, the recommendation is to carefully consider appropriate individuals to engage in the learning process. Each user is encouraged to do a self-assessment available on the Democracy Reloading platform and identify organisational/individual strengths and weaknesses concerning youth participation in decision-making. Democracy Reloading has already delivered more than 10 international webinars to inform and sensitise target audiences to join and upvote capacity-building as proposed by the initiative. It has thus developed and implemented 2 long-term training-of-trainers courses to encourage professionals and youth associations to support municipalities to enhance their abilities. Finally, it developed 3 pieces of international training for the municipalities and municipal workers. In addition, the initiative has developed a pilot training course aimed at young people between 15 and 20 years to support their self-empowerment so they can gain stronger self-efficacy in having more impact in their municipality in the long-term.

2.3 Stakeholders' Engagement

The relevant stakeholders such as municipalities, municipal workers, youth, youth workers, youth associations and other experts were mapped out early in the process through the existing frameworks and initiatives of the Erasmus+ Youth and European Solidarity Corps National Agencies. The agencies also mobilised their pool of trainers to create in-house experts. The stakeholders continue to have opportunities on different occasions to participate in capacity-building, become partners and co-hosts of local/regional events, validate and iterate the proposed methodology and co-create more effective methods and tools that become a repository of good practices. Annual events such as conferences and stakeholder meetings are developed to share the learning outcomes from participating countries and to sustain community growth.

2.4 Scaling Up, Out and Deep

Reflecting on the progress made thus far, the initiative has achieved success in raising awareness about youth participation relevance and introducing the Democracy Reloading approach to a significant number of municipalities and municipal workers. However, the most formidable challenge encountered was engaging decision-makers in positions of authority, to drive tangible actions within the municipalities and facilitate the practical implementation of the approach. This process of scaling up and deep required concerted efforts to develop customised roadmaps, tailored to the distinct procedures, laws, and cultural nuances surrounding youth participation in each local environment. Furthermore, the placement of trained professionals, who had completed the Democracy Reloading training-of-trainers, within the municipalities play a crucial role in achieving long-term capacity-building and mentorship of staff. These professionals exhibited greater success in transferring knowledge and effectively integrating the Democracy Reloading approaches by transforming existing organisational structures.

The subsequent section delves into the process of scaling out, where trainers-in-training of Democracy Reloading adopt and apply the approach within their respective local and national contexts. Each co-author contributes by elucidating the appropriation of the approach and the subsequent knowledge transfer that took place.

3 Four Cases of Democracy Co-design

3.1 Co-design in Democracy Practice in Lister, Norway

Context. In the Lister region, the Norwegian National Agency of Erasmus+ Youth on behalf of the Democracy Reloading initiative has organised a pilot for capacity-building of four Norwegian municipalities. The capacity-building workshops took place in April, May and June 2023, attracting 40 enthusiastic participants, including directors, municipal managers, unit managers, and key youth workers. By involving influential leaders, the initiative aimed to effectively anchor the trajectories and drive positive changes within institutions. The primary objective was to enhance knowledge and inclusive development of youth participation in municipalities. Two experienced trainers in this and the Democracy Reloading project were invited to develop a workshop model for testing the Toolkit's relevance and providing valuable learning experiences to the municipalities involved. Before the events took place, a preparatory meeting with the young people in the youth councils was made (see Fig. 4). The consulted young people provided inputs on what was important to them to emphasise in the workshops.

Problem statement. The core issue identified is the lack of knowledge and skills related to youth participation among young people themselves, hindering meaningful involvement in decision-making processes. Conversely, there is a will to involve young people, but because there is lack of knowledge about what it entails and actual practical skills, participation does not occur. The law requiring all municipalities to have a youth council came in 2019 and is therefore fairly new [16]. Typically, a single municipal worker is responsible for youth participation, leading to insufficient time for proper implementation. Lack of support from management and other municipal departments further hampers systematic youth participation. When there is no commitment from youth, it is perceived as the young people's disinterest and one does not see the connection between the lack of such commitment and the municipality's lack of apparatus to facilitate participation. The pilot workshops aim to address these challenges. The workshops were elaborated by an appropriation of the Democracy Reloading approach to correspond to the national framework and alignment with existing laws and regulations. Also, collaboration with Statens Hus [17], a pilot project on behalf of the Ministry of Local Government and Regional Development to test enhanced collaboration between public sector organisations in

Fig. 4 Young members of the youth councils reflect upon what they thought was the most important to facilitate their local participation

the same living and labour market region, facilitated the establishment of a "cluster of knowledge" dedicated to youth participation in the Lister region.

Design methodology. The 2-day workshops consisted of four parts: (i) law and framework, (ii) culture and support for youth participation, (iii) strategies, plans and visibility of youth participation, and (iv) learning objectives and learning plan. The methodology was appropriated to municipalities, therefore, in some cases when there were less participants and availability, the workshop was adapted and delivered in a single day. In exchange, participants were required to bring their plans and strategies for reflection and discussion during the workshop. The workshops were based on the co-design principles outlined in Fig. 5.

Throughout the workshop, participants explored the Reference Framework and reflected on how these competencies are present in their current work and organisation, as well as identifying areas for further development (see Fig. 6).

Various methods were used, such as analysing selected plans or strategies to assess the expression of youth participation and its application in their work. This allowed participants to reflect on the clarity of their message and its impact on their work management. Rating the content of plans and strategies helped gauge how well the competencies are reflected. The workshop also utilised a deck of cards representing different skills, which prompts conversations and dialogues (see Fig. 7). Participants prioritised the organisational environment competencies and used the cards to determine which competencies were aligned with their municipality and department. Experiences were categorised into green (good), yellow (improvement needed), and red (work required) piles, fostering reflections and different perspectives.

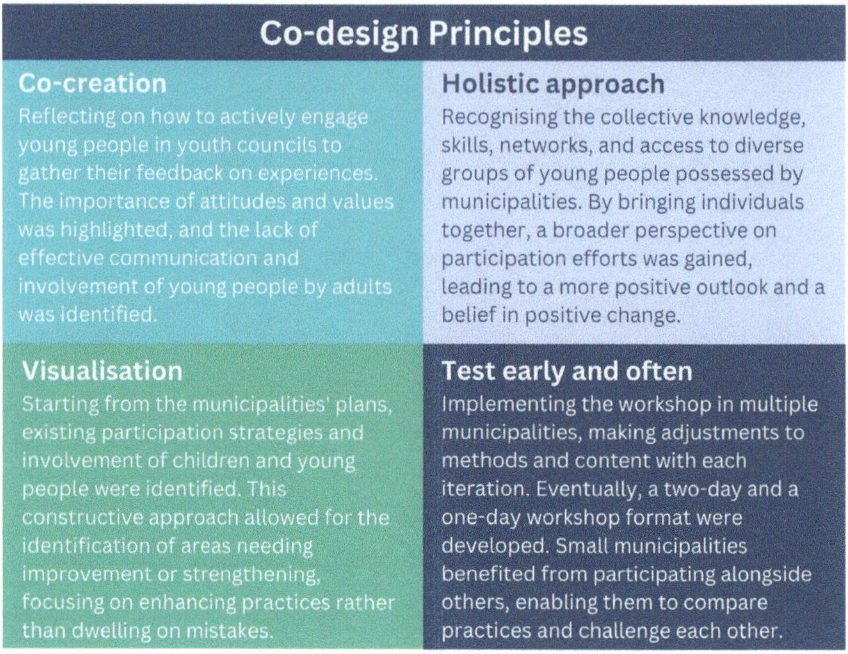

Fig. 5 The co-design principles are integrated in the content of capacity-building workshops

Fig. 6 Employees from different parts of the municipality met to discuss how to improve youth participation

Results. By breaking down the general objective of youth participation into concrete knowledge and skills required by employees and organisations, the workshop enabled a structured and targeted approach to success. The aftermath of the workshop expects to have more municipalities develop competence plans and strategically work towards enhancing youth participation. The workshop also aimed to establish a common language and coordinated approach to youth participation within organisations and cross-departments. Through collaboration, participants could tap into the collective knowledge and skills available, realising the potential for engaging

Fig. 7 Exercise with cards to determine the alignment of competencies with each municipality

vulnerable groups of young people and creating a youth-friendly municipality. The participants expressed that they have not previously reflected on the content and usefulness of youth participation for their organisation. They also highlighted a lack of collaboration within the organisation and across departments to facilitate participation. This initiative helped municipal workers to understand how the work of different departments and workers complement each other in knowledge and skill set. The workshop successfully addressed these gaps and raised awareness of the necessary structural transformation.

Sustainability. Sustainability is a key strength of the trainers as workshop providers, as their shared experience within the municipality equips them with a deeper knowledge of processes and challenges. They acknowledge the need for effective communication between trainers and the National Agency to ensure alignment on expectations and project continuation. They plan to present the workshop to various stakeholders and emphasise its relevance to municipal decision-making processes. Despite challenges in obtaining support from leaders, the trainers believe the workshop aligns with legislative expectations for municipalities. They aim to produce a comprehensive report showcasing the workshop's content and practical value. They intend to maintain communication with participating municipalities and arrange a study visit to share experiences and assess long-term impact. The trainers aspire to replicate pilot workshops to multiple municipalities in the Agder region.

3.2 Co-design in Democracy Practice in Flanders, Belgium

Context. In Flanders, the Democracy Reloading initiative has launched a service composed of a six-month learning trajectory aimed at promoting youth participation and integrating it into the municipality's structure. The trajectory commenced on 4 May 2023, and consisted of sessions held on 13 June, 25 September, and 9 November and mentoring follow-ups (see Fig. 8).

Over six months, the trajectory pursued the following objectives:

1. Facilitating acquaintance among participants.
2. Familiarising participants with the provided toolkit.
3. Identifying the competencies participants needed to develop further.
4. Encouraging participants to initiate local experiments promoting youth participation.
5. Sharing lessons learned among participants.

This trajectory was intentionally co-designed by the national agency, municipal workers and other experts as an experimental approach, acknowledging the value of learning from trial-and-error. A group of six participants from five municipalities in Flanders was involved to ensure a safe environment and ample space for mutual learning in Beveren, Sint-Niklaas, Menen, Izegem and Kortrijk.

Through this trajectory, the aim is to encourage municipal workers to engage with various competencies from the Toolkit. The expected outcome is to not only create

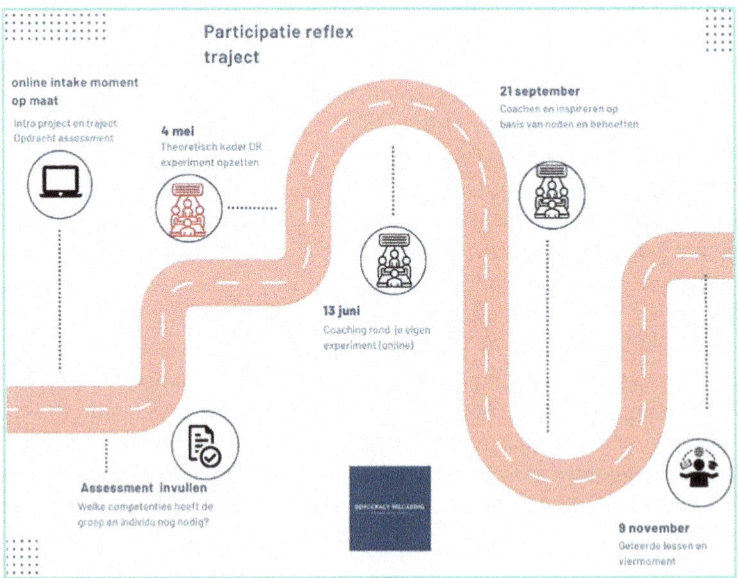

Fig. 8 A roadmap of capacity-building trajectory

an awareness about a need to develop competencies for youth empowerment but also to advocate for youth participation and embed it systematically.

The national practice in Flanders endeavours to actively engage children and young people in decision-making processes that affect them, aligning with the growing recognition of their civic participation in society. One of such examples are youth officials who are following the pilot programme together with the trainers (see Fig. 9). This is seen as an important step towards an inclusive and democratic society. The normative context in Flanders is increasingly emphasising the right of children and young people to be heard and to participate in matters that influence their lives. This is aligned with international treaties such as the UN Convention on the Rights of the Child of 20 November 1989 [18].

At the political level, there are various initiatives and programmes aimed at promoting civic participation of children and young people. For example, advisory councils and youth parliaments are established where young people can have a say in policy decisions. Additionally, subsidies and support are provided to organisations that encourage children and young people to make their voices heard.

Societally, there is an increasing appreciation for intergenerational cooperation through co-creation. There is a growing awareness that involving young people in decision-making processes leads to better policy outcomes and strengthens the culture of participation in society. The current institutional behaviour at the local level varies, but there are municipalities and organisations actively working to involve children and young people in policy development. In Flanders, there are many youth

Fig. 9 The youth officials and the coaches

organisations, like Bataljong, De Ambrassade and Kind & Samenleving that actively contribute.

Overall, there is an ongoing development in Flanders regarding the civic participation of children and young people. Efforts are being made to strive for an inclusive society where the voices of young people are heard and taken seriously in decision-making processes. However, it is up to each municipality to autonomously decide for itself how much it can invest in participation. An investigation in Flanders demonstrates that the participation of children and young people is usually promoted ad hoc rather than systematically. The study "Participation of Children and Young People in Flanders: An Overview" conducted by the Flemish Children's Rights Commissioner was published in 2017. The study analysed the participation opportunities for children and young people at various policy levels, such as schools, youth organisations, municipalities, and provinces. The findings indicated that participation often remains limited, such as consulting children and young people on specific topics or events, rather than being structurally embedded in decision-making processes.

Problem statement. In Flanders, many enthusiastic municipal workers are working on the civic participation of children and young people. They often have the knowledge to engage with the target group and employ appropriate methodologies to gather their opinions. The co-design practice addresses the lack of formal integration of youth participation within broader city policies. The Toolkit offers a comprehensive approach to acquiring the necessary competencies. It challenges municipal workers to work with various stakeholders, disseminate results within and outside the organisation, and develop strategies for systematic embedment of participation.

Design methodology. The six-month-long learning trajectory is a pilot programme co-designed by Bataljong and a freelance trainer and Sint-Niklaas Municipality in collaboration with Jint vzw as a step-by-step process:

- Warm-up: As a warm-up and prior to the launch, the selected participants were asked to complete the self-assessment available on the Democracy Reloading website.
- Introductions: The introductory session on 4 May welcomed cities and municipalities. This allowed them to familiarise themselves with the Reference Framework and encouraged them to work on competencies that strengthen youth participation within their local policies.
- Contextualisation: According to the results of self-assessment, the five municipalities elaborated their topics for experimentation that could have a positive impact on their local contexts (see Fig. 10).
- Benchmarking: In the second session on 13 June, a coaching call took place where the participants were asked to define different steps/milestones in realising their experiments. Together with the trainers, they created their action roadmaps.
- A talk: On 25 June, a physical gathering was organised in which an inspiring speaker introduced nudging techniques, drawing from teachings of Socrates.
- Conclusions: On 9 November, there is a final meeting with the participants, where the lessons learnt and insights are shared. An exploration on dissemination of results in Flanders will be made.

Fig. 10 The participants analyse the assessments and consider which competencies from the Reference Framework they want to base their experiment on

Through an experiential learning approach, each participant prioritised the competencies from the Reference Framework relevant to their practice and conducted practice as an experiment. After the experimentation and conclusion of this trajectory, the lessons learnt were shared with other Flemish cities and municipalities, encouraging wider use of the proposed approach and Toolkit.

Results. The participants reflected on their key challenges and reframed them into the six topics and real-life experiments that will be implemented as local pilot co-design projects (see Fig. 11).

These experiments are being planned and monitored through an online collaborative platform MIRO (see Fig. 12). This allows trainers to keep track of the development of each participant's progress, as well as for participants to get inspired one by another by checking out each other's planning.

The key result is to strengthen the competencies of the six participants so that they are equipped and motivated to pursue actions necessary to embed youth participation in their municipalities. By having participants as in-house ambassadors competent to bring change, it could be sufficient to reinforce structural changes towards involving young people in policy-making. There is also an expectation that within these five municipalities, young people will also notice the outcomes and impact of their participation in the pilot projects.

Sustainability. In the reflection with six participants, the trainers will consider whether they will organise a follow-up after November 2023 to ensure the impact assessment. First impressions are positive as the youth officers recognised the opportunity for peer learning and exchanges across municipalities. The programme's insights will be shared within Flanders, and if successful, it may be repeated annually with a larger group of participants. The process can be enhanced by incorporating

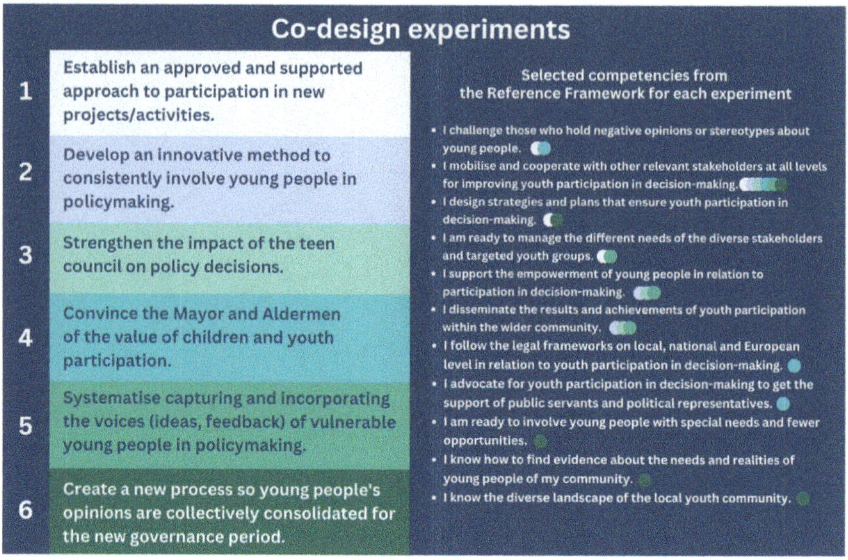

Fig. 11 The topics of participants' real-life experiments (pilots) and associated competencies

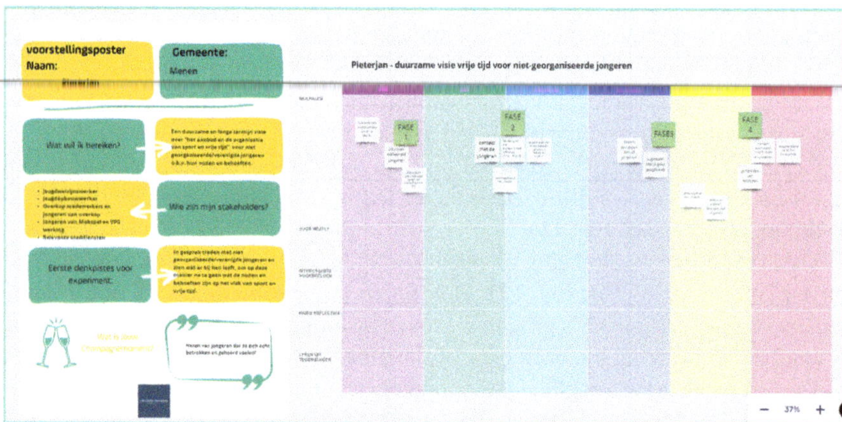

Fig. 12 The MIRO board of one of the participant's real-life experiments. This planning is shared with other participants so they can get inspired from each others' work

feedback from participants and stakeholders, continuously evaluating the impact, and refining the Toolkit and methodologies accordingly. Local and national partnerships with organisations like Bataljong, Jint vzw, and the involved trainers significantly contribute to the successful implementation of the pilot programme.

3.3 Co-design in Democracy Practice in Wallonia, Belgium

Context. Recognising the significant role that municipalities as public authorities closest to citizens should in fostering youth engagement in local decision-making processes and empowering them to actively contribute to problem-solving, it is evident that many municipalities lack the necessary tools for effectively including young people in participative processes. Based on the exchanges with municipal workers, it is apparent that they often operate at the levels of manipulation, decoration, or tokenism according to the Hart ladder [19], which impedes meaningful young involvement.

To address this challenge, the Bureau International Jeunesse—BIJ, in collaboration with CRECCIDE asbl, an organisation that focuses on educating children and youth in citizenship and democratic values, aiming to cultivate responsible, active, critical, and supportive citizens, and trainers from Belgium, have co-designed a training programme as part of the strategic partnership Democracy Reloading. This training journey is specifically tailored to individuals engaged in participation and youth-related work within municipalities. The primary objective is to foster youth participation at a local level as well as provide guidance to local organisations that support young people and municipalities themselves.

This three-day programme, taking place in Federation Wallonia-Brussels, Belgium, aims to equip youth actors, including municipal workers and connectors, with the necessary skills to effectively use the Toolkit. The programme not only provides valuable networking opportunities and knowledge sharing with peers from different cities but also extends support in implementing participatory activities by exploring diverse financial avenues, such as funding options available through programmes like Erasmus+ Youth.

The structure of the three-day programme revolves around three key actions: informing, training and empowering, and engaging. By conducting such actions, the capacity of youth actors to actively involve and support young people in local decision-making processes and the implementation of youth-led projects is enhanced.

The first edition of the training cycle commenced on 18 November 2022, followed by sessions on 9 December 2022 and 27 January 2023. Held in Namur, the inaugural edition witnessed the participation of 14 actors representing various municipalities, including Bouillon, Brussels, Forest, Grez-Doiceau, Ixelles, La Louvière, Les Bons Villers, Molenbeek, Ohey, Pepinster, Soumagne, Uccle, and Verviers (see Fig. 13).

Building upon its initial success, a second edition of the training programme was launched in 2023, with sessions scheduled on 22 June, 30 June and 13 July. This time, the programme took place in the city of Brussels, allowing for continued development and implementation of impactful initiatives.

Problem statement. In the Federation Wallonia-Brussels, numerous municipal workers are keen to locally engage young people in their youth projects and promote their active participation in local decision-making processes. However, they encounter challenges in effectively implementing youth participation approaches,

Fig. 13 Workshop session implemented in Namur on 9 December 2022

accessing funding opportunities, and establishing connections within the municipalities network.

To address these challenges, the co-design practice has emerged as a solution. This approach emphasises the inclusion of young people in the design and decision-making processes, while also providing essential information on available funding sources and facilitating networking and sharing of best practices.

Design methodology. The development of this three-day programme was initiated following initial informal discussions with various Belgian French-speaking municipalities, taking into account the unique local context and needs.

Before the start of the training cycle, potential participants were invited to attend a Democracy Reloading webinar to gain an overview of the tool. Following this, the training cycle was opened to individuals or organisations involved in or closely working with municipalities on youth participation, allowing for a diverse range of participants to benefit from the programme.

This 3-day programme is structured around three modules, each focusing on a different aspect of utilising the Toolkit:

- Module 1: Discovering the tool and how to use it
  - Exploring the transition from theory to practice by understanding the 24 competencies framework.
  - Facilitating exchanges and discussions to delve into the realities faced by municipalities, including their challenges, needs and ongoing actions.
- Module 2: Tool in hand, where do I stand?
  - Providing access or/and reviewing of participants' usage of the Democracy Reloading platform.
  - Developing an action plan to optimise the utilisation of the Democracy Reloading toolkit.
  - Examining study cases and discussing participants' roles as content contributors to the toolbox.

- Module 3: Let's seize the opportunities!
  - Providing an overview of funding opportunities, specifically focusing on the Bureau International Jeunesse youth programmes and Erasmus+ Youth programmes. This includes exploring activities of participation and European Corps Solidarity projects.
  - Bridging the gap between theory and practice by guiding participants on how to submit a youth project and access financial opportunities.

Through these three modules, participants gain a comprehensive understanding of the Toolkit, learn practical strategies for utilising it effectively, and discover funding opportunities to support their youth projects.

This programme incorporates non-formal education approaches and activities to cater to the needs, availability, and workload of participants. It prioritises their experiences and fosters active learning with dedicated moments for practical use of the Democracy Reloading platform and networking among municipalities (see Fig. 14).

Results. This programme has been proven to be highly effective in providing municipal workers with valuable knowledge about the BIJ and Democracy Reloading and the wide range of funding opportunities available for supporting the implementation of their youth projects.

Moreover, participants were granted access to information regarding youth participation and concrete examples of projects that have been implemented within Federation Wallonia-Brussels cities as well as the challenges faced.

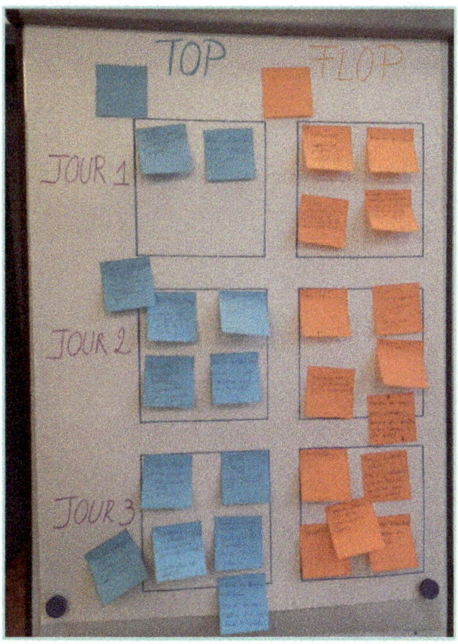

Fig. 14 Workshop session implemented in Namur on 27 January 2023

In addition, the programme achieved one of its key objectives, which was to foster connections among youth actors from different municipalities. Often, due to limited communication and heavy workload, municipal workers tend to operate in isolation. However, these three days have provided an invaluable opportunity to meet, exchange ideas, network, and establish connections with fellow participants, breaking down the barrier of working in silos and facilitating collaboration and the sharing of experiences and practices among participants.

In conclusion, while the primary of this training cycle was to inform and train municipal workers, BIJ also placed a strong emphasis on raising awareness among participants about the available funding opportunities and encouraging them to actively engage in utilising them for their projects. As a result of these two pilot cycles, it was noticeable that the municipal workers networking semestrial day, increased registration and participation in activities and training on participation, and a willingness to contribute to the Democracy Reloading platform by sharing study cases.

Sustainability. Upon initial evaluation, it was noticed a low participation rate in the programme, with 14 participants for the first edition and 7 participants for the second edition. However, there is a genuine interest in this programme. The next step is to adapt the programme and accommodate it to the limited availability of municipal workers. Making accessible youth participation methods may increase the overall participation rate and upskilling of 262 municipalities of Federation Wallonia-Brussels.

Additionally, there is an expectancy of a rise in the number of project submissions within the context of Erasmus+ Youth activities of participation and European Corps Solidarity projects. To ensure sustainability, the team will focus on adaptability and flexibility in programme design, considering the constraints of limited availability among municipal workers. The communication efforts will be placed to engage youth and/or participation councillors and encourage their teams to participate in this three-day training programme. The collaboration between BIJ, CRECCIDE and the involved trainers created a good combination of expertise, experience, and a wide network.

3.4 Co-design in Democracy in Portugal

Context. The Portuguese National Agency Erasmus+ Youth together with the DYPALL Network, organisation in charge of communication and dissemination, has hosted a few international events of the Democracy Reloading initiative in Portugal. These were conferences to launch the Toolkit in 2021, international training for the municipalities in 2022 and stakeholder meetings to evaluate and plan future steps of the partnership in 2023. The agency mobilised four trainers from its pool of trainers that concluded a long-term training of trainers in Democracy Reloading to organise national practice at Eurodesk (European youth information network) [20] reunion in

June 2023 gathering 30 national participants of which the majority were municipal workers, youth workers representing youth associations, and young people.

Problem statement. In Portugal, children and young people are encouraged to participate in civic life inside their schools and in the city, through youth councils, consultation initiatives, youth associations and events dedicated to youth participation at local and national levels. At schools that have regulated procedures on consultation of youth, any child and young person can have a say and co-create to some extent their learning experiences and leisure (extracurricular) activities. The schools of basic education also teach students citizenship throughout the disciplines. Conversely, at the city or national level, most youth participation activities are based on representation and include only a few youth—e.g. few young people from selected schools are invited to the national youth parliament and/or as members of the youth associations are often represented by few other young people or even young professionals who represent the voice of youth per specific organisation in youth councils. Therefore, sensitisation of municipalities and municipal workers about more inclusive approaches to including any young person interested to provide their opinion and having diversification in citizenship practice is expected. Thus, decision-making implies fostering critical thinking and dealing with more ambiguous tasks that have moral and emotional attachment to it [21].

Design methodology. The four trainers from the pool of trainers developed a half-a-day workshop for the participants taking into consideration their level of experience. The workshop was composed of five parts, (i) contextualisation and team building, (ii) exploration of the concepts of participation and youth involvement in decision-making, (iii) mapping of participants' organisational context and existing practices for youth involvement in decision-making processes; (iv) introduction and exploration of the Toolkit, and (v) evaluation of the workshop.

The common definition of concepts was made through an energiser in which the participants needed to explain to each other in a non-verbal way what youth, participation and democracy means to them. The participants were then challenged to reflect to which extent they agree or disagree with proposed statements (see Fig. 15), e.g. "In my youth, I had the will to improve the lives of the people in my community," or "I often found spaces receptive to sharing and discussing my ideas among friends and family."

An individual reflection on the necessary competencies for each of the four categories was made. Participants were reflecting on their practices and trainers would organise them according to the Reference Framework (see Fig. 16). A copy of the framework was provided to participants to reflect on and match their ideas with 24 competencies.

The participants were divided into smaller groups and invited to select a challenge relevant to the group and address it by identifying why it exists, what are the possible solutions and target groups that should be involved in solution development, as well as what type of activities and resources they need to implement them (consult Fig. 17). Finally, the trainers demonstrated the use of the online Toolkit and the platform and answered any questions from the participants.

Fig. 15 Agree-disagree continuum to tackle perception of participants when reflecting on their life youth experiences

Fig. 16 Ideation of competencies from the participants' perspective

Results. The Eurodesk gathering of municipalities, youth association representatives and young people was a favourable environment for opening up discussion on youth participation in local co-governance and developing exchanges on good practices and deepening synergies between municipalities and all involved actors. The mapping of competencies according to the framework structure in an exploratory way, by allowing participants to identify key competencies and organise them according to their understanding before showcasing the Reference Framework was a good reflective exercise. It helped participants to identify gaps in their knowledge and practice. Thus, the ideation exercise has helped them to focus on a single problem with multiple perspectives and experiences and discuss different approaches in order to understand, reframe and solve it. The workshop demonstrated positive results but

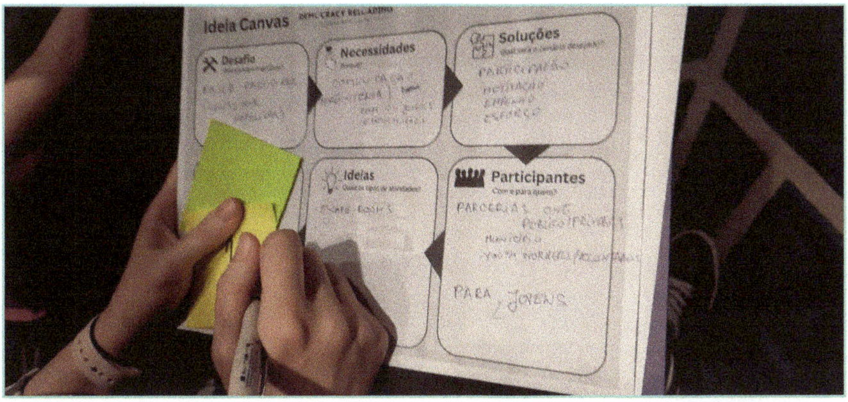

Fig. 17 Ideation of solutions according to the selected challenge

was time limited to go deeper into the elaboration of concrete competencies, activities and other potential actions of interest to the Eurodesk community.

Sustainability. The workshop was a short-term pilot event to test and see the responsiveness of participants toward the subject and introduce the Toolkit. The trainers believe that a more long-term approach to mentoring and coaching could be employed, similar to the ones already implemented in Norway and Belgium.

4 Conclusions

In conclusion, this paper has addressed the problems outlined in the introduction, shedding light on the importance of sustainable practices in youth participation and local co-governance. The authors emphasise the importance of adopting Democracy Reloading as a case-by-case approach, as each municipality is unique and requires tailored strategies. The presented co-design practices of capacity-building and outlined local co-design experiments in various regions shed some light on appropriation which not only depend on the accessible resources (Reference Framework, Toolkit, Case studies, Self-Assessment tool) but also the expertise of facilitators, the efforts placed by the participants and willingness of participants to advocate and pursue for structural changes in their municipalities [22]. The practitioners such as municipal workers, designers, consultants and/or researchers may benefit from these presented and discussed examples whether they work on local youth participation, public sector innovation or any other related field in which they wish to intervene through a systemic co-design. Figure 18 provides a general roadmap on how to apply the Democracy Reloading approach.

While short-term endeavours in capacity-building and defining experimentation are effective in raising awareness and sensitisation on youth participation across

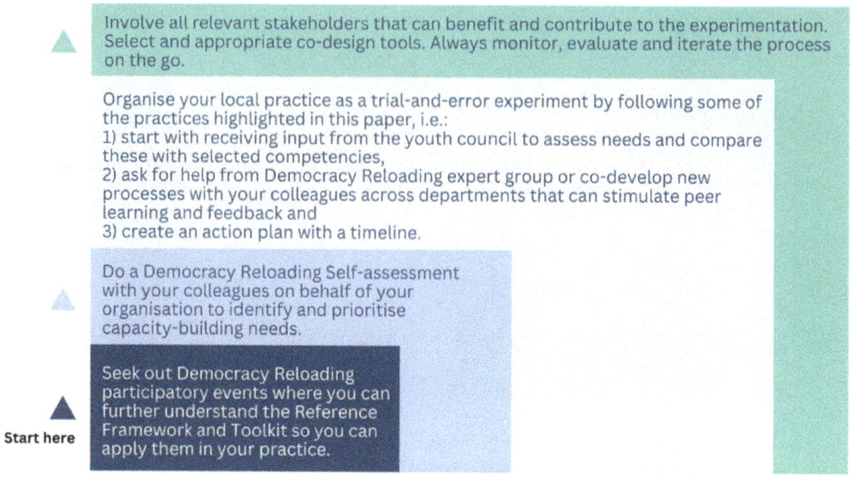

Fig. 18 A roadmap on how to apply the Democracy Reloading approach in the local context as a municipal worker, designer, consultant and/or researcher

municipalities, many times they do not provide long-term solutions due to the requirement for longer training and mentorship.

Additionally, municipal workers in training are required to be aware of and prioritise the lack of competencies in their departments and municipalities at the early stages of the capacity-building process to better appropriate the capacity-building. Upon finalising their training, municipal workers are to share their knowledge with their departments and contribute to the municipalities with a vision of structural changes for which additional mentorship by facilitators (intermediaries) might be needed. Such support can help motivate municipal workers to develop roadmaps of actions for needed change.

The pilot practices have shown that peer-to-peer learning between municipal workers across departments and also among municipalities is appreciated. Peer learning has proven to be highly beneficial, particularly in small group settings where participants can learn from one another.

When working with youth participation, it is important to consider the diverse perspectives and networks that young individuals possess. By bringing young people together in workshops and providing them with a platform to express their experiences and needs, municipalities can foster a more positive relationship with youth.

The use of co-design to co-develop Democracy Reloading, national capacity-building practices and finally real-life experiments in youth participation in local decision-making has ensured that various perspectives and expertise are embedded into the design of new processes that may bring about social change and innovation.

In the continuation of municipal workers' endeavours, co-design continues to play a pivotal role in system gap identification and its systemic transformation. The use of design methods and tools also facilitates more effective prototyping of change inside municipalities and the operationalisation of intergenerational co-creative practices.

5 Future Work

The findings of this paper have provided a solid foundation for future work in the co-design of capacity-building of municipal workers for inclusive and effective youth participation in local decision-making. Building upon the lessons learnt from the regional/national pilots conducted, the next step would be to transition from short-term endeavours to long-term support, provided that it will be possible to secure the necessary backing. One key aspect of moving forward is to share the recommendations generated within the Democracy Reloading network. This knowledge-sharing process will enable authors and other experts to collectively enhance their understanding of sustainable democratic practices.

The Democracy Reloading initiative and the network of experts dream big at envisioning a future where municipalities actively participate and share their best practices at larger national and international events. By engaging at this broader level, municipalities can transcend local concerns and contribute to shaping a bigger picture of how daily practices can be transformed and strengthen democracy as a whole.

Moreover, it is crucial to speed up the process of owning the sustainability issue. By exposure to a larger pool of individuals and municipalities actively addressing sustainability concerns, the pace of learning and aspiring changes could be enhanced. This exposure will not only inspire municipal workers and municipalities but also provide valuable insights into how to handle challenges effectively.

Disclosure Statement The authors thank the participating national agencies that have commented on this chapter and provided their views.

References

1. Glumac O, de Sousa Morais MRC (2021) Codesigners of classroom 52: a case study for codesign in active citizenship. In: Advances in design, music and arts: 7th meeting of research in music, arts and design, EIMAD 2020, May 14–15, 2020. Springer International Publishing, pp 31–49
2. Del Gaudio C, Franzato C, de Oliveira AJ (2020) Co-design for democratising and its risks for democracy. CoDesign 16(3):202–219
3. Dorst K (2015) Frame creation and design in the expanded field. She Ji: J Des Econ Innov 1(1):22–33
4. Manzini E (2015) Design, when everybody designs: an introduction to design for social innovation. MIT Press, London

5. Augsberger A, Collins ME, Gecker W (2018) Engaging youth in municipal government: moving toward a youth-centric practice. J Commun Pract 26(1):41–62
6. Sintomer Y, Herzberg C, Röcke A (2008) Participatory budgeting in Europe: potentials and challenges. Int J Urban Reg Res 32(1):164–178
7. Palmy David N, Buchanan A (2020) Planning our future: institutionalising youth participation in local government planning efforts. Plan Theory Pract 21(1):9–38
8. Glumac O, D'Arcy G, de Sousa Morais MRC (2022) Co-creation and co-design of educational programmes with young people: a comparative study between Dublin and Porto. Perspectives on design II: research, education and practice, 61–76
9. Nesrallah S, Klepp KI, Budin-Ljøsne I, Luszczynska A, Brinsden H, Rutter H, Bergstrøm E, Singh S, Debelian M, Bouillon C, Katanasho MB (2023) Youth engagement in research and policy: the CO-CREATE framework to optimize power balance and mitigate risks of conflicts of interest. Obes Rev 24:e13549
10. Mainsah H, Brandtzæg PB, Følstad A (2016) Bridging the generational culture gap in youth civic engagement through social media: lessons learnt from young designers in three civic organisations. J Media Innovations 3(1):23–40
11. Glumac O (2018) Lab of collaborative youth: shaping a learning framework in active citizenship. Doctoral dissertation, Universidade do Porto (Portugal)
12. Zeldin S, Camino L, Calvert M (2003) Toward an understanding of youth in community governance: policy priorities and research directions. Social policy report. Volume 17, Number 3. Society for Research in Child Development
13. Democracy Reloading homepage. https://democracy-reloading.eu. Last accessed 13 July 2023
14. European Youth Portal. https://youth.europa.eu/strategy_en. Last accessed 13 July 2023
15. Coombs PH, Prosser C, Ahmed M (1973) New paths to learning for rural children and youth. International council for educational development
16. The Local Government Act. https://lovdata.no/dokument/NL/lov/2018-06-22-83. Last accessed 13 July 2023
17. Statens Hus homepage. https://www.listersamarbeidet.no/tjenestesamarbeid/statens-hus. Last accessed 13 July 2023
18. United Nations. General Assembly (1989) Convention on the Rights of the Child, 20 November 1989. Annual Review of Population Law 16:95–501
19. Hart RA (1992) Children's participation: from tokenism to citizenship
20. Eurodesk homepage. https://eurodesk.eu/. Last accessed 13 July 2023
21. Piedade F, Neves T, Loff M, Menezes I (2023) Emotional and critical citizens: Portuguese students' engagement with wicked issues in contemporary EU policy. Educational Review, 1–21
22. Barbero S, Bicocca M (2017) Systemic design approach in policy-making for sustainable territorial development. Des J 20(sup1):S3496–S3506

Speculative Interactions: Educational Contribution for Hypothetical Design Practice

Marco Neves, Sónia Rafael, and Ana Melo

Abstract University master's degrees in design are specialized teaching–learning opportunities, where acquiring professional skills are intertwined with design research. Interaction design, an activity close to technological apparatus, to human–computer interaction and human factors, promotes objective notions of project development where designers act as problem-solvers. Still, interaction design training at a university can benefit from an approach which privileges broad creative skills, critical thinking and reflection, stimulating designers to be agents of change, through speculative proposals. We devised a curricular unit with initial research, practice-led methods and proposal presentation, with the intention of developing a course structure based on work phases, where research through design and speculative design come together to allow hypothetical, but socially aware design proposals. Three proposals are presented as case studies of this educational approach, which demonstrate the possibility of conducting speculative and reflective practice while addressing expected professional skills.

Keywords Speculative design · Research through design · Design education

M. Neves (✉) · S. Rafael · A. Melo
CIAUD, Research Centre for Architecture, Urbanism and Design, Lisbon School of Architecture, Universidade de Lisboa, Rua Sá Nogueira, Polo Universitário do Alto da Ajuda, 1349-063 Lisboa, Portugal
e-mail: mneves@fa.ulisboa.pt

S. Rafael
e-mail: s.rafael@belasartes.ulisboa.pt

A. Melo
e-mail: amelo2@edu.ulisboa.pt

M. Neves · S. Rafael
ITI/LARSyS—Interactive Technologies Institute, University of Lisbon, Lisbon, Portugal

D. Raposo et al. (eds.), *Perspectives on Design III*, Springer Series in Design and Innovation 34, https://doi.org/10.1007/978-3-031-43516-4_2

1 Introduction

Research in design is still recent when compared to other areas of knowledge. In absence of specific methodologies, the discipline of design has been integrating research methodologies, conceptual frameworks and proven practices from other areas of knowledge to gradually establish epistemological bases of research and define its operating methods and procedures. This framework highlighted the importance of defining own research methodologies, as well as a "design science" [1] that would advance knowledge in the field of design.

Frayling [2] clarified various stereotypes about research, what it involves and what are expected results, by identifying a need for greater awareness of cognitive, social and technical contexts in the field of art and design to foster the production of knowledge. Research became regarded as a practice, somehow as writing, science or design also are; and design became regarded as research—either applied research, where resulting knowledge is useful for application, or action research, where the action is calculated to generate and validate new knowledge or understanding. As 'research' seems to be an activity much less diffuse and more convergent than what might have been anticipated, it may be perhaps the most important nourishment for the practice and teaching of design. It offers a way to move forward in an apparent regular circle between design professional practice and design education [3].

Three main principles have related research and design for this matter: research into design, research for design and research through design [2, 4]. Since the last one was announced, design methodologies and processes leading to creative production as legitimate procedures in research have been widely debated and discussed [5]. This relationship is of interest to design education, not only because research can represent an advance in design training, but also research is included in the role of universities. Universities are nowadays meant to create and disseminate knowledge, to train people in cultural, scientific and technical ways, to carry out research and serve the community. The Bologna process helped to implement a compatible educational system throughout Europe, based on a few lines of action, namely the adoption of an education system based on three cycles; establishment of a credit accumulation and transfer system (ECTS); and involvement of higher education institutions and students as partners. All of them implied changes in design education paradigms: abandonment of the *magister dixit* culture to a teacher/tutor system, who assumed roles of guidance and support; a training process no longer centered on teaching but rather on learning, promoting students' autonomy and responsibility for the time they dedicate to all training activities; study programs are now organized based on skills students must attain at the end of the study cycle.

Learning methodologies should provide development not only of specific skills to an area of study but also horizontal and transversal skills that enable critical thinking, analysis of situations, communication skills, innovation or adaptation to change, just to mention a few.

This confluence has been relevant in master's degrees, as it is a study cycle situated between specialization of an area and introduction to research. Therefore, within the Interaction Design master's degree in the University of Lisbon, we propose an approach to training interaction designers that combines acquisition of technical skills with a design practice oriented to complex situations of social and cultural concern, where students are invited to create proposals that fit the speculative spectrum. Such speculation is expected to be obtained by a good amount of knowledge as retrieved from research methods and research through design altogether. We have assembled a combination of exploratory qualitative initial methods to gather information on individual research themes and interaction design methods for creating and shaping individual proposals. Our suggested process comes as an opportunity for students to elaborate on their research interests and develop speculative interactions, as possibilities to tackle situations in a way they were not dealt with before.

2 Design Areas for Speculative Proposals

'Research' and 'design' have come together as operative terms in a methodology that recognizes the design process as an appropriate research activity—Research through Design (RtD) [6, 7]. A research based on the design process itself, on recording and disseminating all stages [8], grounded on the claim that knowledge can sometimes be acquired more effectively through practice, i.e., through experience and consequent critical reflection of this experience [4, 9–12]. In this way, we learn through dynamic articulation of practice with theoretical research, and from it we generate a systematic reflection on the whole process.

Initially applied to art and design, RtD gained a position in other areas, such as Human–Computer Interaction (HCI) and Interaction Design (IxD), being considered a relevant research way [13], as it integrates models and theories with technical knowledge in the design process [14].

Practice-led methods can favor interaction design training as they accommodate the development of creative skills, from idea generation to prototypes. Indeed, an interaction design project is characterized by an understanding of interaction, as a succession of actions and physical reactions between a human being and his surroundings, whether objects or other human beings [15]. An action triggers a reaction and from there, an alternate exchange of messages between both parties and an interpretation can be generated [16], which varies according to context. As such, interaction design is based on products or systems that change state over time [17] and where experience and behavior are important notions to consider, as to prepare the conditions for interaction with and through products and services [18].

Within the scope of interactive systems, besides shaping artefacts, RtD also allows to expand knowledge by creative, speculative and experimental perspectives that help designers to deal with the complexity presented by our contemporaneity. It is therefore an approach to consider, especially in a design learning context to foster the conception of one's own ideas.

There is in design a conformist sense in reproducing the way one thinks and resolves [19], which moves away from the need to train people for a non-immediate period of time, for contexts that will change and for situations where flexible thinking is required. Therefore, design with a critical tone does not address solutions, but rather speculation and possible scenarios [19]. A critical and speculative approach can alter our connection with the surrounding [20] and bring us closer to the necessary skills interaction designers could acquire. Speculative and Critical Design (SCD) tries to stimulate the discussion around alternative proposals and not the reproduction of current understanding [21].

Like RtD, a critical and speculative approach is transposed through design, based on its possible materiality or on the creation of evidence, to the conception of future alternatives [22]. Its importance in teaching may be to help break the cycle of design as business as usual [23], framed by a conformist model, of which it is simultaneously cause and consequence and whose result is 'defuturing' [24]; and thus contribute to a reorientation of design as a field who responds to environmental and social sustainability needs—as transition design or the practice of 'counterdesigning' [25].

Both the concern with themes of a larger social scale and the necessary ability of designers to deal with them imply alternative approaches [21]. Moving away from commercial pressure and aiming for social and experience change, brings SCD a need to relate with everyday life and engage people [26], something somehow ensured by the positioning of interaction design with its potential users, collecting information about who they are and how they deal with systems. People are, at least for the time being, a considerable part of interactive systems, individually or accompanied [27, 28], as they intervene in the system and are involved in behavior.

However, used as a teaching–learning approach, it poses the challenge of articulating the development of expected design skills while addressing more complex situations [29].

3 Interaction Design Education at the Crossroad of Design and Research

Educational programs in design still try to follow a modernist approach to designer's practice, dominated by a technical rigor, typical of industrial production and addressing problem solving as based on functionality. Lack of process progression and an updated self-perception makes design teaching unprepared for students who need to think for a complex world and reinvent it.

Although an approach based on practice-led research and speculative posture presents adequacy with training goals for future interaction designers and there is agreement that it is necessary to work on complex themes [30], the effort of such a program collides with students' expectations.

Difficulty of relating expectations for technical skills with complex situations that provide proposals for alternative futures is present in the pressure higher education institutions feel to train students for a notion of professional success in interconnected commercial contexts, filled by the lack of sustainability and defuturing [22].

This challenge, to combine research and alternative design practices on a design degree, also faces a conventional education [25] based on disciplines of execution and production and not necessarily of social or cultural transformation. If, on one hand, design education bypasses the complexity of design itself and the world in which designers operate [24], on the other hand it shows difficulty in keeping up with emerging design practices [31] or that stand out in design research.

In its entangled beginning with trades and craft guilds, design education history is deeply connected with systems of apprenticeship aimed at acquiring technical know-how, and only in the early twentieth century, increasing demand led to industrial, graphic and interior design becoming professions, and also to the need of college-level programs of design education [32]. Bauhaus and other design schools in Europe and in the United States established a modern and functionalist approach for design practice, intertwined with art, technology and social concerns [22]. In the mid-1980s, technological innovations and computer-assisted design gave rise to new practices such as interaction design and many design schools reformulated curricula, adjusting to focus on enabling user participation and using simulations and stories as experience enablers [32]. Keeping pace with continuous technological change, interaction design contributed to shifting design focus from artifact-oriented projects to more open-ended outcomes and expanded practices, such as designing systems, services, conversations, co-creation or communities. Although many design school curricula still apply an artifact-based, market-oriented, and master-apprenticeship pedagogical approach rooted in historical circumstances, this will not be enough for design education to respond to radical changes in context and in emergent design practices [32].

Considering design takes part in creating, circulating and reproducing cultural meanings, shaping digital networks, information and communication technologies [33], a speculative approach in interaction design education can significantly contribute to questioning and making sense of technological, cultural and social transformation.

Therefore, there is a need to introduce space for reflection in interaction design education, so that future designers can better understand the situations for which they are going to create [22] and that they can call into question already known practices and solutions, to foster new knowledge that opposes them [24].

By their descriptions, RtD and SCD are able ways to create new knowledge, although lacking scientific dimension [34]. Not having such recognition was not however a concern, as RtD and SCD were mainly used to allow students to experiment on two converging approaches: students use design means and methods to search and formulate distinct project proposals, while simultaneously grounding their work in complementary research methods, so that design as a process can accommodate a knowledge contribution for their research area.

Our concern was distant from a strict point of view where the classroom should provide context for professional development, as 'profession' is not a single straightforward understanding, but rather a multiple gathering of diverse experiences. Students were not imposed to consider some professional factors when developing their work. There was no limitation for notions of budget or a requisite for fully developed high fidelity prototypes, considering all necessary materials, systems requirements or production process. There was also only a slight concern about available technologies. Media, devices or technological circumstances, whether known by the student, commercially available or easily considered as belonging to the area should not represent a limitation.

4 Teaching Plan for What Is Yet Unmade

4.1 Interaction Design Master's Degree and Interaction Project Units

Interaction Design master's degree in the University of Lisbon lasts four semesters, with a total of 120 ECTS. From the first to the third semester there are 'Interaction Project' curricular units devoted to interaction design project development. The fourth and last semester is dedicated to a final project, dissertation or internship report.

'Interaction Project I' is the curricular unit with the highest number of ECTS, contact hours and estimated total work hours for the first semester of the degree, which gives it the importance of establishing early purposes for the master's degree and conditioning students' academic presence in following semesters.

It is an introductory course in interaction design, in a university master's degree, which is distinct from other types and levels of education. In this situation, we assumed the nature of interaction is multidisciplinary [35] and training should contribute to the designer's ability to think and act in different circumstances.

4.2 Setting the Stage

Perception of RtD and SCD and their approaches, places them as foundations but also as instruments to achieve two purposes, worthy of attention and which combine concerns of teaching interaction design in the 2nd cycle of higher education studies: (a) enabling design training and design practice by students, ensuring contact with structuring concepts, with the process of developing proposals, with the means and tools necessary for an autonomous constitution of their ideas; (b) stimulate knowledge and research in areas of individual interest, promoting deeper reflection on each theme and experience with methods of collecting and generating information.

We suggested phases for developing projects in interaction design that followed SCD concerns mentioned by Dunne and Raby [20] and summarized by Johannessen, Keitsch and Pettersen [21], namely problem finding, construction of narratives, changing the perception of products and services, aiming at social transformation and modification of experiences.

Methods and phases to generate speculative proposals can vary according to established purposes. In this case, our intention was to enhance critical thinking and reflection on individual creation, maintaining the firm need to experience a process as a requirement for introducing knowledge of interaction design activity. This process mainly consists of moments of practical development, as starting from an initial collection of information. For each individual work phase, a set of methods was proposed to provide the class with: (a) knowledge about various methods of possible use in each work phase (research, generation of ideas, development of prototypes, evaluation of proposals); (b) allow each student to make an informed, conscientious and adequate choice of methods that could provide best quality for their individual work; (c) ensure contact with work episodes close to the process followed in professional activities in interaction design, as well as contact with tools that facilitate execution of each step.

However, these methods did not serve as matrix for repetition of results, but rather as a possibility to help individual creation and stimulate emergence of proposals that do not have to comply with an accommodated thought, understanding, elaboration and presentation.

The process then starts with identification and selection of themes, where there is a social, cultural or technological relevance and where students recognize motivation to develop work phases. Considering possible resistance of students to a goal distant from regular solutions they know, individual choice of the topic and maintenance of personal motivation, seemed to be a positive condition. This was followed by collection of exploratory information; conception and generation of ideas through methods that allow building a discourse, an approach to potential users and elaboration of a future; development of prototypes and proposal communication. We left 'what' they would design open and 'how' would be something partly perceived during the semester and to be later explored throughout the degree. As for 'why', it would insistently be questioned during research and ideas generation.

4.3 Briefings and Work Phases

We devised briefings for school years 2019–2020, 2020–2021 and 2021–2022 with a 4-phase structure for project development, based on research, idea conception, idea development and proposal presentation.

Briefings framed students in theoretical and speculative backgrounds, suggesting as a starting point themes of social or cultural concern, or different places in the city of Lisbon, with which students identified themselves with. Students were encouraged to find an interaction design approach around each subject, focusing on connections and behaviors and challenging digital or physical/digital hybrid artifacts. Projects should aim to create innovative and speculative ways for determined audiences to experience each theme, generating novel modes of interaction with subjects, places and their objects. Scenarios, products and systems were expected to arise from this purpose of infusing new meanings, deploying strategies of place-making and activating communities.

For project development we detailed goals, deliverables and tutoring/evaluation moments for each phase, as observed in Table 1.

During the first phase, students were led to do research about places, contexts and users. By conducting desk-research, interviews, ethnography, direct and indirect observations, and other exploratory methods [36, 37] they were expected to gather relevant and insightful information that could lead to a definition of a project scope and goals. Later, students developed other exploratory methods, like mind maps and affinity diagrams, to make sense of their research material, displaying visually their storytelling and enabling them to communicate their initial ideas to colleagues and faculty. This phase revealed to be challenging for most students, since not having a previously defined problem to work with originated some difficulties in directing research, setting project constraints and being able to move forward to subsequent tasks. Students often questioned the relevance of their own critical and speculative design approaches, revealing some discomfort with more open-ended and less market-oriented projects.

A second phase followed to generate ideas through sketching [38], information architecture, wireframes and low-fidelity prototypes. These initial sketches and prototypes were subject to discussion with colleagues and faculty, striving for the development of artifacts that would enable hypothetical users to experience meaningful interactions. In the third phase students were motivated to translate their ideas into material evidence, such as interactive digital prototypes, demonstration videos or simulations of possible interactions [39]. Prototypes were then advanced to medium

Table 1 4-phase structure for project development

	Research	Idea conception	Idea development	Presentation
Goals	Research about places, contexts and users	Gather relevant information leading to project scope	Translate ideas of possible interactions into material evidence	Develop strategies to present proposals, while enabling to practice communication skills
Deliverables	Mind maps, affinity diagrams	Sketching, information architecture, wireframes and low-fidelity prototypes	Medium and high-fidelity prototypes	Storytelling to guide the audience through concept and project development
Tutoring/evaluation	Communicate initial ideas to colleagues and faculty	Weekly individual tutoring	Sketches and prototypes were shared with colleagues and faculty	Presentation-like compilation of the entire process

and high-fidelity versions, incorporating visual identity development and interface design.

Last phase consisted on development of strategies to present the created proposals, and students were encouraged to use storytelling as a means of guiding the audience through their project conceptual starting point and project development, making all the design process visible. Although throughout the semester, after each one of the three work phases, students had to compile their progress in a presentation-like manner, the final presentation should be designed as an independent project of sorts using visual and multimedia elements. This strategy was used by faculty to facilitate critical self-assessment milestones, while enabling students to practice their communication skills.

4.4 Difficulties and Limitations

Work carried out by students in these three years does not correspond to a homogeneous set, although they respect our proposed approach. Lack of common aspects in some proposals may be due to the fact that each followed theme is distinct in its characterization. However, most proposals were framed for the purposes of each phase and obtained results are compatible with criteria of practical procedures and critical thinking. During each semester, in tutoring students, some difficulties and limitations emerged, which may be due to two circumstances: student specific; or gaps in the teaching plan.

Students. Our approach has faced resistance from some students, namely regarding: individual prejudices about interaction design; lack of basic or fundamental knowledge about interaction design; lack of experience in design processes.

Many students tend to consider interaction design as the study of terms most verified in professional context, especially 'UX/UI' (User Experience/User Interface). Not only in terms, designations and considerations about them, but in the expectation, that projects to be elaborated fit within their personal interpretations of 'UX/UI' and that any other practice, arrives as something unexpected and confusing.

The 2nd cycle of study at higher education allows each student to choose a master's degree, in a scientific area distinct from their bachelor degree. Other students, with professional experience, and holders of training at bachelor level, prior to the implementation of the Bologna process also enroll sometimes. This, associated with the lack of 1st cycle training in interaction design, translates into an initial difficulty in transmitting structural knowledge to students to start an informed and conscientious practice in interaction design.

Students felt comfortable in following defined methods, mostly present in interaction design literature, with described procedures and observable examples and in using conventional or expected techniques and technologies. But they revealed great difficulty in initial stages, in generating, evaluating, deepening and improving ideas and in understanding the importance of creative auxiliary methods, namely visual records, as decisive steps for the elaboration of valuable proposals.

Teaching Plan. We also observed and noted curricular unit planning issues for possible change or improvement.

One of the initial doubts was whether the methods we followed for conception would be the most adequate to stimulate in all students the ability to generate proposals that moved away from expectations and dominant commercial and professional contributions. Especially when facing students' difficulty in generating and expressing initial ideas.

It also occurred to us if our plan, based on a relationship with social concerns, while maintaining space for individual engagement, would be sufficiently aligned with the needs of creative futures and contributing for improved situations.

A limitation is on how to improve assessment of proposals and student performance, through criteria that may reflect horizontal and broad creative skills, while maintaining more structural skills in developing an interaction design process.

5 Proposals as Case Studies

To better understand our approach, we present a summary description of a selection of three student proposals, which demonstrate and clarify the training plan. One responding to the 2021–2022 briefing, "Origin" (student #1, Ana Faria), and two resulting from the 2020–2021 briefing, "The Invisible Library" (student #2, Lívia Teixeira) and "The Underground" (student #3, João Abrunhosa).

5.1 Proposal #1

Student #1 started the project in Tapada da Ajuda, which is one of the largest green spaces in the city of Lisbon and a territory with a strong connection to nature. Tapada has an Astronomical Observatory and it was from this place that the Origin project emerged. It intends to create a journey in space–time, revisiting the past and preserving the present so that it is eternalized. However, this project sets its own direction by preserving memories on Earth so that they can be explored and observed in the space of the Astronomical Observatory.

The project has two components that allow users to revisit any time in history, browse in space to analyze it and leave their own testimony so that it can be revisited later. First component has a solar clock, present on the floor of the observatory, as main interface, from which users can choose a period in time to visit. First sketches (Fig. 1) represented ways to encode information from the present (which would be stored in the clock) so that it could be decoded in the future. Images/videos/texts of the past would be displayed in the own Astronomical Observatory of Ajuda building, in a way to immortalize the characteristics/events of Humanity.

The second component deals with collaboration, where users, by means of a mobile application can leave their own memory/testimony/input so that it becomes

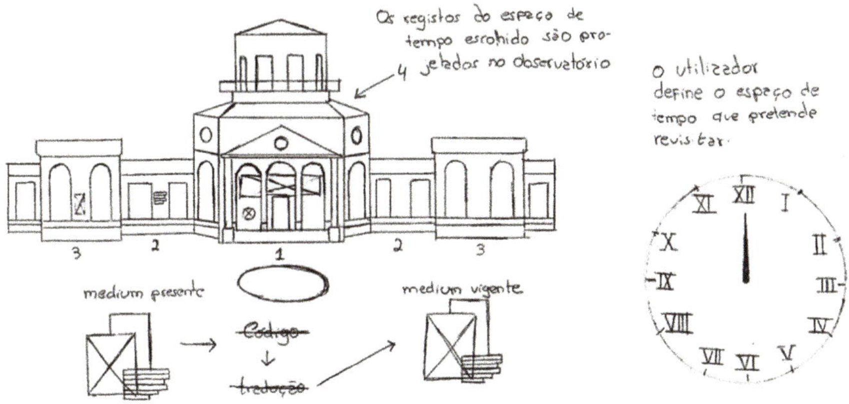

Fig. 1 Sketching the first ideas

Fig. 2 Interface of the solar clock and simulation of displays in the Astronomical Observatory area

a time capsule and can be seen in the future. Prototypes for the system were created and can be seen in Figs. 2 and 3.

5.2 *Proposal #2*

Student #2 initiated her research with Tram 28 route, one of the most emblematic transports in the city of Lisbon that runs through a series of places of great historical

Fig. 3 Mobile application screens—interactive prototype

and cultural relevance. One of those places is Jardim da Estrela, a public garden where in the mid twentieth century outdoor libraries became popular, at the same time as censorship was installed in the country. Student #2 aimed to explore how lost memories of a public space can be accessed to make it possible for users to reflect upon such issues.

The project proposed an interactive experience situated on the garden, through which users could explore a digital portal to simultaneously discover the physical space and censored books in a playful and poetic manner. A design system using beacons, digital installations and users' mobile phones allowed visitors to listen or read excerpts of various books virtually hidden throughout the garden and learn about censorship years in Portugal.

Student #2 used design ethnography methods to make direct observations of how people spent their time in the garden, as well as empathy maps, personas development, sketches and storyboards (Fig. 4), all of which granted her insights that helped to move project definition forward.

Information architecture, wireframes and user-flows helped define features, functionalities and content, followed by visual identity and interface design development. The "Invisible Library" produced high-fidelity prototypes of both the mobile portal (Fig. 5) and of a game-like digital installation (Fig. 6).

5.3 *Proposal #3*

Student #3 had as a starting point Baixa-Chiado, an underground station in downtown Lisbon, a modernized and busy spot populated by hurried or wandering passers-by. The project aimed at creating a synesthetic experience using color, shapes and sound for people who would cross the underground tunnels by devising a digital system

Fig. 4 Sketches used to visually materialize ideas during conception stage

composed of multimedia projections on tunnel walls, an interactive multi-user display wall and a mobile phone application (Fig. 7).

Strollers would be able to create visual and musical sequences made up of predefined modules, share results with other users through the app and experience their creation on the underground walls. Questioning our relationship with non-places [40] and projecting possibilities of place-making through technology and digitally mediated conviviality, “The Underground” project speculated on whether we can expand commuting urban spaces in a meaningful way. Student #3 applied various interaction design methods such as sketching and storyboards, low, medium and high fidelity wireframing, 3D scenario simulations and prototyping (Fig. 8).

6 Discussion

6.1 Interactions as Speculative Proposals

These proposals do not stand as the work students expected at the beginning of each semester, driven by concerns of professional, commercial and technological achievement. In following up on the projects, our effort was placed on combining the current understanding of each chosen situation with visions of possible futures, improved from the designer’s aggregating and critical vision.

Carried out work is a set of potential proposals, which could be produced and distributed, through progressive detailing after completion of this curricular unit. But, more importantly for us, they are also a double provocation. They are provocative as

Fig. 5 Mobile portal prototype

Fig. 6 Video simulation screenshots of an interactive game installation

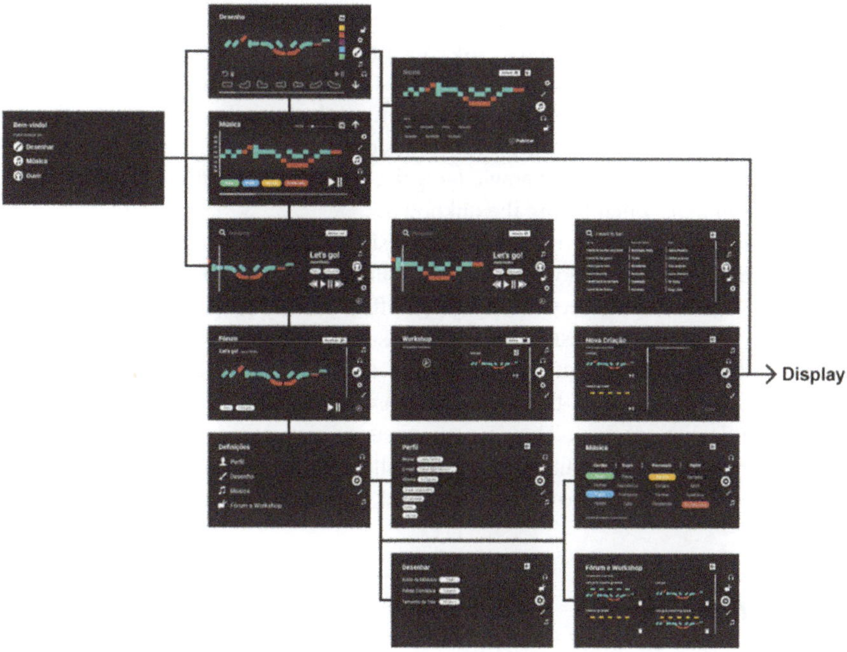

Fig. 7 Mobile application user flow

Fig. 8 Various work stages of the 3D simulation of a digital totem designed for multiple user interaction

a work suggestion, challenging students' expectations and changing an anticipated stability of work, which, in an university education context, caused its own knowledge since it was unforeseen. Individual results stand as a demonstration of acquired knowledge, different from what each student might initially anticipate and not a confirmation of what they already knew. This confirmation often awaited by students does not really translate into knowledge gain, but rather a guarantee not to trigger anxiety in students when facing the unknown.

They are also provocations given the existing understanding of each student's starting theme. Results do not represent the solution that will solve a problem, whatever it may be, in its entirety—something difficult to achieve by just one designer in a single semester. But results are a demonstration of reflection on each situation and a critical position on it, which assumes a contagious side of communication and sharing with others. In this sense, they are established as clues to future work based on a design practice. They are moments of exploratory research, which can support future research on the same topics, allowing the student/researcher to have background information and a conceptual and methodological mapping to work on.

6.2 SCD Approach

SCD is more a position taken by the designer than a methodology [21], which must be followed unequivocally. Which makes 'speculative' and 'critical' to be more of a goal or an approach than an area assumed by structural factors or with common results. This approach can then be associated with design practices, especially those involving social, cultural or technological themes. Interaction design practice that we have stimulated is made up of these ingredients, where unusual or hypothetical proposals, which lead to student or class reflection and discussion, are combined with methods and techniques that have become more regular in interaction designer's activities.

SCD is based on a discursive side, on stories told or implied, above all because of the evidence of what is conceived. This helps in articulating the SCD approach with individual themes and practice-led methods throughout project development. Students were asked to build this discourse from the beginning, with phases and support materials, in order to be communicated, shared, understood and discussed with faculty and colleagues.

However, SCD is provocative [20, 41, 42] and mainly understood by design students as an incitement at the beginning, as it originates confrontations with past educational experiences. Design students tend to acknowledge past learning experiences as unquestionable. Also, learning in interaction design has been profoundly influenced by recent technologies. Student attention to such technologies leads them to objectivity, limitations and predictions on what is achievable, what can be produced and replicated. They understand design as a problem-solving activity dedicated to 'real situations' and devoid of critical awareness, hypothetical capability and imaginary (not yet created) proposals.

6.3 Teaching Plan of What Was Made

The process we have devised was intended to nurture an informed interaction design practice, that may differ from individual to individual, but always based on constant questioning. Learn by doing, although as a regular expected way of guiding work phases, was accompanied by dialogue with faculty and filled with questions that went far beyond what can be merely seen, confronting students with a sense of purpose, of knowledge and reflection, of crossing first established proposals, of providing meaning beyond utilitarian or immediate solutions.

7 Conclusions

In design, as in other areas, speculation brings uncertainty. Something contrary to students' safe expectations, when looking for correct and definitive answers and for stable ways to operate in an area surrounded by progressively objective knowledge and criteria. Nevertheless, our intention of arriving at speculative proposals in interaction design was fulfilled through constant, discussed and reflective practice, which involved individualized paths through common phases to all students.

Such an option for critical vision and speculative creation does not intend to place the designer as an agent with superior or more enlightened perspective. Rather, it is an option that aims to engage students in concerns they can later pursue in their differentiated professional paths, enabling the acquisition of critical thinking skills, informed choices, broad creation and ideation and permanent reflection on the work they develop. These skills do not replace others of technical, methodological or objective nature, on the contrary, they aim to accumulate in students the purpose and clarification of designers as social protagonists, prepared to act with technical and technological resourcefulness of the time in which they live.

Accordingly, the presented proposals are not solutions to problems that meet consensus, they do not obey a semi-professional briefing and they may not even be possible to produce. Still, they position themselves as a way of questioning each situation for which they were designed. They emphasize the need to think, discuss and ultimately intervene in them. In a reasonable way, it was difficult to prevent students from not considering their proposals as solutions. One of the immediate difficulties is the sense of obtaining, of finishing something, of ending the challenge. Which somehow departs from the SCD's assumptions of promoting discussion.

However, results go beyond interactions or visualizations developed by each student and which helped them shape their ideas. Each element conceived in the various phases of individual projects are moments that are part of the proposal, which describe and detail components of these interventions that raise questions and foster positions.

We realized that in the Interaction Design Master's Degree at the University of Lisbon, stimulus to complex situations and project development that do not reflect commercial and business factors of professional activity, gives rise to works that are alternative proposals for social and cultural themes and allow students to train broad creative skills that brings them closer to become autonomous in their field.

SCD and RtD approach also demonstrates our intention of regarding the designer not as a technician, a technology informed and driven professional, but rather as a creator, a mediator, a cultural and social agent of change. What seems important to us, especially in areas so related and dependent on new or upgradable features which face a challenging horizon of autonomous systems, large amounts of information, physical/digital ubiquitous presence, with fast developing possibilities, multiple devices and multimodal interactions. Designers stand as contributors, both skeptical and inventive, to approach such numerous possibilities, anticipating consequences, regarding qualities and dangers, balancing humans and media and as main protagonists in proposing adequate but unexpected ways of living with such an environment.

Acknowledgements This work is financed by national funds through FCT - Fundação para a Ciência e a Tecnologia, I.P., under the Strategic Project with the references UIDB/04008/2020 and UIDP/04008/2020.

References

1. Gregory S (1966) Design science. In: The design method. Springer, Boston, MA, pp 323–330
2. Frayling C (1993) Research in art and design. Royal College of Art Research Papers, vol 1, number 1, Royal College of Art, 1–5
3. Logan C (2006) Circles of practice: educational and professional graphic design. The Journal of Workplace Learning 18(6):331–343
4. Archer B (1995) The nature of research. Co-design 3(1):6–13
5. Niedderer K, Roworth-Stokes S (2007) The role and use of creative practice in research and its contribution to knowledge. In: IASDR international conference 2007, vol 795, Hong Kong Polytechnic University, Hong Kong
6. Giaccardi G (2019) Histories and futures of research through design: From prototypes to connected things. Int J Des 13(3):139–155
7. Herriot R (2019) What kind of research is research through design? In: IASDR 2019 conference proceedings, Manchester, 11
8. Burdick A (2003) Design (as) research. In: Laurel B (ed) Design research: methods and perspectives. MIT Press, MA
9. Stappers P, Giaccardi E (2002) Research through design. In: The encyclopedia of human-computer interaction, 2nd edn, Chapter 43. Interaction Design Foundation
10. Frens J (2007) Research through design: a camera case study. In: Michel R (ed) Design research now. Essays and selected projects, Birkhauser, Basel, 135–156
11. Zimmerman J, Forlizzi J (2014) Research through design in HCI. In: Olson JS, Kellogg WA (eds) Ways of knowing in HCI, Springer, New York, 167–189
12. Durrant A, Vines J, Wallace J, Yee J (2017) Research Through design: twenty-first century makers and materialities. Des Issues 33(3):3–10
13. Fallman D, Stolterman E (2010) Establishing criteria of rigour and relevance in interaction design research. Digital Creativity 21(4):265–272

14. Zimmerman J, Forlizzi J, Evenson S (2007) Research through design as a method for interaction design research in HCI. In: Proceedings of the SIGCHI conference on human factors in computing systems, 493–502
15. Heeter C (2000) Interactivity in the context of designed experiences. J Interact Advert 1(1):3–14
16. Davis M, Hunt J (2017) Visual communication design: an introduction to design concepts in everyday experience. Bloomsbury Publishing, Sydney
17. Goodwin K (2011) Designing for the digital age: How to create human-centered products and services. Wiley
18. Arvola M, Artman H (2007) Enactments in interaction design: how designers make sketches behave. Artifact: J Des Pract 1(2):106–119
19. Kaethler M, Boelen J (2020) Social matter, social design
20. Dunne A, Raby F (2013) Speculative Design: Design, Fiction, and Social Dreaming. MIT Press, Cambridge, MA
21. Johannessen L, Keitsch M, Pettersen I (2019) Speculative and critical design—features, methods, and practices. In: Proceedings of the design society: international conference on engineering design. Cambridge University Press, 1623–1632
22. Escobar A (2018) Designs for the pluriverse. Duke University Press, Durham, NC
23. Tonkinwise C (2014) Design's (dis) orders: transition design as postindustrial design
24. Fry T (2017) Design for/by "The Global South." Des Philos Pap 15(1):3–37
25. Willis A (2015) Transition design: the need to refuse discipline and transcend instrumentalism. Des Philos Pap 13(1):69–74
26. Dunne A, Raby F (2001) Design noir: the secret life of electronic objects. Springer Science & Business Media, New York
27. Forlizzi J, Ford S (2000) The building blocks of experience: an early framework for interaction designers. In: Proceedings of the 3rd DIS: processes, practices, methods, and techniques, 419–423
28. Battarbee K, Koskinen I (2005) Co-experience: user experience as interaction. CoDesign 1(1):5–18
29. Helgason I, Smyth M, Encinas E, Mitrovic I (2020) Speculative and critical design in education: practice and perspectives. In: Companion publication of the 2020 ACM designing interactive systems conference, 385–388
30. Irwin T (2015) Transition design: A proposal for a new area of design practice, study, and research. Des Cult 7(2):229–246
31. Sanders E, Stappers P (2008) Co-creation and the new landscapes of design. Co-design 4(1):5–18
32. Davis M (2017) Teaching design: a guide to curriculum and pedagogy for college design faculty and teachers who use design in their classrooms. Simon and Schuster
33. Balsamo A (2011) Designing culture: the technological imagination at work. Duke University Press, Durham, NC
34. Encinas E, Blythe M (2018) Research fiction and thought experiments in design. Found Trends Human-Comput Inter 12(1):1–105
35. Stolterman E, Blevis E (2008) The confluence of interaction design & design: from disciplinary to transdisciplinary perspectives. In: DRS conference
36. Plowman T (2003). Ethnography and critical design practice. In Laurel B (ed) Design research: methods and perspectives. MIT Press, Cambridge, MA, pp 30–38
37. Biskjaer M, Dalsgaard P, Halskov K (2010) Creativity methods in interaction design. DESIRE 10:12–21
38. Bressa N, Wannamaker K, Korsgaard H, Willett W, Vermeulen J (2019) Sketching and ideation activities for situated visualization design. In: Proceedings of the 2019 DIS conference, 173–185
39. Buchenau M, Suri J (2000) Experience prototyping. In: Proceedings of the 3rd DIS: processes, practices, methods, and techniques, 424–433

40. Augé M (1995) Non-places: introduction to an anthropology of supermodernity. Verso, London
41. Bardzell S, Bardzell J, Forlizzi J, Zimmerman J, Antanitis J (2012) Critical design and critical theory: the challenge of designing for provocation. In: Proceedings of the DIS conference, 288–297
42. Galloway A, Caudwell C (2018) Speculative design as research method: from answers to questions and "staying with the trouble". In: Undesign. Routledge, London, 85–96

What Should Be Known About Design if We Only Know Design?

Carla Paoliello

Abstract Porous liquids are a new class of porous materials. They combine the permanent porosity of solid sorbents with liquid fluid properties. Their basic unifying principle allows them to reinvent materials syntheses, eliminating separations. Are these characteristics used in our Design Education? Design is already an activity associated with other study fields. It is potentially transdisciplinary and transversal. It uses contributions from other areas in its objects and forms of communication. It applies other questions, brings new searches, and constantly expands its reality. But is the Portuguese Design Education System open to further knowledge? Is it a porous system? What should be known about design if we only know design? These are the questions this paper investigates. Five different Portuguese Product Design Courses were studied. The study program's objectives and intended learning outcomes were analyzed. Each curricular unit—syllabus and teaching methodologies—was compared. The conclusion is that the design educational system gains with these porous, liquid, plural, and hybrid programs that embrace different expertise, practices, and cultures.

Keywords Porous liquid · Design Education · Interdisciplinary

1 Introduction and Main Concepts

Two essential concepts are the basis of this paper's discussion: the definition and characteristics of Interdisciplinary and Porous liquids materials. They are the key to answer this paper main questions: Is the Portuguese Design Education System open to further knowledge? Is it a porous system? And the most important one: What should be known about design if we only know design?

Interdisciplinary education involves integrating knowledge, methods, and concepts from different fields to create a more comprehensive and innovative approach to education. A porous education system is open to interdisciplinary

C. Paoliello (✉)
Fine Arts Faculty, Lisbon University, Lisbon, Portugal
e-mail: carlapaoliello@gmail.com

D. Raposo et al. (eds.), *Perspectives on Design III*, Springer Series in Design and Innovation 34, https://doi.org/10.1007/978-3-031-43516-4_3

approaches and constantly seeks to improve and expand its knowledge base. The investigation hypothesis is that the Portuguese Design Education System is open to collaboration and integration with other fields and continuously seeks to improve and expand its knowledge base.

1.1 Inter- and Transdisciplinary Concepts and Approaches

The concepts and research practices of intra-, multi-, inter-, and transdisciplinarity are becoming more pertinent in the academia. It is recognized that many of society's most pressing challenges require an approach that goes beyond the boundaries of any single discipline. While intra-disciplinary means working within a single discipline, people from different disciplines work together in a multidisciplinary approach, each drawing on their knowledge. The integration of knowledge and methodologies from various disciplines to tackle intricate problems is what defines interdisciplinary approach, while transdisciplinarity involves the integration of intellectual frameworks that go beyond traditional disciplinary perspectives, resulting in a cohesive whole. The last three imply collaboration among the parties involved (Fig. 1).

So, intra-disciplinary work focuses on deepening the understanding and advancing knowledge within a specific discipline, often through specialization or expertise in a particular subfield. It involves collaboration and communication within a discipline, rather than between different disciplines or fields. Its work is important because it allows experts within a discipline to deepen their knowledge and understanding of a specific area of study, which can lead to advancements in the field and ultimately benefit society as a whole.

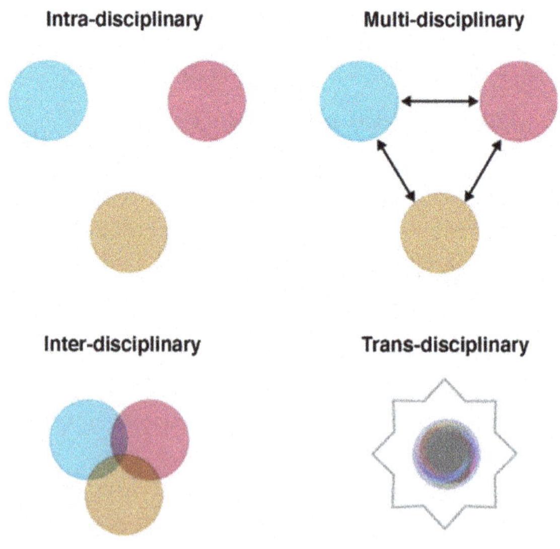

Fig. 1 Differentiation between intra-, multi-, inter-, and transdisciplinary concepts

Multidisciplinary refers to the approach of incorporating knowledge and perspectives from multiple disciplines or fields of study to solve a problem or address a complex issue. In multidisciplinary work, experts from different fields come together to collaborate, each bringing their own unique expertise and knowledge to the project, and it can be particularly effective when dealing with complex issues that require expertise from multiple disciplines. By bringing together experts from different fields, multidisciplinary teams can gain a more comprehensive understanding of the problem and develop more effective solutions. However, its work can also present challenges, such as communication barriers between team members from different disciplines, and the need to navigate differing perspectives and approaches to problem-solving. To be successful, multidisciplinary teams require effective communication, collaboration, and a willingness to learn from and value the contributions of team members from different fields.

Interdisciplinarity is a way of breaking down the barriers between academic fields and fostering collaboration and communication across different domains of expertise. It can involve bringing together researchers from different disciplines to work on a joint project or the development of new fields of study that draw on multiple disciplines. Bringing together diverse perspectives and approaches helps to identify new research questions, facilitates the integration of different types of data and methods, and promotes the development of more comprehensive and nuanced understandings of complex phenomena.

The struggle of interdisciplinary study started with the growing specialization of science into various branches and disciplines during the nineteenth century [14]. However, until today, it enables and fosters collaborative exchange between different scientific disciplines to operate side by side.

On the other hand, transdisciplinary is credited to Jean Piaget. As Patrocínio stated, "discussions about the future of knowledge and research were sparked at that time by the revolutionary notion of a system of relationships between various fields without clearly defined limits" [12].

Nonetheless, transdisciplinary collaboration with a continuous exchange and active cooperation between different disciplines is still rare [17]. It refers to an approach that goes beyond multidisciplinary collaboration, by integrating knowledge, perspectives, and methods from different fields into a new framework that transcends traditional disciplinary boundaries. In transdisciplinary work, experts from different fields work together with non-experts and stakeholders to address complex problems that cannot be solved by a single discipline alone. It can be characterized by the following features:

1. Integration of diverse knowledge systems: transdisciplinary work integrates diverse knowledge systems, including scientific, local, and experiential knowledge, to develop a more comprehensive understanding of the problem;
2. Focus on real-world problems: transdisciplinary work is driven by real-world problems, and seeks to address them in a way that is relevant and meaningful to society;

3. Co-creation of knowledge: transdisciplinary work involves collaboration between experts and non-experts, including stakeholders and community members, to co-create knowledge and develop solutions that are socially and environmentally sustainable;
4. Development of new methods and frameworks: transdisciplinary work often leads to the development of new methods and frameworks that can be used to address complex problems in other contexts.

Transdisciplinary work is important because it allows for a more comprehensive and holistic approach to addressing complex problems, and can lead to more innovative and effective solutions that are socially and environmentally sustainable. However, it can also be challenging, as it requires collaboration across different knowledge systems and perspectives, and may require new methods and frameworks to be developed to address the problem.

What is an interdisciplinary designer? What are its main characteristics? According to the World Design Organization definition:

> Industrial Design is a strategic problem-solving process that drives innovation, builds business success, and improves life quality through innovative products, systems, services, and experiences. Industrial Design bridges the gap between what is and what's possible. It is a trans-disciplinary profession that harnesses creativity to resolve problems and co-create solutions with the intent of making a product, system, service, experience or a business, better. [19]

The definition strengthens the idea that Design can and (actually) transcends disciplinary boundaries. It is an activity associated with other study fields. It uses contributions from other areas in its objects and forms of communication and applies other questions, bringing new investigations and constantly expanding its reality.

The designer has a mediating character, enabling interaction and relations with others' professions and expertise essential to deal with themes such as sustainability, equity, adaptation, justice, and social responsibility. Its transversal characteristic helps society when it faces complex social, ecological, and economic challenges that require collaborative approaches.

Repko [15, 16] claims that interdisciplinary instruction promotes cognitive advancements, and other educational researchers [3, 8, 11, 13], have identified several distinct educational benefits of interdisciplinary learning, including improvements in the ability to recognize bias, think critically, tolerate ambiguity, and acknowledge and appreciate ethical concerns.

Fink [4] identifies six elements of an interdisciplinary educational process that lead to significant learning: foundational knowledge, application, integration, human dimension, caring, and learning how to learn (Fig. 2).

In other words, interdisciplinary instruction promotes the acquisition of structural knowledge, integrating ideas from multiple disciplines, and applying knowledge, all of which advance a student's learning to understand. Furthermore, when analyzing problems, students are encouraged to account for the contribution of disciplines that emphasize the roles of caring and social interaction. As a result of the consistent interdisciplinary learning with the core features of significant learning, students are

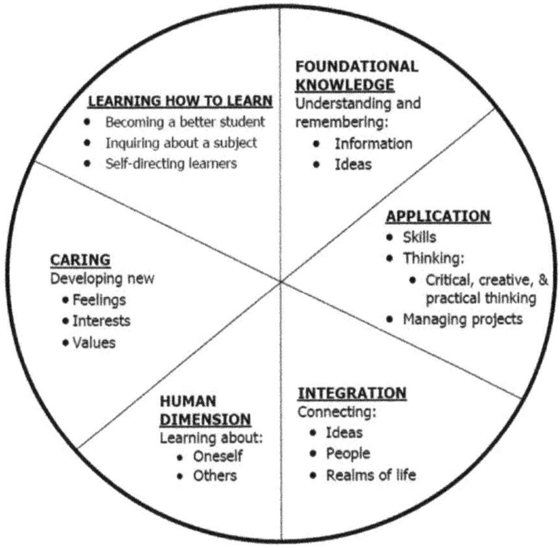

Fig. 2 Fink's taxonomy of significant learning

expected to find interdisciplinary education engaging and, thus, an effective way to advance their understanding of topics under investigation.

However, interdisciplinarity has its challenges. It can be difficult to bridge the language and epistemological differences between different disciplines, and there may be differences in research cultures, norms, and practices that can create barriers to collaboration. Interdisciplinary research may also require more time and resources than traditional disciplinary research, as researchers need to develop a common language and methodology and may need to spend more time learning about other disciplines. Despite these challenges, the potential benefits of interdisciplinarity are significant, especially in Design.

Designers often work across different domains, such as technology, engineering, psychology, and anthropology, and need to be able to collaborate with experts in these fields to understand and solve problems. Interdisciplinary design education involves bringing together students and faculty from different disciplines to work on joint design projects. For example, it can involve collaborations between designers and engineers, designers and social scientists, or designers and artists. By working in interdisciplinary teams, students are exposed to different perspectives and approaches, which can help to broaden their understanding of design practices. In addition, by working with experts from different fields, students can learn to consider various factors when designing products, services, or experiences. They can also learn about the social, cultural, and environmental implications of Design and how their designs can positively or negatively affect society.

1.2 Porous Liquids Materials: Is It Interdisciplinary?

Intrinsically porous materials, consisting of molecules organized in cage-like structures, are generally ordered and crystalline solids at usable temperatures. However, their cavities, channels, or interstices are regions of emptiness, spaces where guest materials can be selectively adsorbed and occasionally chemically changed. Differently, fluidity interprets the rheological behavior of amorphous materials. They have an unsettled or unstable state that presents their constant changeability.

Porous liquids are a new molecular material class combining permanent porosity and fluid properties. The concept of liquids being able to retain porosity permanently was introduced by Giri et al. [5], but other authors have also studied them [1, 2, 6, 7]. They are composed of a liquid solvent, which acts as a host for a network of pores within its structure. The pores can be filled with a variety of guest molecules, allowing for control over the size and properties of the pores (Fig. 3).

According to Mahdavi et al., all liquids are porous; that is, "molecules in liquids are not rigid and well packed; they continually tumble over each other arbitrarily" [10, p. 1578]. It leads to transient pores that consistently appear and disappear. However, Porous liquids generate permanent, unoccupied cavities in the liquid phase.

Conceptually and practically speaking, introducing well-controlled "empty" space into liquids is very appealing. The ability to precisely control the size and shape of the pores within the liquid allows for the investigation of structure–property relationships and the exploration of new chemical phenomena. In addition, the

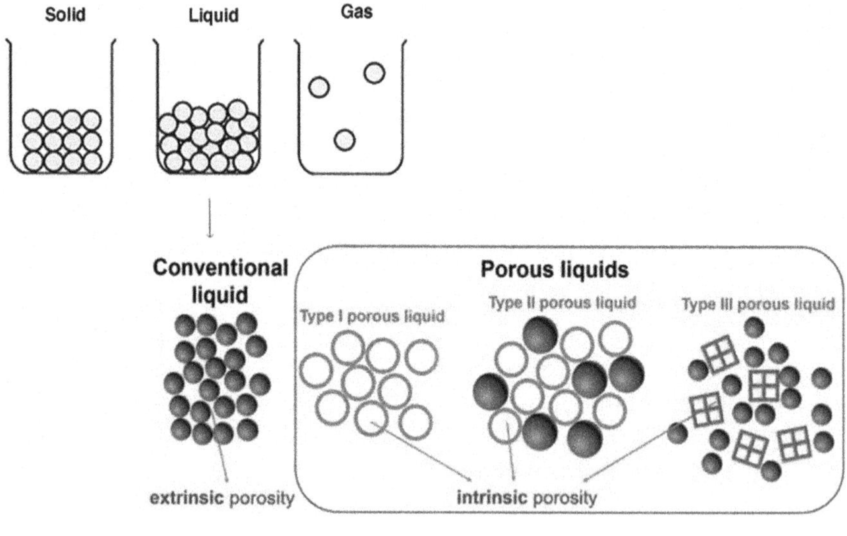

Fig. 3 Arrangement of particles in solids, liquids, and gases and schematic showing conventional liquids and the three types of porous liquids proposed by James [7]. Conventional liquids have only extrinsic porosity, while porous liquids have intrinsic porosity

possibility of absorbing, assimilating, or incorporating something emerges while maintaining the tendency to flow when subjected to stress.

Moreover, studying porous liquids materials also involves collaborations between researchers from different disciplines. Their interdisciplinary study integrates knowledge and methods from multiple fields, including chemistry, materials science, and physics. Nevertheless, it could also be called an interdisciplinary material that reflects or carries out other materials while remaining fluid.

2 Research Method and the Case Studies Information

Is Portugal's Design Education interdisciplinary? Does it have a porous liquid system? These are the questions that this paper investigates. After the literature review phase, the method was to select, study, and analyze five Portuguese Product Design Courses. The study program's objectives and intended learning outcomes were highlighted. Each curricular unit (syllabus and teaching methodologies) was compared.

The investigation focused on Product/Equipment or Industrial Design Courses in Portugal. According to the General Direction of Higher Education—DGES,[1] there are nineteen courses in Portuguese territory. A criteria list was established to reduce them to 5 universities:

1. It should be a public institution. Public universities are higher education institutions (HEIs) financially maintained by the state and, therefore, have the public and collective interest as their main characteristic. Portuguese higher education is organized into two legally different subsystems: universities and polytechnics, and both are of this investigation interest.
2. It should be a master course. A master's degree is a postgraduate degree that allows specialization in a particular subject. It is a continuous improvement toward expertise. It helps strengthen critical thinking and access to new working methods and techniques.
3. It should be dispersed throughout Portuguese territory. Despite being a small country, cultural, social, economic, and environmental differences exist.
4. The information about each course should be readily available and trustable. There is a document (Accreditation of New Cycle of Studies by A3ES) that presents each course, each unit curricular study plan, and the competencies to be developed by students, among other important information that should be used to analyze the interdisciplinary approach.

By using all these five requirements, the following courses were selected: Product and Services Design Master Degree in EA-UMinho, Product Design Master Degree in FBA-UPorto, Engineering and Product Design Master Course in UAveiro, Interior and Furniture Design Master Course in IPCB, and Design for Sustainability Master

[1] https://www.dges.gov.pt/guias/indcurso.asp?letra=d.

Fig. 4 Portugal map with the chosen HEIs location

Degree in FBA-ULisboa, located as on the map in Fig. 4. It is essential to emphasize that all institutions provided evidence that they are reference study cycles in the Design European Higher Education Area.

The Master in Product Design and Services by UMinho promotes an alternative and complementary postgraduate education centered on Design. It provides an innovative proposal for incorporating Design as a strategic tool. Furthermore, it supports innovation as a sustainable methodology and refocuses the designer's role in the global R&D strategy. As in its presentation text, "this study plan arises from the interdisciplinary relation of classical methods and tools of design, as well as design thinking, valuing the role of the designer as a strategic member in the construction of services responding to social innovations".[2]

It brings other scientific areas, such as Psychology, Communication Sciences, and Social Sciences Education, into three curricular units of 5 ECTS. The main scientific area is Design, which is present in all curricular units (105 ECTS). Seminars I and II are also places (curricular units) for other voices and knowledge presence.

The Master's Degree in Product and Industrial Design at FBA-UPorto allows students to deepen their understanding of design practice in specific contexts. In addition, students engage in educational activities to help them develop the skills needed to work independently and in multidisciplinary teams.[3]

It also brings, along with the design area (111 ECTS), other scientific areas: drawing, engineering, and investigation and research methodologies (with a total of 9 ECTS). A particular emphasis can be given to The Design Project unit. It promotes

[2] https://www.eaad.uminho.pt/en/Study/masters/mdps.

[3] https://www.up.pt/portal/en/fbaup/fbaup/2021/.

skills, acquiring and articulating knowledge in implementing and managing projects, whether products or services, in articulation with engineering and management.

The Master in Product Design and Engineering by UAveiro[4] aims to provide the necessary competencies for product optimization and innovation by taking a more integrated approach. It thus provides insight and knowledge on two core scientific areas, namely Design and Mechanical Engineering. Furthermore, this transversal core consolidates the knowledge acquired within the two mentioned scientific areas by exploring their synergies. Therefore, it values the interdisciplinary when establishing a bridge between a new concept and the constraints arising from materials and industrial and productive capacities.

Its scientific areas are Design (30 ECTS) and Mechanical Engineering (24 ECTS), a mix between both areas—EMEC/DS (54 ECTS) and the optative units (12 ECTS). The teaching methods of Project in Product Design I and II emphasize a critical praxis. They are heuristic, with knowledge being shared and developed in tandem with and through the resolution of exercises. The practical resolution and research of real-life problems are also requested.

Aware of the higher polytechnic education mission regarding the nature of training and ministering to the needs of changing world institutions characterized by complexity and uncertainty, IPCB continues to focus on offering targeted training for the labor market. It is shaped by concerns relating to the need to reconcile the requirements of an increasingly specialized (employability-based training) with more solid scientific training. Its Interior and Furniture Design Master Course aims to develop the student's ability to research and the innovation applied to interior design and furniture; train professionals capable of developing technical advice and expertise in interior design and furniture; develop the ability to coordinate projects of interior design and furniture and the expertise in the management, control, and definition of production systems.[5]

Its scientific areas are Design (84 ECTS), Technologies (32 ETCS), and Humanities (4 ECTS). In the curricular unit, Interior Design Project I, the intended learning outcomes (knowledge, skills, and competencies to be developed by the students) are developing the conceptual component, application of interdisciplinary knowledge, particularly in the implementation/creation/transformation and detail; communication skills and motivation of the project; and acknowledge organizational dynamics. Moreover, in other units, there is also the aim to develop good relationships with multidisciplinary teamwork.

At last, the Design for Sustainability Master Degree in FBA-ULisboa[6] has its primary objective: to provide postgraduate training in Design in the context of sustainable development, understood in the transversality of the disciplinary framework of environmental, social, and economic sciences. It also intends to promote

[4] https://www.ua.pt/en/course/329.

[5] https://gri.ipcb.pt/en/master-interior-and-furniture-design.

[6] https://www.belasartes.ulisboa.pt/en/cursos/mestrados/design-para-A-sustentabilidade/.

reflection and debate on specific sustainability issues that allow the Design, development, and implementation of local, regional, and global projects within the framework of the United Nations Sustainable Development Goals—moreover, developing Design Projects in real context and collaboration with public and private entities in environmental, social, and economic sustainability.

The interest in this proposal results from a partnership with the following organic units of the University of Lisbon: Faculty of Fine Arts; Faculty of Sciences; Institute of Social Sciences; Institute of Economics and Management; Architecture Faculty. Because of this scenario, the scientific areas are Design (18 ECTS), Environmental Sciences (6 ECTS), Economics and Management (6 ECTS), Social Sciences (18 ECTS), and the last one is a potpourri with Design and Environmental Sciences or Life Sciences; or Engineering, Energy Technologies, Environmental Engineering and Technologies of Geoinformation or Statistics or Informatics; Design and Economics and Management; Design and Science Social (42 ECTS). There are also the optative units responsible for 30 ETCS.

3 Analyzing Interdisciplinary

Interdisciplinary teaching involves the application and integration of methods and analytical frameworks from various academic disciplines to explore a theme, issue, question, or topic.

This characteristic could be seen by exploring these five curricular study plans. Their curricula were examined by and with other disciplinary approaches, synthesizing insights from various relevant disciplines that contributed to understanding each scientific area in a more complete and coherent analysis framework.

It is essential to highlight that there are several vital elements to consider when analyzing interdisciplinary work, including:

- Research question: What is the central problem or question being addressed, and why does it require an interdisciplinary approach? Understanding the research question helps clarify why different disciplines are being brought together and what each contributes to the overall project.
- Disciplinary approaches: What disciplines are involved in the project, and how do they contribute to the overall approach? Understanding the epistemological and methodological differences between different disciplines and how they are being integrated into interdisciplinary work is important.
- Collaboration and communication: How are researchers from different disciplines collaborating and communicating with each other? Interdisciplinary work often requires effective communication and collaboration across disciplinary boundaries, which can be challenging due to language, terminology, and cultural differences.

- Integration and synthesis: How are the findings and insights from different disciplines integrated and synthesized to address the research question? Interdisciplinary work often involves synthesizing knowledge from different disciplines to develop a more comprehensive and nuanced understanding of complex phenomena.
- Implications and impact: What are the implications and impact of interdisciplinary work? Interdisciplinary work can have implications for policy, practice, and future research, and it is crucial to consider the potential impact of the work beyond the specific research project.

In analyzing interdisciplinary work, it is also important to recognize that it is a dynamic and ongoing process. Interdisciplinary work often involves learning and adapting as the project progresses, and it may require ongoing communication and collaboration between researchers from different disciplines.

The reason for having an interdisciplinary approach in Design Education and its benefits are clear. Designers often work across different domains and need to collaborate with experts in various fields to understand and solve problems. This approach acknowledges that design involves problem-solving and decision-making processes that draw upon a range of knowledge domains. Because of that, there are several reasons for having an interdisciplinary approach in design education, including:

- Diversity of perspectives: An interdisciplinary approach allows students to explore a variety of perspectives and disciplines, it exposes students and faculty to different perspectives broadens their understanding of design practices. And it can lead to a more holistic and well-rounded understanding of design problems. This approach can help students to develop a more nuanced understanding of the social, cultural, and environmental contexts in which design solutions are applied.
- Integration of different skills: An interdisciplinary approach allows students to integrate different skills and knowledge domains to solve complex design problems. By working with experts from different fields, students can learn how to consider various factors when designing products, services, or experiences and understand their solutions' social, cultural, and environmental implications.
- Innovation: An interdisciplinary approach can foster innovation by encouraging students to think outside of their own discipline and explore new approaches to design problems. This approach can help students to develop creative solutions that may not have been possible within a single discipline.
- Real-world relevance: An interdisciplinary approach can help students to develop a more realistic understanding of the challenges facing designers in the real world. By integrating perspectives from different disciplines, students can gain a better understanding of the complexities of design problems and the need for interdisciplinary collaboration.

In summary, an interdisciplinary approach in design education can provide students with a more diverse set of perspectives, integrate different skills, foster innovation, and develop a realistic understanding of the challenges facing designers in the real world.

The integration and synthesis of different perspectives could be seen in the exercise proposals; they consist of complex considerations with multiple viewpoints. A single disciplinary viewpoint can lead to hegemony, preventing critical evaluation of other perspectives. Interdisciplinary education, on the other hand, draws on multiple voices and knowledge to gain a deep and thorough understanding of complex issues. It challenges students to synthesize what each discipline offers before attempting to design efforts to address noted concerns.

Unfortunately, comparing the words that occurred several times at each HEIs study plan, the maximum number of times a word repeated in the case of interdisciplinarity was three, transdisciplinary appeared two times, and multidisciplinary occurred eleven times. Fifty-four words were also used to describe those concepts (i.e., cooperation—9×, integration—34×, perspectives—9×, and stakeholders—2×).

Words such as coproduction, cocreation, and knowledge sharing are also associated with interdisciplinary, but they did not appear in the documents. Lang et al. [9] establish a list of keywords such as system, society, complex, framework, perspective, disciplines, participatory, transformation, and negotiation. This list describes the design principles for transdisciplinary research and could lead to the interdisciplinarity concept. Some of those words appeared in the selected HEIs study plan but were not to present these concepts.

Nevertheless, this scenario could also be their weakness due to the complementary human and material resources coordination needed. An interdisciplinary curriculum plan can establish tools to assess alternative activities, but it is just the baseline of participation, not its imposition.

Interviews with each course's coordinators, teachers, and students could have been conducted to deepen each reality. This practice would bring the voice of these actors and a description that many times needs to be documented. It would also help in understanding the spaces that the design students inhabit and if their cultural background reflects in the classroom and exercises proposed. However, the premise of this article was to assess whether the concept of interdisciplinarity existed in the course plan documents. Therefore, this suggestion is left for future work.

Another research possibility is to map and study solutions that "can serve as catalysts to increase motivation or even effectiveness in fostering inter- and transdisciplinarity" [18]. It has the potential to transform science itself, allowing for the structural changes required for collaborative work both inside and outside of academia.

4 Conclusion or What Should Be Known About Design if We Only Know Design?

The conclusion is that these five courses (Product and Services Design Master Degree in EA-UMinho, Product Design Master Degree in FBA-UPorto, Engineering and Product Design Master Course in UAveiro, Interior and Furniture Design Master Course in IPCB, and Design for Sustainability Master Degree in FBA-ULisboa) are porous, liquid, plural, and hybrid. Furthermore, they considered interdisciplinary as a way of connecting design knowledge with different ones to embrace other expertise, practices, and cultures.

The Portuguese Design Education System is open to further knowledge; it acts as a porous liquid material. The five studied programs' interdisciplinary character and inter-departmental nature are their strength. They have a flow pedagogy, creating an environment where learners can immerse totally into the art of learning in areas beyond Design. They also facilitate collaboration, exchanging, and sharing ideas in different scientific areas.

What should be known about Design if we only know Design? That is not an easy question and further research is needed to visualize the establishment of inter- and transdisciplinarity in the real-situation course day by day. It would demand conscious and reflective facilitation to foster interactions.

Acknowledgements This work is financed by national funds through FCT—Fundação para a Ciência e a Tecnologia, I.P., within the project «UIDB/04042/2020».

References

1. Bavykina A, Cadiau A, Gascon J (2019) Porous liquids based on porous cages, metal organic frameworks and metal organic polyhedra. Coord Chem Rev 386:85–95. https://doi.org/10.1016/j.ccr.2019.01.015
2. Bennett TD et al (2021) The changing state of porous materials. Nat Mater 20:1179–1187. https://doi.org/10.1038/s41563-021-00957-w
3. Field M, Lee R, Field ML (1994) Assessing interdisciplinary learning. New Dir Teach Learn 58:69–84
4. Fink LD (2003) Creating significant learning experiences: An integrated approach to designing college courses. Jossey-Bass, San Francisco
5. Giri N et al (2012) Alkylated organic cages: from porous crystals to neat liquids. Chem Sci 3(6):2153–2157
6. Giri N et al (2015) Liquids with permanent porosity. Nature 527:216–220. https://doi.org/10.1038/nature16072
7. James SL, Hutchings B (2019) Porous liquids. In: Nakanishi T (ed) Functional organic liquids. Wiley, pp 39–52. https://doi.org/10.1002/9783527804948.ch3
8. Kavaloski V (1979) Interdisciplinary education and humanistic aspiration: a critical reflection. In: Kockelmans J (ed) Interdisciplinarity and higher education. The Pennsylvania State University Press, University Park, PA
9. Lang D, Wiek A, Bergmann M et al (2012) Transdisciplinary research in sustainability science—practice, principles, and challenges. Sustain Sci Pract Policy 7(1):25–43

10. Mahdavi H (2022) Practical considerations in the design and use of porous liquids. Mater Horiz 9:1577–1601. https://doi.org/10.1039/d1mh01616d
11. Newell WH (2001) A theory of interdisciplinary studies. Issues Integr Stud 19:1–25
12. Patrocinio G, Filgueiras E, Nunes, Gonçalves JM (2022) A new role for design in the 21st century: from operational to tactical and strategic. In: Virtual and augmented reality for design and architecture. Boca Raton, Estados Unidos: 94. CRC Press, Taylor & Francis, 88–119
13. Pennycook A (2005) Teaching with the flow: fixity and fluidity in education. Asia Pac J Educ 25(1):29–43. https://doi.org/10.1080/02188790500032491
14. Pombo O (2004) Interdisciplinaridade. Ambições e Limites. Relógio d'Água, Lisboa
15. Repko A (2008) Interdisciplinary research: process and theory. Sage Publications
16. Repko A (2009) Assessing interdisciplinary learning outcomes. Working Paper, School of Urban and Public Affairs, University of Texas at Arlington
17. Stokols D, Misra S, Moser RP, Hall KL, Taylor BK (2008) The ecology of team science. Understanding contextual influences on transdisciplinary collaboration. Am J Prev Med 35(2 Suppl):96–115
18. von Wehrden H, Guimarães MH, Bina O et al (2019) Interdisciplinary and transdisciplinary research: finding the common ground of multi-faceted concepts. Sustain Sci 14:875–888
19. WDO—World Design Organization (2015) Industrial Design definition. https://wdo.org/about/definition/

Sustainable Artistic Practices in Graphic Design for Visual Communication

Krasimira Borisova Drumeva

Abstract Graphic design has concentrated in itself the quintessence of all visual arts. It absorbs the most synthetic means of expression in order to unequivocally unfold the author's idea. It is closest to people, at the front line of communication, because it is positioned in all spheres of public and personal life. It is these qualities that make it responsible for the formation of sustainable attitude in consumers towards environmental and social problems. This article elaborates on important ethical aspects of graphic design and draws the attention on a vision of sustainable future in design. The main study is focused on the essential communicative means of graphic design—image, composition and symbol—in the context of the advertising industry. They are analysed as an expressive and artistic means of graphic design for communication, which uses the transformation of colors and shapes. As a result, the practical research offers a summary of the most common approaches applied in visual communication with the audience.

Keywords Visual communication · Graphic design · Visual metaphor · Symbol · Composition · Colour · Images · Associations · Sustainability

1 Introduction

The modern understanding of graphic design and advertising is gradually evolving from a mode of information and persuasion for consumption, to a mode of conceptual communication. The goal is not only to achieve more favourable sales conditions, but to earn the buyers' trust, to promote the true values of our times. This is achieved by applying the so-called "added value". In this article we will examine it as sustainable graphic design in view of its specific main objectives. This type of authentic communication seeks opportunities to share and teach reasonable consumption of natural resources, tolerant attitude towards differences, empathy, aesthetics and many other

K. B. Drumeva (✉)
St. Cyril and St. Methodius University, 5000 Veliko Tarnovo, 48 Nezavisimost, Tarnovo, Bulgaria
e-mail: drumevika@abv.bg

D. Raposo et al. (eds.), *Perspectives on Design III*, Springer Series in Design and Innovation 34, https://doi.org/10.1007/978-3-031-43516-4_4

qualities that are important for the civilized society. To influence the target audience groups, it applies the means of expression of art, technology and psychology. It is characterized by an unobtrusive presentation of the advertised object, which may not even appear in the composition. A new approach is sought to avoid trivial channels for communication with users and to create a new level of connection and empathy. In this aspect, many companies have realized that inciting their customers to consumerism causes the opposite effect of rejecting the advertising messages, even if they are dressed in the brightest packaging. A number of campaigns have been created that address global topics related to current problems of mankind. Such are the advertising messages of Benetton—against racial discrimination, Globul—for saving paper, H&M—aimed at recycling textiles, and many others.

1.1 Critical Analysis of the Interaction Between Graphic Design and Industry

Looking in perspective, several problem areas can be identified in the development course of graphic design and its products. Worldwide, large quantities of printed promotional materials are produced, which generate a lot of waste. Competition among manufacturers provokes the design of ever more attractive and long-lasting packaging, catalogues, leaflets and so on. This trend forces designers to put more and more resources into presenting products, which on the other hand leads to production of unreasonably large volumes of waste, which is not recycled. These practices pose a difficult dilemma for design and marketing professionals to find a holistic approach maintaining the balance of high sales through spectacular design and environmental responsibility. A successful design in this regard is the sustainable packaging of Puma called by its authors "smart little bag" (see Fig. 1). The purpose of its design is to reduce the material used for shoe boxes, to avoid the need for a plastic bag and to use only recycled materials. The design approach is based on the concept of optimal transportation of the product from the production facility to the consumer's home. Once the shoes are in use, the bag can be reused several times. This is a project that aims to preserve, to reduce the weight and volume of the product, to use environmentally friendly materials, and to offer a multifunctional eco-friendly shoe container.

Through such creative solutions, designers seek effective strategies to exert influence on the target groups and to apply feasible planning aimed at fostering a culture of reasonable consumption of short-lived products. Designers are involved in the industry cycle and the guild should unite, provoked by its environmental responsibility, to offer standards and optimal configurations for reducing pollution with plastic and other synthetic materials. Contribution to the industry takes our thinking a step forward in the direction of sustainable development of the advertising industry and introduction of innovative creative solutions to reduce carbon emissions.

Fig. 1 Packaging contents: The Clever Little Bag, Designer: Yves Behar, Brand: Puma SE

Another important aspect of visual communication is that graphic design should engage the attention of users, but this is becoming increasingly difficult because people are set to dismiss advertising as intrusive and redundant information. In any case, at this stage of its existence, the industry is not able to develop without the mediation of advertising. Designers are assigned with the difficult task of overcoming the apathy of the audience and arouse the curiosity of the users. For that reason, it is necessary to search for new channels of communication that break the stereotypes and use new approaches to persuade. It is in this respect that the communication between advertising and graphic design is becoming an increasingly fundamental element for the success of many campaigns.

A major factor determining the quality of graphic design is its ability to form and implement an effective concept in any new project. In the last decades, the lack of creativity has brought the advertising industry to the level of decorating the advertising object without any element of contribution. There are trends towards depreciation of these qualities by turning graphic design into a multiplier of numerous unnecessary and even intrusive images. The lack of a creative element, which entertains, provokes and surprises, has a negative effect on the consumers' desire to perceive advertising. In this process, creativity is the factor to stir people's interest, to make them like and recognize the trademark in all its advertising forms.

These basic characteristics, such as innovation and creativity, outline several advantages that sustainable graphic design has over traditional forms. It is the way to provoke the intelligence of the audience by applying indirect methods and relying on curiosity about the unknown and the non-standard that is inherent in the human mind. It is not perceived as intrusive advertising, but as a useful and interesting means to improve everyday life. It hides behind the screen of the designers' creative energy and the surprising suggestion. Its purpose is to make customers feel that they need or want a particular product or service. In some cases, this is achieved without even presenting the specific product, but only through presenting an intriguing situation related to it.

Graphic design has concentrated in itself the quintessence of all visual arts. It absorbs the most synthetic means of expression in order to unequivocally unfold the author's idea. It is closest to people, at the front line of communication, because it is positioned in all spheres of public and personal life. Often, these places are overflown with graphic images and it is extremely difficult to attract the attention of the audience. This requires a combination of powerful expression and laconic form without anything superfluous and decorative. As a result, the works are charged with dynamism, bold compositions and characteristic details. Stylized and recognizable shapes, dynamic lines and focus on the most expressive elements are sought. The artistic symbiosis between composition, image and symbol attracts attention and provokes associations based on the depicted objects. Through a creative interpretation of reality, the viewer is introduced to a new world of fantasy. It is an approach that provokes visual intelligence to convey content.

This article elaborates on important ethical aspects of graphic design and draws attention to a vision of sustainable future in design. The main study is focused on the essential communicative means of graphic design—image, composition and symbol—in the context of the advertising industry. They are analysed as an expressive and artistic means of graphic design for communication, which uses the transformation of colors and shapes. As a result, the practical research offers a summary of the most common approaches applied in visual communication with the audience.

1.2 Expressive and Artistic Means of Graphic Design for Communication

In addition to being an advertisement generator, graphic design is also a medium that delivers a message. This characteristic defines it as a means of communication in constant dynamic development. It is particularly important for it to find direct, clear and untraditional channels to connect with the audience. It is an important part of promoting events, institutions and campaigns. Good design is a synthetic art, which uses a specific visual language and can influence the audience on an intuitive level. The process of "deciphering" the author's idea from the viewer's standpoint is a challenge, creating a special intellectual connection between designer and recipient.

1.2.1 The Image

Images are the main means of expression in graphic design because they can easily convey a message. They are among the first elements that engage the attention and have a huge potential for transmitting feelings, moods and information. Compared to other elements of expression, they are perceived subconsciously and easily. No matter how many text messages we send, they will not be able to attract attention the way visual announcements do.

In brief, the process of visualization consists of recreating real images within the work surface plane, thus building a conditional space in which three-dimensional images are represented in two-dimensional form. As a result of this, and after being refracted through the prism of the author's creative perspective, the images become highly conditional. In order to weave an author's idea into the final project, it is necessary to create the so-called synthetic image. It is a new, unique object that has been created specifically to serve the needs of the creative process. The mastery of the author lies in finding the most appropriate angle, colour harmony and composition in order to create a convincing illusion of space in the printed format plane. While building the synthetic image, the author aims to exclude every superfluous element from reality, in order to emphasize the main idea. In fact, such frames do not exist in visual perception, and people merge what they see in one general picture. A great deal of the visual information is not even registered and gets overlooked. Often things that impress some are trivial to others. The designer's skill is expressed also in the ability to cut the boundaries of the form to limit and direct the eye to a specific object of his choice in order to impart a specific value or meaning. This approach should be synchronized with a clearly defined centre of meaning that enhances the impact of the main idea. The author's concept is conveyed more directly by placing the additional elements in the background. This is achieved by blurring, dimming or brightening the non-essential aspects. All objects are organized around this centre of meaning, and they in turn represent the context and indirectly complement the suggestion of the design.

A major factor in ensuring synthetic communicativeness in graphic design expression is the stylization and simplification of images. In order to achieve simplicity, the idea should be unravelled to the core and the unimportant things should be excluded. The best design solutions are simple because they do not contain unnecessary elements. On the other hand, simple does not mean boring and useless, but on the contrary. Simplicity is a design philosophy, an approach that guarantees high aesthetics and functionality. Achieving simplicity is not a matter of formal reduction of the information volume, but of systematizing and analysing its important aspects.

Image stylization is a major tool in the hands of a graphic designer. It is a graphical simplification of an object while still retaining its characteristic features so that it remains recognizable without being too "chatty". According to Umberto Eco, "stylizations are certain apparently iconic expressions that are in fact the result of a convention establishing that they will be recognized because of their similarity to an expression-type, which is not strictly compulsory and permits many free variants" [1]. This approach allows the author to visualize details, silhouettes and reflections without burdening the composition, and thus to convey unambiguous messages. In this aspect, images do not need translation, they are perceived instinctively and leave their imprint on the subconscious of the audience. Such projects do not present ready-made solutions, they generate more questions than answers. Viewers are involved in an unusual graphic communication and are able to interpret the author's concept themselves.

Globally, the advancement of digital technologies leads to transformation of values, to search for new methods and means of expression in art and design. Photographic images and the variety of processing software tools, as technological alternatives, have long been occupying their solid place in the evolution of visual communication. A point has been reached where software and hardware have become a visible and basic imaging technique. The photographic image integration is one of the main practices where modern digital and analogue means of expression combine and interact [2]. This trend allows a qualitatively new twist in the development of communication in its essence. With the help of computer graphics, animation and video, images become interactive, thus allowing large-scale reproduction and distribution of content. The visual communication of our time is an open space for exchange between all members of the global network. Actually, the territory of creation and the territory of perception of graphic information are united in a qualitatively new environment: the virtual space of computer networks. In this context, the fixed places of author and perceiver do not exist—they are interchangeable. Communication on the web establishes interactive connections for inter-cultural collaborations, and the diversity and democracy of the media presupposes the connection of a complete virtual society.

1.2.2 Composition

Graphic design incorporates images and typography into a common composition. They complement each other with a certain predominance of one or the other. The composition deliberately employs the visual power of the different properties of forms to convey the desired impact. The individual elements are united into one artistic whole, which reveals the content most vividly through the respective form of expression. All parts of this whole need to have proportion, rhythm, colour harmony and contact with the surrounding environment. Each composition is distinguished by: individuality, entirety, containing elements of the designer's creative imagination and fantasy. The expressiveness of a good design is achieved by skilful use of the contrast between colours, size and saturation of elements.

Composition in graphic design is not an end in itself, but a structure of logically interconnected elements that build and organize content into a form that is clear and easy to perceive. The combination of multiple elements requires their organization along leading lines. Depending on the desired suggestion, they can be developed vertically, horizontally, diagonally, in different variants of ovals, zig-zags, etc. In addition to ensuring the integrity of composition, these leading lines move the focus of attention in the sequence set by the author. This approach provides for visual separation of the primary piece of content that carries the main idea. This effect can be achieved also by inserting the main elements in a basic geometric figure—a square, a rhombus, a triangle, an oval, etc. In his research on design theory, Pavel Popov differentiates between several main types of compositions. These are: frame, cross, spiral, stack, star, snake (chain), mother and child (planet and satellite), rooster (dragon). He calls them archetypal schemes, and among them he defines the characteristic archetypes of plot uncertainty—hieroglyph (small, complex, categorical, with hidden suggestions) and chaos (large, free, disordered, indefinite, threatening). No matter how hard the artists look for new and unique solutions, they are all reduced to those listed by Popov. Based on this really limited number of compositions, an infinite variety can be achieved by changing only one property or mixing it with others [3].

An important feature of graphic design composition is unity. It is achieved by synchronizing all participating elements so that each of them is stylistically and thematically interconnected with the others. Two main types of unity are applied—visual and conceptual. Visual unity consolidates a group of elements by colour, shape, axis of symmetry, texture, alignment, etc. The use of too many heterogeneous elements makes the composition fragmented and inconsistent. The lack of uniform formatting of all images and texts can create the feeling that some of them do not belong or are not related to the main composition.

The conceptual unity combines the symbolic meaning of objects. For example, unity can be achieved between common traits or origins that are compatible and have identical or reciprocal relationships. An image of a diamond, a palace and a pile of money could be united around the idea of wealth. The design elements are matched to a certain convention, such as size, similarity, or scale. Complex structures have a number of repelling and attracting sides, which is good for the composition, but makes is difficult to explicitly determine their compatibility. In graphic design, simpler geometric shapes are preferred. It is necessary to choose a single leading line to be repeated and further developed throughout the composition structure.

An interesting example of visual and conceptual unity are the so-called "smart advertising facilities". Their purpose is to improve the urban environment by assigning an additional utilitarian function to advertising. Designed for IBM, the "Smart Ideas for Smarter Cities" campaign employs the strategy for creating a new level of smart advertising. A series of "useful" billboards have been created that are a functional addition to the infrastructure, such as benches, shelters and ramps (see Fig. 2). Clear and simple graphics in bright colours are used to emphasize the function of the facility more effectively. The campaign is not so much focused on aesthetics, but rather on the additional value that results from the pragmatic combination of idea and utilitarianism. The billboards were initially located in London and Paris, and later on—in many other cities around the world. IBM is committed to creating solutions that help cities become comfortable, accessible, and better places to live.

Fig. 2 Smart advertising facilities. Client: IBM, "Smart ideas for smart cities", Advertising agency: Ogilvy & Mather

1.2.3 Symbols

A symbol is an essential element for recreating concepts in graphic design. The connection between the concept expressed by the symbol itself may be purely arbitrary, subjective, but may also stem from the internal similarity, relation between the object depicted and its allegorical meaning. In fine art, the use of the symbol is especially relevant, when it is necessary to express a very broad, very extensive concept in a laconic, concise form [4]. It appears in incredible combinations and transformations. Finding the right symbols and placing them in a new context gives them extrinsic meaning. This unusual and characteristic approach unfolds new cultural layers for the viewer and opens vast unexplored perceptions. It presents a new unique view of life and art through abstract metaphorical images. Contemplating the projects of recognized graphic designers, the boundaries between reality and illusion are blurred and we fall into the infinite world of fantasy. Design becomes a means of self-expression, a transmission of ideas, a call to reason. In this respect, the mission of this broad-spectrum art goes beyond the utilitarian and unleashes its potential. There is an artistic synthesis between the idea, the symbol and the text that transforms reality by creating new notional connections between objects. The aim is to evoke associations in the viewer and to stimulate direct and natural communication. The reliance is on ideas that are already established in the recipient's mind, gained from their life experience. The collision between associations and ideas causes the emergence of new concepts in the mind. This process acts as a generator of creative thinking and innovations, and develops the imagination. The spontaneously emerging connections invoke unusual and curious images in the mind, which amuse and fascinate.

Graphic design, with the help of its expressive means, establishes creative non-verbal communication with the audience. For that purpose, it needs the expressive power of images and symbols, which visualize the content in an understandable form. Attracting attention on its own is not effective enough, it is necessary to transform concepts into notions. The implied meaning and its transformation by the viewer are the constructive side of communication. Objects that are incompatible at a first glance are transformed into images that create visual metaphors. The meaning of symbols becomes figurative and depends on a number of narrative, spatial and causal relationships. This complex communication provokes emotional and mental interaction with the audience.

Understanding the creatively presented content in graphic design depends both on the proper visualization and on the logical thinking of the recipient. In order to achieve full knowledge, one needs to perceive the surrounding world as a set of accumulated information and to research and analyse it. The application of visual metaphors relies on this acquired visual intelligence. To a large extent, it is also formed by the specific cultural and national affiliation [5]. Therefore, the application of symbols requires a deep knowledge of the characteristics of the target groups to which the content is intended.

Symbols are the subject of research in the scientific discipline of semiotics. It studies signs and sign systems, their meaning, decoding processes and their application in communication. In this article, they are analysed as a means of effective visual communication with the users. The diversity of creative interpretations is immense, but we could summarize a few basic approaches to integrating them into graphic design.

The symbol, being an object of visual research in graphic design, can be studied according to its application by similarity and analogy. Symbols that are heterogeneous at a first glance can be united by constructive, semiotic and spatial consonance. Emphasis on elements of common form or meaning generates associations in the mind that lead to the emergence of a new object, a figment. Multiple meanings are combined into one creative image in order to present the concept in its full depth. This approach allows to recreate the content beyond the literal representation of reality, which is much more multi-layered and wide-ranging. The originality of the presentation attracts the interest, stirs the curiosity and stimulates the interaction with the audience.

A particularly powerful approach to the use of symbols in design is to utilize the differences in shape and colour in order to highlight the conflict of opposites. This is a technique that has long been known to visual artists. In order to emphasize the positive qualities or the beauty of an image, it is positioned against the background of its antipode. Striving to recreate powerful suggestions, authors hyperbolize the qualities of the central object and sometimes even lend surprising characteristics to it.

The creative solutions designed on the basis of structural transformation of the objects are quite curious. The most characteristic features are brought to the forefront, elements are taken away, new ones are added, thus creating an illusion of incompleteness and development of the leading idea. Bizarre interactions are created between construction, fusion and destruction, which provoke the viewer to find out what is wrong with the image. The act of grabbing the attention aims to stimulate the viewer to think and build their own position based on their individual perceptions. Thus, in parallel with the designer, the viewer becomes a co-author, refracting the content through the prism of their individual needs and beliefs.

A successful example of sustainable design is the green Coca-Cola billboard installed in Makati City, Philippines in 2011 (see Fig. 3). It adequately presents the brand through the idea of environmental protection. The visual metaphor used in the composition represents a vast field of tea plants that form the silhouette of the iconic bottle. This billboard helps to reduce the air pollution in its nearby areas as plants absorb carbon dioxide from the atmosphere. The rest of the structure is equally environmentally friendly. The plants were potted in 3,600 containers made of used Coca-Cola bottles. The soil was composted from industrial waste products and organic fertilizers. A drip irrigation system was installed to save resources. "We are proud that we have brought to life the first plant billboard in the country", said Guillermo Aponte, president of Coca-Cola Philippines. "It is an embodiment of our company's Live Positively commitment to making a positive difference in the world by incorporating sustainability into everything that we do. With this, we hope to inspire Filipinos to join us in our journey, because we know that together, we can make a positive impact."

The proper context has a leading role in the work with symbols in design. The environment is a background that can muffle or amplify a suggestion. It can rely on the principle of similarity or the contrast of incompatibility, it can highlight or soften the expressive power of the selected elements. The same images and symbols may carry suggestions of different meaning thanks to the unconventional thinking of artists. Designers are a peculiar kind of researchers of human nature, behaviour and living environment. Based on their knowledge, they manipulate images to lead the thought into a particular direction chosen by them. They are able to create surreal worlds that are easy to perceive and subtly introduce the viewer into the parallel universe of fantasy.

The advertising campaign for the Mini Cooper cars focuses on the small size of the model and the advantages that it has in the overcrowded urban environment (see Fig. 4). Ads are unusual and fun, but they emphasize the car's main features well enough. The leading design concept relies on the carefully selected architectural environment to achieve conceptual, functional and stylistic symbiosis.

The main means of expression of graphic design is the form. It is an important carrier of meaning, emotions and ideas. Striving to find the most synthetic form, designers study and analyse objects in detail. After the sketches are transformed

Fig. 3 Media agencies: McCann Erickson Philippines, Momentum and Starcom MediaVest Group

by the creative thinking of the author, only the most characteristic elements remain in the form of a clean line and a laconic expression. The mastery of the artist is to visualize the idea in a generalized and understandable artistic image. Often, the composition lacks many of the elements with which the symbols are associated, but the visual memory is able to draw the whole shape and to complete the complex semiotic structures in their entirety.

The application of colour is also of great symbolic importance. It has the ability to act upon the audience on the emotional and semantic level. Each tone has its own characteristics, such as the degree of saturation, intensity and brightness. The everyday use of colours in visual communication has imposed certain stereotypes about the way they are perceived depending on their nuance and importance. The combinations of colour harmonies in design are practically inexhaustible, they can

Fig. 4 Client: Mini Cooper, Advertising agency: Jung von Matt, Switzerland

convey content, inspire respect, trust and continuity. Their application is to a great extent arbitrary, because it is synthesized on the basis of implied meaning. Colours with different symbolism are combined to give a new value to the object on which they are applied. In order to achieve the desired impact, when designing the overall vision, it is important to accurately calibrate colours and to analyse the strengths and weaknesses of colour solutions.

2 Conclusion

In today's world, where consumers are overwhelmed by information, sustainable design is a direction for adequate development of visual communication. It presents messages in unexpected forms that captivate viewers. The means of expression it employs are symbol, image and composition. Applies the expressive power of visual language to create highly impressive and memorable campaigns. Facilitates the process of information transmission by adapting all details to the specific nature of human perceptions. Design is not an end in itself, but a powerful initiator and communicator for sharing content, values and spiritual messages. Possesses means of expression that deal with holistic approaches, a product of the creative interpretation of meaning, form and colour. Its works are present in all spheres of the professional and personal life of modern man and it is inevitably an important factor in the development of mass culture. For these reasons, every designer should realize the key role of their work and dedicate their efforts to creating value-added design. Creativity in visual communication is a key component in the quest to create a positive living environment and a sustainable future.

References

1. Eco U (1978) A theory of semiotics. Indiana University Press, USA
2. Tsanova B (2014) Kinetichnite grafiki na Susumu Endo. Academy of Music, Dance and Fine Art, Plovdiv 2:447–453
3. Popov V (2007) Kompoziciqta kato abstrakcij. ArhLibri, Sofia.
4. Konova M (2021) Ornament and symbol. Main symbols in the decorative composition of the church's orthodox art. Visual Stud 5(2):219–226.
5. Kaftandjiev H (2013) Harmonia v reklamata komunikaciq. University Publishing House "St. Kliment Ohridski", Sofia.

Waste Management: Designing a User-Centered and Sustainable Mobile Application

Bruno Justa, Nuno Martins, Leonardo Pereira, and Daniel Brandão

Abstract The textile industry is one of the most polluting sectors worldwide. The purchase of clothing has been on the rise, but it's not accompanied by the recycling process. In Portugal only 1% of textile waste is recycled. However, several initiatives seek to reduce this problem. The "Escola Oficina," established in 2015 in Vila Nova de Gaia, is dedicated to producing sustainable products from the reuse of industrial waste such as leather, fabric, paper, and cardboard. This study proposes, therefore, a digital solution to improve the management of this waste through the development of a mobile App that connects the "Escola Oficina" with its suppliers. This project uses the Design Thinking methodology, focusing on understanding the users' needs and employing the iterative development of the solution. The App's design choices are supported by theories and principles established in the literature review. Through this App, validated through usability tests, it has been demonstrated how digital technology can help optimize textile waste management and, consequently, improve the sustainability of this sector.

Keywords Interface design · Sustainable web design · Mobile App · Textile waste · Waste management

B. Justa (✉)
School of Design, Polytechnic Institute of Cavado and Ave, Barcelos, Portugal
e-mail: brunomajusta@gmail.com

N. Martins
Research Institute for Design, Media and Culture, School of Design, Polytechnic Institute of Cavado and Ave, Barcelos, Portugal

L. Pereira
University of Aveiro, DigiMedia, Aveiro, DeCA, Portugal

D. Brandão
CECS, Institute of Social Sciences, University of Minho, Braga, Portugal

D. Raposo et al. (eds.), *Perspectives on Design III*, Springer Series in Design and Innovation 34, https://doi.org/10.1007/978-3-031-43516-4_5

1 Introduction

The textile sector is among the most polluting ones globally. According to the Portuguese Environment Agency (APA), approximately 200,756 tons of textile waste were collected in Portugal along with municipal waste in 2017 [3]. In comparison to the year 2000, clothing purchases increased by an average of 60% in 2019, resulting in an expansion of textile waste production and, consequently, environmental impacts [3]. This increase, however, was not proportionally reflected on waste recycling. Only approximately 1% of textile waste produced in Portugal is recycled [3]. In the same year, the European Union determined that from 2025 on, selective collection of discarded textiles will become mandatory, enabling better control of these waste materials [6]. This action will have a tangible impact on reducing textile waste and carbon emissions as, according to the European Commission, repurposing one kilogram of textile material can prevent the emission of approximately 3,169 kg of CO_2 into the atmosphere [6].

To fight these figures, several companies and associations have sought alternatives, whether through the implementation of sustainable projects or by donating waste materials. One such organization is Escola Oficina (EO), established in 2015 in Vila Nova de Gaia. EO dedicates itself to the production of sustainable products by reusing industrial waste such as leather, fabric, paper, and cardboard. This initiative follows a training-action methodology, creating opportunities for unemployed individuals to integrate into the job market through the acquisition and improvement of new professional skills. EO adopts a community-focused approach, emphasizing environmental sustainability and economic growth based on the circular economy. Due to these approaches, EO has already produced over 32,000 items from industrial waste, with almost 90% of their production being traded [4].

Escola Oficina collaborates with over 400 companies that donate their waste materials to serve as raw materials for EO's product manufacturing. In doing so, they contribute not only to the production of sustainable products but also to waste reduction. However, the management of this network is currently done in a rudimentary way, using a Microsoft Excel document that aggregates the contact list of several partners. Whenever EO identifies the need for raw materials, they are obliged to individually contact these partner companies to check for raw material's availability. As EO's managers acknowledge, this process is too time-consuming and inefficient.

The goal of this study is, therefore, to address this problem by creating a digital solution that allows for more effective management of textile waste for both EO and its partners. Specifically, the study focuses on the development of a mobile application (App) for textile waste management, that aims to ease the donation and management process of these waste materials provided by EO's partner companies. By making it digital, one expects not only to significantly improve EO's management process but also to contribute to the environmental sustainability of the textile sector in Portugal, as this solution could be replicated in similar cases within this industry.

This document is, therefore, structured around the various subjects related with the development of the mobile App for textile waste management. It explores Gestalt principles [27, 28], Nielsen's heuristics [18], and research subjects such as User-Centered Design wich is studied by addressing the approaches to it of authors such as [5, 13–15, 17, 21, 25, 29, 30, 34]. It also explores concepts of Information Architecture, Human–Computer Interaction [24, 31] and the Design Thinking process [26, 33, 35]. Additionally, sustainability concepts in web design are also addressed, with insights from Greenwood [2], Budiu [10] and Hussain [12].

2 Literature Review

2.1 Gestalt Principles

The Gestalt principles play a crucial role in interface design as they describe how the human brain groups similar elements, recognizes patterns, and simplifies complex images. They explain how design elements can be visually organized to achieve visually understandable results and, in the specific case of interface design, improve information organization and visual perception. This theory consists of eight fundamental principles, namely: Proximity; Similarity; Closure; Common Fate; Continuity; Symmetry & Order (also known as Prägnanz); and Figure-Ground. The use of these principles allows for enhancing specific features of Apps without modifying their functionality [27]. According to Ripalda et al. [27], their use increases users' ease of perception and speed of use by 31.3%.

Furthermore, by combining the principles of Gestalt with Nielsen's heuristics, it is possible to develop even more effective Apps. This approach provides a solid theoretical foundation that supports the practical application in design, justifying design choices and enabling a better understanding and optimization of interfaces [28].

2.2 Nielsen's Heuristics

Nielsen's heuristics are a set of 10 principles formulated by Jakob Nielsen and R Molich [20], in the 1990s, to evaluate the usability of interfaces, websites, software or applications. These principles, however, have evolved and are updated as further technological advances occur. During interface usability's assessment, designers apply these heuristics to provide insights that can help design teams improve the usability of their products. These principles enable the development of interfaces with fewer errors and adversities, improving navigability and user intuition. In Nielsen's words [18], "even the best designers produce successful products only if their designs solve the right problems. A good interface for the wrong features will fail" [18].

By considering the specific challenges of EO, we can adapt, enhance, and refine interface prototypes, relying on the theoretical and visual references provided by these concepts. However, if the main goal is to prioritize user's needs, one has to explore the underlying theory of User-Centered Design, understanding how this approach can further enhance the design.

2.3 User-Centered Design

User-Centered Design (UCD) emphasizes the importance of understanding human needs and behaviors, placing them at the center of the development process. UCD relies on data to inform design decisions and focuses on satisfying user needs [15]. Applying UCD is advantageous for companies and associations like EO, which face challenges in managing their extensive network of partners. The methodology helps with the development of digital solutions that enhance user experience [34].

One of the approaches in this methodology is called Usability testing. Its goal is to assess a product or service from the user's perspective. Usability tests involve observing users interacting with the product under controlled conditions [21]. They are conducted to identify usability issues, gather user feedback, and understand how users interact with the system [14]. The insights obtained are crucial for improving user experience, meeting their needs, and developing objective interfaces [29]. Direct user feedback is highly relevant as it can inform and guide design and development decisions throughout the project [30]. Nielsen [23] emphasize that these tests should occur early and continuously in the design process to identify and solve usability problems. Adopting an iterative approach and constantly refining the digital solution based on user feedback is necessary to achieve the best results. It is essential to listen to users throughout the design process, even if some of their suggestions may be set aside [1]. Lowdermilk [15] highlights the importance of filtering the information collected through usability tests, determining what is useful and what should be discarded.

Understanding cognitive processes is also fundamental for the creation of objective products and user experiences. Cognitive load theory is an example that argues that people have a limited capacity to process information. Therefore, design should minimize cognitive load to facilitate understanding and usage of a product or service. A practical example is the use of contrasting colors and well-structured visual organization in a website or App, which enhances user understanding and interaction [14]. Behavioral psychology, on the other hand, focuses on how people interact with products and services. A notable example is the implementation of immediate feedback and rewards in the design of a mobile App, increasing user motivation to use it [25]. Accessibility and inclusion are also relevant aspects that aim to develop digital solutions that meet the needs of a wide range of users, regardless of abilities, ages, and backgrounds. Accessibility refers to the ability of a product or service to be used by people with disabilities [13], while inclusion focuses on creating products and services that satisfy the needs of diverse users [17].

To achieve these goals, UCD adopts various design practices, including the use of accessible colors and fonts, as well as the adaptation of intuitive interfaces for all users, regardless of their limitations. According to Clarkson et al. [5], applying inclusive design to product development increases user satisfaction and minimizes the risk of excluding minority groups. Therefore, a commitment to accessibility and inclusion in the design process contributes to creating digital products that are simple and clear for all users, regardless of their age or digital experience.

To ensure success in applying UCD, it is essential to adopt an iterative process of continuous improvement based on user feedback. This approach allows for the identification and solving of usability issues, saving a digital product's designers and stakeholders time and resources. However, to ensure a comprehensive design of digital solutions, it is crucial to consider other relevant issues, such as Information Architecture, which deals with the organization and structure of information displayed and provided by the App.

2.4 *Information Architecture*

Information Architecture (IA) aims to structure and organize the information of an App in a logical way, improving user navigability and comprehension. In the context of this project, achieving successful IA requires a User-Centered approach, taking into consideration both partner companies and textile waste recipients. Ausubel's theory of Meaningful Learning (1963) plays a fundamental role in this process as it suggests that learning is most effective when new information relates to users' prior knowledge and experiences.

Applying this theory within the textile waste management project can offer numerous benefits in developing a digital solution that facilitates interaction among the involved stakeholders. One of the benefits is connecting new information and functionalities to users' prior knowledge, establishing meaningful and familiar contexts. This facilitates understanding and adaptation to the platform, providing a smoother experience that ultimately increases information retention rates. Ausubel's theory (1963) can also be employed to organize information and navigation options in a logical and coherent way, optimizing platform navigation and usability, and simplifying users' ability to locate desired information. Lastly, considering users' experiences and prior knowledge, also enables the creation of personalized solutions that meet their needs and expectations, leading to a more rewarding and successful experience for all the involved stakeholders.

Human–Computer theories can be applied to improve interface efficiency. Fitts' Law [7], a theory that describes the relationship between distance and the size of elements in an interface, suggests that frequently used objects should be larger and easier to reach, allowing for faster and more accurate interaction. Miller's Law [16], on the other hand, advises designers to display information in groups of up to seven elements, as it facilitates users' cognitive capacity and working memory. The Principle of Visual Perception, based on Gestalt psychology, highlights the importance of grouping visually similar elements (similarity principle) to promote organization and comprehension of the presented information.

By, in this project, combining IA with the UCD methodology, it becomes possible to develop an effective and user-accessible digital solution. Applying these theories and laws contributes to the creation a digital platform that answers to users' needs, providing them with a smoother experience. Furthermore, integrating this methodology with interaction design is crucial to achieving a higher degree of usability and user satisfaction.

2.5 Human–Computer Interaction

Human–Computer Interaction (HCI) is a methodology focused on the design and implementation of interactive digital products, with the goal of improving the interaction between users and computers, tailoring them to their needs [31]. In the development of the mobile App for textile waste management, the use of various theories from Human–Computer Interaction (HCI) played an important role in improving its usability and accessibility.

One established theory in HCI is the Theory of Cognitive Load, which states that interfaces that require a high cognitive load can lead to frustration, fatigue, and poor task performance. Therefore, it is crucial to reduce cognitive load to enhance the App's usability and improve the user's experience. The theory of visual perception, as explained by Don Norman [24], is fundamental in HCI to understand how users perceive and process displayed information. According to Norman [24], visual elements such as color, contrast, and organization significantly influence how users perceive and interpret information. Therefore, the use of visual cues can enhance the interfaces' usability, making information more accessible and easier to understand. Participatory design, another approach in HCI, leads to more beneficial and satisfactory products as it brings users into the design process, allowing them to communicate their requirements and provide feedback, thus playing an active role in defining requirements and evaluating the design. The use of these HCI theories further contributed to improve the usability and overall effectiveness of the App.

While its primary goal is to ensure effective textile waste management, a secondary objective is to support the creation of sustainable products. The App itself should incorporate a sustainable approach, so it was relevant to explore the concept of sustainable design. This involved understanding how it is possible to integrate this concept along with the discussed interface design theories, harmonizing the App's usability with a sustainable vision.

2.6 Sustainable Web Design

Sustainable web design aims to achieve eco-efficiency when creating Apps and websites by reducing carbon emissions and optimizing energy consumption. The development of such low-emission platforms is increasingly relevant, given the trend of rising energy consumption. Specifically, in the case of digital platforms, a study by Greenpeace predicts that they'll account for 13% of global energy consumption by 2030 [36]. Greenwood [9] defines sustainable web design as adhering to the principles of cleanliness, efficiency, openness, honesty, regeneration, and resilience. During the design processes, it is possible to apply the principles of efficiency and resilience. Efficiency is achieved through feature management, retaining only those that are truly relevant and simplifying the project [9]. Following this principle improves the user's experience by keeping consumer journeys (the sequence of steps a user takes when using a product until they achieve their goal) short and objective. This helps prevent users from having to navigate through multiple pages to find what they need.

The principle of resilience is applied through a clearly structured information architecture. In this regard, essential data is selected, while irrelevant one is discarded. By limiting the information to the essential, the amount of data transferred to load the page is reduced. This improves website performance, enabling access to the platform even with slow internet connections. On the other hand, the more data is loaded, the slower the App will be, resulting in more CO_2 emissions [9]. Ensuring optimized resources is important to ensure the efficiency of digital platforms. Lightweight images and the use of appropriate typography for the web are small issues that make a big difference. Currently, according to data from the HTTP Archive [11], an average of 23 images with a weight of 1 MB each, are loaded per page. Considering that the recommended maximum weight is 200 KB (80% smaller than the average) [32], it is clear that the high number of existing websites that accumulate these values are leading to significant CO_2 emissions. Therefore, file format should be considered, where the SVG format is the most efficient for icons, and WEBP format is preferable for photographs, being approximately 30% lighter than the JPEG format [8].

Greenwood also argues that a high bounce rate is positive for sustainable web design. The bounce rate refers to the percentage of unique users who visit only one page of the platform. So, when users visit fewer pages, they consume less data processing and emit less CO_2 [9]. However, considering current trends where websites strive for maximum engagement, this factor may lose relevance.

Finally, the cost of color in our project should also be taken into consideration, as some colors are more efficient than others. The type of screen each user has also influences this efficiency. Many projects have popularized the idea of using both dark and light modes in their color schemes. Dark mode emits less light than light mode, saving more energy and being more sustainable. However, this also depends on the type of screen being used. For example, LCD (Liquid Crystal Display) screens are more energy-efficient, with a single backlight illuminating the entire surface, and even with any color displayed, this light is always fully on [10]. With this screen type, dark modes end up being more of a user preference than a sustainable act. However, for OLED (Organic Light-Emitting Diode) screens, where each pixel is illuminated by a small LED (Light-Emitting Diode), using dark mode is a significant advantage in reducing energy consumption, especially on mobile devices where energy consumption directly affects battery life [10].

On the other hand, not all users feel comfortable with dark mode. As we age, our pupils tend to decrease in size, which affects our ability to read in dark environments

[2]. In this sense, our eyes become more susceptible to brightness. Therefore, it is best to incorporate the functionality that allows users to switch between dark and light modes themselves, even if it may result in increased energy consumption [2]. When developing web products, we must always prioritize the user experience. While having a sustainable web design is important, a poor user experience is not desirable. One way to strike a balance between a good user experience and energy consumption is to adopt a design that uses darker colors but keeps white as the background for areas of the site where reading may be affected by color, thus providing a more comfortable experience for the user.

Another way to incorporate sustainability into projects without sacrificing certain features, animations, and aesthetics is to include the option to activate a sustainable mode. Once the user activates the sustainable mode, certain colors, animations, and functionalities are changed, presenting the project in its most economical state [12]. It is understood that many users aren't yet fully aware of the use of sustainable products. However, by providing this option, we provide a small emotional reward to users who choose this mode. With a deeper understanding of all these theories and how they can assist the development of this study, it is equally crucial to determine which methodology to adopt during the development process. In this regard, the design thinking process has been identified as a relevant methodology due to its potential to energize and structure its development, making it a more organized process.

3 Methodologies

3.1 Sustainable Web Design

Design thinking is a non-linear and interactive method used to understand users, challenge assumptions, redefine problems, and create innovative solutions for prototyping and testing. It involves five different stages: empathy, definition, ideation, prototyping, and testing. One of the advantages of synthesizing the design thinking process into stages is that this model becomes more accessible, explicit, easily understandable, and applicable to organizations and businesses [33]. According to Pressman [26], the ability to use design thinking can be difficult to acquire, but once acquired, it allows for creative problem-solving. Wolniak [35] also argues that using this organizational approach enables the development of better products that meet user's needs (Fig. 1).

In the empathy phase, it was necessary to understand in detail the difficulties, needs, and expectations of the users, in this specific case, the members of EO. This stage involved a meticulous analysis of the issues they faced and an attempt to understand their expectations and what they value in an App. In the definition phase, the identified problems were interpreted again to obtain useful insights and a concrete definition of the problem. During the ideation stage, an environment conducive to

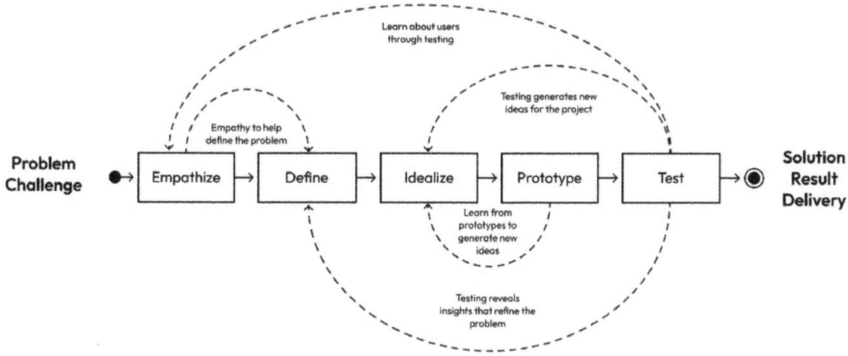

Fig. 1 The various steps of the Design Thinking methodology

generating a wide range of potential solutions was created. This stage was characterized by creative freedom without restrictions, encouraging innovation and originality. In the prototyping phase, the ideas generated earlier were converted into tangible models. This step allowed for the visualization of the proposed solutions through prototypes that provided a physical representation of the solutions, encompassing all the theories and concepts explored thus far. Lastly, in the testing stage, the team collected feedback from users. These tests involved real users using the prototypes and providing their opinions. The goal of this stage was to evaluate the effectiveness, usability, and attractiveness of the proposed solutions. The gathered data was, therefore, essential for refining and improving the product's interfaces and functional features, ensuring that they met the needs and expectations of the target audience.

3.2 *Mobile App Development*

The development of the mobile App for textile waste management, when shaped by the Design Thinking process, involved a collaborative, interactive and user-centered approach. The development process started with initial exploratory interviews with members of the organization. These interviews helped to shape an understanding of the needs, challenges, and the App's design requirements. The insights gathered during these interviews served as a foundation for the subsequent steps of the process. Based on the data collected from these initial interviews, personas and user scenarios were created.

Personas are fictional representations of the target audience, and scenarios are stories that describe how these personas would use the App in their daily lives. These tools helped maintain a user-centric focus throughout the development process. With a solid understanding of the users, low-fidelity sketches were created to visualize and explore different concepts for the App.

After reviewing and selecting the sketches (Fig. 2), more detailed and structured wireframes and wireflows (Fig. 3) of the App's interface were developed. These wireframes and wireflows helped define the Information Architecture, user flow, and key interface elements.

At the beginning of the design process, a Design System was created in Figma to ensure faster and more efficient creation of the different App's screens. The Design System established a consistent foundation of design elements, such as colors, typography, icons, and reusable components, which were consistently used across all screens. This allowed for greater agility in design creation while ensuring visual consistency throughout the App's visual design (Fig. 4).

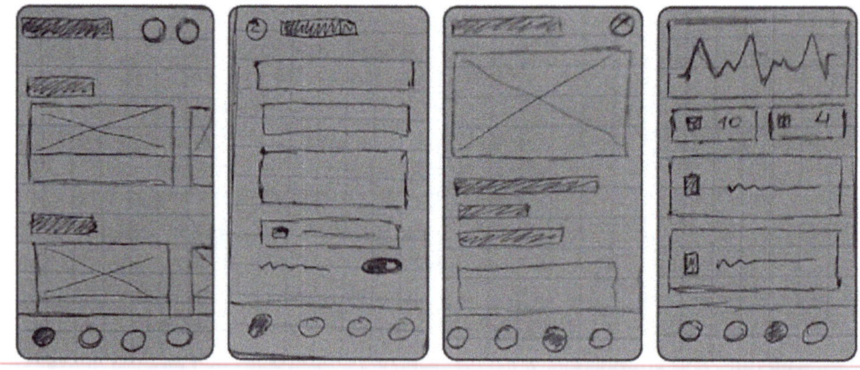

Fig. 2 Initial sketches of the EO waste management App. Self-source, 2023

Fig. 3 Wireframes and Wireflow of the EO waste management App. Self-source, 2023

Fig. 4 Design System developed in Figma. Self-source, 2023

With the wireframes and Design System finalized, the initial versions of the prototypes were developed. These prototypes allowed for testing and validating ideas, for usability issues detection, for task flows confirmation, and for ensuring that the solution was indeed meeting EO's needs. The feedback and data collected was used to make changes and improvements to the design. After several iterations, the final prototypes were ultimately developed, incorporating all the improvements and adjustments that were brought about by the tests, thus representing the most complete and refined version of the textile waste management App to date. These final prototypes not only meet the user's functional requirements but also offer an intuitive and pleasant user experience, considering all the studied theories (Fig. 5).

In this regard, the Gestalt principles, namely the principles of proximity, similarity, continuity, and closure, allowed for the creation of an easily understandable interface. The principle of proximity aided in grouping content, buttons, and functionalities so

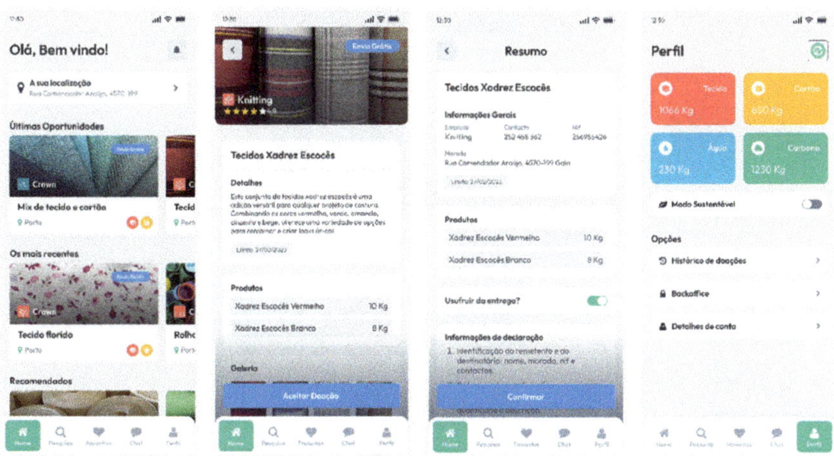

Fig. 5 Some of the final screens of the App. Self-source, 2023

that users can easily identify their relationships. Similarity was used to differentiate different types of waste through similar colors and icons, facilitating their identification. Continuity contributed to creating a sense of flow and direction, guiding users through the steps of the textile waste donation process. Lastly, closure was applied by creating simple closed shapes, using areas to group information related to textile waste donation, such as delivery details and instructions, conveying a sense of organization and coherence. This application of the Gestalt principles can be visualized in Fig. 6. By combining these principles, it is possible to facilitate the identification and selection of options by users, providing a clear and fluid experience.

Regarding Nielsen's Heuristics, they proved to be fundamental for the development of the App's interface. The heuristic "Visibility of system status," which refers to the need to keep users informed through feedback, was implemented through the adoption of status updates, informing users whenever a donation is registered, processed, or sent.

In turn, the principle of "User control and freedom" highlights the fact that users can make mistakes, and it is necessary to provide a clear way to undo undesirable actions. In that sense, page exit buttons and options to delete or cancel donations were applied to the interface.

The heuristic "Error prevention" consists of avoiding problems by eliminating error-prone conditions. In the App's behaviour and feedback to user's interaction,

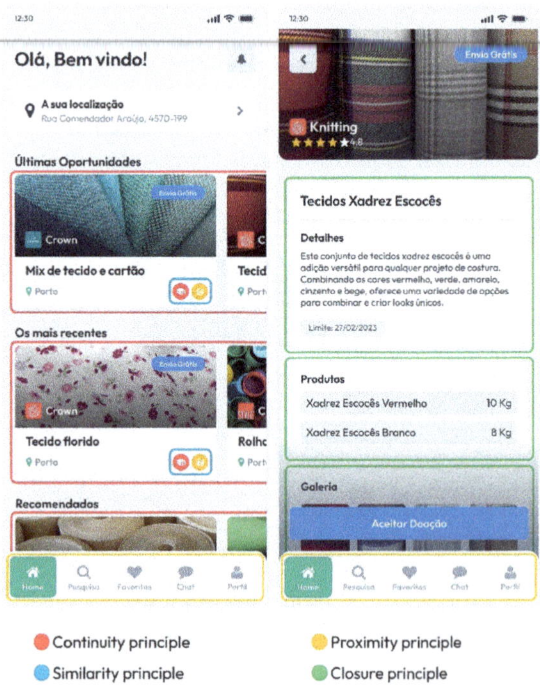

Fig. 6 Gestalt Principles applied into the App's interface design. Self-source, 2023

this heuristic is clearly embedded into the various confirmation alerts that the App prompts the user with, before any important actions are taken.

Finally, the principle of "Aesthetic and minimalist design" ensures that interfaces do not contain irrelevant information. Thus, a simple and clear layout was developed, only displaying the necessary information for making donations, avoiding clutter and information overload. The application of Nielsen's Heuristics to the App's interface design is featured in Fig. 7.

In this way, the EO's textile waste management App project followed a Design Thinking process, incorporating the creation of personas, user scenarios, wireframes, prototypes, and, finally, usability testing. These usability tests were conducted with the goal of assessing the users' experience and identifying issues or problems that needed improvement.

Following Nielsen's recommendation [19, 22], the tests were conducted with five participants. These were selected based on their lack of prior knowledge about EO's management to ensure unbiased results and an objective assessment of the App. It is important to note that all participants had experience and familiarity with various web and mobile Apps, regularly using them in their daily lives, providing an informed perspective during the tests.

Each test session had an average duration of 30 minutes and included the completion of 10 tasks, rated on a scale of 1–10, along with a satisfaction survey. The average score obtained in the usability tests was 8.76 out of 10. Although users were

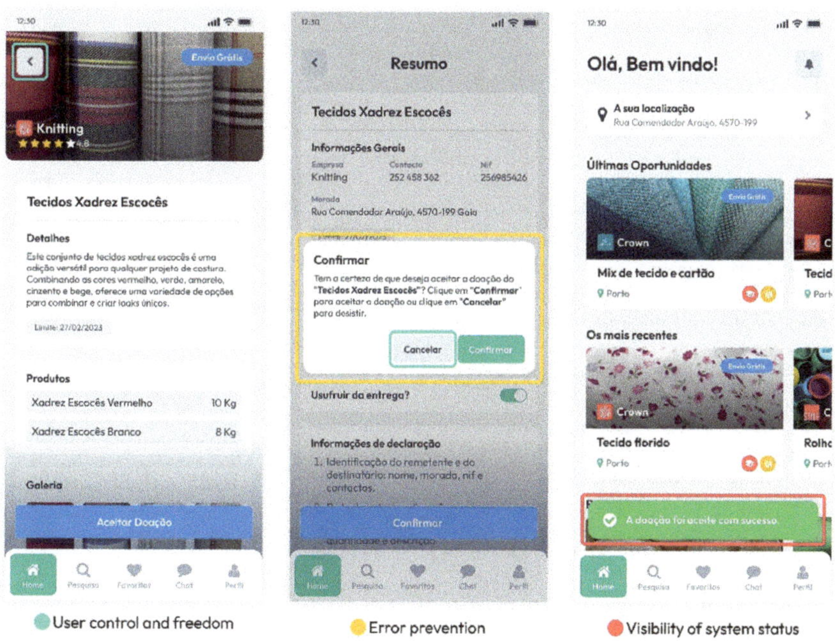

Fig. 7 Heuristics applied to the App's interface design. Self-source, 2023

able to complete the tasks, some usability and functionality issues were identified. On the other hand, the satisfaction survey revealed an average score of 4.18 out of 5, indicating an overall positive experience. Figure 8 shows the table containing the individual and collective results of the usability tests, referring to the tasks performed by the participants.

Based on the results of the usability tests and the satisfaction survey, it was possible to extract insights about the users' experience with the App. Although the scores were high, some specific issues that needed improvement and enhancement were identified. Two tasks received the lowest scores (8.2): switching the App to sustainable mode, which, according to participants' feedback, should be located inside the settings' page instead of the profile one; and filling in the profile page's general information, where participants found it tedious to edit each detail on separate screens, suggesting that these steps could be grouped into a single screen.

These usability tests revealed valuable information for the App's continuous improvement. Based on the results obtained, adjustments and enhancements can be implemented in the identified areas, aiming to provide users with a more satisfactory and efficient experience.

Usability Test

#	Tasks						Average
	Partner Company Mode						
01	Register as a new company.	7	8	10	8	10	8.6
02	Fill in the general information on your profile.	8	9	8	8	8	8.2
03	Create your first donation.	10	8	9	8	10	9
04	Log out from application.	9	10	10	9	10	9.6
	EO Mode						
05	Search for a company and view its details.	9	9	8	8	8	8.4
06	Switch the application to sustainable mode.	7	8	10	7	9	8.2
07	View the details of a donation and accept it.	9	10	8	8	9	8.8
08	Send a message to a partner company.	8	8	9	8	10	8.6
09	View your donation history.	8	10	9	8	10	9
10	Rate a donation	10	10	10	7	10	9.4
Total							8.76

Fig. 8 Usability test results table. Self-source, 2023

4 Conclusion and Future Work

The Escola Oficina (EO) faces significant challenges in managing its extensive network of partnerships, involving more than 400 companies that provide textile waste for EO's product production. To overcome these challenges, this study was conducted with the aim of developing an innovative solution materialized on a mobile App, in order to facilitate the donation and management process of these waste materials for both stakeholders. The process' digitalization is expected to, not only optimize EO's internal management, but also to contribute to the environmental sustainability of the textile sector in Portugal, creating a solution that can be replicated in similar contexts within the industry.

With the developed mobile App, EO's partners will be able to easily register and offer their textile waste, while EO will have a clear and updated view of the available raw materials. This will enable more agile and efficient communication between EO and partner companies, reducing the time required for raw material acquisition and enhancing EO's production process of sustainable products.

However, to ensure that the mobile App adequately meets the users' needs, it is recommended to make improvements based on the results of usability tests. These improvements may involve adjustments to the user interface and workflow optimization. Additionally, it is important to conduct further testing with internal user groups within EO to ensure that the App fully addresses the specific needs of its employees. These users have a deeper understanding of the organization's operations and processes, which can lead to insights that optimize the App's design.

Another issue to consider is the development of a simple back-office system and interface to give the EO's managers management control over the different areas of the App. This back-office system will allow for efficient management of all activities related to textile waste, such as partner management, donation tracking, and monitoring of raw material stocks. It will provide a comprehensive view of essential information and facilitate strategic decision-making by EO. Additionally, implementing monitoring and data analysis features related to textile waste can also be considered. This functional feature will allow for assessing waste management performance, such as the quantity of donated waste, the efficiency in utilizing recycled raw materials, and waste reduction.

In conclusion, the development of the mobile App for textile waste management at Escola Oficina has demonstrated the importance of seeking digital solutions to address organizational and environmental challenges. Through this solution, EO can enhance its partnership management, streamline the textile waste donation process, and contribute to waste reduction and environmental sustainability. The mobile App project is not limited to efficient textile waste management but can also become an essential tool in the textile sector, inspiring other similar initiatives. The developed project highlights the importance of a collaborative and user-centered approach based on solid design principles. By following this method, it is possible to create an effective solution that meets user needs and offers an enhanced experience.

Finally, it is essential to raise awareness about the importance of proper textile waste management and encourage active participation of companies and individuals in this process. Through awareness campaigns and education, the benefits of recycling and reusing textile waste can be emphasized, encouraging the adoption of more sustainable practices throughout the textile production chain.

References

1. Brandão D, Martins N, Cooper R (2023) Design e Comunicação: Desafios e Dilemas do Digital. Comunicação e Sociedade 43. https://doi.org/10.17231/comsoc.43(2023).4830
2. Budiu R (2020) Dark mode vs. light mode: which is better? Obtido de Nielsen Norman Group. https://www.nngroup.com/articles/dark-mode/
3. Capucho J (08 de Abril de 2019) Portugueses deitam fora 200 mil toneladas de roupa por ano. Obtido em Junho de 2022, de Diário de Notícias. https://www.dn.pt/edicao-do-dia/08-abr-2019/portugueses-deitam-fora-200-mil-tonelasas-de-roupa-por-ano--10764484.html
4. Cavaleiro A (25 de Janeiro de 2021) Escola Oficina, o lugar onde tudo se transforma. Obtido em Julho de 2022, de Jornal Mundo Atual. https://mundoatual.pt/escola-oficina-o-lugar-onde-tudo-se-transforma/
5. Clarkson PJ, Coleman R, Keates S, Lebbon C (2013) Inclusive design: Design for the whole population. Springer-Verlag, London
6. Costa AR (16 de Maio de 2019) Recolha Seletiva do têxtil passa a ser obrigatória em 2025. (Abilways Portugal) Obtido em Julho de 2022, de Distribuição Hoje. https://www.distribuicaohoje.com/producao/recolha-seletiva-do-textil-passa-a-ser-obrigatoria-em-2025/
7. Fitts PM (1954) The information capacity of the human motor system in controlling the amplitude of movement. J Exp Psychol 47(6):381
8. Google (2022) WebP compression study. Obtido de Google Developers. https://developers.google.com/speed/webp/docs/webp_study
9. Greenwood T (2021) Sustainable web design. A Book Apart
10. Greenwood T (2022) The Dark side of green web design. Obtido de Whole Grain Digital. https://www.wholegraindigital.com/blog/dark-colour-web-design/
11. HTTP Archive (2022) Page weight. Obtido de HTTP Archive. https://archive.org/reports/page-weight#reqImg
12. Hussain A (2020) Carbon-aware vs. carbon-efficient applications. Obtido de Microsoft. https://devblogs.microsoft.com/sustainable-software/carbon-aware-vs-carbon-efficient-applications/
13. Henry SL, Abou-Zahra S, Brewer J (2008) The role of accessibility in a universal web. In Proceedings of the 11th international conference on Human-Computer Interaction
14. Krug S (2014) Don't make me think, revisited: a common sense approach to web usability. New Riders
15. Lowdermilk T (2013) User-centered design: a developer's guide to building user-friendly applications. O'Reilly Media
16. Miller GA (1956) The magical number seven, plus or minus two: Some limits on our capacity for processing information. Psychol Rev 63(2):81
17. Newell A, Gregor P (2002) Design for older and disabled people—where do we go from here? Univ Access Inf Soc 2(1):3–7
18. Nielsen J (1994, April) Enhancing the explanatory power of usability heuristics. In Proceedings of the SIGCHI conference on Human Factors in Computing Systems, pp 152–158
19. Nielsen J, Budiu R (2012) Mobile usability. New Riders
20. Nielsen J, Molich R (1990, March) Heuristic evaluation of user interfaces. In Proceedings of the SIGCHI conference on Human factors in computing systems, pp 249–256
21. Nielsen J, Loranger H (2006) Prioritizing web usability. New Riders

22. Nielsen J (2000, March 18) Why you only need to test with 5 users. Nielsen Norman Group. https://www.nngroup.com/articles/why-you-only-need-to-test-with-5-users/
23. Nielsen J (2012, June 3) How many test users in a usability study? Nielsen Norman Group. https://www.nngroup.com/articles/how-many-test-users/
24. Norman DA (2013) The design of everyday things: revised and expanded edition. Basic Books
25. O'Brien HL, Toms EG (2010) The development and evaluation of a survey to measure user engagement. J Am Soc Inform Sci Technol 61(1):50–69
26. Pressman A (2019) Design thinking: a guide to problem soolving for everyone
27. Ripalda D, Garido A, Guevara C (2018, June) Gestalt framework in the design of interfaces for mobile devices: theoretical approach. In 2018 13th Iberian conference on information systems and technologies (CISTI). IEEE, pp 1–4
28. Ripalda D, Guevara C, Garrido A (2021) Relationship between gestalt and usability heuristics in mobile device interfaces. In: Karwowski W, Ahram T, Etinger D, Tanković N, Taiar R (eds) Human systems engineering and design III. IHSED 2020. Advances in intelligent systems and computing, vol 1269. Springer, Cham. https://doi.org/10.1007/978-3-030-58282-1_25
29. Rogers Y, Sharp H, Preece J (2011) Interaction design: beyond human-computer interaction. John Wiley & Sons
30. Rubin J, Chisnell D (2008) Handbook of usability testing: how to plan, design, and conduct effective tests. John Wiley & Sons
31. Sinha G, Shahi R, Shankar M (2010) Human computer interaction. 2010 3rd international conference on emerging trends in engineering and technology, Goa, India, pp 1–4. https://doi.org/10.1109/ICETET.2010.85
32. Sophia (2021) Best image size for websites 2021 | The ultimate guide. North West Media Collective. Retrieved June 23, 2023, from https://northwestmediacollective.com/blog/best-image-size-for-websites/
33. Tschimmel K (2012) Design thinking as an effective toolkit for innovation. In: Proceedings of the XXIII ISPIM conference: action for innovation: innovating from experience. Barcelona. ISBN 978-952-265-243-0
34. Vredenburg K, Mao J-Y, Smith PW, Carey T (2002) A survey of user-centered design practice. In Proceedings of the SIGCHI conference on human factors in computing systems (CHI '02). Association for Computing Machinery. https://doi.org/10.1145/503376.503460
35. Wolniak R (2017) The Design Thinking method and its stages. Systemy Wspomagania w Inżynierii Produkcji, 6
36. Ye L (2020) Onlign. How might we shape the future of a greener internet? Obtido em novembro de 2022

Building Bridges Between University and Responsible Practices in Design: A Case Study on a Campaign Against Dating Violence

Maria Luisa Costa and Maria Cristina Pinheiro

Abstract This article presents a case study of a campaign developed in the context of university teaching in Communication Design to raise awareness among young people about the problem of dating violence, which is part of domestic violence and gender violence, behaviors that are a concern in our society. Gender equality is one of the 17 Sustainable Development Goals (SDG) identified in the United Nations (UN) 2030 Agenda, equality that will not be achievable as long as gender violence exists. The ethical thinking and social responsibility of the Designer can be applied in the design and development of campaigns that inform and sensitize the public and educate young people. Designers, as promoters of culture and disseminators of information, can thus contribute to a better future aligned with the United Nations Sustainable Development Goals. With this Case Study, we have promoted responsible design practices, with a focus on a social impact cause, helping Victim Support Association through pro bono design work, and we believe it fits into the principles of service learning. This campaign helped to make students socially responsible agents aware of the importance of their civic action and their active role in changing mindsets in a society that is still confronted with problems of violence between young couples.

Keywords Design and social responsibility · Dating violence · Gender equality · Education · SDGs

M. L. Costa (✉)
CIAUD, Lisboa, Portugal
e-mail: design.luisacosta@gmail.com

M. L. Costa · M. C. Pinheiro
Instituto Superior Miguel Torga, Coimbra, Portugal

M. C. Pinheiro
UNIDCOM/IADE, Lisboa, Portugal

D. Raposo et al. (eds.), *Perspectives on Design III*, Springer Series in Design and Innovation 34, https://doi.org/10.1007/978-3-031-43516-4_6

1 Introduction

This paper presents a project developed in the first semester of the academic year 2022–2023, by student Ricardo Ribeiro of the degree in Communication Design of Instituto Superior Miguel Torga, under the course unit of Project II. The main objectives were to respond to a need for the Portuguese Association for Victim Support (APAV); to promote the debate around the problems that victimize Portuguese nowadays; to develop campaigns to sensitize society about these issues; to make students aware of the importance of socially responsible design practices.

The presented case study is about dating violence, for having been one of the best-rated campaigns in academic terms and has been selected by the APAV and already disclosed through the media this entity regularly uses.

The APAV is a national non-profit organization whose purpose is to promote and contribute to informing, protecting, and supporting citizens who are victims of criminal offenses, providing free and confidential services [1].

Dating violence was one of the problems most worked on by the students, probably due to their proximity or experiential awareness of these practices. *APAV defines dating violence* as an act aimed at controlling, dominating, or having more power than the other person involved in the relationship. It can be practiced unilaterally or bilaterally by the partners involved in the relationship, taking physical, verbal, sexual, psychological, and social forms [2].

As part of Domestic Violence, Dating Violence is a problem that threatens the future of young people and social peace, so the awareness of young people and the early combat of this type of practice is strongly justified in higher education.

Training someone to be a designer implies on providing students with tools and strategies to question the current *status quo*, increasing their skills in thinking and developing design proposals for a better world. Designers today work on organizational structure and social problems, on interaction, processes, services, and human experiences. Many problems involve complex social and political issues [3].

In the process of teaching and learning Communication Design, the work about Violence in dating is doubly justified because more than raising awareness among young people, we are preparing future professionals for the development of ethical and socially responsible practices.

2 Contextualization of the Issue

The Green Paper on Social Responsibility and Higher Education Institutions, 2018 [4], highlights the importance of training socially responsible individuals by including curricular content that stimulates critical and reflective thinking in students. Social project-based learning plays a fundamental role in developing these competencies, allowing students to reflect on the needs of contemporary society, the role of designers in this society, and what impact and contribution their work can have in creating a more just and sustainable society.

Based on these principles, the development of a campaign was proposed to promote practical training and learning in a social context within the scope of the Project II discipline. This campaign allowed students to become aware of the values of solidarity and social responsibility, articulating a professional intervention with a real social problem, a process that we believe fits into the principles of service learning, as defined by Gaete Quezada [5].

The students were free to choose an area to develop the awareness campaign, and gender violence, with a particular focus on dating violence, was the topic that aroused the most interest among the students.

Issues related to violence in general, and gender violence in particular, are serious problems that affect all of society and hinder the sustainable development of humanity.

The 2030 Agenda, adopted by the United Nations (UN) and all Member States in 2015 [6], includes 17 Sustainable Development Goals (SDGs) to be achieved by 2030. Gender equality and empowering all women and girls is one of the priorities presented in SDG 5. This agenda aims to ensure the prosperity and well-being of all women and men while protecting our planet and strengthening the foundations of peace.

We know, however, that achieving gender equality and empowering all women and girls is a complex challenge that all nations will have to face because the subordinate status of women has been imposed for centuries in most cultures, restricting opportunities and freedoms of women and that even in the face of current achievements, women continue to be subordinated, which is reflected in stereotypes arising from a cultural burden that worsens and legitimizes discrimination and violence against women.

The 3rd article of the Council of Europe Convention on Preventing and Combating Violence against Women and Domestic Violence [7] states that domestic violence covers "all acts of physical, sexual, psychological or economic violence that occur within the family or domestic unit or between former or current spouses or partners, whether or not the perpetrator shares or has shared the same residence with the victim", it is also recognized that men are also victims of domestic violence. However, this convention highlights the reality that women are disproportionately affected. In Portugal this reality is confirmed by statistical indicators [8], which we present as a guide:

Analyzing these data, we can see that, on average, in every 10 victims of domestic violence, 8 are women (74.9%), while only 2 are men. Most of the aggressors are male. On average, for every 10 people reported for domestic violence, 8 are men (81%), and 2 are women.

It is also mentioned that domestic violence cases occur mainly in intimate relationships (current or past) or sons/daughters and parents relationships.

Of the reported cases, 63.7% involve couples, partners, ex-couples, or ex-partners. The remaining 36.3% are related to fathers/mothers, step-parents, children, and step-children.

These data also remind us that as long as domestic violence and gender inequality exist, it will not be possible to achieve the SDG 16 [6], which aims to promote peaceful and inclusive societies, provide access to justice for all, and build effective, accountable and inclusive institutions at all levels. As noted in 16.1 "significantly reduce all forms of violence and related mortality rates everywhere."

We can not achieve gender equality (SDG 5), nor peace and social justice (SGD 16), while domestic violence persists while this violence is legitimized by behaviors and sociocultural patterns that normalize dating violence and domestic violence, legitimized by popular ideas that can be verified in phrases like: "*the more you hit me, the more I like you*" or "*between husband and wife, no one puts a spoon*", among many others, which reinforce stereotypes and make women the primary victims of domestic violence.

In the context of this case study, we believe that the topic addressed is framed by SDG 5 since dating violence is a form of gender violence that, according to the Portuguese Commission for Citizenship and Gender Equality [8], restricts and violates the rights of citizens and their quality of life, and may cause severe physical and psychological damage and even death, being women, for historical and cultural reasons, the most affected by this sort of violence.

3 Design and Social Responsibility

Social responsibility is based on ethical and sustainable practices that aim to improve the life of human beings and the planet, and both institutions and individuals must commit to these principles.

According to Papanek [9], ethics is the philosophical basis that guides our moral choices and values. In the case of designers, it is essential to exercise ethical thinking, which must be punctuated by an exercise of reflection that analyzes what they do, why they do it, and what will be the consequences of what they do, constantly bearing in mind the concern for the planet, the environment, and people, and Margolin [10], in the same sense, states that by adopting these ethical principles Design will be, as it was in the past, a powerful tool that allows human beings to survive and evolve.

The products resulting from the practice of Design have a significant impact on society, influence social and cultural behaviors, shape opinions and promote consumption practices. Therefore, designers have a huge social responsibility and can play a valuable role in raising awareness about the need to build humanity based on ethical and sustainable values [11]. They can, by their privileged position, collaborate in building a more humane future, provided they are committed to it, making use of bold ideas and positive visions, oriented toward a future in which a culture of sustainability and social justice prevail [10].

If these design capabilities are a reality, it is no less true that the professional practices of designers do not always correspond to these needs. Due to historical factors or the need for work, designers give answers to the consumer society, which makes them be seen as agents at the service of practices that aim exclusively at a profit instead of individuals who put their knowledge at the service of people and the public interest. This perception causes Design to be frequently associated with commercial advertising and marketing and the creation of products that do nothing for the well-being of individuals.

This perspective on Design, long observed and rejected by groups of designers, has resulted in manifestos, the first dating from 1964 and signed by Ken Garland along with many other designers, the second, published in Emigre 51, under the same name as the previous First Things First Manifesto 2000, was signed by Jonathan Barnbrook and an extensive list of Designers, Art Directors, and Visual Communicators who reiterate their dissatisfaction for the predominance of commercial advertising in the practice of Design, and defend the need for designers to reverse their professional priorities, directing them towards a more functional, democratic and lasting communication, that is, towards environmental, cultural and social issues [12].

If the Designer's practice is shaped by ideals and beliefs that create values and guide their actions [10], the work developed with Design students will undoubtedly contribute to a new vision of the profession and the future where Gender Equality and many other social and cultural problems will have priority.

The shift in the focus of designers will inevitably have to go through the teaching and learning of Design, which should be framed in the typology of Design for social change, which, as mentioned by Souleles [13], encompasses multiple activities focused on social issues that can also be referred to as "public interest design, social design, social impact design, socially responsive design, transformation design, and humanitarian design," all these different designations have a common denominator, that is to achieve collective and social goals rather than focusing on consumer goals [13]

Since the sustainability crisis that the world is facing is mainly due to the practice of Design associated with consumption, it is now urgent to change the teaching of Design in order to prepare future designers to contribute to its economic, social, cultural, and environmental development. These practices cannot happen in isolation because only multiple experiences make Design students deal with real problems and prepare them to adapt quickly and respond to situations that society will present to them to help build a more sustainable future and promote well-being through Design [14].

Future designers face numerous challenges, and the sustainability of the world and human beings should be a priority. Looking at human rights as a starting point, promoting education in this sense, not only through the transmission of information but the practical applicability of skills at the service of the active defense of these rights, will strengthen non-discriminatory and inclusive practices.

According to Ideo [15] "Designing more inclusively means designing products, services, and systems to benefit those who are marginalized, and impacted most by our work. We used to design for people. Increasingly, we are designing with them".

Thus, we believe that the teaching of Design committed to sustainability and inclusiveness, particularly in the context of gender equality addressed here, will have results in the practice of future designers, creating professionals more aware and committed to behavioral and social changes. Communication Design may play a decisive role in constructing an egalitarian society, avoiding gender stereotypes, and promoting diversity and inclusion.

4 Methodology

This campaign was developed on the curricular unit Project II, of the 3rd year of the degree in Communication Design, and intends, in curricular terms, that students apply and consolidate the knowledge acquired in the previous two years, while acquire new skills, such as to know how to produce and model different communication design pieces at all stages and in various media, whether digital or printed, or skills at the level of critical awareness by understanding the role of communication design as an agent that can serve social causes.

It is also expected that students develop creative thinking supported by research, that they acquire practice in design project and, that they know how to respond adequately to the demands of a briefing, raising their awareness for social and cultural responsibility of design.

Thus, the developed campaign encompassed the creation of several pieces of communication in different supports. The analogical materials included the respective art-finalization, and the publications for social media (posts and stories for Instagram and Facebook), also included videos with different purposes and duration.

It was a transdisciplinary project that involved different curricular units and it was launched to 9 students supervised by Professor Cristina Pinheiro, responsible for the curricular unit, with the participation of professors Júlio Costa Pinto of Graphic Production, pre-printing and final artwork of analogical materials and Bruno Carnide supporting production and editing of the videos.

4.1 Process and Development

The project was carried out in phases with following steps: launch of the briefing; research phase; concept; design development; evaluation (in academic context and with APAV) and implementation of the selected project.

The briefing was created by the professor in charge and was built according to the needs listed by APAV but has included other elements considered relevant to make the final project of the Curricular Unit more complete.

The following pieces have been developed: One poster, one magazine advertisement, one flyer, a small, stapled brochure, several posts for social networks (Instagram and Facebook) and two videos, (20 seconds version and another with a maximum of 3 minutes).

A street action was also included, freely chosen by the students, as a way of attracting attention and making the general population aware of the proposed subjects.

APAV has proposed 3 themes: Violence in Dating, Crimes against property and IRS Consignment.

The research phase was based on data published by APAV, with gathered information about the three themes, identification of the target audience and published numbers on the types of victims. It also included a critical analysis of other campaigns previously carried out and published by APAV.

This research was the first step to establish contact with the Portuguese situation, numbers and types of violence between young people. This made them aware of situation and gave them information to work with.

The conceptual phase and generation of ideas included discussions in the classroom with the participation of all students, in a first phase, and later the individual monitoring of each project, with the selection of the best ideas and solutions to be developed by each student. Final works were composed by six campaigns on dating violence, one on IRS consignment and two on crimes against property.

The design development of the various pieces was also carried out in phases – The first piece that has determined the entire line of the campaign was the Poster. This was followed by a magazine advertisement, the flyer, the stapled brochure, that were all printed. This was followed by posts for social networks, the production of videos and finally a street action inspired by the guerrilla marketing actions.

Despite not being related to marketing, the inspiration came from this idea. Guerrilla marketing is a set of marketing actions to launch a campaign at a fraction of the price it would normally cost. The impact should obviously be more significant regardless of the low budget invested. "Guerrilla marketing is like the Banksy side of marketing". Whether you use a sticker or a stencil to get your message across, it all comes down to how much it impresses and impacts your target group [16].

The more unconventional, the more impressive it will be in the eyes of the audience.

This sequential development made it possible to carry out the communication pieces, increasing their complexity, maintaining formal coherence and visual language, while adding more information. The main idea was developed with formal consistency throughout these phases, seeking to add other perspectives.

4.2 Evaluation in an Academic Context and with APAV

In the context of the classroom, the three best projects were chosen and then presented to APAV. They were evaluated according to the following criteria:

- Creativity and originality in solving the proposed exercises
- Application of concepts and appropriate language to the target audience
- Fulfilments of all the phases of the entire project process and delivery deadlines.
- Quality of printing and final presentation.
- Ability to argue and defend the project ideas.

When the best campaigns were presented to APAV, those responsible highlighted the quality of the chosen works and selected three of them as the ones that best suited their purposes. The other two works to be published soon.

4.3 Implementation and Publication

The Case Study presented here was selected by APAV, to be published on Instagram and Facebook and other social networks, on February 14, 2023, Valentine's Day. The campaign will be presented further in this paper.

5 The Original Campaign and the Implemented Campaign

One of the most interesting aspects of this campaign was the interpretation by those responsible for APAV of the original message created by the student.

What he considered to communicate with the initial slogan, "Foi só uma vez" (it was only once), that is, it will never happen again because it is intolerable for it to be repeated, was not exactly the understanding of those responsible of APAV.

They have considered that the general public could accept "It was only once" and could suggest a complacent and excusing attitude and that wouldn't even be very serious because it happens *only once*.

This kind of attitude, which excuses violence over and over again, is responsible for the successive and repeated aggressions, because the victims naively believe that violence will not happen again, that there will not be a second time.

Unfortunately, this is not what happens, and the aggressions are recurrent, repeated, forgiveness and apologies follow one another, "it was just this time". In the end they become a pattern of behavior.

This difference in interpretation could have opposite consequences to those initially desired.

We were facing with the first confrontation between what was expected by the student and what actually happened. In this case, the tone and modulation of the voice when saying "it was just once" would make all the difference if Instagram posts had been accompanied by sound.

Since it was only visuals and no audio, to avoid misunderstandings those responsible considered that the slogan should be changed to "Violence is not Love". The student agreed to make the changes and replaced all the pieces for publication.

Not always the messages that we think are clear and obvious to us are read and interpreted otherwise. This was another lesson that the student took away from this experience.

5.1 The Original Campaign

As presented here, see below the poster (Fig. 1) and printed materials as student initially has proposed (Figs. 2, 3, and 4).

Finally, we present here one street action whose idea is based on the premise that “we only know when it’s up to us”. From there, the intention would be to place people and observers in the center of the situation, where there would be an explanatory text of the campaign. This action in the streets of Coimbra is a mock up, and was not implemented. Despite the guerilla actions have this component of surprise, this action was not implemented because it would have had to involve the

Fig. 1 Original campaign—posters

Fig. 2 Original campaign—flyer

Fig. 3 Original campaign—stapled brochure

Fig. 4 Original campaign—story

autarchy in the process or it would not have been allowed. It was also not within the scope of APAV's request, but we believe that posing this challenge to students was an opportunity to make them think a little beyond conventional solutions. We consider it's unconventional and creative in its use of space (Fig. 5).

Fig. 5 Original campaign—street action

Videos can be seen here: https://www.youtube.com/playlist?list=PLBU5vMNdaSPjJCcDMW2KeYG_uc4w9Hisc

5.2 Implemented Campaign on Social Media

APAV predominantly uses social networks to present awareness campaigns in the various areas in which it operates. Despite the intention revealed at the meeting for the selection of work to print the poster, we are not aware that it has done so.

Thus, the works were presented on social networks, and the changes requested from the student and introduced were those intended for these means of dissemination (Figs. 6, 7, 8, and 9).

6 Results

The results presented in Tables 1, 2, 3, and 4 were provided by APAV and showed the interactions and reactions to the publications made within the scope of the campaign.

However, these data alone do not allow us to draw a conclusion since, according to what this institution informed us, they had never been a campaign launched exclusively to address this issue, so there are no comparative data.

Still, on the social network Instagram, where we followed APAV and saw the followers' interactions, we realized that there was high adherence to this campaign compared to the regular interactions with APAV.

Fig. 6 Implemented campaign—Instagram Carousel

Fig. 7 Implemented campaign—individual post

Fig. 8 Implemented campaign—individual posts

Fig. 9 Implemented campaign—story 1 and 2

Beyond the numbers, which, as we stated earlier, did not allow us to draw conclusions, analyzing the whole process from an empirical perspective, we can figure that this type of work made it possible to improve the training of university students through:

- Scientific and civic training in the field of social design.

Table 1 Instagram results

Instagram	Achieves	Shares	Profile views	Likes
Story 1	1926	1600	37	N/D
Story 2	538	470	5	N/D
Post 1	9646	N/D	N/D	1390
Post 2	1454	N/D	N/D	115
Post 3	1892	N/D	N/D	119

Table 2 Facebook results

Facebook	Achieves	Reactions	Shares
Post 1	8695	389	110
Post 2	881	17	0
Post 3	1739	22	11

Table 3 Twitter results

Twitter	Views	RT	QRT	Likes
Tweet 1	2198	20	1	25
Tweet 2	1082	8	0	15
Tweet 3	190	1	0	3
Tweet 4	203	2	1	5

Table 4 LinkedIn results

LinkedIn	Impressions	Clicks	Reactions	Shares
Post 1	25591	235	923	165

- Encourage students to learn in an extra-academic context to acquire an awareness of the society in which they will operate.

They fulfill the learning objectives identified in the design course, acquiring knowledge, skills, and competencies identified in the Curricular Units.

At the same time, they were aware of social problems and how designers can positively impact society.

7 Conclusions

Designers must be aware of their impact on society when developing new products, system or services. One possible way to success on this endeavour passes by rethinking design education, where: Students must be solving problems related to their local realities and face real problems [3].

With these projects, the students fulfilled the learning objectives identified in the Design Course, as they acquired knowledge, skills and competences that were foreseen in the curricular units.

For the students, one of the most relevant aspects of this experience was the awareness of their real contribution as they saw the positive impact of their work, when the projects left the classroom to be implemented. By doing this, they apply the design solutions, they deal with real situations and problems, bridging the gap between good and interesting ideas developed in the classroom and the world of professional practice with all its constraints.

We consider that the work developed by the students stimulated critical thinking and individual awareness of a problem that concerns humanity. Besides fulfilling the immediate goals of acquiring knowledge and project skills, the development of the campaign to promote and raise awareness of the need to eradicate disparities, prejudices, and violent practices against others will stimulate student's ethical and critical spirit, which will make them capable of channeling their ethical capacities towards social activism directed towards the creation of a better world.

"Education is a process in which the environment changes the learner, and the learner changes the environment. In other words, both are interactive" [17].

References

1. Associação Portuguesa de Apoio à Vítima. https://apav.pt/apav_v3/index.php/pt/apav-1/quem-somos. Last accessed 8 June 2023
2. Associação Portuguesa de Apoio à Vítima. https://apavparajovens.pt/pt/go/o-que-e1. Last accessed 8 June 2023
3. Rocha H, Ferreira M, Azevedo J (2017) Paradigm shift in design education to drive strategic innovations, sustainable solutions and social change. Proceedings of IADE doctoral conference'17, Emília Duarte (Ed.). Lisbon, pp 151–157
4. ORSIES (2018) Livro Verde sobre Responsabilidade Social e Instituições de Ensino Superior. Press Forum, SA – Comunicação Social, Lisboa
5. Gaete Quezada R (2015) El Voluntariado Universitario como Ámbito de Aprendizage Servicio y Emprendimiento Social. Un Estudio de Caso. Última Década 43:235–260. https://www.redalyc.org/articulo.oa?id=19544220009. Last accessed 11 June 2023
6. Transforming our World: The 2030 Agenda for Sustainable Development (2015). https://sdgs.un.org/2030agenda. Last accessed 11 June 2023
7. The Council of Europe Convention on preventing and combating violence against women and domestic violence - Istanbul Convention (2011). https://www.coe.int/en/web/gender-matters/council-of-europe-convention-on-preventing-and-combating-violence-against-women-and-domestic-violence. Last accessed 11 June 2023

8. Comissão para a Cidadania e a Igualdade de Género "Igualdade de Género em Portugal: Indicadores Chave (2022). https://www.cig.gov.pt/area-igualdade-entre-mulheres-e-homens/indicadores/. Last accessed 18 June 2023
9. Papanek V (1995) Arquitectura e Design. Ecologia e Ética. Edições, Lisboa, p. 70
10. Margolin V (2014) Design e risco de Mudança. Verso da História, Vila do Conde
11. Berman DB (2009) Do good design: how designers can change the world. New Riders and AIGA Design Press, Berkeley
12. Emigre (2020) Essays first things first manifesto 2000. https://www.emigre.com/Essays/Magazine/FirstThingsFirstManifesto200. Last accessed 6 June 2023
13. Souleles N (2017) Design for social change and design education: social challenges versus teacher-centred pedagogies. Des J 20(sup1):S927–S936
14. Rocha H, Ferreira, M, Azevedo, J (2018) Benchmarking higher education in design for social innovation and sustainability: state of art and future challenges. Proceedings of the 5th design doctoral conference, DDC'18: transgression. IADE - Universidade Europeia, 20–22 June. Lisboa
15. Ideo. https://cantwait.ideo.com/inclusion. Last accessed 6 June 2023
16. Dimitriou M (2023) https://moosend.com/blog/guerilla-marketing-ideas/. Last accessed 6 June 2023
17. Papanek V (1984) Design for the real world: human ecology and social change, 2nd edn. Academy Chicago Publishers, Chicago

The Contribution of Interface Design on the Promotion and Sales of Social Institutions' Products: The Case Study of Escola Oficina

Rita Lobo, Nuno Martins, Leonardo Pereira, and Daniel Brandão

Abstract This paper focuses on the case study of Escola Oficina (EO), a non-profit, socially-oriented organization that supports unemployed citizens by offering training and employability in the fields of sewing and cartonboard making, with an emphasis on circular economy and environmental sustainability. Although EO is successful in training and integrating their trainees into the job market, it faces external communication challenges and issues selling its products. This study aims, therefore, to tackle the stigma associated with unemployed individuals, while promoting the high production quality of its products. The adopted strategy was to create an online store to, thus, promote the products produced by EO's trainees. This study focused on Interface Design and in the identification of the requirements and strategies that best help to fight the prejudice that traditionally lives amongst citizens associated with products that are produced in the context of social institutions. This project adopted a Design Thinking methodology, using a user-centered approach that was validated through usability tests. The results obtained are intended to serve as a basis for potential replication in analogous cases.

Keywords Design de interfaces · Plataforma digital · E-commerce

R. Lobo (✉)
School of Design, Polytechnic Institute of Cavado and Ave, Barcelos, Portugal
e-mail: ritavlobo@gmail.com

N. Martins
Media and Culture, School of Design, Research Institute for Design, Polytechnic Institute of Cavado and Ave, Barcelos, Portugal

L. Pereira
University of Aveiro, DigiMedia, Aveiro, DeCA, Portugal

D. Brandão
Institute of Social Sciences, CECS, University of Minho, Braga, Portugal

D. Raposo et al. (eds.), *Perspectives on Design III*, Springer Series in Design and Innovation 34, https://doi.org/10.1007/978-3-031-43516-4_7

1 Introduction

Escola Oficina (EO), located in Vila Nova de Gaia, Portugal, is a social, non-profit organization that focuses on supporting long-term unemployed citizens, with poor work habits, through employability training. EO primarily acts in the sewing and cardboard fields, also offering courses in other fields, according to the trainees' demands and interests. EO is based on the principles of circular economy and environmental sustainability, working with repurposed materials from textile, paper and cardboard waste that is donated by textile companies. This project is grounded in values such as sharing economy, environmental education, good citizenship practices, qualified social integration and job market integration opportunities [30].

The knowledge gathered by the trainees is applied practically in a workshop where they develop real projects that transform industrial residues into final products with added value. These are later sold by EO, where the generated profit is payed to the trainees themselves.

EO is a well-known success case in both their employability training for unemployed citizens, as in their integration in the job market. Nevertheless, EO's exterior communication barely exists—a problem that makes it hard to promote and communicate both its activities and the selling of the items produced by their trainees.

EO's managers believe that their clients generally distrust the quality of their products since they're produced by unemployed trainees, generally in a socially vulnerable situation, having low income resources and low academic education levels. These image and communication problems unavoidably harm the products' value and, therefore, its sales. Sales which, in turn are fundamental for the sustainability of EO's project.

In 2022, EO's website was deactivated by its managers as it didn't properly portray the institution's brand. Given the significance of the online presence as a means of communication, EO recognized the need to develop a digital platform with an online store, as a way to build a new communication tool able to correctly portray the institution's values and to promote their products' sales.

In order to address this problem, the here presented study was developed within the field of User Interface Design, as a way to design a new online platform (to both be EO's institutional website and online store) and as a way to identify a set of recommendations associated with Communication Design and Interface Design in the development of an online store for a social institution. Through the designed interface it was intended to combine EO's values with e-commerce's efficiency and consequently, help to counteract the "lack of quality" prejudice associated with products purchased from social solidarity institutions.

In order to achieve these goals, this study centred itself in user interface design, namely in the potential contribution that an online platform can exert on the purchasing and positive evaluation of products. Thus, firstly interface design principles were identified [8, 15], particularly, interface design applied to e-commerce [8, 14, 23, 24], we also seeked to relate interface design with online purchase motivation

[2, 16, 29, 39], lastly, a new digital platform for EO is presented, based in Design Thinking methods [4, 6, 7].

2 Interface Design

Interface Design seeks to establish harmony between the aesthetics and functionality of online platforms. It's about creating a pleasant and intuitive experience for the users, by the means of a well thought out interface. User interface design (UID) is the visual part of an online platform, through which the users interact. In the context of electronic commerce, according to Deng and Poole [8] the concern with the interface aesthetics of a platform helps to predict the emotion, perception and action of the e-commerce client. Gao [12] state that the most interesting and easy to use interfaces stimulate the users, while keeping up the platform's interest and efficacy.

Thus, it's essential to understand the needs and expectations of the users, which involves detailed research to understand the target-audience and how they think and interact with similar online platforms. This information guides the design decisions and helps to develop interfaces that meet the users' needs [15]. This way, after the study of a set of authors [16, 18, 24], the following principles were established: visual hierarchy, consistency, simplicity, intuitive navigation, visual feedback and usability testing.

One of the key aspects of user interface design is an effective visual hierarchy. By properly using colour, size, typography and other visual elements, it's possible to highlight important information and to guide the user's navigation through the interface. This visual organization facilitates user comprehension and makes for a more pleasant experience [27].

Consistency is another fundamental user interface guideline. An interface should maintain a cohesive visual language across the whole platform, using elements such as colour, icons and buttons in a coherent way. This promotes familiarity and facilitates user interaction, helping them recollect certain patterns [24].

Another interface property to be valued is simplicity. Avoiding complex and unnecessary elements helps to limit user confusion and guarantees efficient task completion. A minimalist and organized design favours usability and user comprehension [28].

In turn, it's important to project clear and logical navigation structures, facilitating and making the user's journey fast and intuitive. Well positioned menus, links and buttons assist in intuitive navigation [16].

According to Huang and Benyoucef [18], providing immediate visual feedback is an important practice. It's necessary to inform users that their actions were executed successfully, be it by the means of subtle animations, colour change or confirmation messages. This feedback reinforces interactivity and promotes users' trust in the platform.

Lastly, usability testing is imperative to guarantee the interface's efficacy and efficiency. By submitting the interface to real users it's possible to get valuable feedback and to identify problems and possible improvements to be made before the final launch.

These principles were considered during the development of this project. We tried to create a simple and visually consistent digital platform that would meet EO's needs. However, given the initial research problem posed, it was essential to study e-commerce interface design in more depth, as the user experience is one of the decisive factors that drives purchases.

3 E-commerce Interface Design

> *Connecting Users to the Platform Through an Easy-To-Navigate Interface May Enhance User Experience, Especially on e-commerce Platforms.* [15]

In addition to user experience, there are other factors that may equally influence the success of the e-commerce user, namely the design of interfaces combined with aesthetics and usability [31]. The main goal of e-commerce interface design is to promote user interaction, support user decision making and to encourage them to return (Helander and Kahlid, 2000).

According to Lee and Koubek [24], content organization, visual organization, the navigation system, colour and typography are attributed to interface design. Context organization is related to the effective delivery of information to its users, visual organization is related with the appearance of e-commerce; the navigation system assists users in knowing their location and position on the website; colour is one of the aesthetic aspects that appeals to the users' emotions and helps to recognize the functions of icons, buttons and boxes; typography refers to all existing texts. Each of these design attributes includes usability and aesthetic issues. Context organization, visual organization and the navigation system are related to the usability quality of an interface, while colour and typography are associated with aesthetic quality [24].

While giving priority to user experience and to the purchasing process during navigation, interface design attributes and principles were applied that motivate the purchase of EO's products.

3.1 Aesthetics and Design

Design and aesthetics play a fundamental role in e-commerce, as they attract and involve users, guaranteeing a positive purchasing experience. It's essential that they're aligned with the organization's values and goals, as well as with the target audience's preferences. The concept of "aesthetics" derives from the Greek word "aesthesis" that means "sensory perception". Therefore, aesthetics combined with interface design transmits sensory information through the platform's virtual environment, influencing attitudes, preferences and user satisfaction [23].

The web pages are viewed holistically by users [3]. These are assessed based on visual appearance and the aesthetics of the platform as a whole, not by its individual elements [8]. It's essential to have an attractive landing page, with a clear information hierarchy and a display of individual and isolated graphical elements that compose the page. These elements (colour, image size, typography, font size, column width, background and text colour combination,video and animations help the user concluding a task with ease.

The concepts of "complexity" and "order" are two important variables in the field of visual aesthetics in the construction of e-commerce web pages. For Deng and Poole [8], order corresponds to the page's interpretations and organization. It's associated with intuition and comprehension, through clarity, cohesiveness and legibility of the pages' information architecture. Complexity is associated with the quantity and diversity of elements in a scenario, such as: usage of images, graphics and animations [14].

Complexity and order of the virtual atmosphere influence users' involvement levels. By providing multiple and diverse information as a stimuli source that demands attention and energy, this increase in complexity in the built environment will make the user more excited and interested in it. This statement lines up with Gulfraz et al.'s [14] ideas, in which they state that the complexity displayed in a virtual environment aids in the involvement process, stimulating the user and maintaining its interest. Lavie and Tractinsky [23] establish complexity and order as two design resources that capture the main influence of environmental aesthetics and point to the important role of these aesthetic properties in the design of digital platforms.

In the development of this project's platform pages, a combination of the two variables of the aesthetic field was considered. Thus, the pages' complexity created visual richness with high quality images showing EO's products, with visual consistency lined up with the brand's identity including the logo, colour schemes and design style of the website (strengthening brand recognition and building a cohesive experience for the users); while the other variable structured the pages' information hierarchy in a clear way, reducing doubts and uncertainty for the user.

A dynamic interface requires greater user attention when compared with a static interface of a digital platform [25]. In this sense, Fortin and Dholakia [11] state that increasing the messages' liveliness through colours, images, graphics and animations has a greater probability of generating a positive impact in the user.

Lavie and Tractinsky [23] claim that the human aesthetics experience is subjective and closely related to emotion. Aesthetics in interface design is built on two dimensions, these being classic aesthetics and expressive aesthetics. Classic aesthetics emphasizes organized, clear and minimalist design, similarly to the other. Expressive aesthetics is characterized by creativity, the usage of special effects, originality and dynamism, similarly to the concept of complexity. Other aesthetic properties, such as equilibrium, symmetry and proportion also play an important role in building the virtual atmosphere. The atmosphere of a digital platform is one the main success factors when it comes to online stores [5].

3.2 The Virtual Atmosphere

Karimov et al. [19] developed a general scheme for designing the virtual atmosphere for an e-commerce, which was divided into three main topics: visual design, represented by the layout and aesthetics, it conveys the platforms first impressions to the client; content design, which relates to the information provided by the platform; social suggestion design, which is embedded in the interface, allowing communication between people;

This way, an e-commerce environment might directly influence the users emotional appeal, humour, perceptions and attitudes, which leads to a satisfactory involvement in the purchasing process in e-commerce [39].

A virtual atmosphere with an efficient navigation design should provide an easy to use navigational hierarchy, which allows users to access the desired pages with ease, speed and minimum effort rate [34]. According to Vance et al. [38], navigation design, associated with organization and a structural page layout and platform content, has a significant impact on the amount of effort needed for a user to navigate an e-commerce website.

Authors such as Hewei and Youngsook [17] adopted a Stimulus-Organism-Response (SOR) model that facilitates the identification of relations between the environment stimulus, organisms and answers, in order to develop a conceptual model for online stores. The SOR model is constituted of three stages. The first state, stimulus (S) involves the layout and atmosphere design of the digital platform, which reflects the emotional excitement and consumer attitude towards the online stores' atmosphere. The stage organism (O) seeks to identify and understand the psychological effects of the users during the use of the digital platform. Finally, in the response (R) stage the users purchase intention is analysed, after their presence in the digital platform. Thus, it aims to understand the reactions and behaviours of the interrelationships of layout, atmosphere, emotional arousal, attitude toward the platform and purchase intention.

According to the SOR model, there's a positive relation between the displayed information in a digital platform and the emotional states felt by users [36]. Mummalaneni [35] claims that the SOR model is viable in online user behavioural research. The behavioural results may be classified as proximity behaviours or avoidance. The positive actions being what approaches the user to the platform, in opposition to the avoidance [29].

Manganari et al. [29], present the Online Store Environment Framework (OSEF), a more comprehensive typology of the e-commerce interface consisting of four components: the layout and visual design; the virtual atmospheres; the virtual theatre; and the virtual social presence. The e-commerce layout defines a big part of the users' navigation. Colour is a ubiquitous visual element of e-commerce and digital platforms that affects and influences the user. According to Gorn et al. [13], cold toned colours convey tranquillity, generating better purchasing results. Colour also affects users' intentions to recommend the platform to other people. Furthermore, Wu and Yuan [40] claim that colour combinations that highlight text affect visual preference and reading performance. Virtual theater is represented by the complexity of the atmosphere with images, graphics, videos and animations.

E-commerce with positive results is generally associated to a high usability, friendly and user centred website, regarding interfaces and functional attributes. Usability, as atmospheres aesthetics, is one of the most important interface design principles [26].

3.3 Usability

During this project's development, it was important to understand the user's needs, preferences and behaviours. These information, provided by EO, were valuable insights for the creation of an interface that guarantees a positive experience during the purchase process.

Usability and aesthetics may be connected through simplicity. And although it's considered a fundamental property in the usability of digital platforms' interfaces, it's also an aesthetic preference. The dimension of classical aesthetics serves as a link between usability and aesthetics, being both an aesthetic concept and a usability principle [23].

According to Lee and Koubek [24] usability may be divided into two distinctive concepts: pre-usage usability and user performance usability. Pre-usage usability is the anticipated comprehension of the interface elements, before the real usage performed by the users. While the user performance is related with the completion, or not, of a specific task, in a given amount of time. Lee and Koubek [24], claim that the users' performance is one of the main usability's variables, and Dillon [9] proves that usability may be achieved by observing how users interact with a digital system and saving their performance data (such as task conclusion rate and task conclusion time). Pre-usage usability is mainly influenced by the visual features of a platform, while user performance is influenced by the interface and its functional attributes.

On the other hand, usability being an interface design property, authors such as Kumar et al. [20] and Matera et al. [32] divide usability in ease of use and user-friendliness.

Ease of use refers to the efficiency of the user's performance while interacting with the interface of a platform [20].

The user-friendliness concept is related to the ease of interpretation of the aesthetic design in terms of the platform's interface [32].

Thus, usability takes into consideration the ease by which a group of users understand the structure of a platform, the simplicity of use, the speed in locating an item, the efficacy in navigation and the ability to move within the platform [10]. There's a notorious connection between aesthetics and usability in interface design in digital platforms. In the development of the EO's website, this matter was considered, in a way to influence users' behaviour and users' purchase intention.

4 Purchase Intention in the Digital Environment

The online purchase experience occurs through the interactions between users and the online environment in the e-commerce platforms (Trevinal and Stenger [37]). According to Mollen and Wilson [33], an interactive client experience with the context, resources, design and interface of an e-commerce platform may influence the online purchasing behaviours.

This way, the platform's design properties play a key role in the development of the initial customers' beliefs and their subsequent purchasing behaviour [17, 39], [16, 21]. So developing pleasing and organized online stores is crucial for raising consumer trust and attracting a high client rate [1, 2, 33].

4.1 *Design's Influence in the Purchasing Intent*

There's a direct relationship between interface design and the interactive user experience. The digital platforms' content may influence user online purchase behaviours, resulting in the e-commerce success [33]. A positive user experience is an essential factor for the success of the expected company results, creating a strong emotional connection with the brand and satisfying the user, leading to customer fidelity towards the company [1].

E-commerce platforms that are capable of creating a positive user experience, can lead to a deep immersion into and with the online navigation [2]. Its main property is entertainment, which becomes an emotional experience when users live an interesting and dynamic interaction [17].

Visual involvement affects the emotional side of the user's experience, while the ease of navigation and research influences the cognitive side of the users' leanings [21]. Wells et al. [39] also suggest that a platform's attractive visual design sends a positive message to the users about the quality of the product and the seller. The layout's design and e-commerce atmosphere arouse significant positive attitudes that directly affect the emotional involvement and attitude towards users' purchase intention. Thus, digital platforms that present a layout with organized contents, a variety of products and a simple workflow, positively influence the relationship between the user and the e-commerce purchase [41]. The involvement with the virtual atmosphere, mirrored in a platform's design, content and graphic perspective, might influence the clients' loyalty (Kim et al., 2004).

A platform's ease of navigation greatly reduces users' mental and physical effort. Providing several navigation resources, such as site maps, navigation bars, shortcuts and direct links, research resources and click options, may reduce the necessary time and effort to conclude purchasing tasks [16].

These guidelines were used while developing EO's platform, with the goal of stimulating users' involvement, immersion, and emotional answers, while influencing the users' behaviour during the online shopping process. Along with the branding developed by this projects group, the platform has an attractive visual design that, not only reflects the institution's values, but also aims to mirror and communicate the quality of its products.

A positive online purchasing experience is a multifaceted, holistic and subjective process that occurs through the interactions between the users and the platform's virtual environment [37]. Although, the excessive or improper use of the e-commerce atmosphere might result in negative and unwanted effects [16, 29, 39].

4.2 The Negative Online Shopping Experience

The first users' impressions are created through interactions with the digital platforms' interface, thus, the UI design of an e-commerce platform can highly impact the user's online shopping experience [39]. This implies that a website with an unpleasant interface might bother the users and cause irritation and lack of understanding regarding the design elements, thus leading the users to abandon it without purchasing anything [16].

According to Lim and Ting [28], a user's irritation refers to the feelings of displeasure, discomfort and frustration which are caused by provoking or annoying stimuli. Such as incidents, pop-up messages, blinking texts, animated banners or sponsored ads may go against what the user expects or anticipates in a particular situation and may lead them to feel negative emotions about the site (Gao et al., 2004). Likewise, design resources, such as confusing layouts, excessively vibrant colours or inadequate graphics may accentuate irritation even further. Irritation in e-commerce environments refers to the degree to which an online shopping website seems confusing and frustrating to the users [16].

Understanding and studying the negative shopping experience was key for this project's digital platform development. By analysing issues that might cause frustration, dissatisfaction or difficulties during the shopping experience, it was possible to identify improvement opportunities and to implement strategies to minimize these problems. The anticipation and solving of possible problems allows the platform to earn the users' trust, improve their satisfaction and raise their loyalty degree.

5 EO's Online Store Development

The conception, design and development, of EO's platform followed the steps of the Design Thinking methodology, with an approach focused on the online store embedded into the platform. Therefore, in an initial stage of the platform's development, fictitious profiles of potential groups of users (personas) were created, the information architecture was defined, wireframes and user flows were drawn and, lastly, usability tests were conducted with a sample of real users.

Taking into account the perspectives of different authors [4, 6, 7], regarding the Design Thinking methodology, we verified amongst them, a similar approach to it.

Through a sequence of stages, a solution was then created that tries to answer efficiently to the users' needs, therefore contributing to the EO's products sales increase. Thus, for the development of this project, three main stages of the Design Thinking methodology were accounted for and implemented:

1. Inspiration: the awareness and understanding of the study's central issue (information gathering and analysis stage);
2. Ideation: the generation of multiple ideas and different perspectives regarding the study's central issue (creation of personas, development of information architecture and elaboration of wireframes and user flows);
3. Implementation: the building of prototypes to further review and validate, through iterative usability tests, contents, functional features and navigation.

The inspiration stage's main goal was to understand what were EO's needs and desires that underlined the creation of the digital platform. So, meetings with the managers and the institution's designers were held.

Based on the information and insights that were collected in the inspiration stage, the ideation stage's main goal was to generate creative and innovative solutions to answer to the identified users' needs. Therefore, the personas' creation played a crucial role as these fictitious profiles of the different groups helped to understand their motivations, needs and expectations.

5.1 Personas

The personas revealed themselves to be an effective method to enhance the user's experience. During the project's initial meetings, a survey and compilation, regarding the information provided by EO, was conducted. This data was about real users' features, needs and goals, and it was collected in order to tailor our personas as similar as possible to the real EO's platform users.

Four personas were, therefore, created based on the EO's target-audience (Table 1), where the female gender arises as the predominant one. Consequently, a single persona of the opposite gender was created, the male one.

Information architecture was the next stage, after the study and creation of personas. Using a brainstorming technique and team collaboration, several ideas were generated for the design and functional tools of the digital platform. During this stage, the development of the information architecture took on a key role, allowing for the logical and intuitive organization of information and interactions displayed in the platform's interface.

Table 1 Personas analyses

Maria	Sara	Ana	Carlos
• Cook, currently unemployed; • 52 years old; • EOs trainee; • Had 2 daughters;	• Works in a clothing shop; • 28 years old; • Sews her own clothes	• Design teacher; • 37 years old; • Supports sustainable brands and projects; • Has 3 children	• Business man; • 43 years old; • Has 1 daughter;
Description Maria was a cook for 20 years, but has been unemployed for the last 3 ones. Sewing has always been part of her hobbies because of her mother's influence. Although she knows how to sew, she has trouble turning her hobby into a job	**Description** Sara didn't have financial resources to pursue university studies. Her dream is to work as a fashion designer. She's a creative person with ambition to develop her own brand. But she needs help to enter the job market	**Description** Ana has been a design teacher for over 10 years. She's active on social media, researches about social projects, participates in solidarity groups. She likes to offer her children sustainable gifts	**Description** Carlos has had a company for over 5 years. He cares about sustainability, social corporate responsibility and social innovation. He tries to offer his employees products with a low environmental impact
Goals • Search for sewing courses; • Search for job opportunities; • Likes to purchase hand-made accessories;	**Goals** • Purchase sustainable products; • Search for courses in the fashion field; • Seeks for job market integration;	**Goals** • Purchase products that support social solidarity institutions; • Find a trustful and transparent online store, with sustainable and quality products	**Goals** • Find an online store that offers products in light with his vision of sustainability; • Obtain clear information on the impact generated

5.2 *Information Architecture*

This project focused on the creation of a new solution for the online store embedded into EO's institutional website, capable of mirroring the institution's values and consequently, facilitating their products' sales.

Based on Table 1 and the information provided during the meetings with EO's managers, two organizational charts were sequentially created. The first one to be created, a full organizational chart of the platform (Fig. 1), gathers and offers an ample view of the organization and structuring of the information. The second one that was later created, the online store's organizational chart (Fig. 2), was developed with the goal of facilitating the navigation and search for information.

The platform, therefore, has a complex information architecture, divided into eight sections: *Home, Online Store; Product page; Courses, Employability, Portfolio, News* and *About us*. Considering this paper's research problem, the study specifically focused on a detailed analysis of the interfaces of the EO's platform online store (Fig. 2).

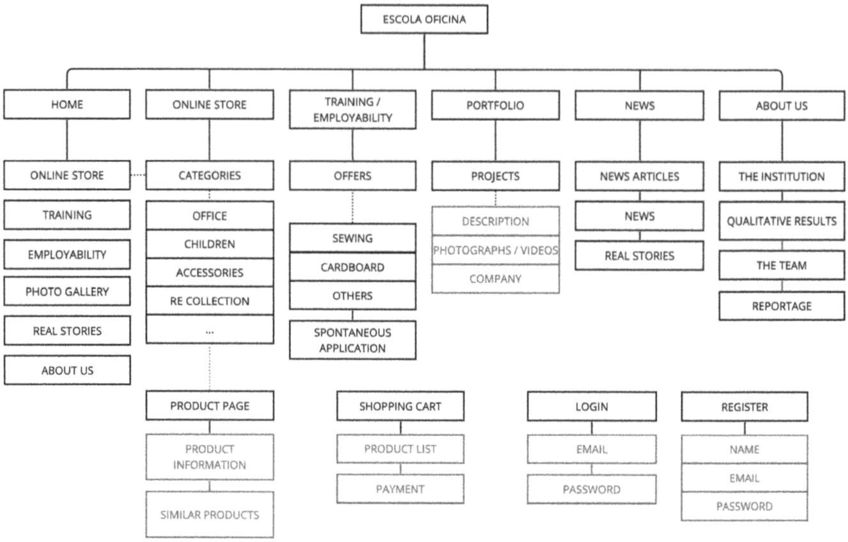

Fig. 1 Organizational chart of the information architecture of EO's digital platform

The platform's *Home* page presents a broad view of the different fields of interest related to the institution. The information architecture of this page mirrors the main fields of EO's operation and explains its mission and values. It's also possible to navigate, from the *Home* page, to all the remaining sections that make up the platform.

The inclusion of a products section in the *Home* page allows for the users to have quick and direct access to the *Online store*. Thus, attracting the attention of users interested in purchasing items through the platform. Or, on the other hand, it makes the selling of EO's products known to new users.

The information architecture of the *Online Store* displays, firstly, the EO's products categories (Office, Children, Accessories and RE Collection) with quick and intuitive access through buttons and links. Immediately bellow, a listing of the products within each category is displayed, showing an image, the name and the price of each product. Still in this page, there's an interactive highlight that allows the user to access to the *About us* section. Here it's possible to access detailed information related to EO's history, mission and values. As well as the presentation of the institution's team of people.

In the *Product* section, the users can access an individual page dedicated to each selected item. This page was designed to provide detailed information about each product, namely images and a full description.

With this information architecture it was intended to create an attractive and intuitive shopping experience on the EO's platform, highlighting the products sustainability and providing detailed information to aid users in their shopping decisions.

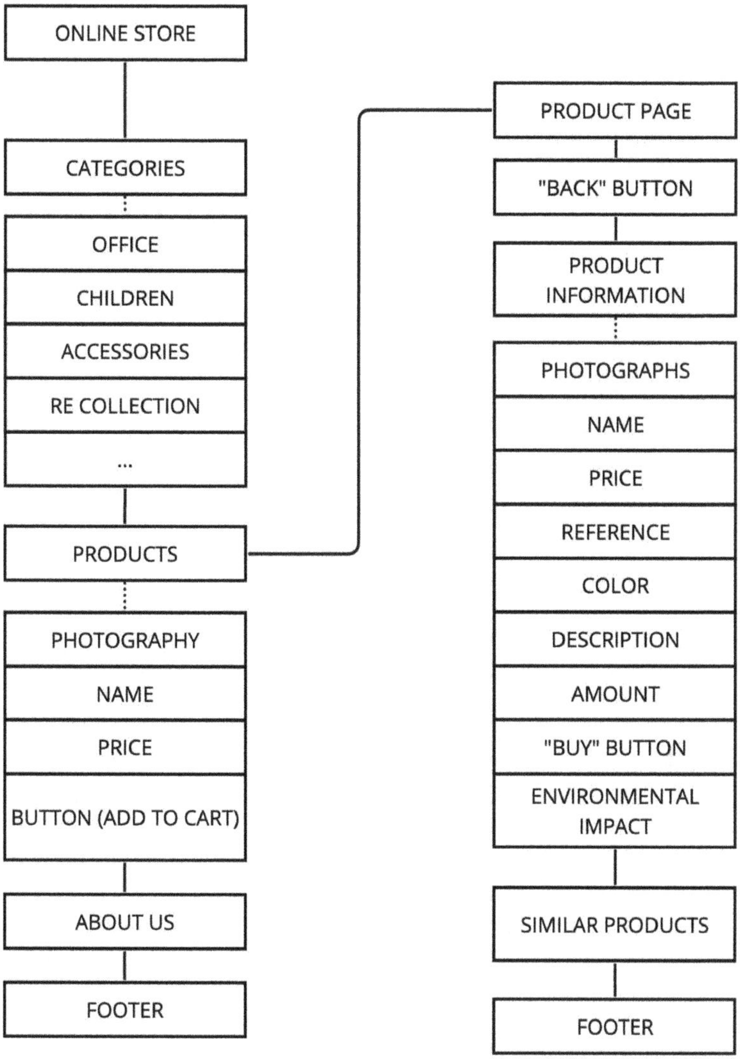

Fig. 2 Organizational chart of information architecture of EO's online store

Once information was organized and well-structured, wireframes and user flows were created, which allowed for a clear and global view of the platform's interactions and possible navigation flows.

5.3 Wireframes and User Flows

The creation of wireframes consists of quickly coming up with several potential solutions for an interface's design. These solutions are simplified schematic representations, generally black and white, that portray the elements that compose a graphical layout of an interface (Buttons, menus, text fields and images). Wireframes were developed to ideate, visualize and communicate the structure and visual composition of the elements displayed by an interface, making use of the least amount of visual details, disregarding colour and real images. In turn, user flows describe the sequence of steps/actions and interactions the user needs to perform in order to complete a particular interaction task, inside an interface. They help to anticipate user needs and allow for designers to conceive the interface in an efficient and intuitive way, thus easy to use by its potential users [23].

The purpose of this stage of the project was to understand how clear and easy to perform the actions required to complete a certain task were for the users or how intuitive an interface button was without applying prominent colours or typography.

This way, wireframes represent the pages and functionalities of a platform. So, the user flows and tasks were conceived for the usability tests.

The development of the first wireframes was focused on the *Home* page. Although the focus of this paper is the *Online store*, the *Home* page is also part of the users purchasing process. This page is the platform's entry point when users want to buy something, providing a broad vision of the institution's activities and values. The page's structure was carefully crafted to convey EO's mission, their fields of action and the relevance of their previous work. In this regard, the inclusion of real success stories on the main page, showcases EO's positive social impact. These stories may inspire and motivate users, by displaying real examples of the good results achieved through the institution's social intervention.

The wireframes of the developed platform were designed to involve and attract users, providing relevant information and sparking their interest in exploring the different sections, having as a main goal the sale of EO's products (Fig. 3).

The purchasing process in the EO's platform was designed to be intuitive and user-friendly, and with the intention of allowing users to perform the purchase task, and its inherent interaction steps, efficiently (Fig. 4).

The *Online Store* section presents the available product categories, which eases user's navigation through the different categories of products sold by EO. Next, there's the product list, made up of a three row layout. Each product is represented by an image, name, price and action button (the *add to cart* button).

By selecting a specific product, users are directed towards the *product's detail* page. This page consists of expanded images of the product, allowing a better viewing of the product's details. Moreover, it displays: the name, product reference, a complete description of the product and additional products information such as materials, production process and environmental impact.

In the shopping cart (Fig. 5) users may verify their selected items, by varying the names, colour, qualities and pricings. They also had the possibility of making

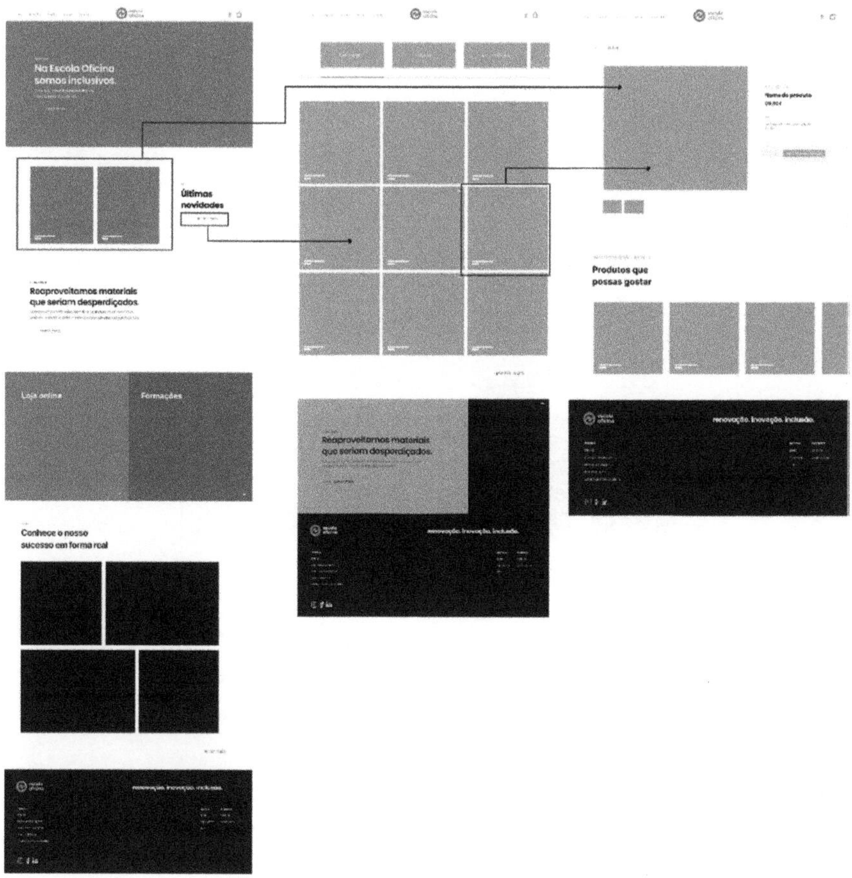

Fig. 3 Wireframes of holistic e-commerce vision

changes to the order, remove items or update amounts, thus guaranteeing that the cart reflects the users' final choices.

Before ending the purchase, users are also prompted with the opportunity to verify all of details of their purchase order. This allows for final adjustments and guarantees that all information is correct before the purchase confirmation.

After the development of the platform's wireframes and user flows, and starting with the project's implementation stage, the *Online store's* prototype was developed. Prototyping is the stage that unites the wireframes and the brand's visual identity. Allowing to create an interactive representation of the interface's design, thus providing a close user experience to the one the user would have with the final product.

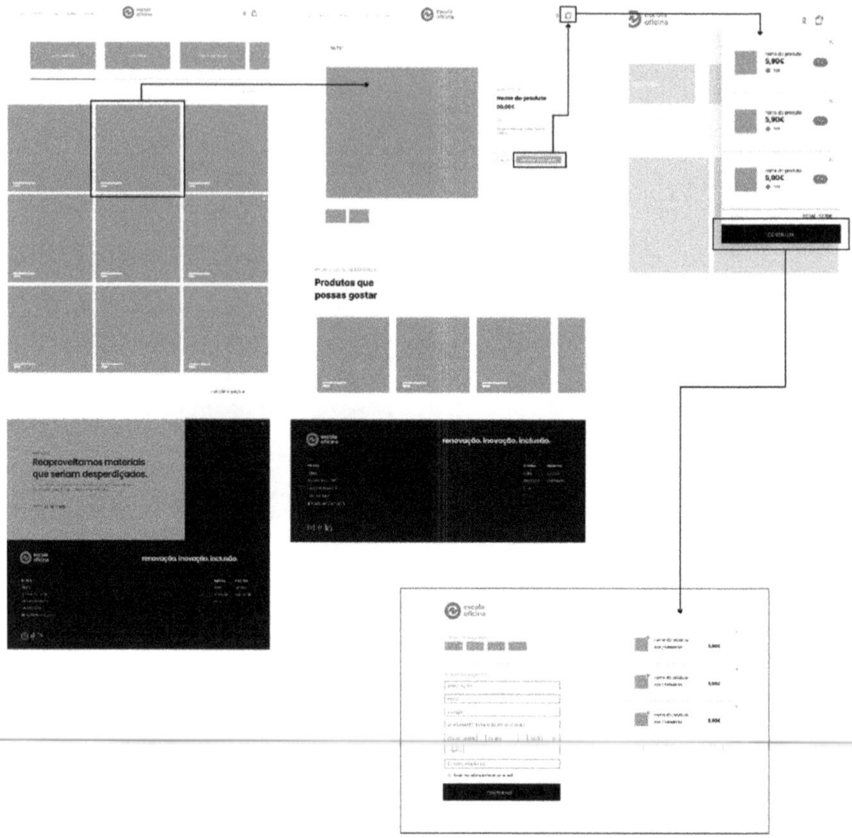

Fig. 4 Wireframes of the purchasing process

5.4 Prototyping

The prototypes play a key role in usability tests, as they offer an experimental and dynamic approach to the procedure. This procedure's goal is to efficiently and effectively test, analyse and validate ideas [6, 7]. This method is an integral part of Design Thinking methodology, which allows a quick and objective validation of the ideas and functionalities conceived for the online platform, before initiation of the final development process. This stage allows, not only to save time and resources, but also to facilitate adjustments and improvements to the platform's design.

A high-fidelity prototype of the final solution was developed (Fig. 6). The prototype was drawn in Figma (an online prototyping tool), where different pages with multiple paths were built and implemented, prototype which in turn provided the user with the needed and desired freedom to navigate through the platform, as that freedom of navigation is a crucial requirement of usability tests.

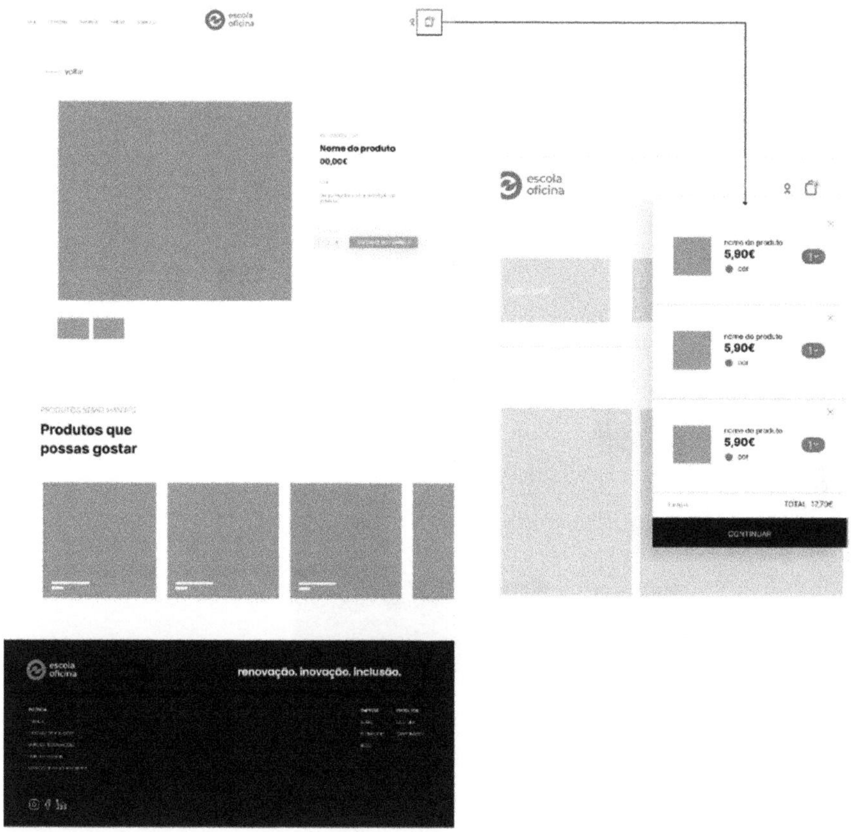

Fig. 5 Wireframes of the product page and shopping cart

With the creation and implementation of a prototype that mimics the platform's final design and behaviour, it was possible to simulate the functional features and interactions required for the usability tests, thus providing the users an immersive experience very close to the real one.

Prototyping allowed us to, therefore, identify efficiency and efficacy problems in the proposed solutions, which in turn indicate the degree of usability an interface has for its users. Thus, the interactive and user centred approach offered a significate contribution to the improvement of the platform's design, providing a better experience for the final users.

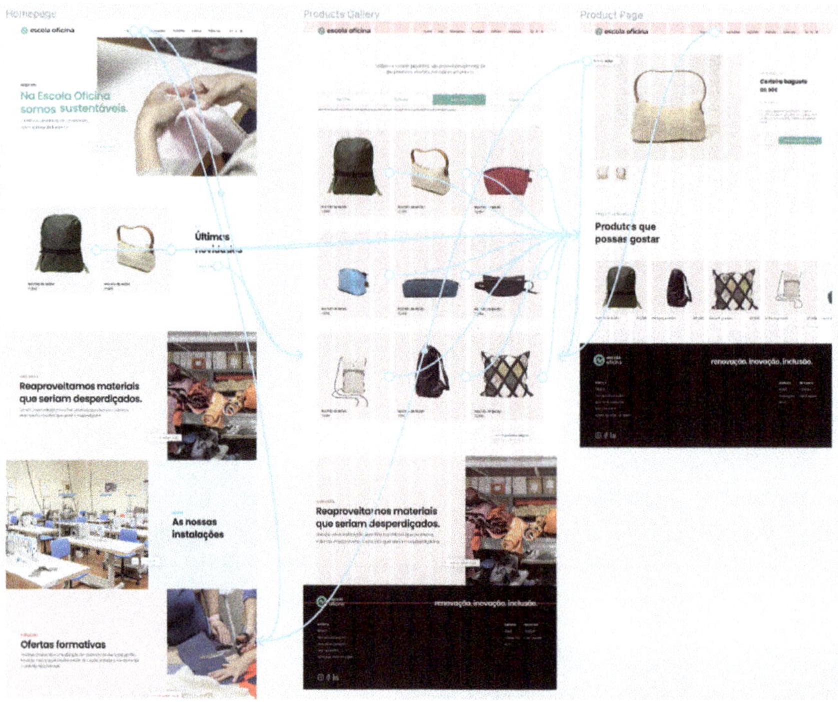

Fig. 6 One of the prototype's flows (Figma)

5.5 *Usability Testing*

Usability testing is a methodology that consists of analysing and observing representative users' behaviours (a sample representative of the target-users), during the completion of interaction related tasks, performed with a digital tool or digital interface. While developing this project, decisions were applied based on continuous feedback from EO's team. This method enabled the final *Online store* prototype to have a low rate of problems or issues regarding the interface's usability the user's experience with it.

Even so, usability tests were conducted with five users: two with profiles generated from Table 1, and three common users, in order to assess the efficacy of the platform's functional features.

For the usability tests of this project, an interactive high-fidelity prototype was developed, in order to gather as much feedback related to the interface's functional features.

At first, it was noticeable that there was no fixed menu at the top (Fig. 8) of the platform. During the tests, three of the users criticized the fact of having to scroll to the top of the page every time they needed the menu (Fig. 7). By creating a fixed

Fig. 7 Homepage without fixed top menu Interface

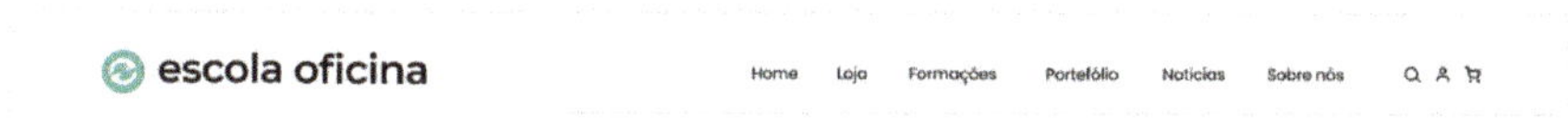

Fig. 8 Top menu interface

menu, the navigation is kept visible, making it easier to access the different sections of the platform.

Inside the interface of the *Online Store* (Fig. 9), the users suggested it would be relevant to add the *News* category to it. It's a convenient category for the user, as it displays the most recent store catalogued items.

Lastly, in the interface of the *Payment* Page (Fig. 10), the lack of a return button was noticed. This page was designed to be the last interface seen by users during the purchase of an item act. For this reason, it didn't contain any direct access to the platform, only allowing the user to navigate with the browser's arrow keys, in case of an order cancellation. This created a non-critical error in the task execution's flow (returning to the *Online Store*) that more than half of the users performed.

6 Conclusions and Future Work

Although EO is a recognized success case, its lack of exterior communication and distrust related to the quality of their products, creates a layer of hardships that hurts their sales. EO recognized the need to develop a digital platform, as to build a

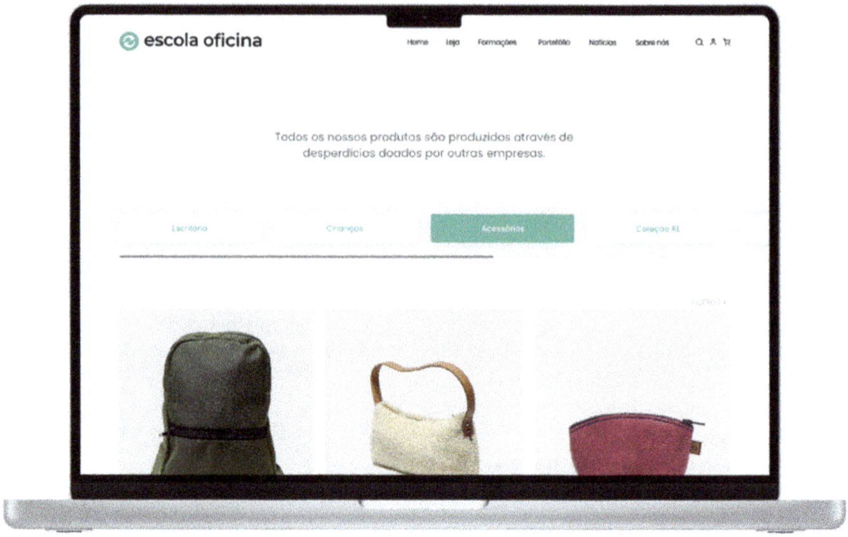

Fig. 9 Online store interface. Product category section

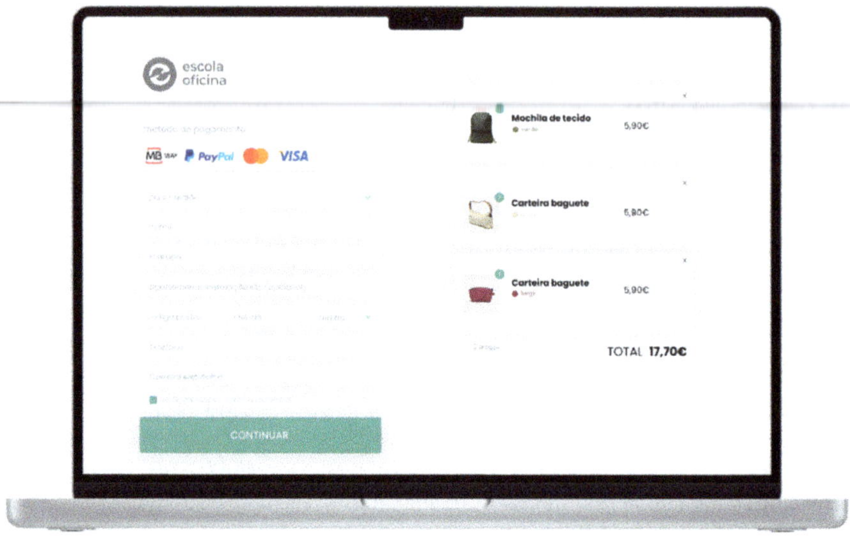

Fig. 10 Payment page interface

communication tool that was able to mirror the institution's values and promote the informed sale of their products.

Thus, as an answer to this problem, this study developed a digital platform with an online store, based on a literature review in the field of Interface Design. A set of recommendations associated with the literature were, therefore, identified for the development of the digital solution, namely:

- a well elaborate visual hierarchy that guides the users while navigating the platform;
- a cohesive visual language that promotes the user's familiarity with the interface;
- avoiding unnecessary and complex elements, as to avoid errors during task completion;
- providing feedback to the user through messages and animations, that help to clarify the success of the performed tasks;
- and usability tests, indispensable in ensuring the efficacy of the interface through user feedback.

Based on the literature and the developed prototype, a direct relationship between interface design and user experience was confirmed. The result of the user's experience is inevitably influenced by the graphic solution designed. So, during the development of the prototype, in addition to the aforementioned recommendations, it was also important to take into consideration design requirements such as ease of navigation, user's mental and physical effort reduction; and achieving an organized layout with only relevant information.

With the designed interface solution, the goal was to combine the values of EO with the efficiency of e-commerce, and, as a consequence, help to counteract the prejudice traditionally associated with buying products from this type of social solidarity institutions.

In conclusion, the creation of the digital platform, with an online store, represents a strategic solution to overcome the communication and selling challenges faced by EO. The platform was designed considering the new visual identity of the brand developed by one of the team members of this research project.

With the new digital platform, it is believed that EO will be able to increase its visibility, therefore reaching a wider audience, increasing sales opportunities and, consequently, helping the circular economy ecosystem.

Given the results obtained in the usability tests to assess the prototype´s interface, the improvements will be implemented in future design iterations of the platform. The next phase of this study will, therefore, consist in the implementation of the online platform. Finally, and as a last step, the sales' evolution and the impact on the target audience's awareness about EO's products quality, will also be tracked.

Acknowledgements This work was founded by the Portuguese Foundation for Science and Technology (FCT) through National Funds under the reference EXPL/ART-DAQ/0037/2021.

References

1. Anshu K, Gaur L, Singh G (2022) Impact of customer experience on attitude and repurchase intention in online grocery retailing: a moderation mechanism of value co-creation. J Retail Consum Serv 64. https://doi.org/10.1016/j.jretconser.2021.102798
2. Barari M, Ross M, Surachartkumtonkun J (2020) Negative and positive customer shopping experience in an online context. J Retail Consum Serv 53:101985. https://doi.org/10.1016/j.jretconser.2019.101985
3. Britannica. (2020, May 26). Gestalt psychology. Encyclopedia Britannica. https://www.britannica.com/science/Gestalt-psychology
4. Brown T, Katz B (2011) Change by design. J Prod Innov Manag 28:381–383. https://doi.org/10.1111/j.1540-5885.2011.00806.x
5. Carroll M (2012). How retailers can replicate the 'magic' of the Apple Store...online. Forbes. www.forbes.com/sites/matthewcarroll/2012/06/26/how-retailers-can-replicate-the-magic-of-the-apple-store-online. Accessed 3 April 2013
6. Dam R, Siang T (2020a) Design thinking: a quick overview. Interaction Design Foundation. Retrieved January 25, 2021, from https://www.interaction-design.org/literature/article/design-thinking-aquick-overview
7. Dam R, Siang T (2020b) Design thinking: get started with prototyping. Interaction-Design.Org. Retrieved May 28, 2021, from https://www.interaction-design.org/literature/article/design-thinking-getstarted-with-prototyping
8. Deng L, Poole MS (2012) Aesthetic design of e-commerce web pages—webpage complexity, order and preference. Electron Commer Res Appl 11(4):420–440. https://doi.org/10.1016/j.elerap.2012.06.004
9. Dillon A (2001). Beyond usability: process, outcome and affect in human computer interactions. https://www.researchgate.net/publication/242176375
10. Flavián C, Guinalíu M, Gurrea R (2006) The role played by perceived usability, satisfaction and consumer trust on website loyalty. Inform Manage 43(1):1–14. https://doi.org/10.1016/j.im.2005.01.002
11. Fortin DR, Dholakia RR (2005) Interactivity and vividness effects on social presence and involvement with a web-based advertisement. J Bus Res 58(3):387–396. https://doi.org/10.1016/S0148-2963(03)00106-1
12. Gao Y (2010) A cognitive model of trust in e-commerce: evidence from a field study in China. J Appl Bus Res 26:27–44. https://core.ac.uk/download/pdf/268103497.pdf
13. Gorn GJ, Chattopadhyay A, Sengupta J, Tripathi S (2004) Waiting for the web: how screen color affects time perception. J Mark Res 41(2):215–225. https://doi.org/10.1509/jmkr.41.2.215.28668
14. Gulfraz MB, Sufyan M, Mustak M, Salminen J, Srivastava DK (2022) Understanding the impact of online customers' shopping experience on online impulsive buying: a study on two leading e-commerce platforms. J Retail Consum Serv 68. https://doi.org/10.1016/j.jretconser.2022.103000
15. Gunawan R, Anthony G, Vendly, Anggreainy, MS (2021) The effect of design user interface (UI) e-commerce on user experience (UX). Proceedings of 2021 6th International Conference on New Media Studies, CONMEDIA 2021, pp 95–98. https://doi.org/10.1109/CONMEDIA53104.2021.9617199
16. Hasan B (2016) Perceived irritation in online shopping: the impact of website design characteristics. Comput Hum Behav 54:224–230. https://doi.org/10.1016/j.chb.2015.07.056
17. Hewei T, Youngsook L (2022) Factors affecting continuous purchase intention of fashion products on social E-commerce: SOR model and the mediating effect. Entertain Comput 41. https://doi.org/10.1016/j.entcom.2021.100474
18. Huang Z, Benyoucef M (2013) From e-commerce to social commerce: a close look at design features. Electron Commer Res Appl 12(4):246–259. https://doi.org/10.1016/j.elerap.2012.12.003

19. Karimov FP, Brengman M, Van Hove L, Van Hove L (2014) The effect of website design dimensions on initial trust: a synthesis of the empirical literature. https://www.researchgate.net/publication/237006618
20. Kumar V, Mukerji B, Francis S, Butt I, Persaud A, Butt I (2007) Factors for successful e-government adoption: a conceptual framework. https://www.researchgate.net/publication/228796407
21. Kuppelwieser VG, Klaus P (2021) Measuring customer experience quality: The EXQ scale revisited. J Bus Res 126:624–633. https://doi.org/10.1016/j.jbusres.2020.01.042
22. Laubheimer P (2018) Beyond the NPS: measuring perceived usability with the SUS, NASA-TLX, and the single ease question after tasks and usability tests. Nielsen Norman Group. Retrieved August 19, 2021, from https://www.nngroup.com/articles/measuring-perceived-usability/
23. Lavie T, Tractinsky N (2004) Assessing dimensions of perceived visual aesthetics of web sites. Int J Hum Comput Stud 60(3):269–298. https://doi.org/10.1016/j.ijhcs.2003.09.002
24. Lee S, Koubek RJ (2010) The effects of usability and web design attributes on user preference for e-commerce web sites. Comput Ind 61(4):329–341. https://doi.org/10.1016/j.compind.2009.12.004
25. Lee W, Benbasat I (2003) Designing an electronic commerce interface: attention and product memory as elicited by web design. Electron Commer Res Appl 2(3):240–253. https://doi.org/10.1016/S1567-4223(03)00026-7
26. Li F, Li Y (2011) Usability evaluation of e-commerce on B2C websites in China. Proc Eng 15:5299–5304. https://doi.org/10.1016/j.proeng.2011.08.982
27. Li Y-M, Yeh Y-S (2010) Increasing trust in mobile commerce through design aesthetics. Comput Hum Behav 26(4):673–684. https://doi.org/10.1016/j.chb.2010.01.004
28. Lim WM, Ting DH (2012) E-shopping: an analysis of the uses and gratifications theory. Mod Appl Sci 6(5):48–63. https://doi.org/10.5539/mas.v6n5p48
29. Manganari EE, Siomkos GJ, Vrechopoulos AP (2009) Store atmosphere in web retailing. Eur J Mark 43(9):1140–1153. https://doi.org/10.1108/03090560910976401
30. Martins N, Brandão D, Guimarães L, Penedos-Santiago E, Brandão D (2023). A importância do Design de Comunicação no processo de disseminação de práticas comunitárias em bairros sociais: o Balteiro", Comunicação e Sociedade, vol. 43. https://doi.org/10.17231/comsoc.43(2023).4455
31. Martins N, Brandão D, Alvelos H, Silva S (2020) E-Marketplace as a tool for the revitalization of Portuguese Craft Industry: the design process in the development of an online platform. Future Internet 12(11):195. https://doi.org/10.3390/fi12110195
32. Matera M, Costabile MF, Garzotto F, Paolini P (2002) SUE inspection: An effective method for systematic usability evaluation of hypermedia. IEEE Trans Syst Man Cybern Part A Syst Hum 32(1):93–103. https://doi.org/10.1109/3468.995532
33. Mollen A, Wilson H (2010) Engagement, telepresence and interactivity in online consumer experience: reconciling scholastic and managerial perspectives. J Bus Res 63:919–925. https://doi.org/10.1016/j.jbusres.2009.05.014
34. Montoya-Weiss MM, Voss GB, Grewal D (2003) Determinants of online channel use and overall satisfaction with a relational, multichannel service provider. JAMS 31:448–458. https://doi.org/10.1177/0092070303254408
35. Mummalaneni V (2005) An empirical investigation of Web site characteristics, consumer emotional states and on-line shopping behaviors. J Bus Res 58(4):526–532. https://doi.org/10.1016/S0148-2963(03)00143-7
36. Shirazi F, Hajli N, Sims J, Lemke F (2022) The role of social factors in purchase journey in the social commerce era. Technol Forecast Soc Chang 183. https://doi.org/10.1016/j.techfore.2022.121861
37. Trevinal M, Stenger A (2014) Toward a conceptualization of the online shopping experience. J Retail Consum Serv 21(3):314–326. https://doi.org/10.1016/j.jretconser.2014.02.009
38. Vance A, Elie-dit-cosaque C, Straub DW (2008) Examining trust in information technology artifacts: the effects of system quality and culture. J Manag Inf Syst 24(4):73–100. https://doi.org/10.2753/MIS0742-1222240403

39. Wells JD, Valacich JS, Hess TJ (2011) What signal are you sending? how website quality influences perceptions of product quality and purchase intentions. MIS MIS Quarterly 35(2):373–396
40. Wu J-H, Yuan Y (2003) Improving searching and reading performance: the effect of highlighting and text color coding. Information & Management 40(7):617–637. https://doi.org/10.1016/S0378-7206(02)00091-5
41. Wu WY, Lee CL, Fu C, Wang HC (2013) How can online store layout design and atmosphere influence consumer shopping intention on a website? Int J Retail Distrib Manage 42(1):4–24. https://doi.org/10.1108/IJRDM-01-2013-0035

Participatory Design and UX Research Methods, Using Interdisciplinary Knowledge From Design, Pedagogy and Nutrition to Promote Food Literacy in Children

Verónica Duarte, Maria João Félix, Miguel de Aboim Borges, and Cláudia Viegas

Abstract Design, as an area of knowledge enabled one to work with creative methods that act in complex situations and can facilitate the combination of interdisciplinary knowledge. To address the need to promote food literacy in children, design research can consider the current ludic context that aims to encourage learning through educational games. The methodology is qualitative and descriptive, based on an exploratory approach. This chapter explores the immersion that elapsed in the field, through participatory design and with the application of design cards about different stages related to foods. Then other UX (user experience) research methods were applied, based on the results of the participatory design experiment, to reflect on the thoughts and feelings of children, generating more specific insights. This allowed the creation of personas and scenarios, as well as user journey mapping, getting a greater awareness of the requirements that should be included in the product design sketch stage, increasing the possibility of the game being successful. As future research work, it is intended to produce and test a prototype of the projected analogue game.

Keywords Participatory design · UX research methods · Children · Interdisciplinarity · Analogue game design

---

V. Duarte (✉) · M. J. Félix · M. de Aboim Borges
Research Centre for Architecture, Urbanism and Design, CIAUD, Lisbon School of Architecture, Universidade de Lisboa, Lisbon, Portugal
e-mail: vmtav.duarte@gmail.com

M. J. Félix
School of Design, Polytechnic Institute of Cávado and Ave, Barcelos, Portugal

C. Viegas
H&TRC—Health & Technology Research Center, ESTeSL—Escola Superior de Tecnologia da Saúde, Instituto Politécnico de Lisboa, Lisbon, Portugal
e-mail: claudia.viegas@estesl.ipl.pt

D. Raposo et al. (eds.), *Perspectives on Design III*, Springer Series in Design and Innovation 34, https://doi.org/10.1007/978-3-031-43516-4_8

1 Introduction

It becomes necessary to ensure that design interventions are based on understanding knowledge from different areas that intersect in order to explore the same problem, especially when the theme is of public interest and socially relevant. This chapter results from an investigation centred on the development of methods that contribute to the idealization of an analogue game that aims to promote food literacy in children and is part of the Doctoral Program in Design, which takes place at the Faculty of Architecture of the University of Lisbon.

Therefore, we present some results of a qualitative methodology still under development that uses knowledge of pedagogy and nutrition to reinforce the design process. Interdisciplinarity is based on the discussion and collaboration of different areas that generate new ideas, methodologies and ways of thinking and teaching [1]. The discipline of design predominates in the context of this study, compared to pedagogy and nutrition, because the methods explored begin with the researcher's cognitive processes as a designer.

This chapter begins by analysing the topic based on the literature review. We recognize the importance of healthy eating for the health of children, who tend to extend their eating habits into adulthood [2].

Learning that is driven by design tools or products can positively affect subsequent behaviours and choice decisions [3, 4]. This research finds in analogue game design and according to pedagogical approaches, the opportunity to promote food literacy in a playful context, conducive to brain development. To illustrate this proposition, an itinerary composed of different complementary methods is suggested.

Firstly, design cards about the Food Life Cycle (FLC) were created, which were applied to children, considering the principles of participatory design and in order to generate qualitative results that were described. After the results, UX research methods used to develop the ability to empathize with children's needs were identified. These methods also allowed one to gain awareness of the tasks inherent in the game and possible situations that may occur in the stages of the user's journey. To characterize the children and their environment, an AEIOU matrix was elaborated, which in turn facilitated the creation of personas, empathy maps and usage scenarios, in order to map the user's journey and determine the requirements for the sketching and manual rendering phase. This last phase focuses on the idealization of possible analogue games that can engage children on the theme of food literacy, in a fun way.

As each method is exposed, its main characteristics are presented, supported by the literature review, to then explain how it was applied in this research. The reflections discussed in the chapter represent opportunities for future research that explore the contribution of design methods that use interdisciplinary knowledge for the development of artefacts aimed at nutritional education.

2 Interdisciplinary Considerations: Design, Pedagogy, Food and Nutrition

Thematic analysis begins by being supported by the literature review, starting from the problematization that recognizes that low levels of knowledge influence bad eating habits, which contribute to the increase of food-related diseases. Healthy eating habits are essential for the development of children's future eating patterns, with a direct impact on health. Furthermore, the nutritional status of children is reflected in the measurement of their productivity based on perceived quality. In that regard, food literacy plays a contributory role in health promotion and refers to the skills and knowledge necessary for healthier behaviours and choices [2, 5].

The promotion of food literacy, inserted in playful approaches, can engage and motivate learning that generates awareness of the impacts on health and the environment [6]. When it is intended to transmit nutritional knowledge incorporated into games, it is possible to create a social environment that promotes motivation, engaging players continuously, as a way to encourage them to change their behaviour [7, 8]. Gamification is the use of game mechanics and dynamics that aim to involve players so that they try to solve problems, improve their knowledge and feel motivated for certain actions and behaviours within the game environment, but is also reflected in their daily routines [9].

This research also uses knowledge in the field of pedagogy to help in the decision-making process. Jean Piaget (1962) stood out as a specialist in cognitive development. According to this author, from 7 to 11 years of age, the period of concrete operations occurs, which corresponds to a cognitive stage in the development of logic and thought. This stage consists of children perceiving and using concepts in their daily routine to solve possible problems that may arise [10]. In this sense, it was decided that this research would be directed to this age group.

Educational games can be used to make children apply in practice concepts they have learned; they can change perceptions, develop both skills and abilities and provide training on the most diverse subjects. Deep down, they inspire and motivate children to learn according to a pleasurable experience [11]. Different types of games have been developed to provide results related to nutritional education. Electronic games can improve eating behaviours through motivation [12] and act as facilitators of significant reductions in the consumption of snacks based on highly processed foods [13].

However, society is increasingly dominated by digital technologies. According to neuroscientist Michel Desmurget (2019), extravagant digital consumption has effects that have a negative impact on the cognitive development of the brain in terms of functioning, development and maturity, that causes difficulties in memory, concentration and language, and also affect the capacity for socialization, which indicates the need to reverse this reality. It is not about repudiating screens, as they have a high potential for countless contexts, but children's time needs to be balanced with physical games which, according to this author, improve children's brain activity [14].

Concerns with the cognitive development of the brain were also considered when choosing the game to be analogue in nature. Analogous practices are a common strategy to facilitate the development of new knowledge, based on players' previous knowledge. They can be implemented into daily routines to guide and apply what children have learned in games [15]. Some experimental studies show that analogue games, such as board, memory and direct interaction with food, can promote healthy eating, encouraging the consumption of vegetables and fruit and modifying eating behaviours [7, 16, 17].

The present study considers the children's collaboration and values the combination of different UX research methods in order to idealize an analogue game that gives a meaningful experience and provides knowledge about healthy eating habits.

3 Participatory Design and UX Research Methods

Participatory design is characterized by the significant involvement of users in the design process [18, 19], so that they can intervene in alternative realities, using different means, tools, techniques and vocabularies [20]. This participation has to make a difference for the participants themselves, the implementation of the results must be likely and the participants need to have fun during the process [21]. It can be understood that participatory design is a process of experimentation and reflection [22].

The application of a participatory design approach through the use of design cards has proven to be an effective way of actively involving children in projected situations, which can be designated as an experience. In this way, the intention is to understand the knowledge and emotions of the children about the different stages of the FLC, listening to them and observing them carefully and without interrupting them. In addition, this approach was also an opportunity to contribute to the transmission of knowledge about the FLC, since explanations and correct answers were provided to the children, after they finished talking about a certain subject present in each design card.

After analysing the results obtained from the participatory design experiment, the chapter describes UX research methods that were used to help support this research, in order to map possible experiences of children in relation to an analogue game that promotes food literacy, according to the different stages of the FLC. In this way, one can probably foresee and evaluate possible representative profiles of children, as well as their journeys at emotional and physical levels, in different contexts of use of the game, considering the problem that anticipates the arrival of the game, the interactions during the use of the game and the effects that the knowledge provided by the game can have on children's daily routines.

UX research methods enable the development of empathy for users' needs. All methods used in this research have a qualitative approach. In this sense, an itinerary is presented below, divided into seven stages.

3.1 Step 1—Creating Design Cards About the FLC

This step focuses on creating a design tool to be used in an accessible and tangible way. More precisely, it is a deck of cards to bring children together and encourage them to talk about issues related to food. Playfulness can be designed into products including cards so that users can enjoy more meaningful experiences while using them [23–25]. The objective was to create design cards with a playful nature to understand children's knowledge about the FLC (including eating habits).

As the theme of food literacy is very comprehensive, it was understood that it should be divided into different subjects, according to each category. Six phases of the FLC and the number of cards in each phase were determined: cultivation and production (6 cards), harvest and acquisition (10 cards), conservation and storage (6 cards), confection (8 cards), ingestion (14 cards) and composting (6 cards). After identifying each phase, the respective theoretical subjects were studied, questions were constructed to be added to the cards and illustrations were made alluding to each subject.

The cards were designed in a rectangular format, with a front (identifying the FLC phase) and a back (containing the question and illustrations). All questions were related to the illustration of the card itself. The typeface chosen was the "Comic Book Commando" so as to allow an adaptation to projects of a playful nature. The textual information present in the cards was written in Portuguese because the group of children involved in the interaction with the cards had Portuguese nationality.

Bearing in mind that the cards would be for an exploration phase, their plastic approach varied in technique (drawing and illustration) and in the materials used (pencils, watercolour and markers) and the finishes and writing were digital (Adobe Photoshop program was used). The illustrated figures and the written content were positioned vertically on each card, which was personalized; that is, within the same deck, no card was repeated. The upper and lower corners of the cards had been slightly rounded to ensure the safety of children. Subsequently, the cards were printed with dimensions of 120 mm × 90 mm (length × width) in a colour printer and then manually cut to form a deck of 50 cards (Fig. 1).

3.2 Step 2—Application of the Design Cards According to Participatory Design Principles and Analysis of the Described Results

The development of this step follows two moments. Moment 1 is about the application of the design cards, according to the participatory design approach, Moment 2 presents the results obtained in this experiment.

Moment 1: Application of the Design Cards. The application of design cards can occur at different stages of the process, from the initial conception of the idea to the evaluation of a given concept. It consists of an interventionist method, innovated in the

Fig. 1 Examples of design cards, from each of the FLC phases

field of participatory design, which aims at exploratory research and implies the need to incorporate empathy, mindfulness, observation, understanding and detachment from prejudices, guiding these aspects in a flexible process [26].

The sample was obtained by convenience and consisted of 43 children from 7 to 11 years old, of both genders. This study was carried out in different rural and urban locations, belonging to the district of Aveiro, in Portugal. When participating in the experiment, the children were observed and heard in order to understand their knowledge, perceptions and memories, as well as their emotional and bodily expressions. A pre-test was carried out on six children (three females and three males), with the authorization of their guardians. With the pre-test, it was possible to understand that the instructions provided to the children were sufficient and the cards did not need to be changed because the illustrated figures and the associated texts were easy to understand. On the other hand, the pre-test allowed one to delineate that the method could be carried out in a maximum time of an hour and a half.

After the pre-test, the study was carried out at the end of 2021, also with the informed consent of guardians. To gather each group of children, the pandemic situation at the time (coronavirus disease) was considered. Contingency measures were adopted (compliance with the national vaccination plan, social distancing whenever possible, hand hygiene, respiratory etiquette and use of disposable masks) and each group was limited to a maximum of three children. Therefore, the children were divided into nine groups of three children, seven groups of two children and two individual children, who lived in more isolated areas and far from other children.

The cards were placed on a piece of furniture with a flat surface and divided and used by order of the six idealized phases, starting with the cultivation and production phase and ending with the composting phase. In each phase of the FLC, the children took the cards randomly, with the challenge facing down. As a child removed a card, he turned it up, leaving the question and the illustration visible to all the children in the same group. He then read the question on the card aloud and all the children observed the respective illustration. Then one of the children started the conversation by sharing his opinion about the content of the card (e.g. he provided an answer to the question that appeared on the card). The children talked about the subjects presented on all the cards, according to their perceptions, feelings, knowledge and memories.

The exploration process of the groups was observed and the sessions were recorded with a voice recorder in order to subsequently analyse the responses, in addition to recording on paper the body language and emotions most perceived in the children. After all the children had answered the questions on each card, they were told the correct answer, because the task required them to understand the subjects discussed through the design cards.

In group sessions, as the children spoke they exchanged ideas and shared memories that were recalled freely. Sometimes when one child provided an opinion, another child would elaborate on the idea with examples. In the two individual sessions, it was often necessary to encourage the children to develop the conversations (e.g. asking the child what he thought and whether he had any memories of a situation that he associated with the card). In all sessions, when there was no more conversation on the part of the children or the topic spoken began to deviate from the theme of the card, the correct answer of the card was provided and the children were prompted to remove another card.

For the cards about the cultivation and production phase, there was talk about the cultivation of different foods and fruit trees that the children were familiar with. With regard to the cards about the harvest and acquisition phase, the children's experience in harvesting vegetables and fruit was debated; namely, whether they knew seasonal food, whether they had a garden or space for cultivation and how they harvested.

In addition, there was talk about children's participation in purchasing food products, their interpretation of food labels, whether they knew what a bulb or root vegetable was, about vitamins, the origin of milk and eggs and the benefits of milk and derivatives in food. In the cards relating to the conservation and storage phase, the arrangement and conservation of various foods were discussed. As for the cards about the confection phase, the importance of food hygiene, the combination of ingredients for healthy recipes and food cooking methods were discussed.

Regarding the cards about the ingestion phase, there was talk about the influence of food on human development, the distinction between healthy and unhealthy foods (including drinks), the foods that children liked the most and the adequate portions for consumption according to the recommendations provided by one of the researchers of this project, who is a nutritionist. As for the cards about the composting phase, there was talk about the composting process and the waste suitable for it.

Moment 2: Results. As this research is qualitative in nature, descriptive analysis was used. A table was built for each card and identical answers were aggregated in order to understand and compare the information provided by the children. In addition, observations made in the field were considered in this analysis, regarding perceived information about how children felt and in which subjects they had more difficulties.

The design cards were an essential tool for successful children's involvement. The results suggested that the use of cards arouses children's interest in the theoretical issues addressed. In this sense, it was noticed that this type of tool can be leveraged as a gamification strategy, which should be explored in the product design sketch phase; that is, in addition to its use being useful in the exploratory research process, it can contribute as part of the end result of a successful analogue game.

The children expressed different perspectives and emotions. In most sessions, children mixed concrete ideas with more abstract ones, and as they expressed themselves, they attributed qualities or made designations based on their personal perception (e.g. they explained how they combined the ingredients for a salad, according to personal taste, either in aesthetic terms or in terms of flavour).

When reflecting on a certain subject, the children conceived or relived in their mind situations that generated different sensations in them; consequently, they attributed their answers, showed interest in learning and surprise at what they learned. During the sessions, the children expressed different emotions at different intensities. Surprise was the most perceived emotion and emerged with more intensity. On the other hand, emotions of fear, anger and sadness were not observable at any time.

In the groups made up of two and three children, it was possible to discuss ideas on different matters, enabling the collection of more comprehensive information with more details involved. In some situations, the children answered questions influenced by the response of the child who had spoken earlier, but when asked to substantiate or justify the answer, they were more thoughtful about the same question and in some cases they changed or deepened the answer they had given. In these situations, only the child's last answer was considered. As for the sessions carried out individually with two children, it was felt that there was a lack of an approach in the disposition for debate, as was the case with the groups. On the other hand, the older the child was, the greater was his ability to develop dialogue.

It was noticed that when children focused on the examples illustrated on the cards, they gave more objective answers (e.g. they defined the term "pulses" based on examples, such as beans, and did not describe the term itself). When the illustrations on the cards encouraged children to make associations, they were more determined to respond and became more capable of deepening their response, including making distinctions and comparisons, as well as providing examples.

During the sessions, younger male children were more agitated compared to female children of the same age, and sometimes some older children who had a cell phone used it to read messages they received. Although children living in rural areas have been shown to have more knowledge about FLC compared to children living in urban areas, it was found that their lack of knowledge or prior knowledge influenced their perception of the different subjects discussed. The seasonality of foods and composting were the subjects in which children showed more difficulties.

Most children do not participate in cooking tasks; however, children who engage in this type of task were very enthusiastic about sharing their experiences and revealed that they felt more motivated to eat what they had cooked themselves.

3.3 Step 3—AEIOU Framework

Information from previous results was synthesized and organized according to the AEIOU matrix. It is a method that consists of an organizational framework, which serves to present and categorize information about certain research and field observations, according to what each vogue (AEIOU) concretely represents and its interrelationships [27]. Therefore, for the construction of this matrix, the following was taken into account:

- Activities—tasks associated with the objectives in which the children were involved were considered.
- Environments—it was taken into account that the shared spaces in the group sessions were more conducive to learning than the individual spaces, where children used the design cards without exchanging ideas with other children.
- Interactions—it is important to note that interactions can occur between children or between a child and an object (e.g. design cards).
- Objects—the elements related to the design cards that made the children more interested were recorded (e.g. illustrations that allowed associations to be made) and possible distracting factors were identified (e.g. mobile phone use).
- Users—the emotions expressed by the children, their perceptions and difficulties were taken into account.

3.4 Step 4—Personas, Empathy Maps, and Usage Scenarios

Personas are specific representations of fictional people and focus on a method that aims at the archetypal description of behaviour patterns of potential users, according to representative profiles, based on field research [26, 28]. The creation of a persona implies understanding the possible users of the product in relation to their motivations and experiences. Moreover, the persona must include information about users such as name, age, marital status (if they are adults), nationality, occupations or hobbies, needs, frustrations, a face image, short descriptions, details of their situation, goals and revealing behaviours depending on the design project [29].

Based on the information categorized in the AEIOU matrix, different personas were constructed, each with an associated empathy map. According to the different perceived characteristics, it became possible to identify different personas, in order to design four potential types of user profiles:

- A 7-year-old female child who enjoys active play but insists on looking at magazines that are not appropriate for her age and needs to improve her eating habits.
- A 9-year-old male child, who practises sports, likes to eat sweets, watch videos, play and win various games (including analogue games) and does not like to eat vegetables.
- A 10-year-old male child with a sedentary lifestyle, who spends too many hours playing on his cell phone, does not like sports and needs to control his appetite in order to have an appropriate weight for his condition and age.
- An 11-year-old female child with type 1 diabetes, influenced by her mother to cook and eat healthily, who enjoys playing, dancing, and cooking.

The personas involve relationships, and therefore the four representative personas of the users were divided into two types of bond: the 7-year-old female child as the sister of the 9-year-old male child; and the 10-year-old male as a friend and classmate of the 11-year-old female.

Empathy maps complement the construction of personas and help to understand the difficulties and opportunities that may arise during experiences, which depend on the cognitive and emotional states of potential users. In this way, empathy maps help in understanding perspectives and developing empathy, so that those who design can act according to what users feel, think, hear, see, do and say [30, 31]. Therefore, empathy maps were created for each of the four personas. As the empathy maps were made, the predictable thoughts of the represented profile were reflected, so that their behaviours and personalities represented the potential users as much as possible (Fig. 2).

The personas must be complemented with the creation of scenarios to humanize the creative design process that is intended to be reproduced. The creation of scenarios must consider possible significant situations that may happen in reality, with the use of the physical product. The inclusion of visual aids or storyboards allows better communication of scenario situations [26]. The creation of scenarios for this research focused on narrating in writing and with storyboards, possible future uses of the analogue game to be developed, considering the contexts in which it can be used.

In view of the characteristics established for creating scenarios, we started by defining the tasks associated with interacting with the game. Therefore, it was possible to create two scenarios: a scenario of use in a family context (focused on the relationship between siblings) and another scenario of use in a school break context (relationship between colleagues and friends). These scenarios include multiple personas (depending on their relationships), who express different emotional reactions across storyboard panels.

The first scenario is composed of two personas that represent two brothers. Both personas don't like to eat vegetables. Furthermore, while the male gender persona spends too much time watching videos, the female gender persona enjoys looking at age-inappropriate magazines. In order to mitigate the negative impact caused by

Fig. 2 Empathy map referring to a persona

these situations, they receive an analogue game from their parents. With this gift, the personas, in addition to getting entertainment suitable for their age, learned about the different stages of the FLC. On the other hand, they spent more time together, strengthening the complicity between siblings. In this step, possible dynamics, rules and rewards associated with the game were considered.

The second scenario brings together two personas representing two children who are friends and schoolmates who play in the school playground, but have different eating and physical activity habits. While the female child dances often and has a healthy diet because she has type 1 diabetes, the male child does not like long walks, spends too many hours playing on the cell phone and cannot control his appetite. The female gender persona buys an analogue game together with her mother, as it is a type of game that identifies with her lifestyle and takes it to the school playground, in order to play with the male gender persona. Personas decide to play together and are quickly engaged due to the variety of challenges the game includes.

It is intended that the game increases the food literacy of the female persona and that the male persona can reflect on their inadequate eating habits, based on the learning obtained from the game, in order to feel motivated to eat more healthily. In order to evaluate these possibilities in detail, the next research method to be carried out was the user journey map.

3.5 Step 5—User Journey Map

This method consists of demonstrating through a visual representation, the user experience and a series of consequent events, in order to evaluate each moment. Throughout the construction of the journey map, a story is told that includes actions, emotions, feelings, perceptions, positive and negative moments and the user's state of mind, depending on their interactions over a period of time [32].

User journey maps were created for the idealized personas. In this sense, all situations studied in the scenarios were deepened, highlighting important and sequential tasks, considering the situations of refusal of vegetables or inadequate eating habits of the personas, access to the analogue game (obtained as a gift or purchased), interactions during the game and acquisition of knowledge or desire to engage in activities related to healthy eating (Fig. 3).

Next, the contact points of each persona were presented, which refer both to interactions between personas (e.g. verbal and body communication) and to interactions between personas and objects (e.g. game); consequently, the possible and predictable thoughts and feelings of each persona for each task or phase of the journey were imagined and described, as well as explained who was the persona who most dominated in each phase, considering the impact of their actions (e.g. who made a decision or won the game).

Finally, the opportunities or insights of each phase were presented, which relate to what results from the motivations of each persona in view of what they felt, thought and learned from the game. With the repetition of the game, the children will be able to better assimilate the concepts about the FLC, so that they acquire knowledge and skills naturally and this has a practical impact, reflected in their eating habits. Transporting the mapped possibilities to real context situations, it is important to highlight that learning about the FLC can be reflected in the children's interest in getting involved in tasks related to food, such as making the shopping list, helping with the acquisition and storage of food [33] and in the preparation of healthy meals, in addition to feeling more encouraged to consume healthy and balanced meals.

Mapping the user's journey was useful because by evaluating and describing the entire trajectory, it became easier to predict eventual benefits and constraints related to the game. Furthermore, as each phase was evaluated, it became possible to plan the necessary mechanics for the analogue game (Figs. 4 and 5).

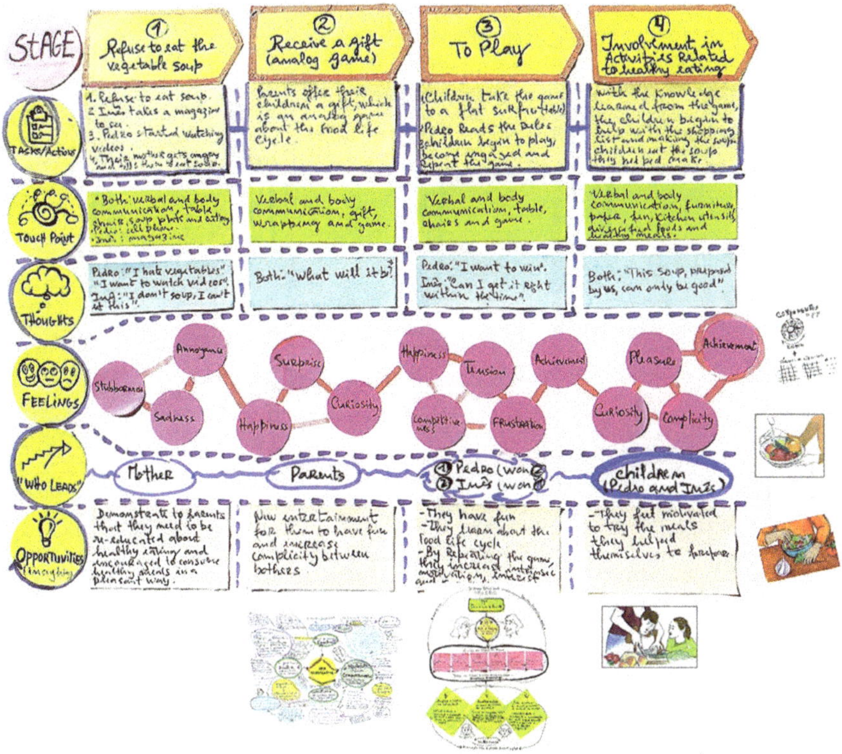

Fig. 3 User journey map

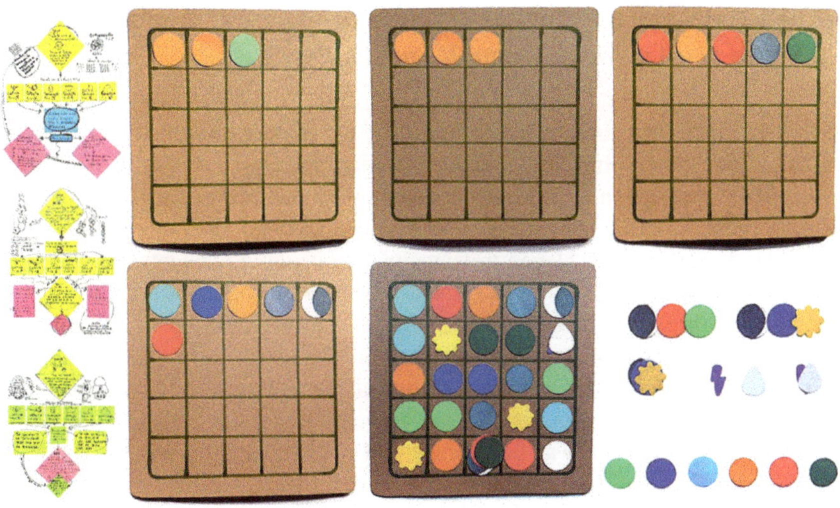

Fig. 4 Planning analogue game mechanics that focus on handling pieces with simple shapes

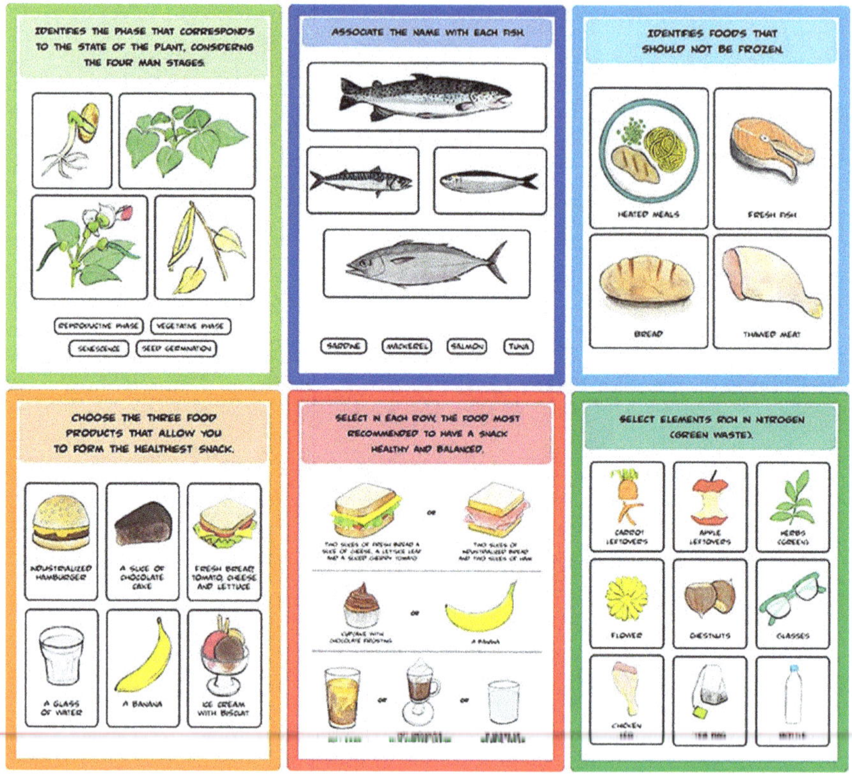

Fig. 5 Planning of game mechanics, which consist of challenges presented in cards

3.6 Step 6—Analogue Game Requirements

Clear identification of users' needs is useful for the coherence of the design process and to facilitate the resolution of a situation that users interpret as a problem [34]. The results of the application of the design cards showed that it is relevant that children's learning about the FLC takes place together with other children. Therefore, the game should be designed to be played in teams of two or three elements. On the other hand, the results suggested that the game needs to have challenges present in cards, to carry the approach of design cards as a gamification strategy, providing children with motivation, entertainment and knowledge at the same time.

In addition, it was found that the association of elements such as illustrated figures, present in cards, can be a promising way to help children to better assimilate the concepts. In this sense, it was determined that the challenges present in cards for the different phases of the FLC have to be based on associations of figures (e.g. associating vegetables with seasons of the year or foods with recommended portions to consume a healthy and balanced meal).

The game's difficulty level must vary between easy and difficult, which requires that the associations on the cards change not only in the subject, but also in the number of associations between elements that the cards can have, from two to six associations. UX research methods were necessary to perceive and evaluate possible experiences of children in interacting with the game and contributed to determining other requirements for the game. It was considered that throughout the game there must be opportunities for children to perform different physical exercises (e.g. dance) in order to encourage them to physical activity, as a complement to healthy eating habits. In this sense, in addition to the cards about the FLC whose phases would be identified in the analogue game by the use of different colours and the name of the written phase, there would also be cards for performing physical exercises.

As for the other game pieces, they had to adapt to different development rates (children from 7 to 11) and therefore it is important that the pieces were practical, easy to handle, transport and understand. For this reason, it was determined that all parts would have simple shapes and with rounded corners to increase safety during use.

The creation of scenarios and the user journey map made clear the importance of considering the use of the game in different contexts. In order to facilitate the transport of the game, it was determined that it should have an accessory consisting of a handbag handle and adjustable straps for the back, so that children could carry it in a way they considered to be most comfortable (on the back or in the hand), this being a way of encouraging them to use the game in different environments (e.g. at home, in the garden or in the school playground).

In order to control the completion time of each challenge and create some tension during the game, it was thought to include an hourglass, which is also important to increase the diversity of emotions provided by the game. The hourglass may present benefits, as it corresponds to the functionalities of a mechanical timer that does not need electricity to function.

3.7 Step 7—Product Design Sketching

In view of the considerations of the requirements for the analogue game, different possibilities of presenting it were designed. Designing products is a task that involves a combination of observing, thinking, predicting and developing according to concrete criteria [35].

There are different types of drawings that a designer can enjoy, from quick sketches to detailed drawings (e.g. fixtures of parts), exploded views, concrete representation of materials and textures, different perspectives or views and in context of use. Informative viewpoints can be used to complement the drawings. These concern important information to clearly communicate the drawings (e.g. textual notes informing intended proportions or scale). The use of colour and different tones can be considered to improve the communication of the drawings and make them more dynamic [36].

Fig. 6 Analogue game drawings

The drawings in this research were made freehand (Fig. 6). The communication and representation of the game through the relationship between thought and sketching was an opportunity to consider all the factors that weigh in the development of a prototype of the game that will be developed in the future.

4 Conclusions

This article contributes to demonstrating the usefulness of UX research methods in the idealization of a product. It became possible to study UX from a perspective generated with the practical approach of participatory design that was successful, as it assumed great importance for including the use of cards and the possibility of directly observing children, to better understand them. Through the application of design cards, it was relevant to realize that this tool can be transformed into a game mechanic (challenges present in cards) and result as a gamification strategy to engage children. The collaborative approach worked better with groups of children than with a single child and facilitated the motivation of children to be actively involved in sharing ideas and emotions, thus contributing to mutual learning about the FLC. The children's learning in a playful context, about the different stages of eating, resulted from an experiment that, in addition to being exploratory, was visceral.

Thus, it is recognized that UX research methods have a multifaceted value due to the immeasurable applications, which are easily adjustable to combine interdisciplinary knowledge and, in the case of this study, generated constructive reasoning about possible future uses of the analogue game. UX research methods can be included in the product design process, and when the product is a game, this inclusion becomes more necessary, because a product designer who focuses on the development of a game cannot only think about tangible aspects linked to production, since a game's main function is to entertain and, for that, it needs to engage the players. Therefore, it is necessary for the designer to balance his concerns regarding the design of the game between the player's experience and the requirements for production.

As for the limitations of the project, it is recognized that there is subjectivity associated with the possible scenarios studied, both for acceptance of the game and for the contexts in which the game can be used. The possibilities will be much greater than those projected in this study; however, this is a non-linear process, so to increase its robustness, it will be necessary, after developing the prototype, to improve the game and reinforce it by creating more scenarios, testing prototypes and making hybrid versions of the game. This will increase the game's possibilities to adapt to the preferences in contemporary society of children, who are increasingly dependent on digital technologies. The idea of thinking about a hybrid version of the game and not a totally digital one stems exactly from wanting to value analogue as a tool that stimulates brain development.

It is intended to apply the knowledge acquired from this research in the next active research phase of this project, which will focus on the design of a physical prototype of the analogue game and on carrying out usability tests. Although this research is still ongoing, the real contribution of the methods used is already verified in the game's idealization phase, because according to the application of complementary methods, it was possible to determine design requirements based on situations thought out and evaluated qualitatively.

Therefore, it is hoped that this chapter will encourage reflections on including more UX research methods in the product design process. In addition, as future work, it is important to think about including more knowledge from the areas of nutrition, pedagogy and even other areas relevant to the project, which could help to materialize scenarios that are significant to encourage children to learn about healthy eating habits, according to a pleasurable experience.

Acknowledgements *This work is financed by national funds through FCT—Fundação para a Ciência e a Tecnologia, I.P., under the Strategic Project with the reference SFRH/BD/05009/2021.* The authors would like to acknowledge the support given by FCT and by CIAUD—Research Center for Architecture, Urbanism and Design, Lisbon School of Architecture, Universidade de Lisboa.

References

1. Kangas M (2010) Creative and playful learning: learning through game co-creation and games in a playful learning environment. Think Skills Creativity 5(1):1–15. https://doi.org/10.1016/j.tsc.2009.11.001
2. Sandell M, Mikkelsen BE, Lyytikäinen A, Ojansivu P, Hoppu U, Hillgrén A, Lagströme H (2016) Future for food education of children. Futures 83:15–23. https://doi.org/10.1016/j.futures.2016.04.006
3. Bhamra T, Lilley D, Tang T (2015) Design for sustainable behaviour: using products to change consumer behaviour. Des J 14(4):427–445. https://doi.org/10.2752/175630611X13091688930453
4. Oxman R (2004) Think-maps: teaching design thinking in design education. Des Stud 25(1):63–91. https://doi.org/10.1016/S0142-694X(03)00033-4
5. Krause C, Sommerhalder K, Beer-Borst S, Abel T (2018) Just a subtle difference? Findings from a systematic review on definitions of nutrition literacy and food literacy. Health Promot Int 33(3):378–389. https://doi.org/10.1093/heapro/daw084
6. Schifferstein HNJ (2023) Supporting food design with consumer research: from inspiration and validation to participation and integration. Curr Opin Food Sci 5:101020. https://doi.org/10.1016/j.cofs.2023.101020
7. Florack A, Haasova S, Hirschauer S, Serfas BG (2018) Playing with food: the effects of food pre-exposure on consumption in young children. Physiol Behav 195:76–81. https://doi.org/10.1016/j.physbeh.2018.07.022
8. Ryan R, Deci E (2000) Self-determination theory and the facilitation of intrinsic motivation, social development, and well-being. Am Psychol 55(1):68–78. https://selfdeterminationtheory.org/SDT/documents/2000_RyanDeci_SDT.pdf
9. Kapp KM, Blair L, Mesch R (2014) The gamification of learning and instruction field-book: ideas into practice. Wiley, EUA
10. Piaget J (1962) Play, dreams and imitation in childhood. W.W. Norton & Company, New York
11. Kalmpourtzis G (2018) Educational game design fundamentals. A journey to creating intrinsically motivating learning experiences. CRC Press, Boca Raton, FL
12. DeSmet A, Van Ryckeghem D, Compernolle S, Baranowski T, Thompson D, Crombez G, Poels K, Van Lippevelde W, Bastiaensens S, Van Cleemput K, Vandebosch H, De Bourdeaudhuij I (2014) A meta-analysis of serious digital games for healthy lifestyle promotion. Prev Med 69:95–107. https://doi.org/10.1016/j.ypmed.2014.08.026
13. Majumdar D, Koch PA, Lee H, Contento IR, Islas A, Fu D (2013) "Creature-101": a serious game to promote energy balance-related behaviors among middle school adolescents. Games Health J 2(5):280–290. https://doi.org/10.1089/g4h.2013.0045
14. Desmurget M (2021) A Fábrica de Cretinos Digitais. Os perigos dos ecrãs para os nossos filhos (translated by Inês Fraga, Portuguese edition). Contraponto, Lisboa
15. Hattie JAC, Yates GR (2013) Visible learning and the science of how we learn. Routledge, Oxford
16. Amaro S, Viggiano A, Di Costanzo A, Madeo I, Viggiano A, Baccari ME, Marchitelli E, Raia M, Viggiano E, Deepak S, Monda M, De Luca B (2006) Kalèdo, a new educational board-game, gives nutritional rudiments and encourages healthy eating in children: A pilot cluster randomized trial. Eur J Pediatr 165(9):630–635. https://doi.org/10.1007/s00431-006-0153-9
17. Porter L, Bailey-Jones C, Priudokaite G, Allen S, Wood K, Stiles K, Parvin O, Javaid M, Verbruggen F, Lawrence NS (2018) From cookies to carrots; the effect of inhibitory control training on children's snack selections. Appetite 124:111–123. https://doi.org/10.1016/j.appet.2017.05.010
18. Bannon LJ, Ehn P (2013) Design: design matters in participatory design. In: Simonsen J, Robertson T (eds) Routledge international handbook of participatory design. Routledge, New York, pp 37–63
19. Ehn P (1993) Scandinavian design: on participation and skill. In: Schuler D, Namioka A (eds) Participatory design: Principles and practices. Erlbaum, New York, pp 41–77

20. Nisha B (2022) Lost in imagined space: a psychoanalysis of participatory design. Des Stud 81:101108. https://doi.org/10.1016/j.destud.2022.101108
21. Ackoff RL (1974) Redesigning the future: a systems approach to societal problems. Wiley, New York
22. Kensing F, Greenbaum J (2013) Heritage: having a say. In: Simonsen J, Robertson T (eds) Routledge international handbook of participatory design. Routledge, New York, pp 21–36
23. Lucero A, Arrasvuori J (2013) The PLEX cards and its techniques as sources of inspiration when designing for playfulness. Int J Arts Technol 6(1):22–43. http://www.funkydesignspaces.com/publications/2013/lucero13_PLEX_cards.pdf
24. Lucero A, Karapanos E, Arrasvuori J, Korhonen H (2014) Playful or gameful? creating delightful user experiences. Interactions 21(3):34–39. https://doi.org/10.1145/2590973
25. Lucero A, Dalsgaard P, Halskov K, Buur J (2016) Designing with cards. In: Markopoulos P, Martens JB, Malins J, Coninx K, Liapis A (eds) Collaboration in creative design: methods and tools, Springer, Switzerland, pp 75–95. https://doi.org/10.1007/978-3-319-29155-0_5
26. Martin B, Hanington B (2012) Universal methods of design. 100 ways to research complex problems, develop innovative ideas, and design effective solutions. Rockport Publishers, EUA
27. Goodman E, Kuniavsky M, Moed A (2012) Field visits: learning from observation. In: Goodman E, Kuniavsky M, Moed A (eds) Observing the user experience: a practitioner's guide to user research, 2nd edn. Morgan Kaufmann, Waltham, MA, pp 211–242
28. Adlin T, Pruitt J (2010) The essential persona lifecycle: your guide to building and using personas. Morgan Kaufmann, Burlington
29. Nielsen L (2019) Persona writing. In: Nielsen L (ed) Personas-user focused design. Human–computer interaction series. 2nd edn, Springer-Verlag, London, pp 55–81. https://doi.org/10.1007/978-1-4471-7427-1_4
30. Cairns P, Pinker I, Ward A, Watson E, Laidlaw A (2021) Empathy maps in communication skills training. Clin Teach 18(2):142–146. https://doi.org/10.1111/tct.13270
31. McDonagh-Philp D, Lebbon C (2000) The emotional domain in product design. Des J 3(1):31–43. https://doi.org/10.2752/146069200789393562
32. Kalbach J (2021) Illustrate: make it visual. In: kalbach J (ed) Mapping experiences. A complete guide to customer alignment through journeys, blueprints & diagrams. 2nd edn, O'reilly, Sebastopol, CA, pp 173–204
33. Félix M, Duarte V (2018) Design and development of a sustainable lunch box, which aims to contribute to a better quality of life. Int J Qual Res 12(4):869–884. https://doi.org/10.18421/IJQR12.04-06
34. Ulrich KT, Eppinger SD (2012) Product design and development, 5th edn. McGraw-Hill Education, New York
35. Baskinger M, Bardel W (2013) Drawing ideas. A hand-drawn approach for better design. Watson-Guptill, New York
36. Eissen K, Steur R (2014) Sketching, product design presentation. BIS Publishers, Amsterdam

From Swiss Modernism to the International Compliant Style: Grids and Graphic Design in the Age of Information Disorder

Anna Kallen Talley

Abstract What role does communication design play in the current crisis of information disorder? What ethical responsibilities and agency might communication designers have in solving the problem? This chapter explores the function of communication design in the era of online information disorder. I argue that when Swiss modernism was remediated on the web as the International Compliant Style (IC-Style), form and content became separated, along with a loss of ideals about the social responsibility of design. In the hyper-capitalist, digital environment of the 1990s, Swiss modernism became a style that, although suited to the technological restrictions of the early web, quickly became co-opted by ideologies of functionalist web design. This resulted in the application of the IC-Style across a variety of information with a disregard for the suitability of form to content and a focus on speed and profit rather than consideration of communication design's responsibility to society as a medium between people and information. The dangers of this can be seen today in the crisis of information disorder, where the IC-Style has been applied to websites peddling mis/disinformation driven by perverse online economic incentives. The chapter concludes by exploring the ethical responsibility of communication designers in the era of information disorder, arguing that the social ideologies of modernism should be placed at the fore and applied to new communication structures that promote dialogue, discourse and slow, considered engagement with information.

Keywords Communication design · Modernism · Web design · Information disorder

---

A. K. Talley (✉)
University of Edinburgh, Edinburgh, UK
e-mail: anna.talley@ed.ac.uk

D. Raposo et al. (eds.), *Perspectives on Design III*, Springer Series in Design and Innovation 34, https://doi.org/10.1007/978-3-031-43516-4_9

1 Introduction

What role does communication design play in the current crisis of information disorder? What ethical responsibilities and agency might communication designers have in solving the problem? This chapter explores the function of communication design in the era of online information disorder. I argue that when Swiss modernism was remediated on the web as the International Compliant Style (IC-Style), form and content became separated, along with a loss of ideals about the social responsibility of design. In the hyper-capitalist, digital environment of the 1990s, Swiss modernism became a style that, although suited to the technological restrictions of the early web, quickly became co-opted by ideologies of functionalist web design. This resulted in the application of the IC-Style across a variety of information with a disregard for the suitability of form to content and a focus on speed and profit rather than consideration of communication design's responsibility to society as a medium between people and information.

The dangers of this can be seen today in the crisis of information disorder, where the IC-Style has been applied to websites peddling mis/disinformation driven by perverse online economic incentives. The chapter concludes by exploring the ethical responsibility of communication designers in the era of information disorder, arguing that although the aesthetics of modernism should not necessarily be scrapped, the social ideologies of modernism should be placed at the fore and applied to new communication structures that promote dialogue, discourse and slow, considered engagement with information. This will require a shift in the education of web designers to not only focus on aesthetics and user interaction but to also understand media and communication theory so as to be more informed about the communications systems for which they are designing. What design for a new communications system might look like is unclear, but attempts at a new kind of web design that combines the democratic and veracity-focused ideologies of modernism with a discursive communications model might be one step towards a solution in solving the information crisis.

2 What is the International Compliant Style?

The International Compliant Style (IC-Style) is a modernist web design style resulting from the combination of technological constraints on early web production due to the restrictive nature of HTML and the adherence to web design ideologies prioritising efficiency. The term 'International Compliant Style' was first used by Clark in 2003 [1]. Clark defines the IC style by both its means of production and aesthetic qualities. Stylistically, the IC-Style is distinguished by its use of black-on-white typography and the confinement of ornament and image to 'a nameplate-like page header'. Overall, the layout is influenced by a highly ordered structure and 'aesthetic cleanliness'. In terms of production, it follows 'official specifications' and is 'an outcome of a sort of ethical uniformity among standards-compliant designers'. However, beyond simple standard-setting, Clark also notes the technical limitations imposed by the 'linear and incremental' markup language HTML. Centring the effect of HTML, Thorlacius has a similar term for these early, standard-compliant sites, calling the style 'HTMinimalism' or 'engineer-based hyperfunctionalism' [2]. Like the IC-Style, HTMinimalism describes websites that emphasise 'technical aspects, functionality, and user friendliness' through a layout replete with 'white space, subdued monochrome and controlled colors, [and] sans serif print types' [2]. Etienne has another, related term, the 'Default Aesthetic' or 'vanilla flavored aesthetic', which Etienne defines by its production as '"ready-chosen" rather than "ready-made"' [3].

Although both 'Default Aesthetic' and 'HTMinimalism' are appropriate to describe the style of web design this chapter investigates, I choose to use Clark's terminology to draw attention to the long history and impact of the International Style on web design as well as the influence of both technological and ideological standards [4].

3 The Development and Dissemination of the IC-Style

The IC-Style developed from its origins in Swiss modernism to its present web application through its remediation within a hypercapitalist, technologically restrictive online environment. Remediation is the 'representation of one medium in another', and has been explored by Bolter and Grusin in the context of re-presentation of images in digital graphics [5]. Although modernism has always operated under the conditions of capitalism, the early web was a crucible for the IC-Style due to the role technological restrictions of HTML played in facilitating hyper-functionalist web designs. As a result, modernism was remediated from print to web to become the IC-Style, international in style and compliant to engineer-driven web ideologies.

3.1 The Style and Ideologies of Swiss Modernism

Post-war modernist design, particularly the use of grid structures popularised by the Swiss style, heavily influenced the development of functionalist web design. Writing on the development of graphic layouts, Cleveland notes that the use of the grid for online layouts has been 'adapted from [a] traditional graphic design approach to print layout' [6]. The magazine *Neue Grafik* and designer Josef Müller-Brockmann are two of the most famous proponents of the Swiss grid. Müller-Brockmann published his book *Grid Systems in Graphic Design* in 1981, which was intended as a teaching guide for designers and includes a number of examples of practical applications of grid layouts. In the book, Müller-Brockmann also expresses an ideological view of the grid, writing that the grid 'shows that the designer conceives his work in terms that are constructive and oriented to the future' [7]. Making an assumption regarding the "objectivity" of grids, Müller-Brockmann writes that design can constitute 'the basis of democratic behaviour' and grids can express, through their formal elements 'factors which are also vital in sociopolitical life' [7]. Müller-Brockmann's statements echo earlier sentiments about the responsibility of designers in public life voiced in *Neue Grafik,* a Zurich-based magazine published from 1958 to 1965 that popularised the Swiss style. In 1963, the designer Hans Hilfiker published an essay titled 'Design and Responsibility' in *Neue Graphik,* in which he wrote that it is wrong for designers not to acknowledge their 'distinguishing authority' and 'corresponding responsibility' [8]. Similarly, the designer Paul Schuitema wrote that the designer 'is responsible for shaping a changing his environment; he is attempting to educate his fellows visually' and should 'contribute to culture through his use of photography and by giving his work an ethical basis' [9].

Connecting grids and early web design, Dilger points out that Tim Berners-Lee, the inventor of the World Wide Web, was based at CERN in Switzerland, where these ideologies from design may have influenced his thinking [10]. Interestingly, Swiss designers' philosophical views of modernist design and its service to society are echoed in Berners-Lee's philosophy of the internet. Like Müller-Brockmann, Berners-Lee postulated that the web could become 'a structure in hyperspace that allows us to work together harmoniously' in a restructuring of society, operating under 'universalist' philosophies of mutual respect and collective creation [11].

3.2 *The Crucible of the Early Web: Technological Limitations and Standards, Economic Concerns and the Ideology of Functionalist Design*

When the Swiss style became remediated as the IC-Style, the socially-driven ideals of modern design became subservient to its aesthetics. The expression of a modernist aesthetic online was due in part to the restrictive nature of HTML, which lent itself to a linear, modular layout. However, rather than retaining a connection between content, form and social responsibility, modernist aesthetics became the visual expression of web functionalism, a design ideology promoted by engineers that emphasised speed and access to content within a commercially-driven information environment.

The technological limitations of the early web heavily influenced the proliferation of modernist aesthetics. Slow download speeds made hyper-functionalist websites the best option for those who wanted to ensure that their websites were easily accessible before the introduction of broadband in 2006 [12]. Internal architectures of the web, like Content Management Systems, the technical development of the web and varying capabilities of different browsers also restricted the design of websites [13, 14]. The 'linear' language of HTML made it difficult for designers to work outside of the norm [1] and HTML's 'tables' function, which expressed the aesthetic of a column, was the only way early web designers could create fixed containers for content [15]. As a result, the tables function established a grid structure for website design, expressing the aesthetics of Swiss modernism, regardless of whether that was the explicit intention of the website designer. This structure soon became the standard for website design, encouraged in part by the introduction of Web Standards by Jeffrey Zeldman in 1998. MacManus and Dilger and Rice note that from 2000, corporate Web sites became more homogenous, which they attribute in part to the introduction of Web Standards that advocated for consistent use of HTML and CSS coding [13, 16].

The establishment of standardised, functionalist websites concurred with the dotcom crash at the end of the 1990s, which saw organisations cut their budgets for unique, custom sites built with Flash, leading to less expensive web designs 'in the form of standard layouts' [17]. Engholm also recognises that demand for user-friendly websites occurred after the dotcom crash in an effort to cement a web page's commercial stability' [18] and MacManus suggests that designers turned toward modernist styles to appeal to businesses as dotcom speculation waned in the late 1990s and they sought to help their clients appear stable and reputable [13].

Nobody did more to suggest that web design and commerce went hand in hand than Jakob Nielsen, an early pioneer of human–computer interaction [19]. The publications of Nielsen, including *Usability Engineering* (1993) and *Designing Web Usability* (2000), had a significant impact on web design and development through their establishment of the conceptual foundations of web functionalism [20]. In *Designing Web Usability*, Nielsen discusses practical methods of web design, like the use of standardised style sheets to 'ensure visual continuity' [21] in an effort of increasing the speed of information search and retrieval. Nielsen associated functionalism with credibility [21], p. 93] and with commerce, claiming 'Usability rules the Web. Simply stated, if the customer can't find a product, then he or she will not buy it. The Web is the ultimate customer-empowering environment' [21], p. 9].

By February 1997, corporate, institutional, and news websites were using the tables function in HTML to create gridded layouts [22]. This adoption of the grid system helped perpetuate Nielsen's concept of the web as a functionalist, content-driven commercial service while expressing a modernist style [22], p. 213]. Since 2003, Samara notes that grids have become 'remarkably prevalent' in web design, driven by the 'practical demands' of efficient, online communication systems and the variability of screen sizes [23]. Thirteen years later, Engholm describes the continued practice of using standardised, gridded layouts as the 'good enough revolution', a kind of 'new functionalism that favours simplicity, ease of use and availability' [24].

3.3 The Dissemination of the IC-Style: The Role of Web Templates

Engholm notes that web design has been heavily influenced by the use of pre-defined standard layouts that are graphically 'neutral' [24], p. 149]. These layouts are the result of a long history of digital templates, beginning in 1985 with the introduction of Aldus' software PageMaker, an early desktop publishing platform. Maudet's work on the history of digital templates reveals how the online web template evolved from templates originally created for desktop publishing software like PageMaker, allowing non-professional users to create professional-quality designs [25]. She describes these templates as an 'invisible architecture' for digital design, a predefined 'extension of the grid' [25]. Templates for websites quickly followed with the release of the first web page creation software, Microsoft FrontPage, in 1996. FrontPage's templates demonstrated the interactivity of digital communication design while at the same time standardising the use-cases of web pages, as templates were sorted by types such as 'personal' or 'employee directory'. Restricted technologically by the limits of early HTML and CSS and adhering to the ideologies of web functionalism, web templates became the de facto evangelists of the IC-style due to their ease of use and replicability.

3.4 The Remediation of Modernism: From Swiss Grids to the IC-Style

Due to limited in technical capabilities, web standards, economic concerns and the ideology of functionalist web design, the Swiss grid system was remediated to become the IC-Style. In the remediation process from print to digital, the modernist grid, something print designers used as 'a visual aid–an underlying, but not prescriptive, layer of guidelines' became a 'core structural limitation' implemented by those designing for the web [26]. However, the Swiss system was never meant to be applied in a mindlessly repetitive manner. In the first edition of *Neue Grafik*, the editorial read 'The constant change in style is a response to the subject matter [...] There are no hard and fast rules for this kind of art' (no.1 1958) [27]. The subsequent homogenising application of modernism to the web has been criticised [28]. However, it has taken until the mid-2000s to understand the disastrous effects such homogenisation can have on our information environment. One particularly negative outcome of the remediation of modernism can be found in the current crisis of information disorder, with the application of the IC-Style to any content posing a particular problem in the dissemination of online news.

4 The IC-Style in the Age of Information Disorder: Newspaper Design and Online Mis/Disinformation

4.1 Modernist Newspaper Design: Aesthetics of Authority and Credibility

What are the 'factors vital in sociopolitical life' that Müller-Brockmann claimed modern design expresses? Authority and credibility—a visual expression of trust and institutional reliability. This is most evident in the evolution of newspaper design. Newspapers have combined modernist aesthetics and historical traditions of newspaper design to establish an aesthetic of trust and authority over the course of the twentieth century. In their history of newspaper design, Barnhurst and Nerone claim that between 1920 and 1940, early modernism became the 'established vocabulary of newspaper authority', which evolved to post-war modernism later in the century [29]. Modern newspapers combined modernist form with 'a journalistic claim to fully and neutrally map the social and with the economic power to make that claim believable' [29], p. 305], which was reflected in the 'rationalisation' of their design [29], p. 22]. The reasons for this shift in the authority of newspapers and interest in credibility is due to a number of professional practice and socio-political reasons too extensive to delve into here [29], p. 221], but suffice to say by the mid-century newspaper designers recognised the authority presented by the printed news page and was understood, if implicitly, by the public [30]. The continued advocation for traditional, modernist principles as applied to both online and print news design can also be found in the work of the influential author and news designer Mario Garcia, who has written several books on the subject, including *Redesigning Print for the Web* [31] and *Contemporary newspaper design: a structural approach* [32]. This visual expression of authority was as true for print newspapers as it was for their digital editions. Barnurst and Nerone write that at the turn of the century, the online version of the *New York Times* 'clearly reflected the newspaper's position of authority as an institution' [33].

The remediation of modernist print aesthetics to the web means that the system of visual codes readers associated with newspaper authority and credibility were also transferred. Although writing about words rather than images, Law's claim that 'similarities, overlaps, stabilities, repetitions, or positive relations between statements tend to increase their authority' is just as applicable to visual culture [34]. Similarly, Honeywill applies McQuail and Windahl's theories on mass communication to his analysis of user interface design, writing that the users perceive information not through discrete messages, but as 'whole sets or systems of messages which have similar features' [35]. As a result, repetition of design can 'provide authority via consistency', as noted by Riley in their analysis of style guides [36].

4.2 *The IC-Style's Application Under Contemporary Commercial Platform Logics*

This aesthetic repetition is possible due to the ability of modernism's form to be applied to any content. Nielsen claimed that the functionalist method of web design can be used in the long-term, writing that 'web usability changes less rapidly than web technology' [37]. This implies a split between the concepts underpinning web functionalism, and the tools used to produce websites. This divergence is echoed in Rileys's observation that *Designing Web Usability* 'presumes a split between form and content' and that design, in Nielsen's view, is purely 'in service of content' [38]. Despite the fact that the technologies used to produce websites have vastly changed since *Designing Web Usability* was published, the IC-Style still dominates due to its ability to be applied to a wide range of commercial content, from paywall news to disinformation websites, as well as its functional prowess that can efficiently transform clicks into cash [39].

The IC-Style is currently applied to news websites that operate under what Andrejevic calls 'contemporary commercial platform logics'. This refers to the economic imperatives of online news sites (all news sites, not only ones producing disinformation) to make a profit through the advertising readers click on. As Glasser et al. note, on the internet, 'the rhetoric of survival preys on the fear that journalism cannot succeed unless it succeeds as a business' [40]. This logic is not without problems. An economics-focused survey for the European Commission on the rise of disinformation concluded that online "fake news" outlets have found an economically sustainable model with online advertising: it is very cheap to produce and distribute just about anything on the internet, and with almost guaranteed access to advertising platforms, there is a clear economic advantage to creating sensational stories that capture readers' attention and entice them to click [41]. More worryingly, the World Federation of Advertisers predicts that the ad-tech industry, the profit model on which fraudulent news relies, will soon become 'second only to cocaine and opiate markets as a form of organized crime' [42].

Operating in this environment of 'perverse incentives', the IC-Style applies modernism's aesthetic of authority to any kind of information, confusing factuality and credibility. These dangers were foretold in 1988, when Moles and Jacobus wrote that in an environment of 'immaterial culture', the conditions of reliability will be dependent on associating both verity *and* credibility with immaterial culture, with the danger being *only* an association with credibility [43]. In the environment of contemporary commercial platform logics, the IC-Style becomes merely a credible aesthetic, not a factual one.

Although historically, modernist designers have understood content and form as essentially connected and related to concepts about social responsibility, authority and verity, in the current online information environment, modernism remediated as the IC-Style has become problematic due to the very merits that made it an attractive option for early web design. Its efficiency and functionality are now applied to any and all content, divorcing content from form, and applying the associations of credibility, verity and authority to untrue and sometimes malicious information.

5 The IC-Style and the Web Environment of Information Disorder: Case Studies

The environment of information disorder that operates within contemporary commercial platform logics is a major research area for journalists and researchers who are concerned with the effects it has on a variety of socio-political issues such as public health and the future of democracy. Information Disorder is described as encompassing three different types of information disorders: 'mis-, dis- and malinformation', which are each defined by their degree of falsity and intent to cause harm [44]. 'Information Disorder' is a broader term than "fake news"'s political connotations, although others argue for the use of "fake news" to encompass a wide variety of mis/dis/mal/information typoglogies [45]. I will be using the term 'information disorder' and 'post-factual news' to refer to the phenomena of twenty-first-century mis/dis/mal/information and a tendency towards sensationalism in a 'post-factual' online media environment. The term 'post-factual' is related to the term 'post-truth', meaning 'circumstances in which objective facts are less influential in shaping political debate or public opinion than appeals to emotion and personal belief' [46]. The following case studies also focus on stories that have a specific reference to US politics in the years 2015–2017 in order to closely examine the application of the IC-Style to one type of news content, the political, as the future of democracy is a particularly pressing issue in the field of information disorder.

5.1 The "Non-Professional" Post-Factual News Website

The following case studies will explore how the IC-Style has been applied to two different websites recognised as contributing to online information disorder. The case studies will focus on what I term "non-professional" post-factual websites. These are distinct from "professional" websites associated with information disorder, such as *Breitbart News*, which has an extensive media presence, multiple bureaus, a clear hierarchical structure with editor and author accreditation and a cohesive brand. In contrast, "non-professional" post-factual news sites are often less clear in their ownership and authorship, appear in other news media only in the context of a particular story, have mixed motives and lack a distinctive brand identity. The common denominator of all non-professional post-factual news websites is that they 'distribute fabricated content' and often repost from other sites 'with or without attribution' [47]. Further, non-professional post-factual websites have a design aesthetic that follows an IC-Style web template. The templates used are sometimes referenced at the bottom of the webpage, something which will be explored in the first case.

Non-professional, post-factual news websites are similar in content, particularly in their focus on stories related to US politics. Craig Silverman's work as BuzzFeed News Media Editor led to a number of stories exposing the harm that post-factual news stories cause to individuals, along with broader analyses of information disorder throughout the 2016 campaign and the Trump administration. In 2016, Silverman found that false reporting on US politics was among the 'top-performing fake news content on Facebook in 2016' and that 'Twenty-three of the 50 top-performing fake news hoaxes we found on Facebook were focused on US politics' [48]. Overall, "fake news" about US politics accounted for 10.6 million of the 21.5 million total shares, reactions, and comments [...] English-language stories generated on Facebook [in 2016]' [48]. The motivation for post-factual websites to spread misleading or false information is not always clear, but it is usually either to outrage viewers on the views of a political party and/or to profit from advertising revenue. Politifact has reported that many fake news sites use online advertising services like Content.ad or RevContent.com, which place 'provocative ads' on their websites so administrators can profit from readers' clicks [49].

The case studies are chosen from BuzzFeed News' "Top Fake News" articles from 2016 and 2017 [50], wherein the authors combined social media data from BuzzSumo with their own list of sites that publish completely fabricated news to determine top-performing posts, as well as from the media scholar Zimdars' 2016 'False, Misleading, Clickbait-y, and/or Satirical "News" Sources' list [51]. I have examined archived copies of the websites from the Internet Archive's Wayback Machine, but because many of the sites were not well established or received much popular media attention, the Internet Archive's scraping of these sites is not comprehensive, and the scraped images and CSS are sometimes incomplete. Thus, some liberties have been taken regarding the consistency in terms of how the websites were chosen, using a purposive sampling technique. Due to copyright restrictions, images of these websites are unable to be reproduced. However, I have provided links in the References to the Internet Archive pages where archived versions of the case studies are available to view online.

5.2 *Case Study: World Politicus*

In 2016, Silverman and Alexander wrote an exposé on young Macedonians who, just in the town of Veles, had launched at least 140 US political news websites [52]. These people, Silverman's article claimed, had purely economic motives, earning from online advertising networks like Google AdSense [52]. A similar study was conducted by *The Guardian*, which interviewed a Macedonian administrator, "Alex", who stated that his aim was to 'influence American policy, especially politics' through his site, and that others, seeing how American politics generated website traffic, copied him with the sole goal of earning money from ad networks [53]. One of these Macedonian-based websites was WorldPoliticus.com. From 2016 to 2017, the website went through four different design changes, all employing modernist aesthetics and an underlying, templated grid structure.

At the beginning of 2016, the WorldPoliticus.com logo used the simplistic design of a white globe imposed onto a red square, with the name 'WORLD POLITICUS' in one line to the right [54]. The overall website design was fairly minimal. Only four generic news subcategories were listed in the menu at the top, and below this menu was a large, central photo gallery. Three top stories were listed in stacked vertical modules in the far right fourth of the gallery, while the left three-fourths rotated through the three headline stories, with a white sans-serif headline superimposed over a focal image.

By October 2016, the website's design and logotype changed [55]. The logo, still positioned in the top left, was redesigned as a blue globe with the name 'WORLD POLITICUS' in two separate red blocks to the right of the globe icon. Beneath the menu, the image gallery, although positioned in the same place, changed in format. The left half of the gallery consisted of one image with a headline superimposed onto a photograph. The right half was quartered, with four different stories and photographs presented, allowing for more variety of photographic content on the page than before. Just beneath, two content dividers were visible. A yellow divider labelled 'News' occupied up the left three-quarters of the page, while an orange divider labelled 'Popular Article[sic]' took up the final right quarter, employing white, sans-serif type on the coloured backgrounds.

In February 2017, the design of Worldpoliticus.com went through a more dramatic change [56]. The logo and news categories were arranged horizontally next to one another in the same bar at the top of the page. The bar was bright red and the logo and sans-serif text appeared in white. The website's logo was simplified, with a white icon of a world standing in for the word 'World' and the name 'Politicus' in white, all capitals sans-serif text. Instead of one image gallery, the page was split into thirds. On the far left were large headline images, headlines and previews of the article content in the centre, and on the right a 'Latest' section that mirrored the left two-thirds of the page in its design. In October 2017, the design changed again [57]. The top bar became blue, and the logo reverted back to the blue globe from 2016.

While WorldPoliticus.com employs a modernist, rational style, it does so in combination with political content that is highly sensational in tone. In 2016, white text is superimposed onto images that are slightly darkened in order to increase contrast. This darkening also adds an ominous tone to the photographs, which feature portraits of leaders looking slightly resigned or suspicious. Although the number of images on the page increases in later layouts, these images become smaller, and there is more negative space on the homepage in 2017 and 2018 than in 2016. Images appear to be primarily of individuals associated with the government. Some of the images are also clearly photoshopped, superimposing portraits of officials onto suggestive backgrounds. For example, on 18 March 2016, the leading photograph with the headline 'Who Controls Obama and US Media?!', at first glance, appears as though Obama is seated next to a Middle Eastern man [58]. However, upon closer inspection, it is clear that the image of Obama on the left is photoshopped, the visual closeness suggesting association. Edited photos appear again on 5 October 2016, with one superimposing Obama onto a background of $100 bills and another of Hillary Clinton's Vice Presidential nominee Tim Kane next to an Islamic state flag in front of the New York skyline collage representing targets of the far right-wing: elites, Democrats and Muslims [55]. Words in all capitals are used to increase emphasis and drama in the superimposed headlines, such as 'BREAKING […] RAPIST […] CHILD' (11 March 2016); 'ITS HAPPENING […] TAKEOVER' (10 April 2016); and 'TEAMSTERS UNION […] GAME CHANGING […] TRUMP […] WELCOME […] REVOLUTION' [55]. The subjects of the headlines follow also typical sensationalist and populist themes such as attacking government officials and suspicion of the media.

The template used by Worldpoliticus.com until October 2016 was created by Themeum, a service that designs responsive WordPress templates. Worldpoliticus.com used Themeum's 'NewEdge' 'News and magazine theme'. Features of the theme included its 'clean, fresh and modern look', drag and drop page builder that made it easy to 'Build your influential news/magazine site in the shortest period of time' and a 'stunning photo gallery' [59]. On 5 October 2016, the words '© Newspaper WordPress Theme by TagDiv' appeared at the bottom of the page. TagDiv is a software company creating news-specific themes for websites [60]. In 2016, in a section on their website featuring their 'most appreciated Wordpress Themes', the 'Newsmag' theme was shown, matching the theme customised by Worldpoliticus.com. Retailing for $49, the Newsmag theme let the user 'write articles and blog posts with ease' [61]. Written at the top of the page description, the theme creators note that 'News mag supports responsive Google Ads and AdSense', which would have been an important asset for those looking to profit from their sites [61]. Scrolling further down, features include the 'smart sidebar' that is 'perfect for ads and for content that the user needs to see', an 'intelligent ad system', 'custom categories', and 'one-click demo install' [61]. It is interesting to note how these web templates use the same language of efficiency characteristic of functionalist web design, agnostic to the content of the news itself.

5.3 *Case Study: Worldnewsdailyreport.com*

Worldnewsdailyreport.com is a unique example amongst non-professional fake news websites due to the depth of the archive, and by extension, how long they were active. The earliest scrape of Worldnewsdailyreport.com is from 18 November 2013, however, this early, text-heavy layout would soon be replaced almost entirely by images [62]. Sometime between 17 December 2014 and 11 January 2015, Worldnewsdailyreport.com underwent a design change that transformed the front page into a grid of images. The homepage from 11 January 2015 is dark with the entire website is set against a nearly black background [63]. The website's logo appears at the top left of the page, consisting of an icon of a blue globe with the letters 'WNDR' in bold, condensed Helvetica to the right. Beneath, the website's name appeared in thin italicised Helvetica. Beneath the logo was a black menu bar, with only the news categories in white, sans-serif text distinguishing it from the background. Whereas Worldpoliticus.com was largely static, WNDR contained a number of kinetic elements. Beneath the menu bar was a grey news ticker bar labelled 'Breaking News', where headlines appeared to type themselves out. Below the ticker was a grid of moving images. On the left was one large slideshow of images, on the right, two horizontal images flashed and changed, and a bar of scrolling images appeared at the bottom. Beneath the scrolling bar of images, the layout broke into three columns, with two columns of stories and images on the left, and white space likely where advertisements would have been on the right. Each article image was overlaid with a news category in a coloured box in the upper left corner of the image, the date on the upper right, and the headline in all-caps, bold, sans-serif text with a text preview beneath.

The stories on WNDR ranged from the slightly political, for example, 'NEW POLL REVEALS OBAMA MORE POPULAR THAN JESUS', combining both politics and religion, to the plausible 'LOGGERS ACCIDENTALLY CUT DOWN WORLD'S OLDEST TREE IN AMAZON FOREST', to the outwardly sensational 'LOUISIANA "DEMON CHILD" BURNS DOWN 4TH HOUSE IN A ROW'.

On 14 April 2016, the design of the website changed again, which would remain the same through 2019 [64]. During the time this layout was in use, Worldnewsdailyreport.com landed a #11 spot on Silverman's Buzzfeed list for a post in October 2016 headlined, 'ISIS Leader Calls for American Muslim Voters to Support Hillary Clinton' [48]. Although I was unable to find a scrape of the website with that story featured on the front page, it is visible in the rotating ticker on 19 October 2016 [65]. In the 2016 design, the ticker was been renamed 'HOT TOPICS' and included a dateline next to each headline. Above the ticker was a black menu bar with news categories in bold, condensed white text. Beneath the ticker, the website is divided into two nearly equal columns with news stories on the left and space where advertisements would have likely appeared on the right. On the left, a large focal image was positioned above a headline in bold, condensed sans-serif text with a dateline, preview text, and large, blue 'Read More' button beneath. Below this main story, the column split into halves again, with two columns of stories. Each story consisted of an image above headline text as before, set in the same typeface as the main story headline.

Examining these two case studies reveals how the IC-Style can be applied to any kind of content, regardless of its verity. Both examples maintain the 'highly structural' layout, 'black and white typography' and 'nameplate like header' characteristic of the IC-Style, while reflecting layout conventions and uses of photography advanced by Müller-Brockmann and the Swiss modernists. In both cases, the websites use columnar structures [66], sans-serif typography [66], p. 19], and 'picture grids' [66], pp. 69–70, 98] promoted by Müller-Brockmann in *Grid Systems.*

In the current online environment of perverse economic incentives, the conflation of modernist aesthetics with post-factual news has in part contributed to the crisis of information disorder, one of the gravest threats to the current system of digital communication.

6 Tackling Online Information Disorder: The Role of Design

In framing the problem of information disorder as, in part, perpetuated by design, it implies that those practising design have a responsibility in addressing the issue. Building upon larger discussions on the ethical responsibility of designers [67], this final section explores the role of the designer in solutions to information disorder. Of course, there are causes of information disorder outwith designers' control. For example, changing the financial incentives that underlie the economic drive of information disorder, which is in the hands of policymakers. Nonetheless, I subscribe to Buwert's assertion that all design involves 'the extension and transformation of potentiality' and here, I ask: how can design 'transform and extend potentiality' in the mediation of online information [68]? I believe this involves designing for an entirely new communication system, rather than designing within the current one. To do so requires an interdisciplinary approach to graphic design and communication design education that integrates media studies as part of the core curriculum. Through this integration of communication theory with design practice, designers can become what Traub and Lipkin term 'creative interlocutors' or an 'integrated' individual whose 'creativity functions as an organic part of society […] to connect for the common good' negotiating 'disparate fields of human knowledge' to 'bring them together in previously unimagined ways' [69].

6.1 *Media Studies, Communication Design and the Future of Online Information*

Writing in 1988 on design in postindustrial society, Moles and Jacobus remarked that the designer 'creates the environment of others' [43]. But what environment is that exactly, beyond the visual? Understanding this larger communication environment, through interdisciplinary study, could help change the conditions in which information disorder and designers are currently operating. Throughout the history of news production in particular, there has been a separation between those who created news (or 'content') and the typesetters or designers who positioned the content on a page. With web design, commercial graphic designers have historically been restricted to concerns over the 'visual appearance' of a website [70]. It must be acknowledged that the skills to design for print do not 'automatically translate onto the Web' [71]. Steven Heller's 2001 edited volume *The Education of an E-Designer*, recognises the different skill sets designers must have when working in a digital environment. However, the book assumes operation under the same communication systems as twentieth-century print mediums. A deeper understanding of the kind of communication structures in which user interface interactions take place, the kind of scholarship found in media studies, will be key to designing truly credible, veritable and discursive online news environments. This suggestion to integrate communication design and theory in interdisciplinary programmes is not new. For example, in 2001, Gromala described the integration of graphic design and cultural theory into Georgia Tech's, multidisciplinary Information Design and Technology programme [72]. What is to be gained from this integration of media theory and design? Ideally, critical reflections on our current systems of communication and the transformation of these systems into new ones.

In his 1978 book *Communicology* (published posthumously in 2022), the philosopher Vilém Flusser proposed a number of such communication structures. Put broadly, Flusser identified that the synchronisation of what he termed amphitheatrical discourse structures (for example, broadcasting) and the structure of network dialogue (public opinion) has to a communication crisis where information is being acquired and distributed, but new information is not being created through genuine dialogue and exchange [73]. The structure of circular dialogue, or of a 'round table' discussion, is one that Flusser considers 'the highest form of communication when it is successful' [73], p. 30]. Although an ideal system, nonetheless, designing for a kind of communication structure that ultimately promotes circular dialogue, with incremental steps to ensure the information attained in the intermediary stages is 'valid' and promotes a progressive dialogue, should be the aim of communication designers working today. The characteristics of Flusser's circular dialogue model align with suggestions for web design models proposed by design critics. For example, early on, Helfhand recognised that the 'urge to race through information' online does not align with 'the speed with which such interaction naturally takes place' [74]. Instead, Helfand provocatively suggests the models of nineteenth-century parlour games that 'were played at a slower and, indeed, a more social pace' [74].

What exactly a new model for web design and communication *looks* like is yet to be seen. However, it should promote slow, considered engagement with content and one another. This is not to say that Swiss modernism needs to be entirely eradicated. One might argue that examples of postmodern or avant-garde web design, such as those advocated by Siegel as early as 1997, are already working against the IC-Style by rejecting modernist principles [75]. Although these can be helpful to reference in terms of aesthetic differences, I see the avant-garde web movement as primarily a reaction against the IC-Style, rather than actively trying to change it. Postmodern design influenced by critical language theories can open up ideas about meaning and alternative readings, but this should be taken further to include critical communications theories more broadly, such as those of Flusser. I believe Swiss modernism's roots as a socially-informed design ideology, tied to an alignment between form and content can be applied to a more 'round-table' model of communication system. However, understanding of the potentiality new communication systems will only be available if design students have a foundational education in media studies and communication theory.

7 Conclusion

As those who create public communication systems, design and designers are implicated in the fight against information disorder. The designer's ethical responsibility rests in their 'constructive contribution to the cultural state of society' through the purveying of public information [76]. The goal of communication designers within the current state of information disorder should not be to create a new aesthetic language or markers for "truth" that operate within our current communication models but to design for new models that promote sociodemographic principles. This aim for communication design aligns with international initiatives for shaping the future of twenty-first-century societies, such as the United Nations Sustainable Development Goals [77]. In each of the seventeen listed goals, communication design can play a role by supporting the distribution of factual information creating online spaces where information can be discussed and debated fairly.

Further, interdisciplinary research into the design of new communications models is needed, along with a deeper understanding of how twentieth-century ideologies of social responsibility and design can be applied to the establishment of ethical principles for communication designers. More historical research could also be done to establish comparative histories between Swiss modernism, post-war corporate modernism and the IC-Style of web design. Detailed visual maps comparing instructional material from Swiss modernists and contemporary post-factual news websites could help us better understand the difference between the intentions and applications of Swiss modernism and its remediation online, exploring in more detail what results when content becomes separated from form.

The information crisis at hand is pressing, and it is vital that designers recognise that 'reality [...], is not independent of the apparatuses that produce reports of reality' [78]. Designers have the ability and responsibility to understand and consider new potentials for the current apparatus of communication, the web, and in doing so, shape our current and future realities.

References

1. Clark J (2003) The IC-style. https://web.archive.org/web/20161223212333/, http://fawny.org/blog/2003/09/. Last accessed 03 Apr 2023
2. Thorlacius L (2009) Visual communication in web design—analyzing visual communication in web design. In: Hunsinger J, Klastrup L, Allen M (eds) International handbook of internet research, Springer, Dordrecht, pp 455–476
3. Etienne C (2002) The default aesthetic: Vanilla flavored beauty. https://web.archive.org/web/20030605134214/, http://www.teleferique.org/stations/Cliquet/Default/default.htm. Last accessed 20 Mar 2023
4. For more information about the evolution of the term 'International Style' from 'Modernism and 'Swiss style', see Hollis R (2006) Swiss graphic design: the origins and growth of an international style, 1920–1965. Lawrence King, London, p 13
5. Bolter D, Grusin R (1996) Remediation. Configurations 4(3):311–358 p 339. See more on remediation theory as applied to computer interfaces

6. Cleveland P (2010) Style based automated graphic layouts. Des Stud 31(1):3–25
7. Müller-Brockmann J (1981) Grid systems in graphic design: a visual communication manual for graphic designers, typographers, and three dimensional designers = Raster systeme für die visuelle Gestaltung : Ein Handbuch für Grafiker, Typografen, und Ausstellungsgestalter. Verlag Arthur Niggli, Niederteufen, p 10
8. Hilfiker H (2006) Design and responsibility. Neue Grafik 15:55–58 (1963) Cited in: Hollis R (2006) Swiss graphic design: the origins and growth of an international style, 1920–1965. London, Lawrence King, p 210.
9. Schuitema P, Neue Grafik 4:43–44 (1960) Cited in: Hollis R (2006) Swiss graphic design: the origins and growth of an international style, 1920–1965. London, Lawrence King, p 210
10. Dilger B (2010) <table>ing the grid. In: Dilger B, Rice, J (eds.) From A to <A>: keywords of markup. University of Minnesota Press, Minneapolis, pp 213, 215
11. Berners-Lee T (1999) Weaving the web: the original design and ultimate destiny of the world wide web by its inventor. San Francisco, Harper, pp 224, 226–227
12. Thorlacious L (2007) The role of aesthetics in web design. Nordicom Review 28(1):63–76
13. MacManus R (2004) The evolution of corporate web sites. Digital Web Magazine. https://web.archive.org/web/20040516055208/, http://www.digital-web.com/articles/the_evolution_of_corporate_web_sites/. Last accessed 03 Apr 2023
14. Koch P (2003) Keep CSS simple. Digital Web Magazine. https://web.archive.org/web/20031203022716/, http://digital-web.com/columns/keepitsimple/keepitsimple_2003-11.shtml. Last accessed 03 Mar 2023
15. Dilger B (2010) <table>ing the grid. In: Dilger B, Rice J (eds) From A to <A>: keywords of markup. Minneapolis, University of Minnesota Press
16. Dilger B (2010) <table>ing the grid. In: Dilger B, Rice J (eds) From A to <A>: keywords of markup. University of Minnesota Press, Minneapolis, p 223
17. Thorlacious L (2007) The role of aesthetics in web design. Nordicom Rev 28(1):63–76
18. Engholm I (2013) Conceptual type—a commentary on the Internet's design development? Artifact 3(1):5.1–5.10
19. Dilger B (2010) <table>ing the grid. In: Dilger B, Rice J (eds) From A to <A>: keywords of markup. University of Minnesota Press, Minneapolis, p 218
20. For a more in-depth discussion of the impact of Nielsen in web design, see: Thorlacius (2007)
21. Nielsen J (2000) Designing web usability. Indianapolis, New Riders, p 81
22. Dilger B (2010) <table>ing the grid. In: Dilger B, Rice J (eds) From A to <A>: keywords of markup. University of Minnesota Press, Minneapolis, p 214
23. Samara T (2017) Making and breaking the grid: a graphic design layout workshop. United States, Rockport Publishers, Rockport, p 7
24. Engholm I (2010) The good enough revolution—the role of aesthetics in user experiences with digital artefacts. Dig Creat 21(3):141–154
25. Maudet N (2023) Une brève histoire des templates, entre autonomisation et contrôle des graphistes amateurs. Systèmes: logiques, graphies, matérialités, Revue Design Arts Medias. https://journal.dampress.org/issues/systemes-logiques-graphies-materialites/une-breve-histoire-des-templates-entre-autonomisation-et-controle-des-graphistes-amateurs. Last accessed 08 Mar 2023
26. Brunborg E (2013) Fuck grids. 8gramgorilla. https://web.archive.org/web/20130715081839/, http://8gramgorilla.com/fuck-grids/. Last accessed 28 Jun 2023
27. Neue Grafik 1 (1958) Cited in: Hollis R (2006) Swiss graphic design: the origins and growth of an international style, 1920–1965. Lawrence King, London, p 210
28. Swanson G (2001) The web versus design: "usability" and the homogenized future. In: Heller S (ed.) Education of an e-designer, Alworth Press, New York, 192–194
29. Barnhurst K, Nerone J (2001) The form of news: a history. The Guilford Press, New York, p 21
30. Arnold E (1956) Functional newspaper design. New York, Harper & Brothers, p 3
31. Garcia M (1997) Redesigning print for the Web. Hayden Books, Indianapolis

32. Garcia M (1993) Contemporary newspaper design: a structural approach. Prentice Hall, Englewood Cliffs
33. Barnhurst K, Nerone J (2001) The form of news: a history. The Guilford Press, New York, p 288
34. Law J (2004) After method: mess in social science research. Routledge, London, p 28
35. Honeywill, P (1999) Visual language for the world wide web, Intellect. Exeter, p 136
36. Riley B (2010) A style guide to the secrets of <style>. In: Dilger B, Rice J (eds) From A to <A>: keywords of markup, 67–80. University of Minnesota Press, Minneapolis, p 71
37. Nielsen J (2000) Designing web usability. New Riders, Indianapolis, p 12
38. Riley B (2010) A style guide to the secrets of <style>. In: Dilger B, Rice J (eds) From A to <A>: keywords of markup, 67–80. University of Minnesota Press, Minneapolis, p 74
39. Andrejevic M (2020) Political function of fake news: disorganized propaganda in the era of automated media. In: Zimdars M, McLeod K (eds.) Fake news: understanding media and misinformation in the digital age. MIT Press, Cambridge, MA, 19–28 p 22
40. Glasser T, Zou S, Varma A (2020) Native advertising as counterfeit news. In: Zimdars M, McLeod K (eds) Fake news: understanding media and misinformation in the digital age. MIT Press, Cambridge, MA, pp 87–94
41. Martens B, Aguiar L, Gomez-Herrera E (2018) The digital transformation of news media and the rise of disinformation and fake news, p 41. https://ec.europa.eu/jrc/sites/default/files/jrc111529.pdf. Last accessed 28 Jun 2023
42. Compendium of ad fraud knowledge for media investors (2016) https://wfanet.org/knowledge/item/2016/06/03/Compendium-of-ad-fraud-knowledge-for-media-investors. Last accessed 28 Jun 2023
43. Moles A, Jacobus D (1988) Design and immateriality: what of it in a post industrial society? Des Issues 4(1/2):25–32
44. Wardle C, Derakhshan H (2017) Information disorder: toward an interdisciplinary framework for research and policymaking. https://shorensteincenter.org/information-disorder-framework-for-research-and-policymaking/. Last accessed 24 Apr 2023
45. Tandoc E, Lim Z, Ling R (2018) Defining "fake news." Dig J 6(2):137–153
46. Post-truth, adj. OED Online. Oxford University Press (March 2023) https://www.oed.com/view/Entry/58609044?redirectedFrom=post+truth#eid. Last accessed 28 Jun 2023
47. PolitiFact's guide to fake news websites and what they peddle (2017) https://www.politifact.com/article/2017/apr/20/politifacts-guide-fake-news-websites-and-what-they/. Last accessed 11 Apr 2022
48. Silverman C (2016) Here are 50 of the biggest fake news hits on Facebook from 2016. Buzzfeed News. https://www.buzzfeednews.com/article/craigsilverman/top-fake-news-of-2016. Last accessed 22 Feb 2023
49. PolitiFact's guide to fake news websites and what they peddle. Politifact (2017) https://www.politifact.com/article/2017/apr/20/politifacts-guide-fake-news-websites-and-what-they/. Last accessed 11 Apr 2022
50. Silverman C (2016) Here are 50 of the biggest fake news hits on Facebook from 2016. Buzzfeed News. https://www.buzzfeednews.com/article/craigsilverman/top-fake-news-of-2016, last accessed 22 Feb 2023; Silverman C, Lytvynenko J, Pham S (2017) These are 50 of the biggest fake news hits on Facebook in 2017. https://www.buzzfeednews.com/article/craigsilverman/these-are-50-of-the-biggest-fake-news-hits-on-facebook-in. Last accessed 28 Jun 2023
51. Zimdars M (2016) False, misleading, clickbait-y, and/or satirical "news" sources. https://docs.google.com/document/d/10eA5-mCZLSS4MQY5QGb5ewC3VAL6pLkT53V_81ZyitM/preview. Last accessed 12 May 2023
52. Silverman C, Alexander L (2016) How teens in the Balkans are duping trump supporters with fake news. https://www.buzzfeednews.com/article/craigsilverman/how-macedonia-became-a-global-hub-for-pro-trump-misinfo#.op95xv35M. Last accessed 11 Apr 2022
53. Tynan D (2016) How Facebook powers money machines for obscure political 'news' sites. The Guardian. https://www.theguardian.com/technology/2016/aug/24/facebook-clickbait-political-news-sites-us-election-trump. Last accessed 22 Feb 2023

54. Worldpoliticus.com (11 March 2016) https://web.archive.org/web/20160311103556/worldpoliticus.com. Last accessed 28 Jun 2023
55. Worldpoliticus.com (5 October 2016) https://web.archive.org/web/20161005065621/worldpoliticus.com. Last accessed 28 Jun 2023
56. Worldpoliticus.com (10 February 2017) https://web.archive.org/web/20170210205021/worldpoliticus.com. Last accessed 28 Jun 2023
57. Worldpoliticus.com (15 October 2017) https://web.archive.org/web/20171015112429/worldpoliticus.com
58. Worldpoliticus.com (18 March 2016) https://web.archive.org/web/20160318210930/worldpoliticus.com
59. Themeum Newedge Wordpress Magazine Theme. https://web.archive.org/web/20160304094408/, http://www.themeum.com/wordpress/themes/newedge-responsive-wordpress-magazine-theme. Last accessed 28 Jun 2023
60. Tagdiv Homepage. https://web.archive.org/web/20160426085019/, http://tagdiv.com/. Last accessed 28 Jun 2023
61. Newsmag theme. https://web.archive.org/web/20160426074442/, http://themeforest.net/item/newsmag-news-magazine-newspaper/9512331. Last accessed 28 Jun 2023
62. Worldnewsdailyreport.com (18 November 2013) https://web.archive.org/web/20131118082224/, http://worldnewsdailyreport.com/. Last accessed 28 Jun 2023
63. Worldnewsdailyreport.com (11 January 2015) https://web.archive.org/web/20150111065220/, http://worldnewsdailyreport.com/. Last accessed 28 Jun 2023
64. Worldnewsdailyreport.com (14 April 2016) https://web.archive.org/web/20160414193000/, http://worldnewsdailyreport.com/
65. Worldnewsdailyreport.com (19 October 2016) https://web.archive.org/web/20161019060803/, http://worldnewsdailyreport.com/. Last accessed 28 Jun 2023
66. Müller-Brockmann J (1981) Grid systems in graphic design : a visual communication manual for graphic designers, typographers, and three dimensional designers = Raster systeme für die visuelle Gestaltung: Ein Handbuch für Grafiker, Typografen, und Ausstellungsgestalter. Niederteufen, Verlag Arthur Niggli, pp 31, 52–56
67. For more on design and ethics, see: Buwert P (2017) Potentiality: the ethical foundation of design. Des J 20(1):S4459–S4467; Dilnot C (2009) Ethics in design: 10 questions. In: Huppatz DJ (ed) Design: critical and primary sources: social interactions. Berg, Oxford, pp 230–245; Rich T (1996) Who needs ethics? Print 50, 18; Monterio M (2017) A designer's code of ethics. https://deardesignstudent.com/a-designers-code-of-ethics-f4a88aca9e95, Last accessed 28 Jun 2023
68. Buwert P (2017) Potentiality: the ethical foundation of design. Des J 20(1):S4459–S4467, pp s4460, s4464
69. Traub C, Lipkin J (2001) Digital humanism. In: Heller S (ed) Education of an e-designer. Alworth Press, New York, p 82
70. Wragg N, Barnes C (2016) Graphic designers' sense and knowledge of the user: is thinking differently the groundwork for acting differently? Vis Lang 50(3):29–62
71. Heller S (ed) (2001) Education of an e-designer. New York, Alworth Press, pp viii, 192–194
72. Gromala D (2001) Learning the languages of Babel: an approach to new media pedagogy and the relevance of graphic design. In: Heller S (ed) Education of an e-designer, 50–55. Alworth Press, New York, p 82
73. Flusser V (2022) Communicology: mutations in human relations. Stanford University Press, Stanford
74. Helfand J (2001) Screen: essays on graphic design, new media, and visual culture. Princeton Architectural Press, New York, p 6
75. Siegel D (1997) Creating killer Web sites: the art of third-generation site design. Hayden Books, Indianapolis
76. Müller-Brockmann J (1981) Grid systems in graphic design: a visual communication manual for graphic designers, typographers, and three dimensional designers = Raster systeme für die visuelle Gestaltung : Ein Handbuch für Grafiker, Typografen, und Ausstellungsgestalter. Verlag Arthur Niggli, Niederteufen, p 12

77. United Nations Department of Economic and Social Development | The 17 Goals. https://sdgs.un.org/goals. Last accessed 28 Jun 2023
78. Law J (2004) After method: mess in social science research. Routledge, London, p 31

Typography: The Legacy of Manuel Pereira da Silva

Vítor Quelhas

Abstract Manuel Pereira da Silva (1930–2008), a Portuguese typographer, researcher, and type designer, made significant contributions to national typographic culture. Despite being relatively unknown, his work deserves recognition and rediscovery. Pereira da Silva learned typography from his father and pursued a career in advertising agencies before establishing himself in the graphic industry during the 1960s. He developed a passion for letter drawing and established a digital workshop in his office in the late 1990s. Self-taught and driven by his love for books, type history, and letterforms, he developed digital revivals of ancient typefaces and original designs. This study aims to shed light on Pereira da Silva's methodology through his typefaces, publications, and untapped archives, emphasizing the importance of documentation in the type design process. Furthermore, it explores how his work influenced contemporary national type designers. Despite limited awareness of his journey and accomplishments, Pereira da Silva's work exemplify his unique approach and enduring impact on the national typography scene. By celebrating his legacy and projecting it into the future, this article seeks to honor his memory and inspire designers today.

Keywords Typography · Type design · Manuel Pereira da Silva · Cultural heritage · Portugal

1 Introduction

Type design and typography, as essential components of visual communication, carry the power to shape narratives and convey emotions.

The typefaces are the formal expression of writing and writing is the physical representation of language [6]. In Communication Design, its study is increasingly

V. Quelhas (✉)
uniMAD, ESMAD, Polytechnic of Porto, rua D. Sancho I, 4480-876 Vila do Conde, Portugal
e-mail: vquelhas@esmad.ipp.pt

ID+ Research Institute for Design, Media and Culture, Porto, Portugal

D. Raposo et al. (eds.), *Perspectives on Design III*, Springer Series in Design and Innovation 34, https://doi.org/10.1007/978-3-031-43516-4_10

relevant, and its importance can be assessed by the difficulty in developing a project that does not involve its use [8].

A typeface is not simply a representation of the alphabet. It results from the combination of thousands of years of collective, social, technological, and economic history, combining the passion, legibility, experience, and paths of its creators [3]. Typefaces are cultural artifacts [2]. Letter forms reflect the style of a period, and its cultural background.

Building upon the legacy of the Bauhaus movement, which revolutionized design in the twentieth century, the New European Bauhaus initiative launched by the European Commission in 2020, aims to integrate sustainability, aesthetics, inclusivity and cultural heritage into contemporary design practices [1].

Within this context, cultural heritage plays a vital role [4]. It serves as a wellspring of inspiration, historical references, traditional craftsmanship and knowledge, informing the design process and providing a sense of continuity. By incorporating elements of cultural heritage into type design and typography, designers can create visually captivating and meaningful expressions of identity, history, authenticity, and cultural diversity.

By studying and incorporating elements of cultural heritage, designers can create typefaces that resonate with specific cultural contexts, paying homage to the traditions, aesthetics, and unique visual languages of different periods and communities.

Moreover, cultural heritage brings depth and meaning to typography. It offers a connection to the past, allowing type designers to explore and reinterpret historical letter forms, calligraphic styles, and typographic techniques. By engaging with cultural heritage, designers can revive forgotten or underrepresented typographic traditions, breathing new life into them through contemporary design approaches. Cultural heritage also enables typography to become a vessel for storytelling, encapsulating narratives, beliefs, and societal values. Through type design, cultural heritage can be preserved, celebrated, and shared, acting as a bridge between generations and fostering a sense of cultural continuity in an ever-evolving design landscape.

This study plays tribute to the life and work of Manuel Pereira da Silva, a Portuguese typographer, researcher, and type designer, who made significant contributions to the national and international typographic culture. His influence recognizes the inherent value of preserving and reinterpreting our collective past while embracing the possibilities of the present and the future.

2 Background

Manuel Rodrigues Pereira da Silva [1930–2008] was born in Póvoa de Varzim and passed away in Lisbon at the age of 78. He began learning the typographer's art and trade with his father when he was five years old, in the printing shop of the newspaper *O Comércio da Póvoa de Varzim* and the Tipografia do Patronato of S. José, both of which were run by his father [7].

At 14, he acquired calligraphy, typewriting, and stereography in a Commercial course, and in the absence of an appealing course, he dropped out and began his professional career as a typographer at A. C. Calafate's Typography and Bookstore at the age of 15. Between 1955 and 1956, he enrolled in a course of study on the History and Design of Letter Forms at the Centro Técnico Profissional in Lisbon, instructed by the calligrapher Alberto Cardoso and overseen by Eduardo Calvet de Magalhães.

In 1955, 1961, and 1963, he was arrested by the International and State Defense Police (*PIDE*), where he was subjected to interrogations, sleep torture, and statuary. With his health deteriorating as a result of the mistreatment he endured in prison, he gave up his jobs as a typographer and a film club animator in 1964, because he couldn't stand on his feet for lengthy periods of time [12].

He worked at the marketing agency Êxito the same year, and as soon as the first forms of computerized typesetting and printing arose, he returned to his prior activity, which was now less physically demanding. In 1966, he started Prograf, a workshop that pioneered the production of type proofs and photocomposed titles as an independent business [5, 7]. In 1977, he went to Trama Artes Gráficas, Expressão and became technical director of photocomposition in Fototexto, Lda., a specialized supplier of photocomposition for the Portuguese graphic, advertising, and publishing markets.

Passionate about books, the history of typography and letter forms, he developed digital interpretations of ancient typefaces, stimulated by a grant from the Calouste Gulbenkian Foundation in 1994.

From the 80's on, he dedicated himself to bibliographic and individual exhibitions related to typographic art. He has attended in national and international seminars and conferences, and in 1999 he taught History of Typography at Alquimia da Cor in Porto.

He dedicated himself to graphic design for private and institutional clients, among them Richard C. Ramer, Teixeira da Mota, Associação Portuguesa de Livreiros-Alfarrabistas, Jardim Infantil Pestalozzi and Fundação Calouste Gulbenkian.

As a researcher, he produced texts, articles, and books related to typographic art, besides the leaflets he distributed to his closest friends (Fig. 1).

Among the most significant publications are Roman Faces (*Faces Romanas…*), edited by Liouher in Lisbon, 1996; the Rotunda catalog (*Rotunda, um semigótico redondo. Recriação de um antigo estilo de Letra*), published by the Municipality of Póvoa de Varzim, 1997 (Fig. 2); The publication Techniques and Materials of the School Press (*As Técnicas e os Materiais da Imprensa Escolar. Casa da Praia. Centro de Saúde Mental Infantil de Lisboa*), author's edition, Lisbon, 2002; Specimen of digital typefaces (*Espécime de fontes tipográficas digitais*), author's edition, Lisbon, 2003 (Fig. 3); and the book 500 Years of Typography and Calligraphy (*500 anos de Tipografia e Caligrafia*), author's edition, Lisbon, 2008. Due to the author's death, his wife published this book in a limited edition of 50 copies in 2018 (Fig. 4).

He was also the protagonist of articles in the press, namely, *Diário Insular*, *Comércio*, *União* newspaper and *Page* magazine, as well as the assistance and

Fig. 1 Leaflets on typography that Manuel Pereira da Silva distributed among his friends

technical-scientific consultations he provided to trainees and researchers, masters' and doctoral students who sought him out and his specialized library [5].

Pereira da Silva's work was informed by his bibliographical passion concerning the History of Letter Forms, Books, and Typography.

From his more technical professional career as a graphic consultant, his visits to the Berthold company in Berlin in 1970, where he acquired the first Diatronic automatic phototypesetter, with keyboard and integrated computer, and his internship at Imprinta in Dusseldorf in 1984, to study the Scantex equipment, had a significant impact on the development of his professional career in Portugal.

The visit to the ATypI conference in Lyon in 1998 will have fueled his already voracious passion for letter forms, its design, and study.

He valued the work done around the classics of calligraphy and typography as reference authors. "Monotype was his primary reference and goal." He admitted to being a fan of Stanley Morison's work" (A. Ferreira, personal communication, July 11, 2013).

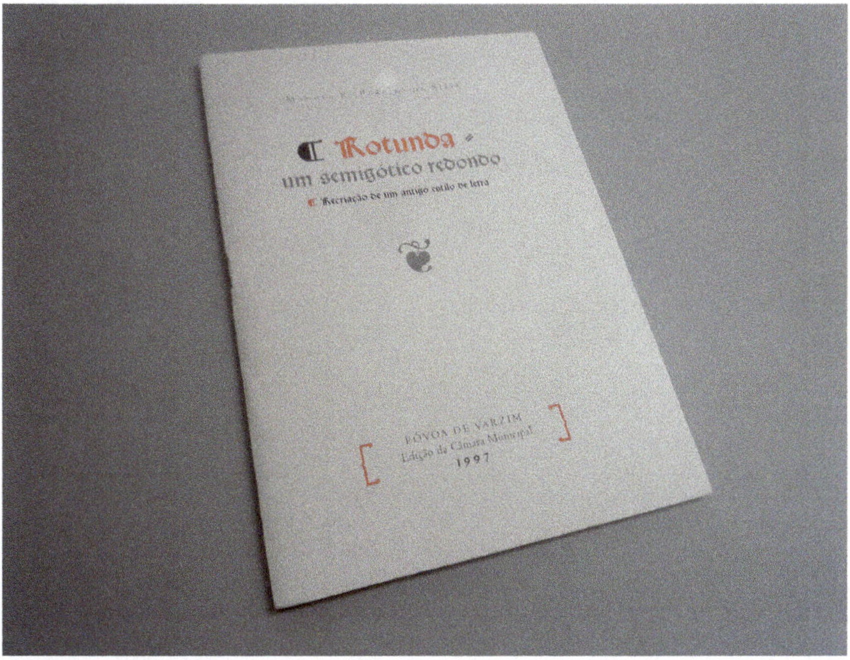

Fig. 2 Cover of the catalog *Rotunda*, by Manuel Pereira da Silva, published by the Municipality of Póvoa de Varzim, in 1997

3 Approach

According to current evidence and validated by exploratory interviews, the working process in the design and production of Pereira da Silva's typefaces began with the fundamental phase of investigating and collecting references.

Pereira da Silva almost always chose not to draw all the characters on the screen, remarking, regarding the Rotunda process, that the finished representation could not escape the appearance of something mechanical [10]. He drew the simplest characters directly on the screen, but for the more complex ones, he used a freehand pencil sketch. He began by photo shooting texts and alphabet reproductions at high magnifications, then isolating each letter for digitalization and treatment. He would next vectorize and made the respective corrections to the fonts before finishing them and editing Type 1 and TrueType versions (Figs. 5, 6, 7).

In other cases, he used a more rigorous and geometric drawing, such as the sketches on squared and millimeter paper for the Tialira typeface (Fig. 8) from around 1983.

Pereira da Silva was aware of the issues that type designers face considering letter forms. As he said, two contradictory aspects concerning their structure come to mind: first, letter forms are necessarily made of lines and curves; second, letter forms are much more than that [11].

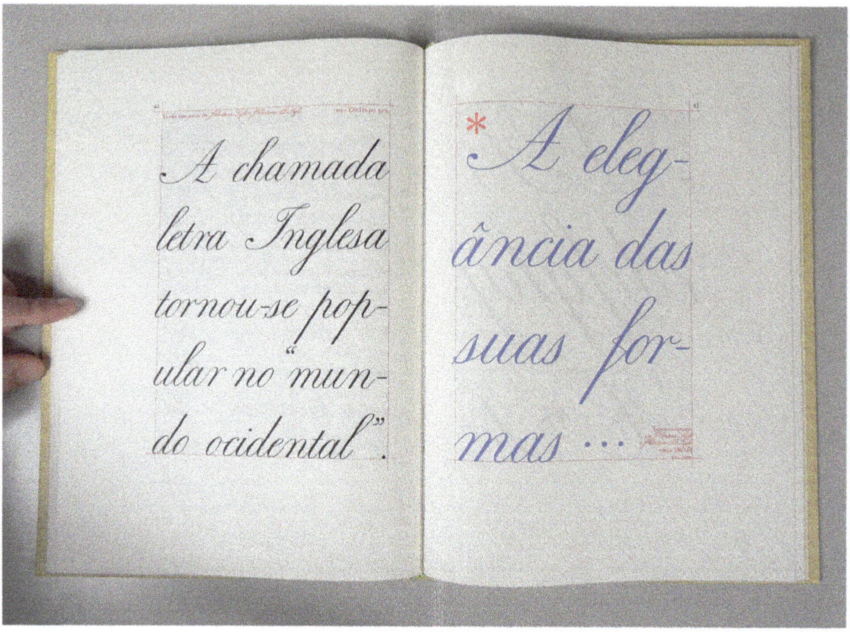

Fig. 3 Spread of the *Specimen of digital typefaces*, author's edition, Lisbon, 2003, showcasing *JVentura Light*

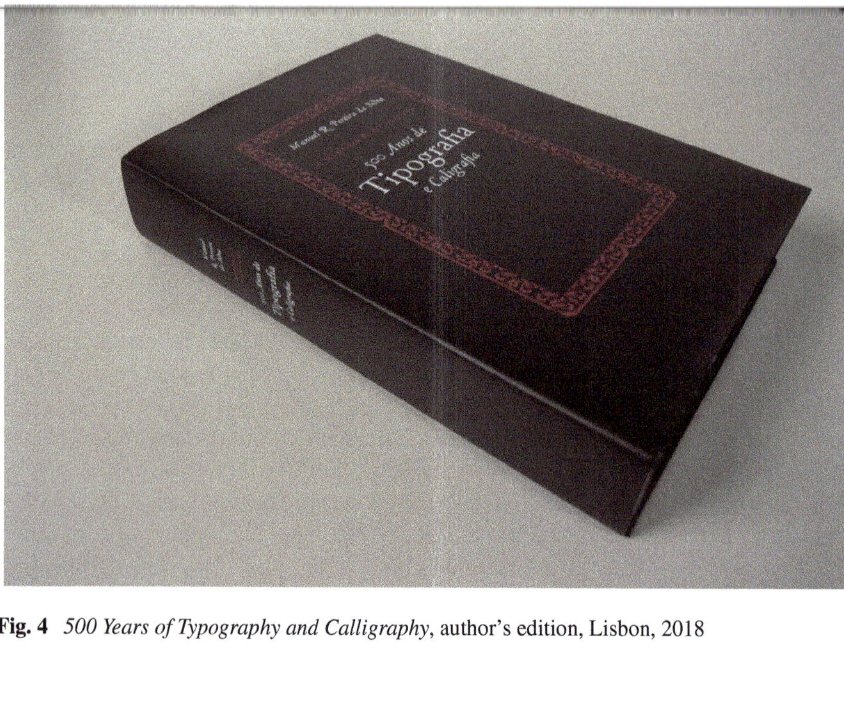

Fig. 4 *500 Years of Typography and Calligraphy*, author's edition, Lisbon, 2018

Fig. 5 Book documenting the design and production process of *JVentura* typeface

Fig. 6 Printed proof of *Rotunda* character with the author's notes concerning the necessary adjustments to the drawing

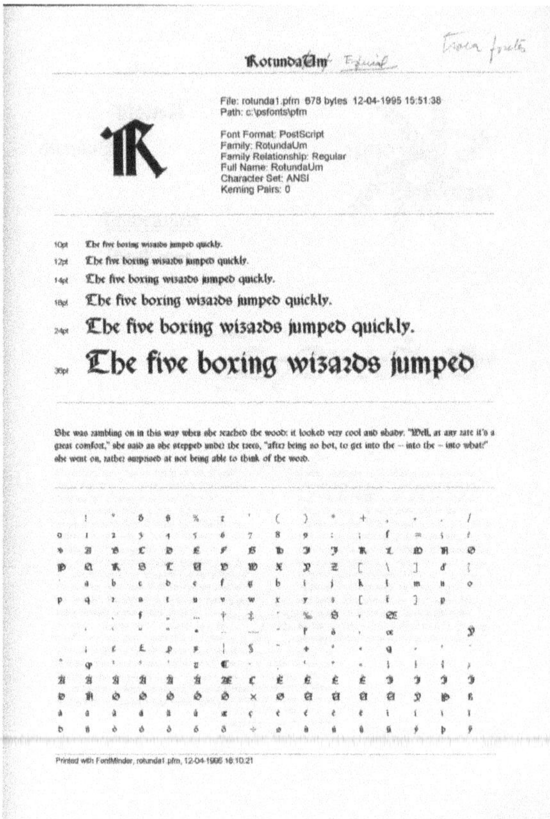

Fig. 7 Printed proof from FontMinder software, with pangram and character map of the *Rotunda Especial*

He worked largely alone and self-taught on his projects, and the advancement of technology organically conditioned the development of his work approach. Around 2003, he built up his workshop at home using digital technologies and equipment such as a computer and a printer, allowing him to write, assemble, edit, design, and print his books himself.

He began drawing digital type in a Windows environment with CorelDRAW. He relied on Corel Photo-Paint for digitizing, Corel Trace for vectorization and correction, Corel Kern for kerning, and Fontographer for finishing his fonts.

4 Outputs

Rotunda, Andrade, JVentura, and the originals Tialira and Fontanela stand out from Manuel Pereira da Silva's type design career.

Rotunda, developed between 1994 and 1996, was a recreation of semigothic typefaces popular in the Mediterranean from the 13th to the sixteenth centuries, with more

Fig. 8 *Tialira* typeface sketches, c. 1983 (M. Silva, 2008, pp. 389–390)

rounded shapes, also known as *Letra de Summa* or *Rotunda*, hence the name given to this typeface, as opposed to the more angular and condensed shapes of Germanic Gothic typefaces. These characters spread in an extraordinary way, almost becoming a national style in Portugal, since other forms of Gothic letters were only found in titles or woodcuts of faces, and this over a long period of time [9, 10].

Pereira da Silva thoroughly summarized the complete sequence of the investigation carried out published in his 1995 work Rotunda (*Rotunda, um semigótico redondo: Recriação de um antigo estilo de caracteres tipográficos, organizados em fontes coerentes*). An expert of this style, Pereira da Silva was also familiar with some digital interpretations of similar typefaces such as Paganini or San Marco. The Rotunda typeface by Pereira da Silva is the outcome of a selection of variants printed in various texts, resulting in a certain formal hybridism, but also a greater fidelity to the calligraphic spirit of this typeface [10].

The Rotunda font is made up of two families: the Rotunda Normal family, which has characters distributed by 256 addresses, as was the standard at the time for Type 1 or TrueType fonts, and the Rotunda Especial family, which has some special signs replaced by abbreviations, ligatures, initial letters, middle letters, final letters, and so on, allowing transcription of any documents and books that used them (Fig. 9).

When compared to the Germanic Gothic, Pereira da Silva's Rotunda type design bears a considerable resemblance to the qualities of humanist writing, as evidenced by the more rounded forms, broad apertures, a smooth transition between curves, and a slightly less condensed spacing. The x-height is high, making it easier to read. This is also why medieval scribes frequently utilized this style of writing in the production of missals. The thickly drawn forms contribute to the text's dense texture and darker tone. The contrast is highlighted by the highly broken stroke

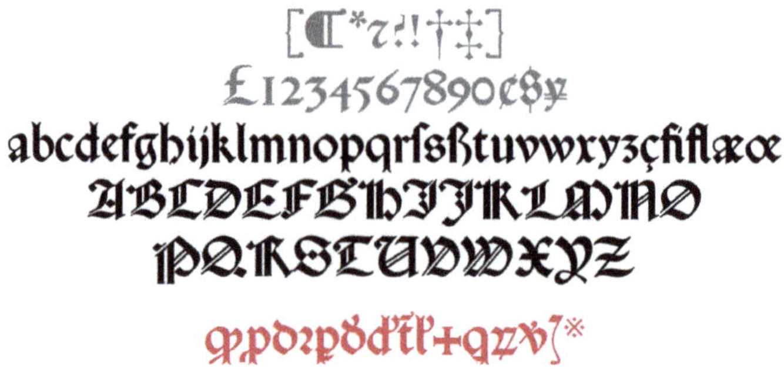

Fig. 9 *Rotunda Normal*. The last line shows special glyphs from the *Rotunda Especial* (M. Silva, 2008, p. 372)

structure. Upper case characters are embellished. The lowercase characters are the result of different sources. However, there are some conventions that allow us to easily identify this style of writing, which Pereira da Silva recreated. The double-storey a with a lower and upper bowl completely enclosing the upper section, or the g, which also has two bowls. Typical forms can also be seen in the design of the r and d, which have a short, curved upward stroke. Among the several cases analyzed by Pereira da Silva, the hyphen, accents, and punctuation symbols were also subject to distinct options. Two new sets of numerals, as well as ligatures, abbreviations, and signs, were produced. Pereira da Silva added the Japanese Yen, cent, and @ characters so that the font may be used internationally.

The Rotunda exhibition (*A memória e o carácter I - Rotunda: um semigótico Redondo*) opened to the public in 1997, also with the support of the Calouste Gulbenkian Foundation, at the Rocha Peixoto Municipal Library in Póvoa de Varzim, Portugal, featuring panels, poster, and a booklet by Pereira da Silva (Fig. 10). In this context, he has also organized and presented conferences on the history of letter forms and typography.

Andrade, developed in 1998, came up with the purpose of creating a digital version of the Roman characters presented by the Portuguese master calligrapher Manoel de Andrade de Figueiredo [1670–1735].

For this mission, it was based on Andrade's essential calligraphic and typographic work, *Nova Escola para Aprender A ler, escrever e contar (…)*, which was most likely produced in 1722. He used the facsimile edition of Livraria Sam Carlos, Lisbon, 1973 as a source [11].

The Andrade typeface, named after the master calligrapher, is made up of two families: the Regular family, which includes the fonts round, regular, and thick, and italic, regular, and thick, and the Special family, which includes the fonts special round, special italic, special thick round, and special thick italic (Fig. 11). The latter group is built similarly to the former, but it includes various glyphs and variants, such as ligatures and numbers, that may or may not appear on the calligrapher's plates. The fundamental distinction between round and italic is that the latter is narrower and has a lowercase that is slightly lower than the standard form. This is a transitional

Fig. 10 Detail of the *Rotunda* type specimen leaflet

style, characterized by the slanting bar of the e and the modern high contrast. The geometric aspect of the letterforms gives them a more static appearance. However, there is a subtle baroque quality present in some details and the play of slopes that distinguish the design of the characters and contribute to their legibility. It has a sharp contrast and a high x-height, when compared to the height of the uppercase.

The finials have some reminiscences of the writing instrument. The apertures are large, and the serifs have a distinct linear pattern that is somewhat convex at the bottom. Because they do not occur on Andrade's plates, the characters J, K, U, W, j, k, w, and others were invented randomly, keeping into account the overall structure of the others.

Following the completion of the Andrade typeface, Pereira da Silva edited a leaflet in which he summarized texts about the History of Calligraphy, Manuel Andrade de Figueiredo, and his *Nova Escola (…)*, while also displaying specimens of the Andrade typeface (Fig. 12).

In 2003, he prepared and executed the graphic materials for the Andrade exhibition (*A memória e o carácter – II: Exposição de Caracteres Romanos criados no início do século XVIII pelo calígrafo português M. Andrade Figueiredo*), which was held at the Casa da Cultura da Terceira, Azores. He also gave a lecture on the subject.

JVentura developed between 2001 and 2002, is another recreation, named after the Portuguese calligrapher, teacher and writer, Joaquim José Ventura da Silva [1777–1849]. As reference material, Pereira da Silva used the calligraphic and typographic alphabets found in the facsimile edition of 1899 (textbook and plates), made by the booksellers-editors Lopes & C.ª, from Oporto, as well as the original editions of the textbooks of 1819 (2nd Ed.) and 1841 (3rd Ed.) [11].

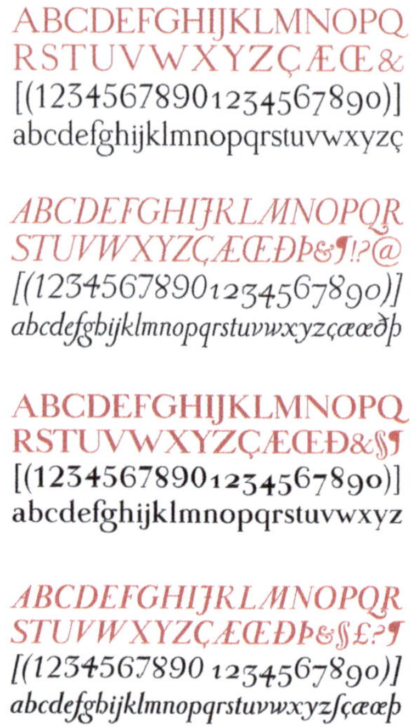

Fig. 11 Specimen of *Andrade* typeface (M. Silva, 2008, p. 379)

JVentura consists of up of six fonts: two for English Letters (roundhand), JVentura-Light and JVentura-AltLight; two for Roman Letters, JVentura-Roman and JVentura Special-Roman; and two for Aldine Letters, JVentura-Aldina and JVentura Special-Aldina (Fig. 13).

Ventura da Silva's models are distinguished for their modernity and mechanical precision. It should be noted that, in contrast to Dino dos Santos' Ventura typeface, which dealt with the less inclined *Letra Portuguesa* model, Pereira da Silva used the *Letra Inglesa* model. As a result, these are not redundant approaches to Ventura da Silva's work, but rather complementary. Pereira da Silva's first two typefaces for *Letra Inglesa* adhere to the requirements of this calligraphic model, with a 35-degree angle to the vertical plane. The contrast between the stems is apparent, and the proportions between capital and lowercase letters, stroke thickness, and curvature coherence are all harmonious.

The Roman and Aldine letterform variants are approaches to what Ventura da Silva referred to as the *Typo Portuguez*. The character design exemplifies the typographic feature of high modularity and homogeneity. The rational slant axis, square uppercase proportions, and high contrast between strokes all indicate the influence of modern typefaces, such as Bodoni. Its forms, however, are more compacted and homogeneous. The counterforms are wide, which contributes to the type's clarity. The ascenders and descenders are extended, and the x-height is medium. The serifs shape are symmetrical and linear, with rounded connections more prominent in the thin stems. The terminals acquire a drop shape, which is seen on the a, c, f, g, or r,

Fig. 12 *Andrade* type specimen leaflet. Author's edition, Lisbon, 1998

and a hook shape, which is apparent on the a or t. Lowercase stems can terminate in linear, unilateral projections with a very slight angle, such as the top of the stem of the b or d, or they can finish in an oblique cut, such as the foot of the stem of the b or the top of the q. The JVentura Special-Roman font includes a collection of old-style non-aligned figures, as well as variants of characters with an alternative design to the one presented in the original Ventura prints. They so reflect Pereira da Silva's desire to produce a text typeface that is useful, consistent, and compatible with the original model.

The assigned angle to the vertical plane is 20-degrees in the variants dedicated to the Aldine Letters. In terms of proportion, it is also worth observing that the uppercase has the same height as the ascending ones, but its stroke is twice as thick. Pereira da Silva also produced a set of alternative characters in this version, which may be found in the typeface JVentura Especial-Aldina.

In 2002, in Lisbon, Pereira da Silva produced a large-format illustrated work, in ten copies, to highlight Joaquim José Ventura da Silva's work (*As Letras Inglesa, Romana e Aldina (…)*), which was totally designed with JVentura characters (Fig. 14).

Fig. 13 Some characters of the digital font JVentura Light and JVentura AltLight and JVentura-Roman, JVentura Especial-Romana, JVentura-Aldina and JVentura Especial-Aldina (M. Silva, 2008, pp. 383–385)

Tialira is a 2003 experimental geometric typeface created by Pereira da Silva from sketches of sans-serif letters that were already two decades old, with the purpose of helping in the education of his children.

Tialira has five weights: Tialira-Thin, Tialira-Normal, Tialira-Bold, Tialira-Ultrabold, and Tialira-Heavy (Fig. 15). The development process began with the thinnest variant and progressed to the thickest, with all weights generated from scratch, without any kind of automatic production process [11].

In Tialira-Thin font (Fig. 16), the characters were structured as a square module with ~40 × 40 mm and ~1 mm stem, similar to the original designs, all shapes being perfectly geometrical, without any correction [11]. In Tialira-Heavy, the inner spaces of the letters disappear to gain more density, contributing to its strong color. The terminals change according to the weight, from a cut perpendicular to the baseline, visible in the C of Tialira-Thin and Tialira-Normal, to a cut perpendicular to the direction of the curvature, therefore, oblique to the baseline, visible in the other weights.

All letters are uppercase and of monolinear construction, with one version coded in uppercase and the other in lowercase. The characters vary both in their horizontal proportions and in design. Alternative variants of some characters are found in special

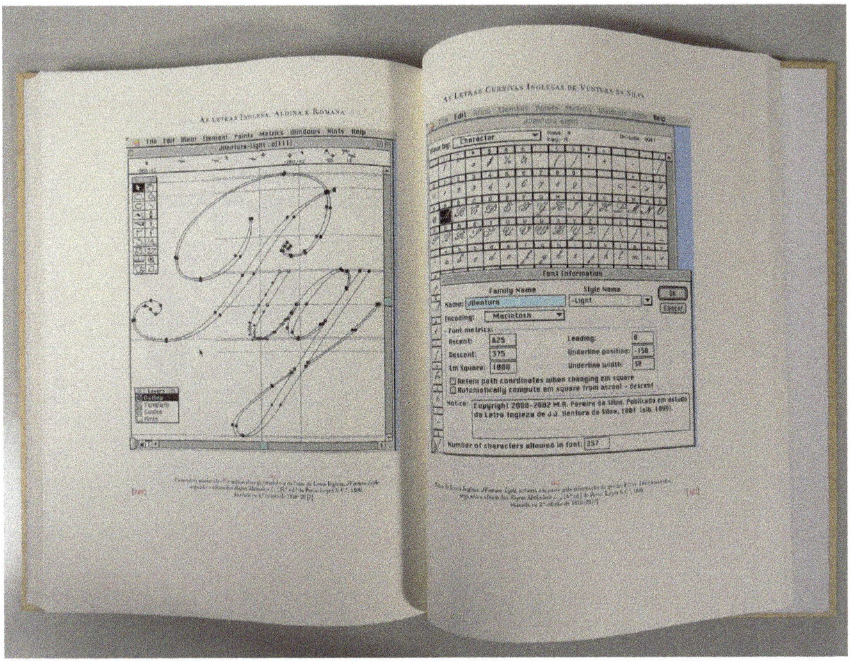

Fig. 14 Spread of the book showcasing JVentura design and production process

Fig. 15 *Tialira* type family (M. Silva, 2008, pp. 392–393)

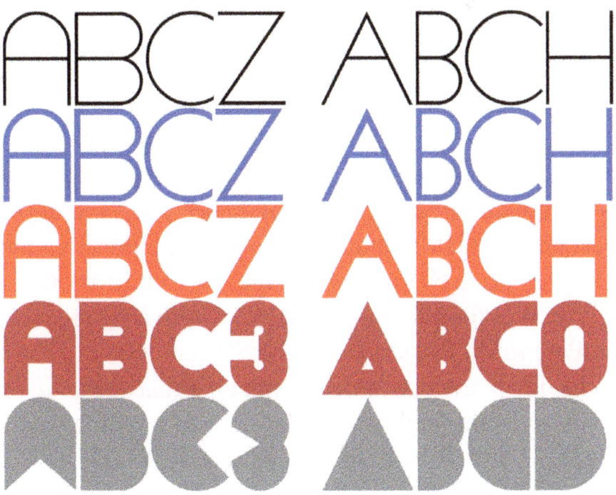

addresses. As Pereira da Silva described it, this is unquestionably an experimental kind. The first sketches, which date from 1983, can be considered Pereira da Silva's early attempts at geometric and modular rationalization of sans-serif letters.

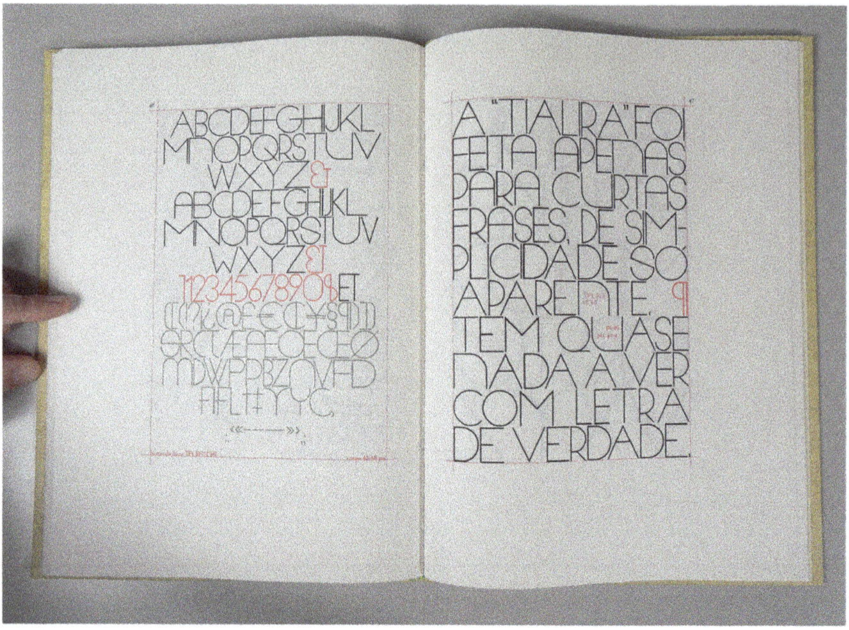

Fig. 16 *Tialira-Thin* in the book of *Specimens* from 2003

Fontanela is a handwriting style typeface designed in 2003 at the suggestion of his wife, Manuela Cruz Silva, with the intention of being utilized in educational purposes or meant for reading by a very young population (Figs. 17, 18).

The character structure closely resembles the handwriting, albeit with a slight typographic rigidity. Its amplitude displays ovoid shapes that are somewhat condensed, bringing them away from the circular shapes themselves. The weight is consistent, though somewhat dense. The lowercase always has connecting strokes between characters, and some uppercase characters can also connect to the lowercase.

Alternative characters include: o (with respective accents); s with no right-hand connection for endings; and b, v, w with a stronger loop, among others.

Pereira da Silva created the *JVilleneuve* font family in 2004, comprising eight fonts, in an attempt to depict the type that Jean Villeneuve produced for over half a century as thoroughly and faithfully as possible (Fig. 19).

The work was based on photocopies of the specimen *Os CHARACTERES*, that João de Villeneuve formed for the service of the Academia Real da História Portugueza, and the booklet *Primeira Origem da Arte de imprimir, dada a luz pelos primeiros caracteres (…)*, and also from several books from the eighteenth century that used his typeface. João de Villeneuve's typefaces were very well known in Portugal and Brazil [11]. Later, the digital typefaces of David Laranjeira (Vilanova, 2001), Paulo Heitlinger (João Quinto, 2008–2014), Rúben Dias (2015), and Mário Feliciano (Villeneuve, 2010–2017) were produced with the same intention.

Fig. 17 Text and character map of the digital font *Fontanela-Normal* (M. Silva, 2008, p. 397)

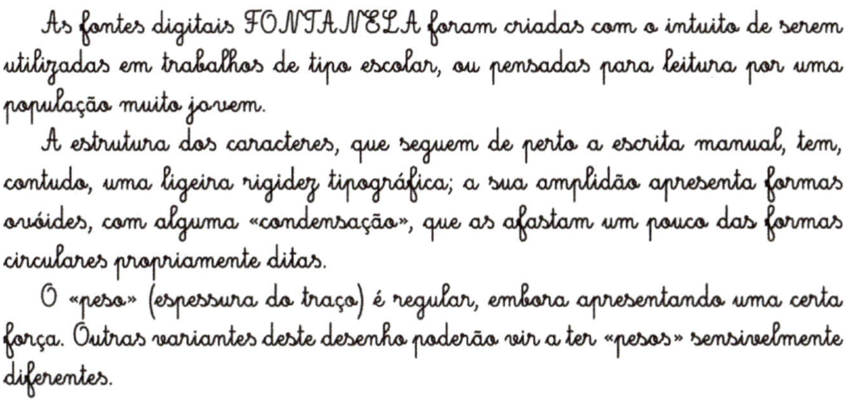

Fig. 18 Text set in *Fontanela-Normal* (M. Silva, 2008, p. 396)

In 2004, he also designed the *MBarata* and *Barata* families, which include six typefaces that differ in minor structural and weight aspects (Fig. 20). While MBarata attempted to be as similar to Manuel Barata's calligraphic plates as possible, the fonts in the Barata family are more open to interpretation, while still close to Manuel Barata's drawings. They were intended to support smaller body sizes, because they have a slightly heavier construction, less contrast, wider proportions, with less curved serifs, a slightly higher x-height, and more regular letter axis.

Fig. 19 *JVilleneuve* type family (M. Silva, 2008, p. 398)

Fig. 20 *MBarata* and *Barata* type families (M. Silva, 2008, p. 402, 408)

He designed the *Elzevir* family in 2005, with three variants for a total of four fonts (Fig. 21). Based on the typefaces used by the Belgian-Dutch family of booksellers and printers. He was interested in the structural aspects, in the narrower but classical proportions, appropriate for small book formats, of greater circulation [11].

In 2006, he developed the *Lusiadas* family, in four variants. Lusiadas was based on the printed version of *Pityographia*, and *Os Lusíadas*, from the greatest poet Luís Vaz de Camões, printed by António Gonçalves, in Lisbon, 1572. He also created three sub-species of decorative monospaced capitals based on the Lusiadas-Titling font. Lusiadas family express the desire to make a tribute to the Portuguese editorial and typographic culture (Fig. 22).

Fig. 21 *Elzevir* type specimen (M. Silva, 2008, p. 413)

Fig. 22 *Lusiadas-Regular* and one set of decorative *Lusiadas-Titling* (M. Silva, 2008, p. 420, 424)

5 Conclusion

Manuel Pereira da Silva's life path reflects an intense thirst for knowledge. His legacy reflects his restlessness and passion for books and the shapes of letters, from the visits he made abroad to acquire innovative equipment for Portugal, to the library of rare books he acquired throughout his life, to his participation in international congresses associated with typography and type design.

Pereira da Silva's typefaces were not created with a business perspective in mind, instead favoring freedom of expression over commercial contracts. He produced small pieces, which he offered to a very limited circuit of interested circles. His typefaces, on the other hand, have characteristics that demonstrate his concern for a broader, even international use demonstrating the desire to create contemporary typefaces, coated with utility and always in coherence and compatibility with the original model. His works, which range from leaflets to specimens, and culminating in his most recent work, published by his wife after his death, illustrate his research capacity and pedagogical concern for the eventual reader. Mário Feliciano became interested in type history and, in particular, Spanish typefaces through Manuel Pereira da Silva's printed leaflet (*Joaquim Ibarra, impressor*, published in 1994, in author's edition) containing texts and illustrations on the life and work of Joaquim Ibarra [8]. Manuel Pereira da Silva's attention to detail in creating and documenting his works was undeniable. The collection that chronicles and discusses the full creation process of his Rotunda typeface is an indisputably important addition to type design today, emphasizing the crucial importance of preserving production documentation, even in these digital days, as a legacy for future projects and research.

The typefaces he developed until the end of his life demonstrate his taste for classic typographic styles, which are most relevant to the history of typography and books, both internationally and particularly at the national level. It is worth noting, however, that his curiosity extended to other styles, such as the more experimental, modular, and geometric design of Tialira typeface and the handwritting style of Fontanela typeface.

However, given the subjects, styles and purposes of the typefaces he developed, especially the revivals, the intention to pursue a path around the main manifestations of letter forms in Portugal demonstrates a strong taste and desire to deepen the national and international typographic culture.

Pereira da Silva's legacy, whether in type design or through publications and exhibitions, exemplifies the essence of a singular author on the national scene. The ability he demonstrated in investigating, dedicating, and adapting himself to various technologies, as well as the influence he exerted on many contemporary digital type designers, such as Mário Feliciano, Ricardo Santos or Rui Abreu, distinguishes Manuel Pereira da Silva as a unique author deserving of national and international recognition.

By fostering creativity, dialogue, preservation and knowledge sharing, his inspiring life devoted to the study of letter forms, paves the way for an ever growing harmonious and culturally rich design landscape in Europe and beyond.

References

1. Culture Action Europe. New European Bauhaus: a promising intention and a much-needed open debate. Culture Action Europe website. https://cultureactioneurope.org/news/new-european-bauhaus-a-promising-intention-and-a-much-needed-open-debate/. Accessed 23 June 2023
2. Drucker J (2004) What is a letter? In: Heller S (ed) The education of a typographer. Allworth Press, New York, pp 78–90
3. Earls D (2002) Designing typefaces. RotoVision, Mies
4. EUROPA NOSTRA. Cultural Heritage as an integral dimension of the 'New European Bauhaus' initiative. EUROPA NOSTRA website. https://www.europanostra.org/cultural-heritage-as-an-integral-dimension-of-the-new-european-bauhaus-initiative/. Accessed 23 June 2023
5. Ferreira A (2009) Manuel R. Pereira da Silva (Póvoa de Varzim, 1930–Lisboa, 2008): o tipógrafo português completo. Grafema 1:3–6
6. Heller S (ed) (2004) The education of a typographer. Allworth Press, New York
7. Matos M (2009) Manuel Pereira da Silva (1930–2008). Revista Portuguesa de História do Livro 23:618–621
8. Quelhas V (2017) Design português de tipos digitais (1990–2010): da procura de sinais identitários à construção de uma plataforma de divulgação. PhD thesis, University of Aveiro. Retrieved from http://hdl.handle.net/10773/19167
9. Silva M (1997) Rotunda, um semigótico redondo. Recriação de um antigo estilo de caracteres tipográficos organizados em duas fontes digitalizadas: Rotunda Normal e Especial [...] [folheto-espécime], o N.º 2 da 2.ª Serie. Author, Lisbon
10. Silva M (1997) Rotunda, um semigótico redondo. Recriação de um antigo estilo de letra. Câmara Municipal Póvoa de Varzim, Póvoa de Varzim
11. Silva M (2008 [2018]) A memória e o carácter – 500 anos de tipografia e caligrafia. Author, Lisbon
12. Silva S (2002) Pereira da Silva. Da letra nasce o livro. Page 29:34–41

The Non-fiction Installation as a Form of *Being-With*

Kenneth Feinstein

Abstract This paper will look at the various aspects of documentaries to look at how they present a relationship of being-with between the viewer and the subject. Starting with Bruzzi's update of Nichol's taxonomy of the documentary. We will analyze how these forms present the documentary subject to the viewer. We will be focusing on how this enacts a relationship of being-with the other through a feeling of presence. We will see how being-with and our responsibility to the other is fundamental to the documentary. From here we will look at contemporary non-fiction installations to see how this relationship of presenting the other to the viewer has helped develop the emerging form. We will see how the documentary form has been transformed by installation. How its nonlinear format has created new ways of presenting this relationship responsibility to the other to the viewer. We will look at our relationship to media as found in Flusser and see how it relates to the idea of otherness as found in Lévinas ontology.

Keywords Installation art · Documentary film · Otherness · Testimony media archeology

1 Introduction

1.1 Immersive Multimedia?

The conventional understanding of the development of art and technology tends to be presented in a very linear path from one point perspective and the easel painting to photography, film, television, to the digital (the internet and virtual reality). Although that is a simplified and useful narrative it leaves out a great deal of technical innovation and popular culture. To not understand the impact of the panorama is to not understand its place in the development of photography and cinema as well as its place as a

K. Feinstein (✉)
Sunway University, No. 5, Jalan Universiti, 47500 Bandar Sunway, Selangor, Malaysia
e-mail: kenf@sunway.edu.my

D. Raposo et al. (eds.), *Perspectives on Design III*, Springer Series in Design and Innovation 34, https://doi.org/10.1007/978-3-031-43516-4_11

forerunner to pop culture. The fact is that elements of immersive media can be traced back to the early Renaissance, the time of the development of one-point perspective and the easel painting [1]. Central to understanding these visual technologies is to analyze and understand what each one tends to valorize, what ways of address and what kind of narratives does each form tend towards. For example, with easel/panel painting we can see how beginning with its use in churches it has been intended to present allegorical meaning as opposed to being literal. Later as Diderot defined its narrative function as being a tableaux vivant, presenting the heightened movement of a known narrative, these narratives are still allegorical. Part of how this format functions is based on the fact that the image is framed it is presented to us as a window unto another world [2]. This allows a specific way of reading the image. One where our separation from the scene gives us a distance so that we can read the image and make judgment of the message. Presenting the viewer with a Cartesian perspective on the image, one where the presence of the image is separated from judgement of the viewer. As such this form of art is one that is centered on that distance of the image from the viewer as found in the presence of the frame. When Diderot talks about the tableaux vivant, he is placing the core if the visual experience into the narrative. The image is centered on the story first and the aesthetics or possible presence are secondary considerations. As much as we read this as the primary way that most people experienced images it doesn't negate the fact that a desire for the experiential existed even before his time. Or that with a desire for the experiential, immersion and a feeling of presence tended to its own forms of address and narrative. As we become wrapped up in the experiential, we start to move away from a Cartesian experience of disembodied judgment on a remote scene into one that exists through our presence. In doing this we will see that the relationship of the image moves from being purely metaphorical into being one that centers on experiential or denotive elements to transmit information. We will see that it presents what Emmanuel Lévinas calls a face-to-face encounter with the other [3] and how that is central to nature of the work.

Let us look at how the immersive has developed from the early Renaissance to our present moment of virtual and mixed reality with an emphasis on how these forms have an important part in the creation of the non-fiction and documentary forms as we know them today. We will see how these forms focus on and present our relationship to the other as a fundamental part of their function and ask questions as to how this understanding allows us to move forward.

1.2 *From the Museo Kircherianum to VR and XR*

In order for us to look at the development of the immersive and see how it has developed we need to find a starting point. We have to ask what qualifies as an immersive work. Do we say that the cave painting found in Chauvet or Maros-Pangkep karst as they are in a closed environment where they are central to the experience? We need to see what are the common elements that allow us to say a work is an immersive installation. As stated above immersive works are ones that bring a feeling of presence to the viewer. This means that there is a sensory stimulation beyond just the visual. It also means that this stimulation is designed to engage the viewer. If we look at what we know of the cave painting or even Greek or Roman mystery cult murals, while the images played an important part in the rituals, they remain supplemental to the events within the rituals. The actions centered on performance (citation). If we take the idea that that the acts relating to the work are centered on a relationship between it and the viewer, we eliminate out most traditional performances, rituals and theater. In these traditional forms the audience is either a separated viewer as in an opera or they are active participants with prescribed roles as in religious rituals.

From this we can start to see that interactive works move away from the frame and create a direct relationship with the viewer. As this idea of interaction of becomes developed so does the need to create technologies that can create and present these actions. As Siegfried Zielinski explains in *Deep Time of the Media*, we can see these beginning in the Renaissance. This begins with the work of such people as Giovan Battista della Porta and Athanasius Kircher [1]. They were part of the movement from Alchemy to Science. Important to this movement was the not just the development of new ways to research and create new technological items, because that was still found within alchemy, but what was more important was the belief in making this knowledge available to others. The presenting of knowledge and the experiments that allow this knowledge to be transmitted is an important basic element of science. For people like della Porta, Kircher or Ramond Llull this transmission included the visual and in Kircher's case the development of an experiential museum (Museo Kircherianum in the Collegium Romanum) for the Jesuits in Rome (ibid.). Here images and sound were used to present to the viewer an experience which would present the great and esoteric knowledge of the world.

As the discipline of science was developing from alchemy and metaphysics, people like Kircher were developing new ways of understanding and depicting the relationships between the physical world and the metaphysical world. Early devices such as the magic lantern and metamorphosis apparatus[1] are made to put us in relation to the image as Other. Where the frame separates us from the image giving us a distance in order for us to understand the image a representation, the metamorphosis apparatus and subsequent devices allows us as viewers to a direct access to the image as a presence. The early uses of the magic lantern by della Porta, Kircher and others still understood the image as one of metaphor of ways of making the metaphysical presentable. It is with later inventions that we see how presence becomes more front and centre as images away from the frame become more immersive.

It is with the invention of the panorama that we start to see the development of a technology specifically designed to immerse the viewer in an environment. As a system it was developed to make a view not accessible to the public where it is

[1] The metamorphosis apparatus was a device described by Kircher in *Pseudo-Euclid* (1671) as device where a viewer sees their body reflected while their head is replaced by a projection of the sun, moon, or astrological signs. It is further describes as allowing another observer to see these images through a peep hole [1].

installed available. The first designated panorama was 'View of Edinburgh' seen in London in 1788. In a purpose built building the viewers enter onto a platform in the middle of a circular room where a 360° painted image displayed on the walls. The images shown were views of other places in the form of a landscape [4]. These images could be remote locations, such as Edinburgh to a Londoner, historical, as in battle scenes of ancient or recent history, or religious such as the scene of the Crucifixion of Jesus. Because the panorama and the later diorama are both frameless and landscape based, they tend towards the evidentiary. We take these images as having veracity. They are placing us into an event and its location for us to experience it. Where the panorama was solely images on the wall, giving the viewer a remote view of an event or place, with the diorama scrims or objects were placed between the painting and the viewer to give a more realistic and immersive experience.

Where Kircher gave us a metaphorical experience now it starts to become a documentary experience. People go to the Panorama/Diorama in order to experience an event as unfolding in time. Since the image is too big to see at once the viewer move around the platform on their own or following a guide. With the diorama adding an extra level of drama to the experience. Still in the end what makes this form of purpose-built installation work is a feeling of being able to experience what is being seen. The story being told may have a moral, it may be one that the viewers know, but it is the experience of it as an event in the world, our being-there in the event that is unique to the form.

Here we see that the experiential brings us to the documentary. It is the placing of us in a relation to what we see and hear that defines the form. This is the beginning of presenting the concept of the documentary as our seeing the event unfolding before us as opposed to having a written narrative which may utilize documents as evidence. This will develop further in the documentary film. With the invention of photography, we were able to experience images that were literal slices of time and space. As Roland Barthes said images are moments of the past captured to be seen in the future [5]. It brought us images of denotation. The veracity of what is before the lens is not questioned. With cinema this relationship was further enhanced by the unfolding of time. We now could experience events as they unfolded as real events. Where the diorama was a recreation based on a theatrical narrative, with cinema just the unfolding of images of reality came before a narrative. As we experienced the world through movement in time, the experiential became an important part of what cinema is. This is why the Lumière brothers first film, their workers leaving their factory had the power that it did. Even in fiction film it is this sense of experiencing the real that captures the viewer. Vilém Flusser says that with the invention of the camera we moved into a post-historical world [6]. We went from history as a linear progression of events recounted and organized by an author in print to a documentary, a time-based presentation of direct evidence in the form of seeing the events in question and the testimony of witnesses. Where the historian finds evidence and documents and then makes sense of it for us in a linear narrative, in the documentary we are confronted with the documentary evidence more directly. This is not to say that the documentarian doesn't try to formulate a linear narrative to make sense of what we see, but we believe it because we see the events and hear the voices of witnesses;

they carry a different weight. The move form history to documentary is precisely an attempt to become more experiential. To make sense of the world through direct encounter with the issue in question. As cinema developed the desire to be more immersive continued. Although the technology was built on being framed images, we can even from the silent film days a desire to make the experience more immersive An early notable example is the ending scene *Napoleon* [7] where a triple screen projection was used. In the 1950s Cinerama and CinemaScope and later IMAX in the 70s were developed for a similar immersive experience. The idea of formats is that the projected image should be larger than the field of view of the viewer so that there is no frame edge. As the technology of Cinerama was difficult to shoot and project Much like the panorama before it, IMAX tends to produce documentary experiential works based on putting us in places we would not be able to normally experience. Again, the form starts with the experience and only after that is established can narrative occur. We find this continuing through to the new technologies of 360° video and mixed reality. There is a draw between the experiential, non-fiction, and documentaries. This is because we are using this technology to place us in the world.

1.3 The Technical Image and How It Places Us in the World

Behind the development of our technologies there are the concepts which encase and frame the technology. They are the ideologies that motivate and reinforce how the technology presents the world to us. They can be very obvious such as how algorithms and universal Turing machines present us with a world that is driven by mathematics, or they can be more metaphorical as in how our understanding of time and self was changed by the photograph. As we look at how the immersive installation has developed, we need to investigate what are the theoretical underpinnings that motivate its development.

Earlier we have mentioned how the immersive work such as the panorama is designed to place us into the presence of an event that we cannot experience in normal life. It is not just the idea of remote viewing like we would find in a framed painting, but the idea that we would feel a sense of presence. That we should feel that we are before the events we are seeing. The fact that the panorama was developed around the same time as the idea of the sublime is linked. As we develop new ideas of how we see and understand the world we need to find ways of portraying that. Edmund Burke published *A Philosophical Enquiry into the Origin of Our Ideas of the Sublime and Beautiful* in 1757, Immanuel Kant's *Critique of Judgement*, where he talks about sublime judgement, came out in 1790 and the patent for the panorama was in 1791. The idea of the move away from the beautiful to something that is all encompassing it is a device that creates the vast visual vista that Burke is referring to.

If the beautiful as we understand it can be found in the framed painting this because the frame allows for a distance between the viewer and the image, while the panorama takes away the frame and places the viewer seemingly in the middle of the scene depicted. It is meant to give the viewer a feeling of being present facing the event before them. It tells us that we are not alone in the world. This is where the feelings of awe and fear arise, in our feeling the presence of an otherness before us. In this both Burke and Kant are in agreement even if they do not use the same terms. What is found in this sublime feeling is the presence of something beyond the self, not just other but other in relation to us. It is this feeling of the sublime as our being overwhelmed by the world as something greater than us that also grounds us in the world. If the framed painting places us in Cartesian space of judgement where we are detached from the image and we can pass judgement on it because of this separation, then the sublime places into the same space as what we are seeing. There is no ability to be separate from what we see. The movement from the beautiful to the sublime is going from a detached view to *being-with* what we see. It places us in the world. It is about the fact that we are facing the world as Otherness. And how that reinforces our understanding that our being is tied to a relationship with the Other. It is this confrontation between Being as self with the world as Other which is what gives us this sense of fear and awe. Fear of losing control of the world and awe of how the world makes a demand on us in our responsibility to it. We are faced with that which is prior to us and that from which we have arisen. For Burke and Kant this is an unnerving occurrence. It goes beyond reason; it places us in a world of immanence. As such it makes sense that the main form of image used is the nonfiction image.

As we developed forms of imaging that allow us direct access to the world, photography, and film/video, they became not just images from the world, but images that place us in relation to the world. They present us with a reality that we cannot ignore. Where the hand drawn image is created through interpretation, these images grounded us in time and place. They are created in a specific moment in the world. They carry the stamp of the denotational with them. Our belief in technical images is based on this fact. As they place us in a situation that emphasises us as *being-in-the-world* it brings forward this feeling we find in the sublime. It is not that every image will give us a sublime feeling, but that by the nature of their relation to the world they have that potential. They bring us closer to our *being-in-the-world* as they draw us closer to the world.

As we develop immersive works, we have two distinctly different directions that we can go, one that places in the world or another that places us in an imagined world. In his book, the *Uncanny*, Freud talks about a what is a feeling of uncanniness (unheimlich) and what its effects on us are [8]. He defines the uncanny as "often and easily produced by effacing the distinction between imagination and reality, such as when something that we have hitherto regarded as imaginary appears before us in reality" (ibid.). It is when our daily experiences are confronted with something that takes us away from our normal sense of self and confronts us with another as beyond meaning. Something that we must first confront as real. His definition has strong parallels to the sublime. Both are situations where we are confronted with an otherness that disrupts our sense of being. This is done because as we confront the Other, we are faced with our responsibility to it as other (an actual entity in the world). For both Kant and Freud this confrontation with Otherness in its reality causes fear and awe. It takes us away from being as the solitary entity long defined in

Western philosophy. It negates the Cartesian world view not only because it places otherness into existence, but it also places being into a physical world of dependency and relationship. In doing so, by revealing us as *being-in-the-world* it also looks to the world as fact, to it as real and not fiction. This the feeling of the uncanny. This is the feeling of coming face-to-face with the other as real. Again, we see how by turning us to face the world as it is and not as symbolic language we are drawn back to non-fiction.

By way of contrast in the same essay, Freud tell us that we can also experience works that are complete world unto themselves. These do not possess the uncanny as they are not tied to the world. The example he gives is the fairy-tale. For him they never give us this feeling because we know that we are not connected to that world. It is wholly imagined and as such remains in the world of the symbolic. We may enjoy experiencing it, but it remains separate from us. We can see this in the gaming and VR worlds. Where we may enter as characters, we may have agency within the world, but that world doesn't touch our world. As cinema has moved away from the real towards the narrative world such as the Marvel Universe, they have tried to create spectacular work in the hopes of having it be overwhelming, but in doing so they have abandoned the feeling of presence. We are kept at arm's length from what we see, it does not present us with a feeling of *being-with* instead it hopes to overpower us to take us to their world where we are merely spectators. The spectacle can be absorbing, and it can communicate meaning to us, but in the end, it depends on the work and the viewer having a distance from each other. This fits with Wagner's Gesamtkunstwerk. It is complete in itself, and we are allowed entrance into it, but this is absorption, but not immersion. We are taken into the story, we identify the with characters, yet we are always aware that there is a separation between us and it. This Wagnerian mould is one where we are given the privilege of presented with a complete world as conceived of by the artist. It speaks to us but never enters into dialog with us. To do this the work and us have to be encounter each other in the world. In *I and Thou* Martin Buber says that the I-Thou relationship can only happen through presence, and this is where dialog happens. Without a capacity for dialog, we are left with an I-It relationship, one where we make sense of the thing before us [9]. In the end while it may seem overwhelming, with the Gesamtkunstwerk we are in its presence and not present with it. Its spectacle distances us from it leaving us in an I-It relationship.

1.4 Engaging with the Audience

Buber talks about the I-Thou relationship as my being engaged with you through dialog as an active event establishing presence. He sees that to be engage with the other we have to be there with it. This is what we are calling presence to be before the other as an event. The nowness of the event is central even if we are encountering images that were created in a past. The encounter is now. To do this we have to enter this relationship as equals or else a dialog cannot happen. The event may be removed from the flow of causal time as Badiou reminds us, but it still places us in-the-world [10]. To feel that we are present in an event is to feel that we are removed from the normal world. This again takes us to Kant's sublime and Freud's uncanny. In all cases we are talking about a moment that removes us from the normal flow of the world, from our being ourselves within the world and places us in a moment where we are confronted with otherness. Being confronted with otherness places us in moral relationship with the work that draws on our responsibility to the other as themselves through and with the work we are confronted with otherness in how it completes us by grounding us in the world. If we look at the work of Shimon Attie, we see that he places the face of the other into our environment so that it calls back to us. In *The Writing on the Wall* (1991–2) we are presented with images of the pre-war Jewish community in Berlin projected back onto the building of the neighbourhood where the images were originally taken. He is placing us in direct relation to these images in a way that emphasises the reality of time and place, both past and present. We are confronted with the people who would be erased from Germany in a way that opens up their humanity to us. We see them in their reality, not as symbols of history first, there is a call to our responsibility to them found in facing them, in not forgetting. While in *The Writing on the Wall* presents historical images as a form of presence, *Night Watch, New York* (2018) & *Night Watch, San Francisco* (2021) present the face of the other in a contemporary situation. Here video images of refugees recently arriving to the US are shown on screens on barges floating the harbours of the two cities. They walk up to the camera and silently look at us. They are on boats in the two major ports of entry in the US. The placement of the video on boats in these harbours adds a context that emphasises our relationship with the faces we are looking at them. We are confronted with otherness in their face. We are called on to respond in some fashion. We cannot ignore their presence. We bear witness to them as their very presence is testimony to what they have gone through. This is how the work makes us see ourselves in relation to them as other it makes us see them and us as *being-in-the-world*. Our relationship with these faces as real people is what we feel first, we see them as people, not symbols of a political issue. We encounter their faces as silent testimony. They are not making a statement; they are just there, and we recognise this when we look at their faces. As in *The Writing on the Wall* a particular physical space is used to present the meaning of the work though its place in the world.

All of this comes together by opening up a space for the voice of the other as testimony. The act of bearing witness or testimony is one that ties us to the witness. For testimony to be given it must be to someone else, it is a call that demands a receiver. This can only be done in some form of face-to-face relationship between the persons involved. Before the creation of recording devices this testimony y could only be in person. But since invention of photography, we have been able to use devise to preserve and present testimony in a meaningful way; one that perseveres the experience of bearing of witness and the responsibility found in being the receiver.

2 The Non-fiction Installation and the Documentary

2.1 The Forms of Documentary and Testimony

What distinguishes the documentary from other forms of non-fiction is that it allows us direct access to the testimonial. Where written history is mediated through a linear text giving access to the events in question through the author, the documentary lets us experience first-hand the data behind the narrative. This is normally done either through direct observation or by allowing participants bear witness to us on camera.

In *New Documentary* Stella Bruzzi updates Bill Nichols' taxonomy of the documentary. They break it down to five forms, expository, observational, participatory, reflexive and performative [11]. For us distinguishes the different modes is their relationship to testimony. How much do they allow the bearing of witness within the work. In the documentary form witnessing manifests itself in two ways, we observe events as they unfold, or we are presented with direct testimony from witnesses. All these forms allow for this in varying amounts. For example, the narrative heavy expository form is based a traditional linear narrative told to us by a narrator as in the series, *The Civil War* by Ken Burns [12]. Here images and diaries are used as supplemental evidence to the singular narrative. Such a form allows for very little in terms of testimony. By contrast observational films like the Maysles brothers & Charlotte Zerwin's *Salesman*, which follows door to door bible salesmen is very heavy in direct observation [13]. In this form while we bear witness to events, we are not privy to the thoughts and motivations of the subjects just their actions. To varying degrees the participatory, performative, and reflexive forms allow for us to have direct testimony from subjects. A good example of the participatory form is found in the work of Erroll Morris, most notably in The Fog of War [14], where we are confronted with the life and career of Robert S. McNamara through a series of interviews conducted by the directed (off camera). The face and voice of McNamara is the core of the film with historical footage used to fill in gaps or illustrate what he is saying. He gets to bear witness to his life and the effects that his choices have had on history. While his bearing witness is the centre of the work his version of reality is not left uncontested by the interviewer instead, we are left to see McNamara's face as he is challenged as a way of judging the reliability of his narrative voice. Another strategy towards the bearing witness of events is found in Claude Lanzmann's *Shoah* [15]. In this nine-and-a-half-hour documentary we see Lanzmann as he goes from place finding different people who are able to bear witness to the systematic annihilation of European Jewry during the Nazi occupation of Europe. Lanzmann talks to perpetrators, survivors, villagers who witnesses the events of this mass murder. Here we see people in their environments talking about events of the past. We see their faces as they speak, we get to judge who they are and what they say as their testimony is presented a fairly objective way. No archival footage is used in the film, the voices of the witnesses are presented in their own environments in the present to emphasise the veracity of their testimonies. That different voices have different perspectives, that they may contrast or contradict is central to the work. As a method of presenting testimony as narrative we can see that this has been picked up in the creation of installation-based work.

2.2 Testimony in the Nonfiction Installation

While the understanding of the act of bearing witness and its relationship to the viewer comes from cinema, it is transformed with installations. The documentary as part of the cinematic tradition still defers to the director as author as the creator of meaning, with the installation the narrative form becomes more open ended. When the director has the final say as to what is real and how we are supposed to draw meaning from what we see then the testimony of the witness remains supplemental on a certain level. Because the installation exists not only as image, but also in a physical space the viewer's relationship to the how we encounter this testimony changes. The documentary as a form comes out of the traditions of written history, the linear narrative and the authoritative voice of the historian. What distinguishes it from this prior form is that it allows us direct access to the voice of the witness, shows us events as they unfold, and allows for non-linear time in its telling. As the documentary practice moves from the cinematic form to multi-experiential installation certain elements recede and others become more prominent.

As we have discussed earlier the work becomes more conversational in the way that Martin Buber lays out this idea. Where the cinematic experience is one of stopping life to be still and have the film unfold before us in a theatre, the installation can be in situ as we say with Shimon Attie or the space can be designed specifically for the work encouraging or demanding movement form the audience. We will see more about this with the two examples we will discuss later. This idea of engaging with the space is tied our second point our being asked to bear witness to the testimony of the subject. Bearing witness demands being in relationship to the other, the witness bearer. We are receiving their testimony. Although mediated it is still a face-to-face relationship. Because as the work becomes more experiential, it removes the control and voice of the director placing the function of creating meaning to the viewer. Yet since the work also is organized around the experiential, we face the witness in their humanity encountering them as real before we are in a position of creating meaning. Being-with comes first and meaning only comes later. In *Into the Universe of Technical Images*, Vilém Flusser says that we are drawn to the technical image because of how it opens up new way for us to be able to be drawn together. That the promise of the face-to-face is what are looking for in the imaging system. This promise is inherent in the technology, it is how we use and develop technology that will valorize this or turn it to other ends such as surveillance capitalism [16]. So, for him the facing of the other is at the core of the technical images that we use. As we develop documentary installations we are adhering to this principle. In both this work and his earlier *Towards a Philosophy of Photography* Flusser also states that as functionaries creating work with and through the technical image that we interact with the technical image to create unique forms, to find all the possibilities of expanding the full potential of our interactions with the technical image and the viewer [6]. If we look at the installations *From the Other Side* (2002) by Chantal Ackermann and *My Head is My Only House, Unless it Rains* (2022) by Ken Feinstein we see how this form brings the testimonial voice forward, employs the experiential, and places the viewer in a relationship with the witness.

2.3 *From the Other Side*

From the Other Side was originally created to be shown at Documenta 11 in 2002. It is based on the footage shot to make the film, *De l'autre côté (From the Other Side)* (2002). The installation is about illegal immigration into along a section of the US Mexico border where the towns of Agua Prieta, Mexico and Douglas, Arizona meet. It is made up of three parts, A single channel video based with a voice over narrative, based on US Border Patrol images from helicopters this leads us to the main body of the work which is 18 monitors arranged in 6 rows or monitors arranged so that one can see the entire work as whole or walk through the work to see the clips individually or as part of a troika. Finally, there is a large screen projection of a screen along the US Mexico border where she projects the film version of this work. The images in the installation are of interviews with people from both sides of the border as well as shots travelling along the border, in the desert nearby and in the two towns. These images give us a feeling of how it feels to experience the trek of the border crossing and of the border police and ranchers who patrol the border trying to find people slipping into the country.

Central to the work is the presentation of the voice of the witnesses, of both sides of the situation. As we hear their testimony, we see the complexity at play here. In the interviews we hear the voice a young man on the Mexico side as he tells the story of an attempted border crossing that his brother took part in that resulted in several deaths. In another clip a border guard expresses sympathy for the people crossing the border, but also states that he needs this job as he feels a lack of opportunities or choice similar to that found with the migrants [17]. This central room is one designed for the viewer to move around through to go from person to person to encounter them on an intimate level. As all the clips are playing at once the narrative arch found in *De l'autre côté* avoided. We are left to encounter each person as an individual, we must look into their face as they testify to their history, situation and perspective. The accompanying images in the towns and along the border region present us with an experience that locates us into this space. The screens are arranged in a way that gives us view similar to what we see driving down the highway with a distant horizon line implied by the road. We become present there, it places us into this world in a more direct fashion than we would find in a documentary. We are experiencing the same thing as witnesses; we are there and cannot ignore what is happening. Even the video footage from the Border Patrol helicopters places us both in the position of the Border Patrol and of those being observed. We see both sides equally in their otherness. We understand this situation as being a web of action and responsibility that all the players are part of and cannot control. In the final space we see a screen in the desert, the sun sets and *De l'autre côté* is projected onto it. Here we see Akerman bringing the conversation regarding immigration back to the site where it plays out. She is adding a form of presence to the border so that we can reflect on what is happening as it defines how we relate to the other and the responsibility that this carries. In case we are not aware of her point the name of the work is *From the Other Side* in the title she is telling us that this is about our relationship to otherness. She is telling us that we have to see the situation form the eyes of the other. In a situation like illegal border crossings the political debate happens through taking the individuals and turning them into signifiers. Making them signs instead of people. Akerman's work is designed to bring forward the face of the other in their humanity.

Akerman's case is interesting in that she had made a documentary first *De l'autre côté*. She created the installation precisely because it addresses the topic in a very different way. It is meant to give us a feeling of journey as experienced by the border crosser. We go from room to room, from antechamber to the border crossing zone and finally away from it to a space that allows for reflection. In her written work on this piece, she has referred to Agua Prieta as the antechamber while getting to a major city such as Los Angeles or Chicago is the goal where the event is over and we can reflect on it. In this way the entire area is a liminal space, and the work is meant to reflect this transition and the final projection place back at the border and also talks of the ability to be on the other side of this liminal space. The installation form here uses both forms of bearing witness as the central element of the work. We are presented with the face and voices of those bearing witness to what happens in this liminal zone, and we are given an experiential movement through space which is parallel to the journey of the migrant crossing the border into the Douglas area. The desire to present this as an installation is because it allows for a different way of giving us this sense of the plight of the other. This is reflected in her essay for the Documenta catalogue [17].

2.4 *My Head Is My Only House, Unless It Rains*

This was another project based on issues of migration, in this case migrants to Lisbon in 2022. *My Head is My Only House, Unless It Rains* was created as part of an artist-in-residence at Carpentarias de São Lázaro, an art center in Lisbon. The project was a look into issues of assimilation among migrants of varying generations. The work was in three parts, interviews with migrants, footage of the Martim Muniz/Mouraria area and video montages of religious tiles on the exterior of buildings transforming from Catholic imagery to Hindu and Buddhist. The last part was meant to reflect the changing nature of the neighborhood as it the population became more South Asian, West African, and East Asian. The work was designed with three projected screens and a single mixed soundtrack. The center screen contained clips of interviews with a group of migrants from Europe, Asia, Africa, and the Americas. This group included recent migrants as well as people whose life was more directly affected by Portuguese colonialism. The group of interviewees split into people whose background was touched by Portuguese colonialism and those who had no cultural connection the country.

In terms of the use of testimony is used in the work the closest parallels are Lanzmann's *Shoah* and Akerman's *From the Other Side*. Like these works the testimony of the interviewee is central to the work. Where *Shoah* and *From the Other Side* were shot to be used in traditional documentaries, this project was conceived of as an installation. The design of the installation was already in mind when the interviews were conducted. The nature of the installation in terms of intent and design was explained to the subjects before the interview. The interviews were conducted around a loose set of questions so that the answers from the interviewees fit together. They were asked about assimilation and any feeling they had relating to becoming part of a new nation and culture. Topics such as language and how they were treated on the streets or at a job/university were covered. In the installation the clips taken from the interviews were programmed to play randomly. This was so that the artist/ director's voice would be diminished if not eliminated. The intent was to bring center the work on the testimony of the interviewees. If there was any direct voice of the artist /director it was found in the montages, which along with the street footage was designed to be supplemental to the testimony presented on the central screen.

The design of the work was that of a three-screen projection with the testimony of the subjects was in the center large screen and the montages, street scenes and random blank image made up the side images. They were all played randomly so as to create a feeling of conversation between the elements to each other as well as including the audience in this conversation. By randomly programming what was being played allowed the images and voices to encounter each other in their own fashion and avoiding the building of a specific argument of view from the artist/ director. This work was designed specifically to enhance a sense of *being-with* the work. As we find with the design of *From the Other Side*, this work is meant to create an intimacy with the subject, bringing us face-to-face with the other. The act of removing us from the daily world and entering into dedicated space is to immerse us in the event as a space. To have us face the other as a nonthematizable face and voice. While the images of the neighborhood help us in seeing ourselves and the subjects as *being-in-the-world*. The work was conceived of as a way to bring present the migrants voices to the viewer, but also have us bear witness to that voice as a way of understanding our responsibility to the other through this act.

3 Conclusion

As we have seen the use of immersive technology has to been used to present Otherness to us since these technologies have been developed. As technology has developed so has the ways that we can present the other to us. From the panorama to the immersive installation, we have seen how we have developed ways of creating presence. This has enabled us to create works that go beyond the rhetorical and metaphoric nature of symbolic language and put us in direct presence with the other. As technology allowed us to see and hear others, we have developed work that allows us to both hear testimony and to directly experience events as they unfold. This puts us in a different kind of relationship with the work than we had with traditional art. Where that work uses metaphorical language to express its ideas here especially in the form of the documentary, we find that we are face-to-face with the other in the form of the witness and our witnessing. As we add in an ability to encounter these images in a more experiential way, we find that the call of the other becomes more central to the work. We have seen and discussed a few examples in order to understand how this facing of the other and its call is brought forward. As we look as we can see how they indicate a way forward for future non-fiction work and the intentions that the experiential carries within it.

Here we have looked at the non-fiction work only and briefly made a distinction between it and the purely fictious immersive work, but we should also acknowledge that some fictional works refer back to how we access otherness through the immersive. Such works that bridge between the two forms is also an indication of how allowing the image to be a form of presence can present us with the face of the other in new forms of narrative.

Here we have looked at the non-fiction work only and briefly made a distinction between it and the purely fictious immersive work, but we should also acknowledge that some fictional works refer back to how we access otherness through the immersive. Such works that bridge between the two forms is also an indication of how allowing the image to be a form of presence can present us with the face of the other in new forms of narrative. As Flusser has said, we develop technologies so that we can make sense of the world. That the communicative drive is central to this desire [16]. Within this drive is a need to reach out to the other and we have been creating form to enable our ability to do this. As artist move forward into new ways of creating this drive is an underlying aspect of what they do.

References

1. Zielinski S (2006) Deep time of the media: toward an archaeology of hearing and seeing by technical means. MIT, Cambridge, MA; London
2. Friedberg A (2009) The virtual window from Alberti to Microsoft, 1st MIT Press pbk edn. American Council of Learned Societies. MIT Press, Cambridge, MA
3. Lévinas E (1998) Entre nous: on thinking-of-the-other. European perspectives. Columbia University Press, New York
4. Oettermann S (1997) The panorama: history of a mass medium. Zone Books, New York
5. Barthes R (1981) Camera lucida: reflections on photography. Hill and Wang, New York
6. Flusser V (2000) Towards a philosophy of photography. Reaktion, London
7. Gance A, Volkov A, Krauss H, Woods L, Hull FE, Krüger J et al (1928) Napoleon, American edn. Metro-Goldwyn-Mayer Distributing, United States
8. Freud S, McLintock D, Haughton H (2003) The uncanny. Penguin classics. Penguin Books, New York
9. Buber M, Kaufmann WA (1970) I and thou. Scribner, New York

10. Badiou A, Feltham O (2017) Being and event. Bloomsbury revelations. Bloomsbury Academic, an imprint of Bloomsbury Publishing Pic, London; New York
11. Bruzzi S (2006) New documentary, 2nd edn. Routledge, London; New York
12. Burns K, Burns R, Ward GC, McCullough DG, Plimpton G, Robards J et al (2011) The Civil War. PBS Home Video; Distributed by Paramount Home Entertainment, Hollywood, CA
13. Maysles D, Maysles A, Zwerin C, Brennan P, McDevitt P, Baker J, et al (2001) Salesman. Criterion collection 122. RSDL dual-layer edn. Home Vision Entertainment, Chicago, IL
14. Morris E, Williams M, Ahlberg JB, McNamara RS, Glass P, @Radical.media (Firm), et al (2004) The fog of war eleven lessons from the life of Robert S. McNamara. Columbia TriStar Home Entertainment, Culver City, CA
15. Lanzmann C, Chapius D, Glasberg J, Lubchansky W, Postec Z, Ruiz A, et al (2003) Shoah. New Yorker Video, Hollywood, CA
16. Flusser Vm (2011) Into the universe of technical images. Electronic mediations, vol 32. University of Minnesota Press, Minneapolis
17. Catalogue = Katalog appendix: Documenta11_Platform5: Exhibition | Ausstellung. Ostfildern-Ruit: Hatje Cantz Publishers (2002)

Fashion Design and Product Design for Sustainability and Collaboration

Empowering Imagination in Design Practice: Focus on Knitwear Design

Giulia Lo Scocco

Abstract This paper explores the role of imagination in the field of design, particularly focusing on its possible applications to the process of Knitwear Design. In this context, knitwear is an example of both artistic design, as it is part of fashion design [Affinito et al. in The Design Journal 20:S2760–S2770, 2017; Stacey and Eckert in International Journal of Product Development 11(3–4):241–255, 2010], and of industrial design, when looking at the technology behind its manufacturing process [Conti in Design della maglieria. Strumenti e Metodologie progettuali, Lupetti, Milano, 2013; Motta in Designing Knit Designers. Teaching tools and methods to train professionals for the knitwear industry, Milano, Franco Angeli, 2019; Underwood in The design of 3D shape knitted preforms. School of Fashion and Textiles Design and Social Context Portfolio, RMIT University, Melbourne, 2009]. The contribution tackles the issue on three levels. Firstly, it focuses on the principal characteristics that the pragmatist philosopher Charles Sanders Peirce attributes to the concept of imagination and how his thought is central to the contemporary debate on semiotic and design. Consequently, it analyses connections between design and imagination [Folkmann in The aesthetics of imagination in design, MIT Press, Boston, 2013] from a philosophical and aesthetical perspective, delving into the contemporary debate on how imagination is evolving in the digital era [Montani in Open Philosophy 3(1):187–201, 2020]. Finally, the focus is on the case of knitwear design, questioning how designers can acquire the skills and knowledge required to engage creatively with digital knit technology on several levels.

Keywords Knitwear design · Imagination · Digital knit technology

G. Lo Scocco (✉)
Design Department, Politecnico Di Milano, 20158 Via Durando, 10, Milan, Italy
e-mail: giulia.loscocco@polimi.it

D. Raposo et al. (eds.), *Perspectives on Design III*, Springer Series in Design and Innovation 34, https://doi.org/10.1007/978-3-031-43516-4_12

1 Introduction

The present investigation, by discussing the contemporary phenomenon of design in the field of aesthetics, argues that designers can acquire the skills and knowledge required to engage creatively with digital knit technology on several levels.

The aestheticological dimension of design, starting from what is considered to be the incipit of its culture, namely the Great Exhibition at the Crystal Palace in London in 1851 [6, 18], is gaining an increasingly important role in the modern debate and has more recently been addressed by several contemporary authors [9, 10, 21, 32].

Mecacci's study [18], the traditional categories of design experience, such as beautiful/useful; shape/function; image/consumption, provide a characterisation of the aesthetic experience of design that tends to be disjunctive as they emphasise either a particular state detectable in an experiential subject or the characteristics that a designed object should possess in order to be positively evaluated from the point of view of aesthetic appreciation.

Instead, overbalanced by new technologies, today's context records a design process permeated by interactivity and relational experientiality principles.

Design cannot therefore limit itself to imagining 'design objects' as entities opposed to the 'subjects' that come into contact with them. In it, the poles of interaction, 'subject' and 'object', cannot be understood in a disjointed manner, but rather in a dialogical relationship involving an iterative process from problem to project, from project to artefact, from artefact to user [33].

The discussion points outlined so far can be profitably transposed to the field of knitwear, an industrial sector where innovation drives are often univocally identified with the technological advancement of machinery, risking to underestimate other types of innovation. By bringing to light the potential meanings hidden behind its method of production, Knit Designers can benefit from this discussion, opening up new perspectives for creativity and, ultimately, practical applications for the industry.

2 Thinking Through the Imagination

In order to discuss the relationship between Design, Creativity and Imagination, it is possible to refer to Zingale's perpective on the relationship between design and imagination [33], which draws on the semiotic analysis developed by Charles Pierce.

The American Scholar, in fact, linked the conception of imagination with the investigating of how reason functions and new ideas arise. According to his thought, imagination appears as something distinct from mere fantasizing as it consists in "the power of distinctly picturing to ourselves intricate configurations" [3].

Given this circumstance, Barrena [3] argues that, within Peircean pragmatism, imagination is not merely the psychological property of having images of absent or non-existent objects, nor does it consist of unlimited creativity beyond any rational comprehension. It is a way forward to organize experience, in order to anticipate the world in a meaningful and satisfying fashion.

Put differently, one must not confuse the great potential of imagination with mere fantasy, since for Peirce, the castles that we build in the air must be diligently reproduced on the ground: "Every man who does accomplish great things is given to building elaborate castles in the air and then painfully copying them on solid ground… Mere imagination would indeed be mere trifling; only no imagination is mere" (CP6.286, 1893).

Imagination allows us to see beyond what is immediately present (CP 1.38,1890) and expands our environment while enabling us to discover unexpected solutions.

Empowering imagination means permitting the continuity of thoughts, since we incessantly need to take new ideas before dropping the old ones (CP 7.429, 1893).

In sum, for Peirce, there is no other quality so indispensable for knowledge as the imagination. Without its creative work, the inquirer would have no world to explore, no determinate hypothetical situation to investigate with the rigor of reasoning.

Further in the discussion, [3] states that since knowledge, for Peirce, starts with experience, one must not forget that the first step to experience something is to imagine it.

A significant part of our reasoning happens through the formulation of hypotheses, which in turn occur through the medium of imagination.

In Peircean pragmatism, imaginary observation is essential for reasoning. We need to appeal to our imagination to explore consequences, clarify concepts and advance in knowledge [3].

According to Iliopoulos [12] the pragmatist theory of Charles Sanders Peirce can be linked as well to Malafouris' perspective, defined by the author "Material Engagement Theory[1]" (MET). Following MET's theorical view, the design intent is considered an aspect that emerges within a material engagement process, implying a cognitive dimension as well as perceptual aspects. The author developed such theory by drawing, among others, on Peircean philosophy. As Iliopoulos argued:

> MET seems to align with pragmatism, a mode of reasoning that grounds the meaning of abstract mental concepts to concrete experience. (…) Peirce, in particular, had described the relation between concepts and facts (of which material objects are a part) by sketching his famous doctrine of phenomenological categories. [12, p. 43]

A further application of Peirce's concept of imagination has been developed by the Italian semiologist Zingale [34], who argues that only by imagining the effects of hypotheses and concepts, it is possible to conceive new objects.

A relationship of reciprocal interdependence exists between the conception of an object and its practical effects. These two aspects stand together and together they merge into the meaning of the entire conception. The raison d'être of an artefact, in this sense, is formed by the potential effects and consequences that artefact holds inside of itself [34].

---

[1] Malafouris, L. 2013. How Things Shape the Mind. A Material Engagement Theory. Cambridge: MIT Press.

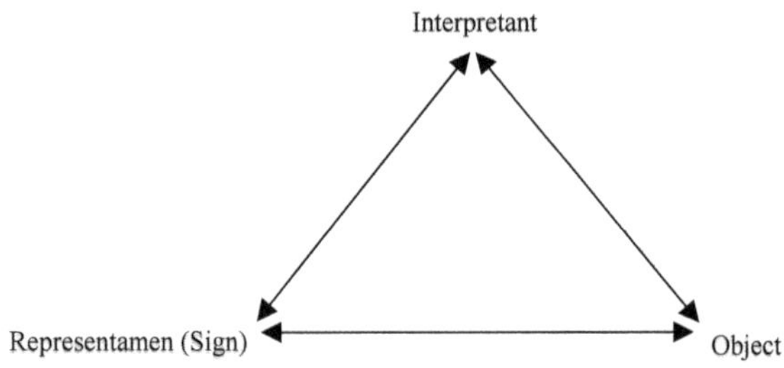

Fig. 1 Peirce's semiotic triangle

Following this reasoning, designers proceed to a reformulation of the existing objectuality through the projection of possible similarities, identifying what could be and prefiguring the presence of an absence of something possible, yet to be achieved [34]. All artefacts before being designed are, in fact, absent and possible and Design is, therefore, an iterative process that ranges from problem to project, from project to artefact, from artefact to user [33].

There is, in the final analyses, a concatenation of three elements always present and necessary: intention, form and objective [33].

The need to reestablish the centrality of the user becomes evident if the process of data analysis is approached from Peirce's semiotic triangle (Fig. 1). According to his view, a concept is formed in our mind via three interconnected elements: a sign, an object and an interpretant.

The sign is everything that can be perceived, the world as filtered by the sensor. The object is what the sign concerns and consists of the physical object. The Interpretant is the acquaintance that the observer reaches about some sign-object relation.

"Consider what effects, that might conceivably have practical bearings, we conceive the object of our conception to have. Then our conception of these effects is the whole of our conception of the object." (Peirce, CP 5. 402).

By incorporating Peirce's triadic vision into the discussion, it is possible to see how innovation in design regularly occurs in a dialogical and, in some ways, collective environment, connecting various levels of meaning, including the meaning the designer intended, the meaning expressed by the product itself, and the meaning understood and claimed by the user [35]. Accordingly, the combination and interaction of these three components provides the meaning of a "designed" product.

The triadic viewpoint that forms the cornerstone of the Peircean semiotic triangle would be lost if even one of them were missing, which would cause the total meaning to lose some of the sense that is assigned to it by their interaction [4].

In the end, the significance of a designed object lies not only in the nature of the artefact but also—and perhaps most importantly—in the potential repercussions or consequences that it may have in the future.

3 Design, Creativity and Imagination

Design breakthroughs originate from a complicated process of choosing shapes and technologies to create the most expressive result. This process of pure creativity exerts an influence on both the meaning and usefulness of an object.

For this reason, this paper argues that design inventions must go beyond the simple display of ground-breaking technologies that streamline the realisation process rather than provide novel functionality or language structures.

As a bridge builder between the worlds of art, technology, and society, the designer's fundamental responsibility is to comprehend not just the practicalities but also the significant implications of new "sign mediations" and "social garments" [33].

Based on these premises, the present investigation here proposes an observation point that, without denying the potential offered by recent innovations and technologies, tends to reaffirm the more humanistic and less technocratic dimension of a designer's inventive capacity. An inventive capacity that is not played out in the aesthetic dimension alone, but must be combined with imagination to define new uses, functions, and languages.

The conceptual fulcrum of Folkmann's contribution on design regards the relationship betweem possible, imagination and aesthetics.[2] The author views "design" as a tool that can spark creative thought processes that ultimately lead to the concretization of novel possibilities, and the aesthetic dimension of design is discussed from three points of view.

Firstly, the conceptual-hermeneutical, which refers to the understanding of the "aesthetic coding" in design modes and structures (essential in this context is the critical-constructive engagement of the imagination in conjuring possibilities through symbols).

Secondy, sensitive-phenomenological. At this level, the communicative aspects of design are emphasized and, more specifically, the imaginative engagement triggered by the sensitive dimension for the creation of new solutions (fundamental, in this context or analytical "platform," is the connection between sensible appearance and conceptual content, or meaning). Thirdly, the Contextual-discursive level. In this context, the author makes use of the aestheticization paradigm, which is a method of deftly staging (staging) and spreading (distributing) meaning. The viewpoint embraced by Folkmann is, in this third case, orientated in a "postphenomenological" sense, but it only seeks to supplement Merleau-Pontean phenomenology, not to replace it. In actuality, the investigation of the capacity of the design object to diffusely and continuously organize experience in conversation with the experiencing subject is what comes into play and shifts the focus away from the conditions of experience itself. Within this perspective, imagination is a central element of the conceptual design framework, and as such it is defined by Folkman as "the capacity or the faculty of consciousness to envision things that are not present in the physical world that surround us" [8, p. 1].

[2] The following analysis is based on Iannilli's review of Folkman perspective.

In the author's view, imagination performs a phenomenological process through different leverages.

On the one hand, he describes the sensual dimension—defined as internalization—where meaning enters the imagination. On the other hand, he identifies a conceptual phase—unrealization—, unfolding when the human mind alters and loses the original meaning.

Thirdly, he conceptualizes a degree where design, in its various manifestations, contributes to a significant paradigm shift in the way people see, perceive, and understand the world. For the author, this phase goes under the name of transfiguration.

As to better understand how the imaginary contributes to the process of making meaning in design artefacts, Folkman furthers the discussion by introducing the concept of symbolic coding defined as "the capacity of design objects to be attributed a dimension of meaning that exceeds the extension and properties of the design object" [9, p. 219].

In other words, he claims how design, by linking materiality and immateriality, transcends the purely functional, denotative elements of an artefact, acquiring symbolic meanings that give space to new possibilities.

Design performs what Folkman defines as "matrices of ideas" through material and immaterial qualities, physical-visual presence, and imaginary meaning. When implemented in design concepts, such matrices impose "coherent deformations" on the appearance of the world.

Delving into the contemporary scenario, where digital technologies permeate many fields of inquiry, the potential of imagination as a formative power of creativity is the object of an ongoing debate [11, 19, 24].

According to Montani [19], the advent of digital technologies is causing a profound re-negotiation in the sphere of the word-image relationship.

With the expression interactive imagination, Montani refers to a very accurate model of interactivity developed by Lambros Malafouris [17] and named MET (Material Engagement Theory).

To this theory, the overall design intent consists in a gradual appearance in the material engagement process and does not constitute an element either planned or constructed in advance. The specific argument that Malafouris is putting forward in material engagement is that cognitive and perceptual-motor elements cannot be treated as separate aspects. On the contrary, Malafouris proposes that we can only understand human beings by understanding the modes of how human minds become (human cognitive becoming).

In other terms, MET encourages the emergence of human ways of thinking through the practical effects of the material world:

> (…) our ways of think-ing are better described as modes of thing-ing. To explain: thinking is usually understood as something we do about things in the absence of things. On the contrary, thinging denotes the kind of thinking we do primarily with and through things. For the material engagement approach whitness and througness takes precedence over aboutness. [17, p. 7]

4 Knitting, Design, and Imagination Tools: 3D Prototyping as a Challenge for the Future

The philosophical categories and theories discussed so far offer sources of interpretation towards the contemporary prerogatives of knitwear design bringing to light the potential quiescent meanings of the technology behind its manufacturing process.

Stacey and Eckert [26] argue that researchers have not put enough attention on how digital knitting practice has evolved within the context of digital manufacturing.

For the two authors, as designers rarely engage directly with the machinery and with the process of knitting making in general, the field of contemporary knitwear seems to be an activity divorced from the idea of "craft".

This circumstance is particularly evident if we consider how the contemporary organization of labor sees knit designers having limited access to hi-tech industrial knitting machinery and their complex and sophisticated software, resulting in a sharp division between the professional figure of Knitwear Software Technicians and that of Knitwear Designers.

Put in other words, the person who manages the practical degree of the process (the software technician) is a different professional from the person dealing with its aesthetical aspects (the designer), the two having very different perspectives and approaches towards the subject.

Nevertheless, technical, and aesthetic design issues cannot be completely separated in knitwear as it is the only textile product where the fabric is created at the same time as the shape [7].

Knitwear design, therefore, remains a collective form of creativity as a knitted object is very rarely the work of a single individual, but rather the outcome of actions by many subjects who contribute to the creative process with their skills and expertise [20].

So how can knitwear designers acquire the skills and knowledge required to engage creatively with digital technology? And what role imagination plays in such a technical industry?

To answer this question, firstly it is important to frame how imagination, within the field of knitwear design, is affected by both fashion and manufacturing constraints.

On the one hand, there are technical and anatomical limitations that restrict the possible design applications of knitwear. As a matter of fact, despite the machine manufacturers' efforts to make knitting technology and software more user friendly, the digital interface and the technical prerequisites remain a significant barrier to designer, who generally access this design field via experienced technicians [27].

On the other hand, fashion trends affect the ranges of acceptable or desirable possibilities shaping the cultural meaning of design products.

As a result, knit designers usually struggle to distinguish their designs from others in the marketplace while, at the same time, trying not to be too dissimilar from their competitors.

Put differently, for fashion and knit designers, the concept of creativity is as much about balance and proportion as about the presence or absence of identifiable hallmarks.

In this context, the emerging 3d virtual prototyping and CAD technologies, when applied to textiles, are valuable tools to support designers in their projects and activities, serving as a medium to fill the skills gap that technicians complain designers are lacking [7, 29]. In sum, such technologies could offer structural assistance to designers in breaking down the technical barrier between them and software programmers, and to reappropriate the artisanal dimension they seemed to have lost in recent years.

4.1 *Knitwear Beyond Fashion*

Besides the aspects described in the previous paragraph, there is a different degree in this discourse on knitwear design to which we could apply the imagination categories so far described.

In a previous work by the author (2022), it has been examined how digital tools allow interdisciplinary applications of technologies and craftsmanship to fields that, before the advent of such tools, seemed very far away and disconnected [27].

In this sense, this investigation questions whether it is possible to assume that knitwear technology bears in itself potential possibilities of application in a broader context, away from the textile, clothing, and footwear (TFC) industry.

In recent years, many authors [23, 28] discussed how knitwear could expand from a purely manufacturing process to a design tool in the field of architecture or in that of biomedical product design, while some experiments and prototyping have been developed at various levels (see Figs. 2, 3, 4 and 5).

Figures 1 and 2[3] show the prototype Knit Candela, an homage to Spanish-Mexican architect Felix Candela (1910–1997) and a collaboration with Zaha Hadid Architects Computation Design Group (ZHCODE), and Architecture Extrapolated (R-Ex).

This structure marks the first application of knitwear technology on an architectural scale. It consists of a concrete waffle shell built using a lightweight, stay-in-place, cable-net and knitted fabric formwork. The heart of the four-metre-tall curved concrete shell is knitted. The structure's formwork is a textile supported by a steel cable-net.

Figure 3 and 4[4] show a bespoke textile installation for the Danish Pavilion at the Architectural Biennale 2018, called Isoropia.

Isoropia, which means equilibrium, balance, and stability, is a carefully calibrated tension–compression balance. These dynamically bent fibreglass rods include custom-knitted fabrics with a range of material qualities that come together to establish their balance and shape.

[3] More information is available at https://www.zaha-hadid.com/design/knitcandela/.

[4] For more information refer to Thomsen et al. (2016).

Fig. 2 Knit Candela Pavilion (External)

Fig. 3 Knit Candela Pavillion (Internal)

Rarely are structures made of a single material or in tension or compression. Instead, they comprise various components, each with a unique performance. In Isoropia, the knitted textile system balances off the stresses that cause the active fibreglass rods to bend. A stable equilibrium is created by these two components interacting. Knit is used as a textile membrane in Isoropia. Compared to conventional laminated membranes, knit is softer and less uniform, and its structure may be changed to produce different amounts of stretch in different places.

Thus, the use of the knit element as a construction material for structures and buildings has been successfully experimented within the field of architecture [23, 25, 28].

Fig. 4 Isoropia Installation (External)

Fig. 5 Isoropia Installation (Internal)

However, it must be recorded how this construction methodology still needs to be improved in industrial practice to avoid being the exclusive prerogative of academic studies.

The reasons for this are to be found at many levels but, according to the writer, the main one consists in the fact that knitting machines are not designed for the creation of large elements (the needle-bed of a CNC flat knitting machine measures between 120 and 220 cm) with obvious difficulties for the design and construction phases of such materials.

Other examples can be cited in fields far away from fashion, such as the biomedical industry [2] or the well-known case of Concrete Canvas [13, 15], a material developed

Fig. 6 Concrete Canvas soil reinforcement

Fig. 7 Concrete Canvas warp knitted material

on warp knitting machines used in emergency engineering to reinforce soil structures (Fig. 6, 7).

Despite the different fields of application, the technology behind this machinery is the same as that used in the production of fashion clothing. If this type of new use of knitwear technology continues to take hold, it will be challenging for companies in the industry to embrace such a change.

5 Conclusions

Throughout the paper, imagination was addressed as a key skill that designers must embrace as a non-institutional method for their intellectual investigation and a strategy for defining new uses, functions and languages.

It is, therefore, worth reaffirming once again how design objects are not closed entities; on the contrary, they are affected and permeably transformed by the experience we have of the world and carry in themselves layers of tacit and explicit meaning where we significantly need our imagination to unfold.

By empowering imagination, designers can envision various elements or scenarios that are not necessarily pre-determined in all their aspects. At the same time, through their imaginary way of investigation, they develop critical awareness about the values of technology.

If it is true that 3D rendering software allows designers to instantly see their idea take shape, on a different level, the resulting concentration of time between conception and realisation proposes an intuitive leap that tends to exclude not only the variety of materials and tools, but also established techniques and traditions.

Therefore, one way to move forward with this scenario might be to affirm, on the one hand, a more humanistic and less technocratic aspect of a designer's invention capacity. A second way consists in reconceptualizing innovation in knitwear as a path that strongly considers the idea that the significance of a designed object is to be found not only in the nature of the object itself but also, and especially, in the future effects or consequences that it is capable of producing.

References

1. Affinito L, Conti GM, Motta M (2017) New vision on Knitwear design: how the traditional craft methodologies are evolving into fashion international scenarios. Des J 20(sup1):S2760–S2770
2. Ahmed U, Hussain T, Abid S (2023) Role of knitted techniques in recent developments of biomedical applications: a review. J Eng Fibers Fabr
3. Barrena S (2013) Reason and imagination in Charles S. Peirce. Eur J Pragmatism Am Philo 115
4. Bonfantini, M. A. (1987). La semiosi e l'abduzione. Bompiani, Milano
5. Conti GM (2013) Design della maglieria. Strumenti e Metodologie progettuali. Lupetti, Milano
6. Dellapiana E (2022) Il design e l'invenzione del Made in Italy. Einaudi, Torino
7. Eckert C (1997) Intelligent support for knitwear design. Open University, London
8. Folkmann MN (2010) Enabling creativity: imagination in design processes. In: First international conference on design creativity, ICDC 2010. 29 November–1 December 2010, Kobe, Japan
9. Folkmann MN (2013) The aesthetics of imagination in design. MIT Press, Boston
10. Forsey J (2013) The aesthetics of design. Oxford University Press, Oxford; New York
11. Frich J, Nouwens M, Halskov K, Dalsgaard P (2021) How digital tools impact convergent and divergent thinking in design ideation. In: Proceedings of the 2021 CHI conference on human factors in computing systems pp 1–11
12. Iliopoulos A (2019) Material engagement theory and its philosophical ties to pragmatism. Phenomenol Cogn Sci 18(1):39–63
13. Jun Z, Wei X, Xingzhong W, Peiwei G, Zhihua Y, Lihai S, Jiang W (2020) Application and research status of concrete canvas and its application prospect in emergency engineering. J Eng Fibers Fabr 15
14. Kaag JCS (2014) Peirce and the growth of the imagination. In: Kaag J (ed) Thinking through the imagination. Fordham University Press, New York, pp 57–74
15. Liu S, Ma X, Ma Y, Chen Z, Dong Z, Ma P (2023) Review on the design and application of concrete canvas reinforced with spacer fabric. J Eng Fibers Fabr 18

16. Lucibello S (2018) Design, ingegno e immaginazionel Design, ingenuity, and imagination. DIID. Disegno Industriale Industrial Design 28–37
17. Malafouris L (2019) Mind and material engagement. Phenomenol Cogn Sci 18(1):1–17
18. Mecacci A (2012) Estetica e design. Il Mulino, Milano
19. Montani P (2020) The imagination and its technological destiny. Open Philos 3(1):187–201
20. Motta M (2019) Designing Knit designers. Teaching tools and methods to train professionals for the knitwear industry. Milano, Franco Angeli
21. Parsons G (2016) Function, form and aesthetics. In: The philosophy of design. Polity Press, Malden, Cambridge
22. Peirce CS, Collected Papers (CP), vols. 1–8, Hartshorne C, Weiss P, Burks AW (eds) Cambridge, MA, Harvard University Press. Electronic Edition of J. Deely, Charlottesville, VA, InteLex (1931–58)
23. Popescu M, Rippmann M, Van Mele T, Block P (2020) KnitCandela-Challenging the construction, logistics, waste, and economy of concrete-shell formworks: making resilient Architecture. FABRICATE 2020: Making Resilient Architecture, pp 194–201
24. Sennett R (2008) The craftsman. Yale University Press, New York
25. Scott J, Gaston E, Agraviador A (2021) Configured Knitting: grafting as an assembly process for knitted architecture. In: 39th eCAADe conference (eCAADe2021). Newcastle University
26. Stacey M, Eckert C (2010) Reshaping the box: creative designing as constraint management. Int J Prod Dev 11(3–4):241–255
27. Taylor J, Townsend K (2014) Reprogramming the hand: bridging the craft skills gap in 3D/digital fashion knitwear design. Craft Res 5(2):155–174
28. Thomsen MR, Tamke M, Karmon A, Underwood J, Gengnagel C, Stranghoner N, Uhlemann J (2016) Knit as bespoke material practice for architecture. Programmable matters. Acadia Post Human Frontiers
29. Vallett R, Knittel C, Christe D, Castaneda N, Kara CD, Mazur K, Dion G (2017) Digital fabrication of textiles: an analysis of electrical networks in 3D knitted functional fabrics. In: Micro-and nanotechnology sensors, systems, and applications IX, vol. 10194. International Society for Optics and Photonics, p 1019406
30. Verbruggen D (2014) The digital craftsman and his tools. In: Luscombe P (ed), All makers now: craft values in 21st century production—conference proceedings, Falmouth University, Falmout, pp 173–177
31. Underwood J (2009) The design of 3D shape knitted preforms. In: School of Fashion and Textiles Design and Social Context Portfolio. RMIT University, Melbourne
32. Vial S (2013) Le geste de design et son effet: vers une philosophie du design in B. Lafargue, S. Cardoso (a cura di), Philosophie du design, "Figures de l'art, revue d'études esthétiques", n. 25, Pau, Recensioni, rassegne, autopresentazioni, note 192
33. Zingale S (2012) Interpretazione e progetto. Semiotica dell'inventiva. Franco Angeli, Milano
34. Zingale S (2015) 'This is my Design'. Lo spazio dell'abduzione nella progettualità. In: Bonfantini MA, Fabbrichesi R, Zingale S (eds) Su Peirce, Interpretazioni, ricerche, prospettive. Bompiani, Milano, pp 257–268
35. Zingale S. (2020). Design o progettualità? Il progetto come trasformazione inventiva. Ocula, 21, pp 51–72

Strategy for Observing Trends: A Tool for Developing Analytical and Critical Skills of Fashion Designers

Layla de Brito Mendes, Ana Cristina Broega, and Nelson Pinheiro Gomes

Abstract This work aims to present a strategy proposal for observing trends directed to the fashion industry based on free content available on the internet. Based on understanding some of the challenges of the fashion design practice in the post-industrial era, especially those related to the dynamics of trends, the strategy was structured and tested in a workshop with a group of students from a Fashion Design undergraduate course. From the results obtained, through observation during the workshop and two questionnaires, it is possible to conclude that the proposed strategy can be presented as a path for the development of the analytical and critical skills of fashion designers.

Keywords Trends studies · Trends directed to fashion · Research directed to fashion

1 Introduction

Throughout history, the role of fashion in the social structure has been much discussed, and authors such as Kawamura [1] and Crane [2] emphasize the importance of the designer in this system. Although the fashion system tends to center on the individual and his social interactions [3–5], fashion changes are also legitimized through the designer's creativity [1]. These changes are at the root of the concept of trends: "A trend is a direction of change in values and needs which is driven by forces and manifests itself already in various ways within certain groups in society" [6, p. 37].

L. de Brito Mendes (✉) · A. C. Broega
School of Engineering, University of Minho, Guimarães, Portugal
e-mail: layla.mendes@ifrn.edu.br

L. de Brito Mendes
Federal Institute of Rio Grande do Norte, Caicó Campus, Caicó, Brazil

N. P. Gomes
Centre for English Studies, University of Lisbon, Lisbon, Portugal

D. Raposo et al. (eds.), *Perspectives on Design III*, Springer Series in Design and Innovation 34, https://doi.org/10.1007/978-3-031-43516-4_13

Through fashion, trends dynamics can be vividly perceived, and it is in fashion that trends guide changes most thoroughly and conspicuously [7, p. 40]. The use of trends as a source of inspiration is a common practice in fashion designers' creative process. Specialized agencies identify these trends through research with methodological rigor [8–17].

Thus, due to the efficiency of the trend reports compiled by these companies, access to this content represents a financial investment [18]. On the other hand, Seivewright [19] states that research is an activity inherent to the design process and Gaimster [20, p. 180] adds that "trendspotting and interpretation have now become a ubiquitous part of being in the fashion industry". When access to paid content is not possible or when designers want to complement it with their own research, they can look for this information online, as trend agencies share some free content in their digital environment (newsletters, blogs, social media, and content sharing platforms) as a way of publicizing their services [8, 21]. As a result, we can see the importance of having opportunities for research practices in design courses and that professors and lecturers seek ways to stimulate students' observation, interpretation, and analysis skills [22].

Therefore, this exploratory research with a qualitative approach proposes a trend observation/review strategy based on free online content to be used by fashion designers. Developed in an ongoing Fashion Design doctorate program, this strategy was tested in a workshop with students of a Fashion Design undergraduate course at a Portuguese university. Through observation made during the pilot study, as well as the analysis of the answers obtained in two questionnaires, it was noticed that trend observation, when taught and stimulated, can contribute to improving the analytical and critical skills of Fashion Design students, essentials for the exercise of their profession.

2 Literature Review

2.1 *The Fashion Design Practice from Modernity to Post-Industrial Era*

As the world moves into the post-industrial era, the challenges designers face in exercising their profession become increasingly complex. Since globalization and technology accelerate transformations in various spheres—social, economic, and environmental, for example—design paradigms need to evolve so they do not remain restricted to the superficiality of the mere desire to reconfigure the world [23]. Cardoso [23] states that fitness for a purpose is an ideal in design practice and that in this endless pursuit, it is necessary for designers to continuously question themselves about what these ideals are and if they meet real-world needs. Thus, it makes sense to bring this debate to the realm of fashion, since it is clear (mainly due to the environmental impacts caused by this industry) that designers can no longer reduce their creations to mere wearable artefacts that seduce by appearance and are disposable [24], even though the fashion system directs them to this path [1, 25].

Kawamura [1] reflects on the legitimacy of the fashion design profession as part of such a complex and constantly changing system. She argues that for a long time, the designer's creativity was defined not by his creative capacity or by the way he uses his technical skills but by his social condition [1, p. 59]. The author also argues that belonging to a high social class worked as "symbolic capital" [4]. In other words, being at the top of the social hierarchy increased the chance of being accepted into the system, within what Crane [2, p. 134] called "class fashion". Despite being an exclusive system, Kawamura [1, p. 63] makes a counterpoint by arguing that the existence of "star creators"—in other words, professionals belonging to the elite, and therefore renowned—continues to be important for the industry as designers personify the clothes and the clothes portray a particular lifestyle [1, p. 63], which attracts the attention of the public—whether belonging to the same social class or not.

The shift from "class fashion" to "consumer fashion" took place in the middle of the twentieth century. In "consumer fashion", the cartesian logic of the social pyramid was no longer the only reference as a dissemination model; tastes and concerns of social groups were incorporated regardless of which class they belonged to [2, pp. 134–135]. This change, which was only possible to be materialized thanks to technology—which allowed mass production [26, p. 41]—contributed to the "geographical dispersion" of the fashion system [2, p. 161], making it increasingly complex and plural, with the consumer at the center of the system. Therefore, the industrialization of fashion supported the increase in consumption, which led to an increase in production and, consequently, an increase in the demand for creation [9]. In the industrial context, the designer's signature ceases to be the central element in legitimizing his work, but Kawamura [1] attests that "creative production has not dissolved into the anonymity of industrial production". Thus, a possible way for designers to become relevant in the market was to start questioning which purposes meet the desires of their consumers so that their creations do not fall into what Godart [27, p. 85] called "social emptiness".

At the end of the twentieth century, the internet and globalization influenced how fashion was produced and consumed. Kawamura [1, p. 113] described it as the "legitimation of an alternative fashion system". Social networks became popular and turned into important spaces for disseminating fashion information, especially through the role of digital influencers, and this contributed to the consolidation of the fact that "fashion is a way for society to take the word" [28, p. 50]. Physical distance is no longer a limiting factor in the global market, as brand/creator and customer relationships can be solidly established in the virtual environment. However, the internet and the figure of the digital influencer contribute, in a way, to the deprofessionalization of fashion [1, p. 117], and this causes the false idea that the fashion designer' specific skills acquired during his academic qualification, are no longer necessary. In this way, it reinforces the need for the designer, in addition to his academic background, to be more socially involved and incorporate themes such as sustainability, ethics and diversity into his professional practice.

2.2 *Trends, Culture and Fashion Consumption*

Trends have become a solution to problems of modernity, as they are a way of perceiving cultural information, from which corporations can make more conscious decisions about the future [7, p. 27]. Therefore, the interest in trends arises from the curiosity to idealize how changes that are taking place today will have repercussions in the short and medium term and from the need to bring the possible effects of these changes closer to the present time, where they can be objects of action [6]. In the meantime, Gomes et al. [29, p. 5] highlight Trend Studies as an approach to Culture Studies, as they constitute an analysis of sociocultural dynamics, such as changes in mindsets and behavior patterns. Or, as Powers [7, p. 34] adds, trends are a way of "domestication of culture"—of identifying, perceiving, and democratizing culture based on its objectification.

Even though it is, in fact, more comprehensive, the concept of trends is intrinsically linked to consumption because hyperconsumption is one of the most striking characteristics of individuals in postmodernity [30]. Powers [7, p. 36] clarifies that mass production and communication were the basis for the so-called consumer culture establishment. Thus, the reading of social changes can be done by observing the consumption patterns. It is not by chance that an important publication in the field, the book "The next big thing" by William Higham [21], begins with the section entitled "The meaning of consumers", even before talking about trends. In this discussion, the author states that trends not concerning consumption are only relevant when they drive consumer behavior [21, p. 15]. Thus, in this complex dynamic where consumption is influenced by trends and trends influence consumption, trends are no longer just an optional strategic tool for the most diverse industries and have become commodities [7, p. 108], especially for the fashion industry.

In addition to the sociology of distinction by Veblen [3] and Simmel [5], fashion consumption, over the years, has contributed to the construction of youth culture and individual claims, still with social purposes, but where aesthetic values will transcend "class rivalries" [24, p. 138]. Powers [7, p. 49] states that, in this context, research on the psychographic profile of consumers was incorporated into research on market segmentation and purchase motivation, already widely used by the industry in general. There is an understanding that fashion consumption has become a means of communicating lifestyles more than conspicuous consumption [3]. Therefore, it is important to mention that Raymond [31, p. 12] refers to trend researchers as "lifestyle detectives" as they seek to identify changes not only in consumption, but also in individual and collective attitudes and mentalities, which will represent the spirit of the time.

The term "trend" occurs in people's daily lives, mostly because the media uses it frequently, mainly when it wants to indicate a probability or novelty. What the media considers a trend is aligned with individuals' massive understanding of it as a noun (in the literal sense). In other words, it consists only of its representations in the visible field [29]. Vejlgaard [32, p. 5] explains that when people show interest and talk about trends, it is because they are looking for information about things that already exist and are in the process of being massively popularized, such as a new style, a new product or service. Concerning fashion, searching for "fashion trends[1]" on the internet will lead to results about colors, prints, shapes, products, or specific styles already materialized in garments, footwear, and accessories. In the post-modern context, where the tastes and opinions of individuals change very quickly, more than ever, the fashion industry makes use of programmed obsolescence and launches many "new" products, which are nothing more than "superfluous updates" [7, p. 49], only intending to stimulate consumption. In this context, Raybould [22] emphasizes the importance for fashion designers to use the so-called short-term forecasts[2] with caution because, despite collaborating for the maintenance and profitability of the business, they contribute to the perpetuation of problems such as excessive consumption, which generates environmental and social problems.

2.3 *Trends as a Tool for Developing Fashion Designer's Analytical and Critical Skills*

Trend Studies are on their way to consolidation in the academic field, while as a business practice can already be considered more established. Although there are still ways to go in its consolidation, some points are already consensual both in academia and in the market, and one of them is the fact that professionals involved in the trend analysis process need specific skills. Because it is a deep and complex research process, it requires skills such as curiosity to conduct data collection and interpretive, analytical, and critical abilities to identify patterns that will point out the trend [6, 7, 21, 31, 34].

One of the issues that academic researchers have dedicated themselves to studying is the pragmatic nature of trend forecasting, especially regarding understanding the methodologies used and under what conditions these methodologies are applied, since Trend Studies articulate concepts and methods from other areas, such as anthropology, marketing, design, and fashion [6, 7, 21, 31, 32, 35]. However, aspects such as the project's particularities, the speed at which the market demands results, and even the researchers' expertise can lead to the adaptation or fusion of methods that are used [6, 7]. In general terms, Gomes et al. [29] systematically present a roadmap for identifying sociocultural trends, summarized in four points. This script was proposed based on an extensive literature review, and it represents the consensus of what is portrayed by the main authors in the area (such as Powers [7]; Dragt [6]; Raymond

[1] Gomes et al. [33, pp. 14–15]; clarify that the usage of the expression "fashion trends" is problematic since fashion and trend are two types of patterns. Therefore, saying "fashion trend" is similar to say "pattern of a pattern", which is redundant.

[2] Short-term forecasts are relative to a time horizon of up to 2 years. For the fashion industry, these forecasts are related to the design elements, such as shapes, silhouettes, textures, and product details [16, p. 32].

[31]; among others): (1) Determining zeitgeist topics, such as space–time contextualization of the research; (2) Data collection, through observation, and subsequent systematization and in-depth analysis; (3) The trend architecture construction, in other words, presenting its nature and main aspects that characterize it; and (4) Analysis validation process, where the title, the trend text and its content are validated by specialists or by the research team itself [29, p. 245].

Based on the Gomes et al. [29] script, reflecting on its four points is valid in the light of trend forecasting aimed at the fashion industry. Regarding point 1, the zeitgeist perception and interpretation are relevant as it directly affects fashion consumption [16, p. 13]. Regarding point 2, it is known that the research practice (observation and data collection) not only contributes to the construction of the designer's reference repertoire—important to stimulate his creative process—but also makes him leave his comfort zone, developing a broader vision of the world [22]. Regarding point 3, being aware of the trend nature and its main characteristics are essential so the designer can, from these aspects, be able to translate them into visual elements (materialize the creations). So, the endogenous logic of fashion change is completed by an exogenous perspective [27, p. 85]. And finally, regarding point 4, the validation process of the analysis leads the designer to review and reassess the nature of the trend, and this critical look can contribute to improving the consumers' relationship with fashion [22], especially concerning their individuality and conscious consumption.

3 Methodology

This article presents part of a doctoral exploratory research in Fashion Design with a qualitative approach. The objective here is to present the results obtained in a workshop, where a strategy proposal for the observation of trends (directed to fashion) from the free content available online was used in a pilot study.

3.1 Trend Observation Strategy to Be Used by Fashion Designers

The proposed trend observation strategy corresponds to a set of activities organized into four stages, to be carried out preferably by a team of professionals. These steps were idealized based on design thinking, as from the literature review it was possible to observe similarities between the convergent (creating choices) and divergent (making choices) phases with the trend analysis process. Figures 1 and 2, respectively, Brown's [36] convergent and divergent thinking scheme and the trend observation strategy scheme.

Step (1) of the strategy corresponds to preparation. It consists of describing the project briefing (supposedly already prepared) and resuming the aspects that will

Fig. 1 Divergent and convergent thinking [36]

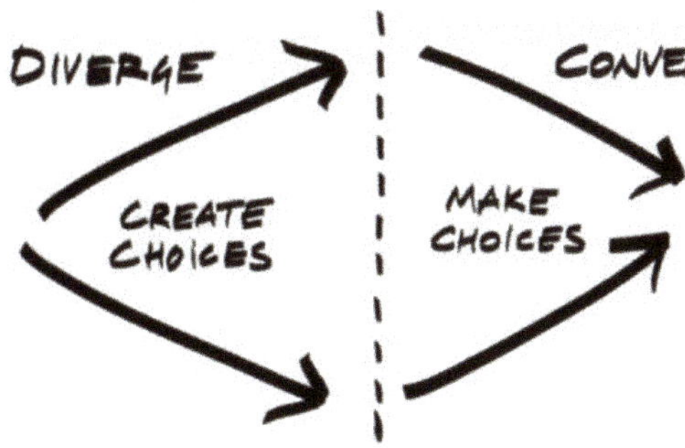

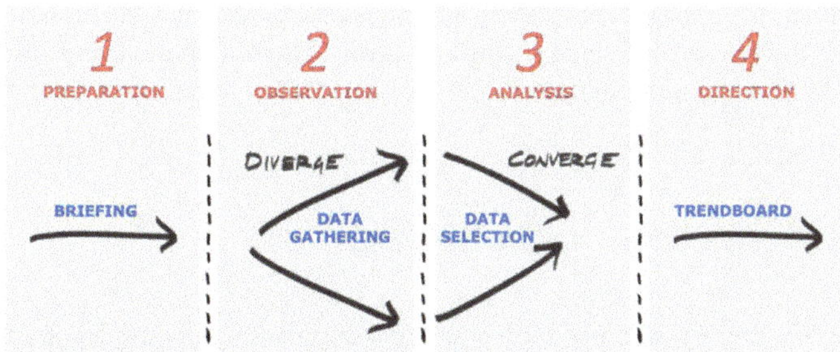

Fig. 2 Strategy for observing trends (2023), adapted from Brown [36]

delimit the creative process. In the case of these participants, the project in question was developing a fashion collection. From the briefing, the team must indicate the objective it intends to achieve with the research execution, and this must be more complex than the superficial curiosity of knowing a color or a style element that will attract the attention of the media in the next season. The research objectives must, then, be linked to some design problem since the solution to these problems can be found in the new patterns that are emerging in society, in the most diverse areas—patterns that characterize the trends.

Next, the team must proceed to the execution of step (2), observation. This is the stage where data collection, such as trend observation through desk research, will be carried out properly. This step was named observation because the directive is that designers should carry out the desk research based on the trends content available online by specialized agencies, free of charge—trends already pointed out.[3] From the trend agencies, the team can expand its search for more free content online, thus building its own list of references. As content is observed and collected, designers must systematize it, as it contributes to the identification of converging points obtained from the most diverse sources consulted (i.e. patterns) and facilitates

[3] In the meantime, Mendes et al. [8] analyzed the content of open-access trends made available online by a sample of ten consolidated trend agencies in the fashion market. The authors attested that these companies provide a significant amount of free content, and this material can be helpful for fashion designers' creative process.

the analysis process. Thus, the observation stage stimulates divergent thinking, where the collected data opens space for the creation of choices [36].

Step (3) concerns the observed trends analysis. At this point, the team should discuss the collected data, considering the aspects described in the project briefing. This phase of the process is important because not everything that seems interesting at the time of observation will, in fact, be useful for the project in question. At this stage, convergent thinking is then stimulated. Based on the analysis, the team should be able to select the trends that will, in fact, support the creative process, in other words, make choices [36].

Finally, the process proceeds to its final step, (4) targeting. From the selected trends, the team must then build a trend board. This board will work as a visual source of inspiration, from which designers can extract elements that will materialize and characterize their creations, such as colors, textures, prints, shapes, and silhouettes—the so-called design visual elements [37–39].

3.2 *The Trends Observation Workshop*

The proposed strategy was put into practice through a workshop by a group of 35 students in the final year of the bachelor's degree in Fashion Design and Marketing at the University of Minho (in the city of Guimarães, Portugal) (Fig. 3). The workshop took place in October 2022 and lasted a total of 8 h, divided into two meetings of 4 h each, with an interval of one week between the two sessions. It is important to highlight that the two sessions took place within the curricular unit "Fashion Trends and Semiotics", so the students previously had a theoretical contextualization about trends. As a resource, participants used laptops connected to the internet and the Miro digital platform (http://miro.com), free to use, where teams could work collaboratively.

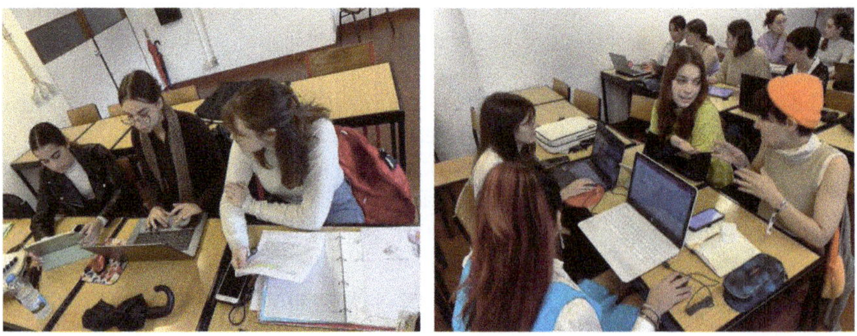

Fig. 3 Fashion Design undergraduate Students attending the trend observation workshop, at the University of Minho, in Portugal, October 2022

The first session began with the workshop presentation and the application of a diagnostic questionnaire, answered by each student individually. This questionnaire consisted of ten questions: seven were closed, and three were open. The objective of the initial questionnaire was to find out about the students' access to trend information and their opinion about the use of trends in the creative process. After answering the questionnaire, the students were divided into teams (seven teams with five members each) and began the execution of steps 1 and 2 of the proposed strategy. At the end of the first session, students were asked to continue with desk research until the next session in their free time. In the second session, steps 3 and 4 of the strategy were carried out, ending with an evaluation questionnaire to be answered individually. The evaluation questionnaire had twelve questions, where 10 were closed questions, and 2 were open questions. The final questionnaire objective was to evaluate the use of the presented strategy and leave space for critics or improvements suggestion.

4 Findings

At the end of the workshop, each of the seven groups created a trend board with the selected contents after observation and analysis. However, the evaluation of the content of these panels, whether the content was really aligned with the briefing of each project, was not part of the scope of this research. The objective here was to evaluate the feasibility of using the proposed strategy so that the results could be verified through observations during the workshop and the answers obtained in the two questionnaires conducted.

4.1 Diagnostic Questionnaire

The diagnostic questionnaire, applied at the beginning of the workshop's first session, was answered by 32 participating students. As they were students in the last year of the Fashion Design undergraduate course and because the workshop took place in the curricular unit "Fashion Trends and Semiotics", they already knew that using trends is a common practice in the fashion industry. When asked how often they look for trend information, 59.4% answered that they rarely look for it, and 40.6% answered that they often look for it. The fact that the majority indicated that they rarely look for it can demonstrate a need to encourage students better to research practices, especially the observation of trends, to contextualize their creative process and support in decision-making.

Then, students could indicate where they usually look for trend information in a multiple-choice question. The options given and their respective incidences were as follows: 71.9% chose specialized media (special edition magazines and fashion websites, for example); 71.9% mentioned fashion events (fashion shows, fashion weeks and fairs); 56.3% chose fashion brands; 56.3% marked social networks; 50%

indicated specialized companies/agencies; 37.5% marked celebrities or influencers; 21.9% indicated making their own observation, personally, in stores and shopping centers; and 15.6% subscribed to the traditional media (newspapers and magazines in general). Based on these responses, it was possible to notice that students search for trends in specific fashion sources. However, in these sources, the content is only sometimes clearly and correctly categorized as a trend, so this identification must be made by those who observe it. Alternatively, it can even be categorized as a trend, but it actually represents just a personal opinion and not an emerging pattern of a social group (as it is common in social networks or through celebrities and influencers). Only 50% of the incidences corresponded to specialized companies/agencies, where the disclosed content is clearly signaled as a trend and was obtained by trained researchers through methodological rigor.

Next, students were asked if they had already had access to some trending content developed by specialized agencies/companies, and 96.9% said yes. When asked where, the incidences were as follows: 100% subscribed to trends portals through subscription access (paid); 41.9% indicated content released for free on the internet; 35.5% indicated free in-person events (courses, lectures, and workshops); 19.4% indicated trend books or other printed material (paid); and 6.5% indicated free online events (courses, lectures, and workshops). There was no incidence of the paid in-person events (courses, lectures, and workshops) and paid online events (courses, lectures, and workshops) options. In this context, students were also asked which trend agencies they had already consulted or used to consult, and 100% of the answers indicated the British agency WGSN (http://wgsn.com). This was because the students had access to the WGSN trends portal during the course through a subscription paid by the university. Another aspect is that, as they are inserted in the academic environment, these students eventually have the opportunity to access paid trends content offered by the university or by trends companies/agencies' actions aimed at students as a form of dissemination of your services. Even so, the high incidence of searches for open access trends on the internet demonstrates interest in this type of content, reiterating the space for using such strategies.

Finally, regarding the use of trends in their creative process, 50% of students indicated that trends help a little, 37.5% indicated that trends help their creative process a lot, and 12.5% indicated that trends do not help their creative process. Moreover, about this issue, some comments were made, such as "they help to decide a direction that may be more appealing to the consumer", "some elements of trends can influence the creative process from shapes, textures and colors that may appeal to the public taking into account the state of society at the time", "a little limiting for the creative process, but very useful for the product development and its commercialization". Therefore, students knew the potential of using trends in the creative fashion process.

4.2 Evaluation Questionnaire

The evaluation questionnaire, applied at the end of the workshop's second session, was answered by 25 participants. Seven of the twelve questions corresponded to evaluation through the Likert scale (where numbers 5 and 4 indicate positive opinions, number 3 indicate neutral opinions, and numbers 2 and 1 indicate negative opinions). In all seven questions, the answers were mostly positive (Fig. 4).

Regarding the workshop duration, 76% of respondents stated that the duration was sufficient, and 24% indicated that the duration was short. Furthermore, when asked if they had used any other research source besides the indicated trend agencies, only 24% answered yes. In this context, even though most respondents indicated that the workshop duration was sufficient, one of the difficulties was encouraging them to expand the search for trends in other sources to deepen their research. This point can be better understood by considering the fact that the age group of the participating students was from 19 to 25 years old, in other words, from Generation Z. Despite being considered 'digital natives', Generation Z people seeks instant results [40]. Another important aspect to underline is that students who reported having consulted other sources indicated Instagram. Djafarova and Bowes [40] state that Generation

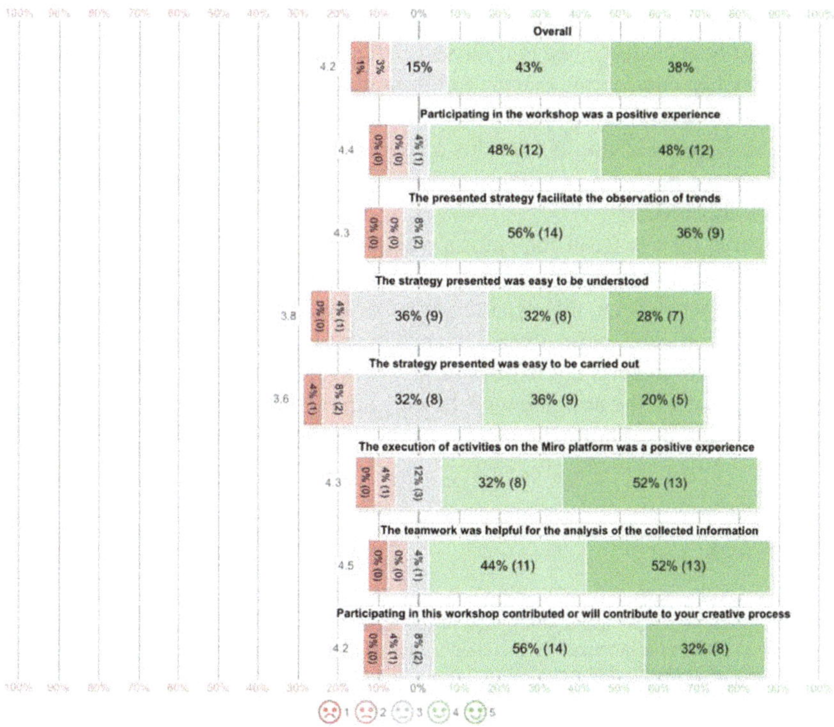

Fig. 4 Overview of the answers obtained in the evaluation questions through the Likert scale

Z people spend many hours connected to the internet daily, especially using social networks and prefer communication through images rather than text. However, the content flagged as a 'trend' on social networks must be carefully evaluated by those who research it, as it may be an advertising tool or an individual's opinion.

Finally, some participants commented about the experience of participating in the workshop, which will be considered in further investigations. In their assessment, they indicated that some content was too far from being incorporated into their creative practice at that time, particularly about technology and sustainable solutions (due to access or budget). Others reported that aspects such as textures and materials took more work to be found. On the other hand, finding references related to colors was straightforward. Furthermore, they showed little concern with content found in idioms they did not master, thus indicating the need to encourage them to include a local view in their research besides the global one.

5 Considerations

The analytical and critical skills of the fashion designer, when well used, can contribute to building and improving the consumer's relationship with fashion in all its nuances. Topics such as sustainability, ethics, diversity, and concern for the future must be included in the daily lives of all professionals in this immense chain, especially when considering that the future is increasingly collaborative. In the post-modern world, reading the spirit of the time is a necessary practice, whatever the professional specialization is, and this activity can be better developed when stimulated from the beginning of their academic path through strategies and tools that streamline this process.

The search for free trend content is a practice that does not intend to discredit the work of agencies and specialized professionals. The intention, then, is to bring the fashion designer closer to this dynamic, reinforcing that, regardless of how time will change this profession, curiosity and interest in research need to remain fundamental practices. Trend analysts are experts in proposing solutions according to society's movements, but it is the designer who, based on the autonomy of his creative process, effectively takes this information to the public through products and services.

References

1. Kawamura Y (2005) Fashion-ology: an introduction to fashion studies. Berg
2. Crane D (2000) Fashion and its social agendas. The University of Chicago Press
3. Veblen T (2018) A teoria da classe do lazer. Conjuntura Actual Editora
4. Bourdieu P (2010) A Distinção: uma crítica social da faculdade do juízo, 1st edn. Edições 70
5. Simmel G (2008) Filosofia da moda e outros escritos. Edições Texto & Grafia
6. Dragt E (2017) How to research trends. BIS Publisher
7. Powers D (2019) On trend: the business of forecasting future. University of Illinois Press

8. de Brito Mendes L, Broega AC, Gomes NP (2023a) Online trend observation: analysis of free content available by fashion-directed agencies. In: Broega AC, Cunha J, Carvalho H, Providência B (eds) Advances in fashion and design research. Springer International Publishing, pp 62–75. https://doi.org/10.1007/978-3-031-16773-7_6
9. de Brito Mendes L, Broega AC, Gomes NP (2023b) Trends in the fashion sector: an analysis of their use and paths for the researcher profession. In: Raposo D, Neves J, Silva R, Castilho LC, Dias R (eds) Advances in design, music and arts II. Springer Nature, pp 298–311. https://doi.org/10.1007/978-3-031-09659-4_23
10. Campos AQ (2021) "Eu não sigo tendência": o uso e o não uso de relatórios de tendências de moda por designers no Brasil e na Alemanha. Dobra [s]: Rev Da Assoc Bras Estud Pesqui Em Moda 32: 153–167. https://doi.org/10.26563/dobras.i32.1371
11. Campos AQ (2017) Of tradition and creation: the discourse of fashion designers on trend report usage [PhD thesis, Universidade Federal de Santa Catarina]. https://repositorio.ufsc.br/handle/123456789/185500
12. Holland G, Jones R (2017) *Fashion trend forecasting*. Laurence King Publishing
13. Rech SR, Gomes NP (2016) Anatomia das tendências e o desenvolvimento de produtos de moda. 12° Colóquio Moda-9A Edição Int 1–13. http://www.coloquiomoda.com.br/anais/Coloquio%20de%20Moda%20-%202016/GT/GT04-DESIGN-E-PROCESSOS-DE-PRODUCAO-EM-MODA/GT-04_ANATOMIA-DAS-TENDENCIAS.pdf
14. Kim E, Fiore AM, Kim H (2011) Fashion trends: analysis and forecasting. Berg
15. McKelvey K, Munslow J (2008) Fashion forecasting. Wiley-Blackwell
16. Brannon EL (2005) Fashion forecasting, 2nd edn. Fairchild
17. Perna R (1987) Fashion forecasting. Fairchild Publications
18. de Brito Mendes L (2014) Metodologias de coolhunting aplicadas à criatividade em moda: estudo de caso empresa tendere [Masters Thesis, Universidade do Minh0]. https://hdl.handle.net/1822/33976
19. Seivewright S (2009) Pesquisa e design. Bookman
20. Gaimster J (2011) Visual research methods in fashion. Berg
21. Higham W (2009) The next big thing: spotting and forecasting consumer trends for profit. Kogan Page
22. Raybould C (2022) Trends forecasting as a tool for sustainable education. Fash Style Popul Cult 9(3):383–396. https://doi.org/10.1386/fspc_00058_1
23. Cardoso R (2013) Design para um mundo complexo. Cosac Naify
24. Lipovetsky G (2009) O império do efêmero: a moda e seu destino nas sociedades modernas. Companhia das Letras
25. Lynch A, Strauss MD (2007) Changing fashion: a critical introduction to trend analysis and meaning. Berg
26. Svendsen L (2010) Moda uma filosofia. Zahar
27. Godart F (2010) Sociologia da moda. Senac SP
28. Erner G (2015) Sociologia das tendências. Editora Gustavo Gili
29. Gomes NP, de Mendonça Cohen SA, Cantú WA, Lopes CMA (2021) Roteiros e modelos para a identificação de tendências socioculturais e a sua aplicação estratégica em produtos e serviços. Modapalavra E-Periódico 14(32): 229–272. https://doi.org/10.5965/1982615x14322021228
30. Lipovetsky G (2007) A felicidade paradoxal: ensaio sobre a sociedade do hiperconsumo. Companhia das Letras
31. Raymond M (2010) The trend forecaster's handbook, 1st edn. Laurence King Publishing
32. Vejlgaard H (2008) Anatomy of a trend. McGraw-Hill
33. Gomes N, Lopes MV, Alves PE (2016) Coolhunting e estudos de tendências aplicados à moda: modelo de segmentação estratégica. ModaPalavra 9(17):06–26. https://doi.org/10.5965/1982615x09172016006
34. Kongsholm LB, Frederiksen CG (2018) Trend sociology 2.0. Pej Gruppens Forlag
35. Gomes NP, de Mendonça Cohen SA, Flores AMM (2018) Estudos de tendências: contributo para uma abordagem de análise e gestão da cultura. Modapalavra e-periódico 11(22). https://doi.org/10.5965/1982615x11222018049

36. Brown T (2009) Change by design: how design thinking transforms organizations and inspires. HarperBusiness
37. Löbach B (2001) Design industrial. Blucher
38. Baxter M (2011) Projeto de produto, 3rd edn. Blucher
39. Treptow D (2013) Inventando moda: planejamento de coleção, 5th edn. Edição da Autora
40. Djafarova E, Bowes T (2021) 'Instagram made Me buy it': generation Z impulse purchases in fashion industry. J Retail Consum Serv. https://doi.org/10.1016/j.jretconser.2020.102345

Concepts and Material Futures in Fashion and Textile

Maria Antonietta Sbordone and Gianni Montagna

Abstract Change in production fields such as Fashion and Textiles, which are complex and intricate by nature, requires a new predictive capacity. Research and experimentation are the most appropriate terms of reference to build advanced perspectives that today, more than ever, look at the fundamental balance between artificial and natural. The approach or posture of design for Fashion acting in the present day cannot disregard multidisciplinary involving different disciplines and productive sectors. In disciplinary, design and production fields such as Fashion and Textile, the culture of design and the critique of the current production and consumption model, result in a digital model that transforms the logic of making in a predictive key. The objectives of productivity and consumption-oriented towards sustainability should consider the paradigm of organic meets digital and the latter expresses a mutualistic behavior that builds a solid perspective to drive change.

Keywords Predictive capacity · Artificial natural · Mutualistic behavior

1 Introduction

A useful speculation on the current content of Fashion and Textile, especially when discussing the necessary revision of the processes that shape the supply of manufactured goods that circulate globally, and from whose circuits it seems impossible to escape, imposes a reflection then an attitude.

The latter requires a *posture* that opposes the current set-up to disrupt unfailing certainties. Otherwise, there is a risk of a general flattening out on issues that are certainly urgent, the effects of indiscriminate action that cannot be definitive and to which concrete and feasible alternatives must be given. The questions coming back

M. A. Sbordone (✉)
Università Degli Studi Della Campania "Luigi Vanvitelli", 81031 Aversa, CE, Italy
e-mail: lncs@springer.com

G. Montagna
Lisbon School of Architecture, Universidade de Lisboa, 1349-063 Lisboa, Portugal

D. Raposo et al. (eds.), *Perspectives on Design III*, Springer Series in Design and Innovation 34, https://doi.org/10.1007/978-3-031-43516-4_14

today more than ever concern: the identity that is divided between many belongings that form a fluid and often inconsistent, and changeable human nature; the individual and collective ability to create a cognitive-technological surplus that is transformed into a productive and consumer surplus; the inability of local economies to be autonomous from the circuits of the world-economy that neutralizes every difference and singularity; the shared urgency to form and transfer knowledge between human and natural ecosystems [3].

These are some of the questions that trouble society and consequently the markets and that have serious consequences on the fashion system and necessitate a change.

These questions require a different perspective that investigates beyond the systems, recognizes the immanent causes whose effects must be responded to and above all remedied. Specialists ask where and when the dialogue between the design and creative culture of Fashion that was revealed in a high cultural, material and manufacturing quality is no longer detectable in the objects that satisfy the need to dress; how is the representation of the self-realized today in the digital era and how do belongings become explicit; how do we reconcile the relationship with the context that is not only social and cultural, but of the human being immersed in the virtual dimension and, despite everything, at the opposite in the natural one; furthermore, bio-digital couture may constitute a profitable ambivalence to access a new paradigm.

Questions that arise within the critical reflection on contemporary fashion, of design and production models inspired and guided by the lead-to-time productivity paradigm that pursues the creation of surplus value that is non-distributable, non-accessible and, at best, a generator of inequalities, otherwise conflicts.

The complexity of the socio-political-economic system, as we live it, implement it, and perceive it today, includes another dimension; from the more sensitive one of experientialization which sets in motion emotional levers with a strong appeal to a different degree of perception of oneself and of the environment, to those, now widely tested, attributable to the neutral acceptance of the innumerable challenges of everyday life. There is an obligation to equip oneself with new instruments of field investigation and speculative/imaginative observation to recover a margin of critical constructiveness which establishes man's ability to prefigure, predict, formulate worlds, to behave like a mystic futurist or better yet, a reliable prescient on the fate of humanity on earth, ever forward into a plausible future [15].

On the side of reflection and criticism of the current model of life and development, the heterodox narrative proposes new methods of indoctrination, understood as a profound reconnection of man to nature which acts in the psychological sphere, representing new possible approaches.

The man-nature relationship is widely described as decisive and on the verge of a clear break [2], recounting the laceration of ties, the devastation of ecosystems, and the impoverishment of the ethno-zoo-botanical genetic heritage. The prefigured scenario outlines a field of reflection on survival by reflecting on the one hand, on the announced disappearance of man on earth, launching an appeal to human persistence,on the other, on the role of the repairman through tools for developing a new thought that requires an awareness that goes beyond data and statistics [2].

Reacting to the current crisis takes various forms, repairing the lost man-nature bond and identifying interventions requires an anthropological change that brings the new approach of doing to its goal, foreseeing all its effects.

On the other hand, the trusted prescient bases his imaginative knowledge on the premonition fueled by the fantasy of an expert futurist; in psychology, these are called 'self-fulfilling prophecies' [9] and lead to finding and interpreting data in such a way that our expectations are met, allowing us to act positively, to raise the level of awareness.

The self-fulfilling prophecy matrix responds to the identification of a purpose that motivates the achievement of a positive result [6], in this case with a strong premonition of the effects that correspond to those causes.

2 Humans and Nature

The design looks at 'real people' [2]. It is developed in a collaborative environment with experts from all fields, ready to test their theories and, thus, with the activation of critical thinking to re-position new constructs. Paola Antonelli's essay 'Vital Design' [1] states that design is about 'life' and guarantees, in an era of great technological acceleration and as many crises extended from the environment to politics, greater attention to human beings, reconstructing their essential values.

The ability to collaborate to produce critical thinking on the current state of the human-nature pair introduces an intricate concept of collaboration with more complex implications. Critical thinking reflects human beings on their role, and not being alone, their actions have effects to anticipate and foresee in every process they undertake.

Ultimately, a new way of creating value moves from deep, critical, and evolutionary thinking, embraces adaptive doing, orienting towards the continuous regeneration of equilibrium, and establishes a relationship of mutuality between artificial systems and living sentient beings. The irrationality of the current model, according to some authors [8], is evident in the face of incontrovertible data on the, by now, ascertained dangerousness of human action, believing that the current model of development is unique and irreplaceable, does not mean that procrastinating its end will never be written or, worse still, never proven.

The issue arises from the intense research activity that leads to profound debates on the evidence of irrefutable scientific data, testifying to irreversible ecosystem transformation processes that, on the contrary, must be kept in balance and for which initial values must be restored as far as possible [4]. Humanity has become such a dominant force in shaping the Earth that the pressing question is how the overall material production of human activities compares with the overall natural biomass.

"Here we quantify the mass produced by humans, referred to as the anthropogenic mass, and compare it to the total living biomass on Earth, which currently equals about 1.1 ternatons 10.11. We find that the Earth is exactly at the crossroads; in the year 2020 (±6), the anthropogenic mass, which has recently been doubling roughly every 20 years, will exceed the entire global living biomass. On average, for every person on the globe, an anthropogenic mass equal to more than their body weight is produced every week. This quantification of the human enterprise provides a quantitative and symbolic characterization based on the human-induced mass of the Anthropocene' [5].

For the first time in the history of our planet, human-designed constructs—materials, products, and buildings—exceed the entire terrestrial biomass. "Although humans are part of the natural world, human activity and the 'goods' we design and build—from our clothes to our cities—have increasingly set us apart from nature, negatively impacting ourselves and our planet" (Oxman, 2020).

3 The Intertwined "Couture Vivant" for Fashion

The paradigm of *Couture Vivant* (Living Fashion) is based on concrete evidence, manifestations of a new way of thinking and conceiving the creation of fashion and textile projects attributable to interdisciplinary knowledge. It is intertwined knowledge that questions the limits imposed by the environment and how to change the way we design, produce, and use tangible and intangible goods that are sustainable and reusable.

The hypothesis is to integrate design and scientific disciplines to make design and manufacturing processes open and modifiable: it is a question of designing the prototype process according to a living biological matrix cultivated in symbiosis with a technological matrix that produces the material in a usable configuration. In general, it is about advanced digital technology combined with biology, or the bio-digital that creates new generations of materials [10, 13, 14].

This matter contains within itself the concept, the process, and the final product, so that the generated or re-generated matter is a matter that falls into the category of configurable one.

Design works with microbiology, it is planned and created with living systems whose bacterial biotechnological applications evolve with fashion and textiles. The aim is to decrease the dependence on petroleum-based materials and processing to achieve technically advanced productions where the idea is not to assemble the materials but to cultivate them [10, 13, 14]. So that, in fashion and textiles, returning to the bedrock of a conception that integrates nature, biology and technology means considering the metabolic activities of bacteria that enrich and transform materials, and help in waste treatment, for example, they break down plastic, or in manufacturing of pigmented dyes.

A new category of configurable materials comes forward that are described as living materials of the future that challenge old categories to impose new ones; the living merges with the non-living, promoting continuously configurable materials that respond only to the rules of cultivation depending on the nourishment that is activated.

The urgency of dealing with complex problems requires a substantial effort in redefining the approach, which, of course, in addition to ensuring crossdisciplinarity must grasp the challenges of current events. It is a matter of redefining the scientific approach by orienting it toward a collaborative model that repudiates the attitude of using many disciplines that do not collaborate but provide a mosaic of many different disciplines in their own right [7]. Disciplines that speak different languages that look at the project as a stand-alone element without connections, without adherence, worse still operational tools are put in place that do not dialogue with each other and others and provide partial results.

4 Reverse Matter Design

Various design approaches make their way, from material innovation to creative technological exploration, to speculative design, a great convergence of intentions and vital energies emerges, coming from different disciplines explored by design [7].

In the innovation of materials, the virtual reality used for the visualization of certain 'concept materials' materializes a new design thinking that responds to an 'inverse' process to the customary design process. The usual practice follows the linear model from design to prototyping, to the choice of materials or the best configuration to produce, use and communicate it, and possibly recycle it; the non-linear model reverses the perspective [11].

The process goes backwards, stemming from an overall idea that is structured in a digital (parametric) matrix that simulates matter in different stages and relative configurations starting from a prediction of its decomposition up to dematerialization; from the creation of matter-second from reprocessing waste; from a concept of hybrid biological and technological structures, through proliferation and mutualistic growth; from data that are organized according to purpose and that inform matter (informed matter). The perspective, then, is the regeneration of natural and artificial cycles that define its purposes and intentions.

In the first instance, a kind of 'virtual raw material' is developed, which traces, by visualizing it, the entire process, according to one or more of the previous options, and subsequently materializes into an object or artefact that contains one or more results, descending from those design intentions. This is the *matiére brute* that stems from a profound knowledge of processes; it is an 'inverse raw material' that has undergone, ideally or rather virtually, all the processes of an ordinary raw material (in the old logic starting point), it observes its memory and for this reason, it is designed to reconnect man and his actions to the regeneration of the natural-artificial cycles of matter and energy.

There are many approaches by designers, critics, creatives, and researchers who pursue one or more options/intentions in their projects. Among the most significant examples, some common traits stand out: criticism of the current production model and, above all, the development of a reflection that goes beyond sustainable or conscious behavior and beyond approaches to the circularity and resilience of systems, with the aim of reproducing ancestral mechanisms that adopt the molecular dynamics of living things.

4.1 Biodesign/"Couture Vivant" for Fashion

Neri Oxman pursues the path of 'matter cultivation as an alternative to assembly' this mode pursues the idea that natural systems can establish a close dialogue with human technology (digital soft) and help to develop living systems from an artificial matrix and vice versa [12].

The idea of a bio-digital era, where "the confluence of computational design, additive manufacturing, materials engineering and synthetic biology is planned, allows for the creation of new generations of materials" [10, 13, 14, 16] (see Fig. 1). One finds here the concept of matter generated and re-generated through the concrete co-evolution of biological living with the engineered artificial. In the co-evolutionary processes, the biological matrix is grafted onto an artificial material or structural matrix that provides direction and naturally interweaves the two together. It is a matter, even though of co-evolution, of intervening on time, on the design capacity to foresee the response of biological growth adhering to the technological structure.

4.2 Subframe Studio

Subframe Studio proposes digital visions and material constructs based on the narration of production processes in various fields of action, the contribution is innovative, creative, and often imaginative of reality as it is presented and envisaged. The future for Subframe Studio is at hand, the construction of the image is a digital fact programmed to provide answers to change, and above all, inspired by virtual reality, it favors design with advanced intentions.

New materials take shape from ancestral matrices, others from raw-secondary materials from waste and the related industrial processes of transformation and reuse, designs that envisage behavior in response to a set of external stresses, ultimately represent the creation of materials and configurations of digital objects whose growth and response is visualized (see Figs. 2 and 3).

Being spaces of possibility, the criterion is to imprint them with internal and external conditions and adaptability to tools and environment.

Among the projects that solicit reflection for their visual, design and construction impact, a significant application has been realized in the field of Fashion, for which it is clear how much distance exists between the custom and habit of Fashion design and that animated by artificial intelligence.

Subframe Studio for Vollebak builds films on inanimate nature inspired by the project 'From the First Clothes Built for Mars, to Gear Built to Outlive You' (https://vollebak.com/pages/ranges) (see Figs. 4 and 5). The experience of one becomes

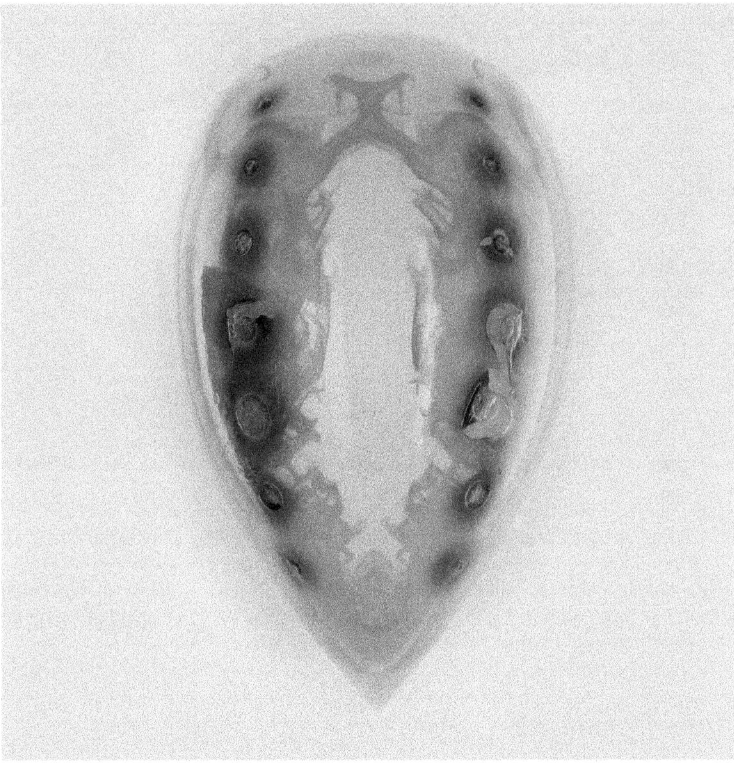

Fig. 1 The masks in Vespers III are habitats for microorganisms and sites for the creation of new life. The third series revolves around death and rebirth, denoting both spiritual incarnation and biological recapitulation. To create the Vespers III masks, novel tools and techniques were developed that enable tight integration between, and control of, designed and biologically derived properties. By combining living and non-living materials using 3D printing and synthetic biology, they are creating new categories of materials, termed Hybrid Living Materials. Research team: C. Bader, R. S. H. Smith, D. Kolb, S. Sharma, J. Costa, J. C. Weaver. Prof. Neri Oxman. Design Museum, 2018, London, United Kingdom. National Gallery of Victoria, 2018, Melbourne, Australia

a mode of narration for the other so that the creation and production of high-performance garments stem from a transfer of knowledge to technologies from sectors far removed from fashion: "Everything they use is so durable that it was originally used as bulletproof vests, ballistic armour for vehicles, mooring systems for giant container ships and ropes used to tie up oil platforms in violent, icy seas. The aim was to show the selected minerals in a creative, abstract way highlighting the characters of each. We focused on celadonite, hematite, ochre and volcanic soil and created four short films' (Subframe Studio).

For its part, Vollebak transfers knowledge of heterogeneous materials into its design and production know-how for advanced clothing: 'Our clothing addresses the fundamental challenges we will face in the next century: from extreme heat waves, floods and fires to resource scarcity and space exploration' (Vollebak).

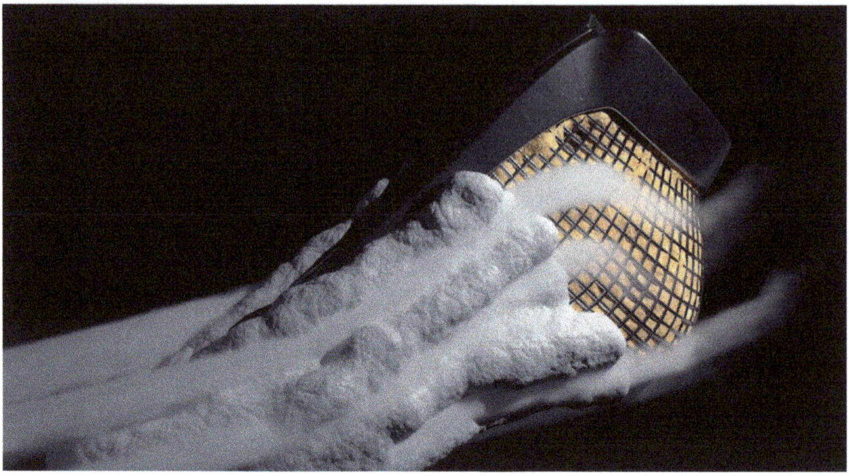

Fig. 2 Next Nature. 'Sculpting with Air' explores design through mycelium foam. The raw materials collected for this project comes from agricultural wastes: corn husk and hemp. Under the conditions of high humidity, high carbon dioxide, proper temperatures and airflow running constantly, a foam-like element is formed and can be used as a material. The project provides another way and opportunity to work with living materials by harnessing the growth instead of fitting them into moulds. Lars Dittrich (icw Eveline Peeters and Simon Vandelook) 2022

4.3 Rosie Broadhead

The scientist Rosie Broadhead has explored the composition of the skin biome, i.e. the ecosystem formed by microorganisms, bacteria, fungi, etc. that live on the skin ed. she explored how it works. Collaborating with the microbiologist Christopher Callewaert of the University of Ghent, you have experimented with the microencapsulation of probiotic bacteria in adherence with textile surfaces in direct contact with the skin.

The textile surfaces, through the rubbing mechanism and therefore by overheating, release the encapsulated bacteria in the presence of sweat. The latter, from laboratory tests, in addition to reducing body odour, can support cell regeneration and increase skin immunity. The Skin II prototype presents interesting innovations, i.e. the positioning of the encapsulated probiotic bacteria has been optimized to obtain a natural rebalancing of the Skin Series (Fig. 6).

The research and experimentation on textiles that Rosie Broadhead carries out can have interesting repercussions on the work of fashion designers in terms of procurement of materials and on the interdisciplinarity that helps to use waste and biological systems to invent processes and concepts of materials completely new.

Fig. 3 Subframe for Adidas makes PRIMEBLUE project provides story about ending plastic waste. The challenge will be how we educate the public as to how PRIMEBLUE is solving the problem. That means showing how the material is made, the technology used, and the final product come to life through seamless, well-composed, live action shots and gorgeously crafted visual effects. "We were working in close collaboration with Bemo Studio to produce CGI concepts, key visuals, and animation as well. Through CGI, we'll tell the important story of the process capture. How we collect the plastic, crush it, wash it, dry, shred, melt and thread it. Since this process has never been seen before, we'll need to create a visual canvas that clearly illustrates the technology. Think stylized and dynamic shots of a piece of plastic being broken down into its simplest elements then transformed into something else entirely. Additionally, the sequence needs to flow where each step hits on the beat like a well-oiled machine"

5 Brief Notes for the Launch of the Discussion

In brief, several points have been highlighted. The reaction to the complex crisis we are experiencing today starts with a substantial anthropological change that brings a new approach to doing to purpose, foreseeing each effect. Acting with the effects in mind will be the perspective of every action; replacing the anthropocentric productivity model with a new way of creating value moves from deep, critical, and evolutionary thinking.

The hypotheses are realistic and possible: adaptive doing, oriented towards the continuous regeneration of equilibriums, establishes a relationship of mutuality between artificial systems and living, sentient beings.

The paradigm of orientation refers to some experiments illustrated in the text that respond to the following reflections on production and processes, focusing on future materials: a prediction of decomposition up to dematerialization; from the creation of raw-secondary-material from reprocessing waste; from a concept of biological and technological hybrid structures, through proliferation and mutualistic growth;

Fig. 4 Subframe Studio for Vollebak in "Parad of minerals" works on the visualisation of some of minerals which they use to create an advanced clothing. Everything they use is so tough that it was originally used in body armour, anti-ballistic vehicle armour, mooring systems for giant container ships and ropes used to tie down oil rigs in violent, icy seas. The goal was to show selected minerals in abstract artistic way with strengths of each. Subframe focuses on Celadonite, Hematite, Ochre and Volcanic soil and created four short films. 2023

from data that are organized according to purpose and that inform matter (informed matter).

The new perspective relapses within the logic of matching natural and artificial cycles and regenerating as much as possible, defining its purposes and intentions, from conception to production, to use and to reuse.

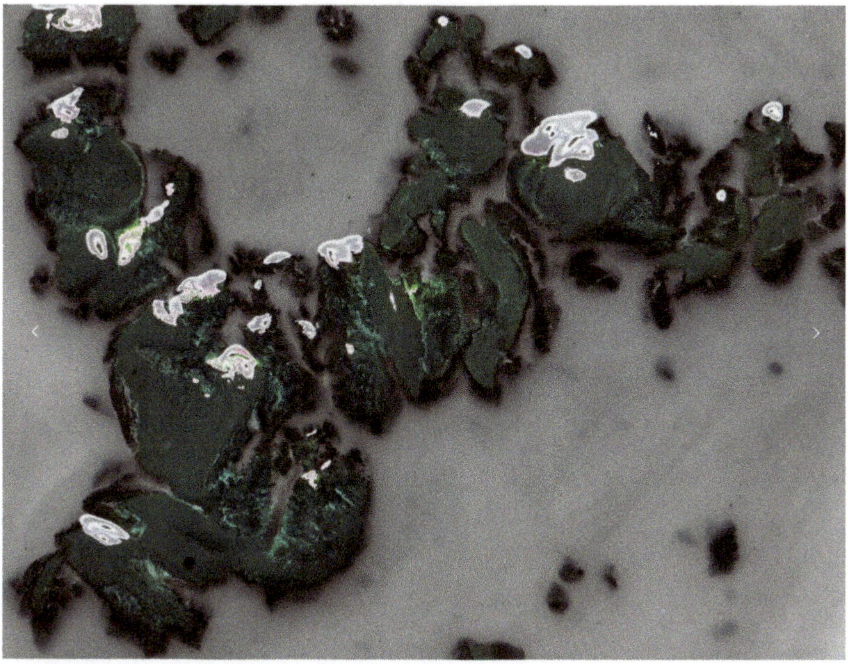

Fig. 5 Vollebak builds black algae T-shirt with biomaterials start up. "With the help of US biomaterials company Living Ink, we've found a method of making black clothing with algae. After its founders discovered that an algae cell is almost identical in size to a carbon black pigment, and can create the same colour, they've been on a mission to replace carbon black ink with a black ink made from black algae waste, 2023

Fig. 6 Rosie Broadhead "Skin Series" Probiotic clothing exemplifies the co-habitation of human and non-human cells, and the importance of these entangled ecologies when designing the future. Material Futures, exposition, Milano Fuorisalone 2023

References

1. Antonelli P (2012) Preview, vital design. In: Myers W (ed) Bio design: nature, science, creativity. Thames & Hudson
2. Antonelli P (2019) Broken nature: design takes on human survival. XXII Esposizione Internazionale della Triennale di Milano (27/02/2019–01/09/2019)
3. Beery T, Olafsson AS, Gentin S, Maurer M, Stålhammar S, Albert C, Bieling C, Buijs A, Fagerholm N, Garcia-Martin M, Plieninger T, Raymond CM (2023) Disconnection from nature: expanding our understanding of human–nature relations. People and Nature Journal published by John Wiley & Sons Ltd on behalf of British Ecological Society
4. De Biase L (2016) Homo pluralis. Essere umani nell'era tecnologica. Codice Edizioni, Torino
5. Elhacham E, Ben-Uri L, Grozovski J, Bar-On YM, Milo R (2020) Global human-made mass exceeds all living biomass. Nature 588:442–444
6. Heidegger M (2015) Quaderni neri, a cura di P. Trawny. Bompiani, Milano
7. Ito J (2016) Design and science. Can design advance science, and can science advance design? J Des Sci (JoDS)
8. Lagioia N (2022) …la natura… Impariamo a non essere i padroni del pianeta. Robinson, 06 agosto 2022
9. Merton RK (1971) La profezia che si autoavvera, in Teoria e Struttura Sociale, II, Bologna, Il Mulino
10. Oxman N (2016a) Age of entanglement. J Des Sci (JoDS) https://jods.mitpress.mit.edu/pub/ageofentanglement/release/1

11. Van Gelder M (1996) The strange case of the electronic lover. In: Kling R (ed) Computerization and controversy. Academic Press, London
12. Museum of Modern Art. Material Ecology: Neri Oxman. New York, NY, 2020
13. Oxman N (2016b) Age of entanglement. J Des Sci (JoDS)
14. Oxman N (2016c) Towards a material ecology. World Econ Forum
15. Rutherford A (2013) Creation: how science is reinventing life itself. Penguin, London
16. San Francisco Museum of Modern Art (2022) Nature X Humanity. San Francisco, CA

Edgar Morin's Vision and the Fashion Design Education. Part II—"Human Understanding: Understanding Each Other" as an Approach to Cultural Sustainability

Fernanda Enéia Schulz and Joana Cunha

Abstract Based on the article published in 2022, "The 7 Complex Lessons from Edgar Morin Applied in Fashion Design Education for Sustainability", and with the aim of looking at local cultural processes (instead of global ones) associated with Fashion Design education, we seek to develop the theme proposed around Edgar Morin's sixth lesson, called "Human understanding: understanding each other". In this way, we propose a reflection around the author's assumption, the urgency of a collective look, endowed with understanding of the other, related to local cultural processes, mainly those associated with the traditional cultural knowledge of each region, as a way of enriching the curricula of Fashion Design. In this way, we discuss approaches that provide future designers with access to cultural knowledge that dialogue directly with creativity and constitute in this relationship, designers and local cultures, not only the perpetuation of ancestral knowledge, but innovation in products imbued with emotional, cultural and historical values. In a reflection, arising from personal experiences in the classroom and from contact with the academic environment, we realized that when we look at local cultures, it is possible to develop sustainable products through fashion design that respond to the expectations of a certain public, providing thus, consumers of their own identities, beyond globalized trends.

Keywords Fashion design · Cultural sustainability · Education · Local culture · Edgar Morin

F. E. Schulz (✉) · J. Cunha
Centro de Ciência e Tecnologia Têxtil, Universidade do Minho, Campus de Azurém, Guimarães, Portugal
e-mail: ferschulz.design@gmail.com

D. Raposo et al. (eds.), *Perspectives on Design III*, Springer Series in Design and Innovation 34, https://doi.org/10.1007/978-3-031-43516-4_15

1 "Human Understanding: Understanding Each Other" by Edgar Morin and Its Contemporary Relationship with Craft Cultural Knowledge and Cultural Sustainability

In 1999, at the invitation of UNESCO, Edgar Morin presented his work "The Seven Complex Lesson in Education for the Future", a compilation of his ideas on education for a sustainable future, with a precept in detecting error and illusion, in principles of pertinent knowledge, in the teaching of human condition, in earthly identity, in the confrontation of uncertainties, in understanding each other and in ethical formation. Associated with these issues, Morin's vision extends to the fundamental relationships of transdisciplinary teaching, as a basis for human development in ethical, social, cultural, and sustainable values, as a solution to deal with the human complexities of the contemporary world. Questions that are also pertinent in the research universe of fashion design and the designer's formative character, as a creative and professional agent of social transformation, who must be able to deal with and solve contemporary problems associated with the ethical and sustainable crisis of the fashion industry and cultural relations pertinent to human heritage and traditions [1].

The relationship between the "seven lessons" by Morin and the fashion design education were emphatically discussed in the article "The Seven Complex Lessons from Edgar Morin applied in Fashion Design Education" [1], where we point out possible paths to sustainability of fashion by relating cases and authors to that proposed by Morin, once we understand the transdisciplinary role implicit in the discipline of fashion design in the relation between clothing-individual-society. By mentioning this triad of fashion design and its direct relationship with transdisciplinarity, we highlight the need for collaborative relationships through multidisciplinary teams, coming from industrial technological universes and cultural craft knowledge as a way to develop solutions for the future of sustainable fashion. In this speech, it is important to emphasize the need to understand the countless cultural languages communicated through crafts, the possible interactions between industry, environment, society, and intellectual creative development. For Morin [2], it is through the university that cultural knowledge and multiple languages are preserved, integrated, re-examined, updated and transmitted. And it is in this environment that complex and transdisciplinary thinking must be inserted from multiple perspectives on past cultures to understand the future of humanity, culminating in new ways of interpreting and creatively reinventing knowledge without the limits imposed by traditional teaching models. That is, to "ecologize the disciplines", as Morin emphasised, to encourage and provide conditions for developing the comprehension of social and cultural conditions [2, 3].

Even though the 'seven lessons' refer to Morin's conceptions and ideas around the complexities of teaching for the future, human understanding, his sixth lesson, is at the core of all his research, which implies the development of cultural relations and the social interactions through complex, non-reductionist thinking and with a character that integrates the various disciplines of knowledge, with the university having a fundamental role in the integration of society and mainly of the cultural values intrinsic to it. Morin highlights the need to teach and understand the multiple "cultures of the humanities" [4], promoting intercultural dialogue through practices that relate the multiplicity of knowledge (history, literature, arts, philosophy, technologies, etc.) and consequently favouring the construction of a more sustainable society, not only with regard to the classic environmental rhetoric, but also with regard to human valuation through traditions and socio-cultural relations.

As referenced by Williams [5], culture from the point of view of sociology, refers to human processes, initially related to the "culture and creation of plants and animals", consequently, by the production and cultivation of the human mind, and finally, by the very "spirit and global way of life of a particular people." For Campello, Santiago and Andrade [6], it is important to emphasize that nowadays, culture also refers to cultural heritage, popular cultures, cultural identities and diversities, as well as mass culture (globalized).

Like Williams, for Edgar Morin, the concept of culture is seen in a complex way, consisting of a body of norms, symbols, myths, and images, since it is related to the various aspects of human life that are transmitted, preserved, and learned from generation to generation [4, 7]. These aspects are composed of knowledge, rules, norms, traditions, values, myths, beliefs, which describe human society, both in the past and in the present, thus meaning for Morin the non-existence of societies without culture and, therefore, the need for human understanding, since the human being is a fully cultural being that is only realized, completed, through culture and in culture [4, 7]. In this context, Morin identifies culture as one of the challenges of education, since it was fragmented at the beginning of the twentieth century, thus being divided into two "blocks, humanities culture and scientific culture". Thus, the humanistic culture becomes generic, fragmented and is often forgotten (or replaced by scientific culture), causing what Morin describes as a "black hole" of knowledge, where we understand a lot about the universe and about objects, but practically nothing about ourselves, since both cultures, humanity and science, do not mutually corroborate for the development of understanding about human culture. On the other hand, corroborating the stagnation of teaching in humanistic cultures, we have the perception that scientific and technical culture itself perceives other cultures as "ornament or aesthetic luxury". Therefore, the connection between both cultures is seen as part of the great challenge of complex thinking proposed by Morin, classified by the author as one of the main missions of teaching, as already mentioned, with human and cultural understanding being fundamental for the education of the future [4, 7, 8]. In his book "La tête bien faite" [4], Morin calls for special attention to the culture of the humanities, since it is through cultural knowledge that it is possible to develop the necessary skills to solve global problems.

It is through this cultural context and its problems that Morin's sixth lesson develops, proposing the need to understand man as a subject and as an individual, through the understanding of the individual issues of each human being, their relationships and social contexts and their natural relationship. Thus, starting to understand man not as an object, but as a subject endowed with empathy, desires, aspirations, and culture. "Human understanding: understanding each other" points to problems in the contemporary world related to human and cultural values, which, for Morin, are necessary to teach and learn, to guarantee the intellectual, ethical, and moral solidarity of humanity [1, 4, 7]. That is, Morin [7] alerts to the problematization of understanding around the theme, addressing two aspects: the planetary aspect that refers to understanding between humans, that is, the cultural origins and the respective cultural relations between peoples; and individual and private relationships, threatened by misunderstanding. In this approach, it is important to refer to the need to develop intellectual understanding and human understanding, both endowed with empathy, identification, and projection.

In his book "The Seven Complex Lesson in Education for the Future" [7], Morin dedicates a chapter to human understanding, in which he lists the obstacles to intellectual education centred on understanding:

- Noise in the transmission of information, that is, a loss of meaning or poor understanding;
- Polysemy of the word culture, which refers to the distortion of the meaning of the word culture itself, which for Morin, means everything that must be learned and acquired, uses, values, beliefs and contributions from the different areas of knowledge;
- Ignorance of the rites and customs of others, which for Morin, leads to self-disqualification or offense to other cultures;
- Misunderstanding of the values of other cultures, which, as in the previous point, leads to offense and disqualification of traditional cultures, as well as the rupture of the cult of the individual and respect for freedoms in contemporary society;
- Misunderstanding of the ethical imperatives implicit in each culture, as cited by the author, misunderstanding of the laws of tribal cultures, for example;
- Impossibility of world view, which leads to non-understanding and lack of vision towards other cultures;
- Misunderstanding of a mental structure in relation to another.

In summary, Morin presents obstacles to human understanding centred on issues of ethnocentrism and sociocentrism, which reminds us of the complexity of the subject, which requires awareness of human complexity and the need for cultures to learn from each other, raising the concepts of understanding, ethics, and culture. In the words of Morin [7], "to understand is also to learn and relearn incessantly", that is, the act of learning also refers to communicating the various existing cultural interactions.

Edgar Morin's approach with regard to 'Human understanding: understanding each other', has a direct relationship with traditional and ancestral cultural knowledge, since it is directly related to human beings and their understanding as individuals and society, therefore, it is also directly related to the Sustainable Development Goals (SDGs) and the UNESCO 2030 Agenda for culture. In this way, we recognize Morin's approach from the perspectives and encouragement of an education focused on cultural diversity, with recognition of multiple cultural communities, as well as the promotion of economic activities aimed at sustainability and the promotion of sustainable consumption practices [7, 8], which leads us to the identification of SDG 4 (Quality education), SDG 8 (Decent work and economic growth), SDG 11 (Sustainable cities and communities) and SDG 12 (Sustainable consumption and production).

When we talk about sustainability in the Cultural dimension, it is important to mention that, according to UNESCO directives, Culture is a strategic dimension to be considered within Horizon 2030, particularly regarding creative development [9]. The connection between culture and sustainable development has been discussed since 1995 with the publication of the World Commission on Culture and Development (WCCD) report "Our creative diversity", but it has gained greater importance since the end of the 1st decade of the twenty-first century [10]. At the beginning of the millennium, the vision of the importance of culture for humanity was consolidated with the UNESCO "Universal Declaration on Cultural Diversity" published in 2001 [11], which considers traditions as an element of Culture. According to Article 1, these are "a source of exchange, innovation and creativity", further clarifying that "cultural diversity is as necessary for humanity as biodiversity is for nature" [11, art. 1].

Still on this topic, it is important to refer to the UNESCO "Convention for the Safeguarding of the Intangible Cultural Heritage" held in Paris in 2003, where the importance of preserving cultural heritage was widely discussed [12]. In the guidelines for this convention [13] it is clear that, intangible cultural heritage is also manifested in the field of traditional handicrafts. And that the safeguarding of this intangible cultural heritage should be done, among other ways, through preservation, enhancement, and transmission "namely through formal and non-formal education, as well as the revitalization of the various aspects of this heritage" [13, p. 6].

Finally, we believe that culture, from the perspective of human relations, goes far beyond what is proposed by UNESCO, as well observed by Skrzypaszek [14], who highlights the constant need to evaluate and adapt concepts and meanings in cultural contexts, since culture is composed of a complex and changeable character [7], thus representing an evolution in the concepts of humanistic cultural traditions, which, as already mentioned by Morin, relate to the various aspects of human life. Thus, based on the transmission, preservation, and teaching of this cultural knowledge, it is possible to redesign new proposals and cultural contexts, coherent and necessary both for education and for a sustainable future.

2 Local Cultures Versus Global Culture: From Micro to Macro Perspective on Artisanal Cultural Knowledge

For Morin [4], "we are no longer primates thanks to culture", which, through interactions between individuals, originating from a cultural set composed of language, symbols, products, and cultural values themselves, constitutes us as a society And, it is through social interactions that it is possible to develop the set of cultural diversity, transmitting knowledge through a system of exchange of ideas and cultural practices, constituting cultural enrichment and cultural miscegenation [7]. Indeed, culture can become universal, "migrate from one culture to another" [7], however, there is always our culture that connects us with the past, with our ancestry. As well clarified by Morin through the cultural examples (here understood as the sum of human and technological knowledge) of the wheel, the compass, the press, religious beliefs and the very conceptions and understandings of ideas. Thus, culture in Morin's conception [7] is not static, much less closed, but mutable and adaptable according to the context, society, period, and technological development. In this way, it is also possible to understand that culture has a transdisciplinary character, since it integrates and influences the various aspects of human life, in a process of transition of cultural traditions, which oscillates either in the global dimension or in the partial (local) dimension [5]. With Pearce [15], it is noted that there is no society without the cultural physical manifestations' characteristic of the ideologies and expressions of each cultural society.

One of the several approaches in the cultural discussion is about the perception of what refers to the local culture and the global culture, both from the point of view of the human understanding implicit in Morin's speeches, "understanding each other", as in the understanding of the complexity of cultural interactions and the various influences caused between and through these cultural encounters. In this reflection, the evolution of studies and discourses around post-Cold War global culture is understood, since in the 1990s we see a global remodelling in political, economic, and cultural terms, which culminates in the academic understanding of global culture, as a set of processes that integrate the world, causing interdependence and interconnection between peoples, cultures and countries [16].

Mirrlees [16] when reflecting on the theme, questions the real existence of a "global culture" in an antagonistic world. For the author, it is complex to think of a "global culture" when the world is faceted by multiple political, antagonistic, and separatist ideas and interests. Instilled in this questioning, Mirrlees analyses three possible articulations of global culture: (1) Society mediated in the global village: where, through the evolution of communication means and technologies, the author visualizes, as a consequence, the process of deterritorialization of society, since cultural interactions and transitions are facilitated through technology; (2) American Empire and cultural imperialism: imposition of a global way of life through the process of the "transnationalized" way of life, without taking into account the particular ways of life and cultures; (3) Global popular culture: refers to global entertainment means and media, such as cinema and television, which when distributed globally contribute to cultural hegemony. Through the discussion of these three points, Mirrlees realizes that for most people, who still live in local, regional, and even national communities, global culture still means a distant horizon, since cultural narratives associated with myths and local affective bonds do not are part of the great mass culture. In conclusion, for the author, in the near future, people will continue to identify themselves as part of their local and national culture as opposed to a global culture.

It is a fact that, if we analyse globalization, mainly from the point of view of the global village, there is a strong contribution with regard to cultural exchange, since the model of globalization facilitates human migrations and cultural ties between peoples. But the influences on local and cultural identities are also part of the globalization processes, which corroborate the loss of local cultural identities, mainly to issues associated with handicrafts, arts, and unique characteristics of each people. For the authors Raikhan et al. [17] and Skrzypaszek [14] with globalization, numerous disadvantages arise for cultures at local and national levels, such as forgetting local cultural and artistic processes to the detriment of a global artistic and cultural model, with "encouragement" to the lack of interest in ancestral cultures, mainly in young groups and more influenced by global cultural massification and, finally, as an effect of globalization, loss or mischaracterization of local and national characteristics (understood by cultural, social, artistic, political and economic characteristics), who no longer receive due attention, which corroborates the already mentioned lack of interest. Campello et al. [6] corroborate the discourse by stating that the advance of globalization also has the effect of social inequalities and the devastation of local cultures, thus requiring greater effort in terms of strengthening measures in favour of valuing multiple minority identities. For Krucken [18], the challenge is to find the balance between global and local cultural relations, since the associated relations are complex, as already exposed in the above discussions, and design must create methodologies that promote these cultural interactions.

In order to find a balance between global and local cultural relations, it is important to emphasize that local craft knowledge is a reflection of the way each community relates to its environment and its historical, cultural and social contexts. Thus, traditional artisanal knowledge is based on practices rooted and accumulated in the knowledge of a community, being therefore unique and forming part of the local culture [19, 20]. Designers must assume their responsibility as actors of social transformations and seek to understand the impact they can have on local communities through the adoption of artisanal cultural practices [19].

As already mentioned, through Morin and reinforced in the discourse of Mirrlees [7, 16], the techniques used in this cultural knowledge can be shared between cultures, and often are, however the products that result from them are, in terms of semantic language, unique in each community, as is the case for example of traditional costumes [21].

For Skrzypaszek [14] the local culture is immersed in the shared experiences and collective memories of a community and, in this way, is also the artisanal cultural knowledge. In order to appreciate the meaning of objects produced from this cultural knowledge, in the ever-changing global cultural environment, it is fundamental to understand the contexts of local cultures and their human experiences. Since the acculturation processes generate a gap between the community that created that culture and the narratives that are associated with it, that is, this acculturation causes the loss of identity, uniqueness and originality of the local culture expressed in the artifacts and their languages.

In terms of valuing local culture, there have been many projects and designers who, in close dialogue with sustainability issues, have resorted to artisanal cultural techniques and knowledge to develop products that transfer local cultural values to global culture [19, 20, 22–24]. However, many times these projects do not become completely successful due to the lack of articulation with the market, but also because they are often very limited projects in time [19]. For the success of this design-local craft cultural knowledge interaction and for the achievement of sustainable development goals, at the level of the agendas proposed by UNESCO and the EU, it is necessary to develop a true understanding of the local context and its human values [19]. Tung [19] proposes a methodology for this type of project, which begins with a pre-development phase in which the activities aim to facilitate the mutual understanding of the actors involved, not only as a motivational strategy, but "to lay the foundations for collaboration" [19, p. 370].

It follows from this analysis that artisanal cultural knowledge plays an important role in our lives, allowing the establishment of relationships with human values as well as the exploration and combination of concepts in an innovative way. This knowledge has come to be recognized both as a process and a way of thinking, which is intrinsically complex given their holistic nature [14, 19, 25].

We denote here the importance of human understanding advocated by Morin, and how this understanding should encompass the understanding of the complexity of cultural interactions starting from the local to the global, through creative languages implicit in fashion design, given that the discipline plays a fundamental role in what refers to cultural, social, and human development through collaborative actions between designers and society [26].

Finally, we observe that new languages and approaches around local cultural processes have emerged, both as an attempt to keep alive the characteristic traits of each community, and due to the understanding of the need for sustainability at local and global levels. New languages and expressions around traditional craft cultural processes instigate young designers to give a new symbolism to processes and cultures that are in the process of being erased [27]. Just as, according to Arizpe [27], it is possible through this methodology to mobilize people, communities and keep their own heritage alive. According to the assumptions already made by Morin, Arizpe also discusses the need for dialogue between the different areas of human and scientific technical knowledge, as a way of shaping new sustainable possibilities for the future. For Moura [28], designers must not only translate multiple global languages into local environments but must also articulate and promote local and peripheral language in an international environment.

There are several cases within the universe of fashion, of brands that differentiate themselves in the market by betting on the integration of artisanal cultural knowledge into their creative and productive processes. In this way, these brands work on the experience by building memories with their consumers, by sharing the history of the product, thus contributing to their products having, through emotional means, greater durability. In this sense, we highlight below some micro cases associated with fashion, which seek, through dialogue between local culture, cultural traditions, and industrial technologies, to transmit heritage, knowledge, and culture to a globalized society, spreading ideologies and concepts of sustainability at the human, ethical and environmental levels.

2.1 *Micro Cases in Fashion: Practice of Local and Global Relationships in a European Context*

In the context of European fashion, there are several initiatives by companies and brands that reinforce the importance of a teaching approach that works with local ancestral cultural knowledge. We highlight two different cases that are relevant to our thinking, one is the Burel Factory, a Portuguese project that unites innovation with tradition, and the other is the case of Italy, which focuses on the way in which the identity of Italian products boost the appreciation of local traditions globally by being closely linked to cultural heritage and artistic craftsmanship.

The Burel Factory Case—Innovation and tradition in Portugal: Burel Factory is a project and a Portuguese brand created by Isabel Costa and João Tomás dedicated to the preservation and recovery of the tangible and intangible heritage of industrial woolen production in *Serra da Estrela.* The Burel Factory recovered the old *Lanifícios Império* factory and its proto-industrial machinery, the old textile patterns produced there and the production of *burel* fabric. The project rescued knowledge that was almost lost by putting the old loom masters to teach the younger ones and introducing color and design in an innovative way in the *burel.* It has a creative center dedicated to the innovation and development of products where they are committed to partnerships with artists and designers to reinforce and develop the region's identity, "weaving with the threads of the past a sustainable, circular and more authentic vision of the future".[1]

The *burel,* an ancestral fabric once used by mountain shepherds, is re-signified into a contemporary product synonymous with design, creativity, and sustainability through the sharing of knowledge and working techniques with ancient looms and spinning machines (craftsmanship heritage) with design thinking.

The Burel Factory case represents, in essence, Portuguese design itself in terms of valuing cultural and technological traits relevant to local cultures, transcribed through design for global contexts. For Moura [28] this model of Portuguese relationship, comes from the existing social legitimation from the global local mediation, that is, for the author, the development of cases like the Burel Factory, start from the responsibility with the past.

It should be noted that, as Portugal is a country made up of countless small communities, the designer's relationship becomes internalized, with Portuguese design par excellence seeking the internationalization of these identities, as occurs through the works of Álvaro Siza and Eduardo de Souto de Moura, who through architecture represented traditional forms and the Portuguese people [28].

When Burel Factory proposes to dialogue with designers, architects, and artists, it seeks new representations of traditions and symbols originating from the community to which it belongs, that is, the designer takes on the creative role associated with the transforming power, as it communicates the cultural representations of this place, role which Moura [28] defines as "designer - active agent".

---

[1] See https://burelfactory.com/pages/history.

The Case of Italy—local traditions valued globally: Italian products are widely recognized for incorporating distinctive elements such as cultural heritage, artistic craftsmanship and the "made in Italy" [29]. According to Tarquini et al. [30], luxury goods companies can play a leading role with regard to the dissemination and revitalization of culture derived from traditional knowledge, as these cultural values play an extremely important role in the experience of consumers with these products.

In an approach to local traditional culture and knowledge, the "hand in hand"[2] project of the Italian brand Fendi develops from the brand's partnership with several traditional workshops to recreate the famous *Baguette* bag, imbuing it with the Italian artisanal culture.

The project is based not only on textile craftsmanship, such as lace (bobbin lace and tatting); embroidery from different regions of Italy; fabrics such as traditional Venisian velvet and other hand-woven fabrics; but also, in knowledge such as goldsmithing, basketry, leather, glass or carpentry, which form part of the Italian cultural heritage. According to the brand, this project aims to transform the Baguette into a "true art object" and value local cultural knowledge as a tribute to "regional craftsmen and their traditions".[3] The brand thus values the local artisanal culture, transporting it across the globe and, therefore, valuing it globally. At the same time, the "hand in hand" project shows how this local craft culture can be preserved, evolving into new products and introduced in new contexts, that of the global market.

Another example is the Dolce Gabbana brand, which traditionally uses elements strongly linked to the Italian national identity and local artisanal knowledge, as a brand marketing strategy [31], but also incorporates Italian artisanal cultural knowledge in the execution of its haute couture collections. For example, in the Haute Couture collection presented in September 2020 in Florence, the brand gave prominence to the artisans who executed it:

> This Dolce Alta Moda collection, they stressed, had been executed by artisans of their own home bottega: A newly assembled corps of 50 employees, all aged under 30 and dedicated to various forms of embroidery, enabled this to be the first all in-house fabricated Alta Moda collection. [32]

The examples cited here show the importance of valuing ancestral cultural knowledge in the creation of differentiated products with high symbolic value.

3 Cultural Sustainability from the Perspective of Edgar Morin and Its Application in Fashion Design Education

In the vast complexity of teaching discussed by Morin and in the challenges for the future of education and humanity, we identify urgent and necessary reflections for the development of human understanding and the way in which the relationships between

---

[2] See https://www.fendi.com/sustainability/people-first/hand-in-hand.

[3] See https://www.fendi.com/sustainability/planet-care/les-journées-particulières.

individuals, society and culture occur. For the author, a reform of thought is necessary, which allows us the intellectual and relevant development, necessary to connect multiple cultures, which the author defines as "paradigmatic reform" [4]. When we approach the issues related to the specific Curricula of Fashion Design, we visualize the dissonances and problems discussed by Morin and the urgency in a reform of thought and curriculum aiming at more humane and sustainable approaches.

When related to fashion and design, as previously mentioned in the article "The Seven Complex Lessons from Edgar Morin applied in Fashion Design Education" [1], we approach 'Human understanding: understanding each other' from the point of view of cultural appropriation, pointing out cultural incomprehension to the detriment of the marketing and economic needs of the fashion industry. It is also important to remember the good point made by Moura [28] about the identity of a designer, which is constituted by many factors, among them, "tradition, language, geography". As referenced by Moura through the words of William Morris, who understood design as a social and political discipline, not as a subgenre of design itself, but rather as the ethical character that forms the discipline, reminding us of the transdisciplinary character implicit in culture and of the importance of these humanist questions from a social, cultural, ethical, and sustainable point of view. Contemporaneously, contributing to the reflection of cultural and artisanal development in fashion, it is important to emphasize that cultural craftsmanship, being intrinsic to human formation, constitutes imagery, historical, intellectual, and artistic background capable of sustaining an ethical and sustainable rhetoric for the future [26].

Only understanding culture from the point of view of human understanding can it transform the future [20, 33]. In this way, the understanding of cultural identity and artisanal cultural knowledge can provide a "motivational structure not only for creative expressions in the present, but also a motivation for creative expressions in the future" [33, p. 9]. In the same line of thought, Tung [19] argues that providing designers with knowledge related to artisanal cultural knowledge translates into an effective way of nurturing their individual creativity and that products that reflect a local identity, or that show cultural values, provide a way of differentiation.

However, inconsistencies are observed in the current educational model that do not encourage intellectual development associated with human knowledge and human understanding (sixth lesson by Edgar Morin). In this way, Morin [4] identifies an inadequacy of the curricula, when analyzing the fragmentation and compartmentalization of knowledge through isolated disciplines. The same situation is observed by Bertola [34], who describes universities in crisis, due to the lack of flexibility to deal with contemporary situations, which range from global factors (macros) to local cultural factors (micros). It is also part of the author's rhetoric, the specific approach of the curriculum grids of Fashion Design courses, of fragmentary and multifaceted nature, as well as approached by Morin in the context of global education. Added to this approach is the need to incorporate a new dialectic into teaching with regard to the culture of the humanities, since this provides solid foundations for solving global problems [4, 34]. For both authors, the solution runs through the concepts of multidisciplinarity and "metadisciplinary"[4] through approaches that contextualize and integrate human, ethical, cultural, social, political, and economic issues, which Morin [4, 7, 35] defines as "ecologizing the disciplines".

For Morin [4], multidisciplinarity is understood as the association of multiple disciplines, connected through a project and with common objectives; Bertola [34] recognizes the complexity of teaching the multidisciplinary context, as well as of fashion designers practicing such contexts in innovative solutions to problems with multiple faces. In this way, both authors resort to the "metadisciplinary" as a way of creating "bridges" between different disciplines of knowledge, generating a dialogue between technical, human, and cultural knowledge and perspectives characteristic of the individual experience of each designer, as a way of solving problems through characteristic perspectives of multidisciplinarity. With regard to Morin's term, "ecologizing the disciplines", Bertola [34] understands, in the context of teaching, the need for universities to open their spaces for dialogue with external agents, bringing culture, society and economic models closer together beyond disciplinary and academic limits. Morin questions us about the role of the university and whether society should adapt to it, or the academic environment should adapt to society and its multiple forms of cultural expression [4, 7, 35].

In the complex discussion of educational innovation through open academic spaces, it is also worth addressing the importance of emphatically including cultural heritage in the education of the future, Skrzypaszek [14], like Morin, argues that the role of cultural heritage needs to be aligned with an approach to education that includes a focus on the whole human being. Skrzypaszek [14] thus proposes a model for the education of the future which he calls the "Pathway of Cohesive Cultural Continuity", creating a link between the past and the present, but also with the future placing at the center of this model "human ingenuity & value and potential".

Among the global complexities, it is worth noting that, as well as various economic, cultural, technological, ethical, and human sectors, fashion has also suffered the effects of globalization, becoming a symbol of an unsustainable market, especially with regard to the environment and human labor relations, associated with fast fashion and exacerbated consumption, with the fashion design education being the necessary means for changes in the sector [36]. In other words, in an era marked by massification, it is urgent to look for solutions to slow down consumption and one of the possible ways is to improve the experience with products. The integration of artisanal cultural knowledge in the fashion design process makes it possible to endow products with added symbolic and cultural value. And in this way expand the experience with these products, their meaning, their appreciation and consequently their emotional durability [37, 38].

In support of Morin's humanistic ideas and ethical and ecological globalization, and as a way of going against the negative current of globalization, Kupisz and Holuj

[4] Term coined by Morin to describe the act of surpassing and conserving—"meta", the discipline, without disrespecting its peculiarities, individualities, and characteristics. In the "metadisciplinary" there is no exclusion of the discipline, but rather its integration with others, as in the multidisciplinary model [7, p. 115].

[36] refer to the importance of highlighting, among others: academic approaches as a support to resources and to local production; the use of local craft skills and traditions; and the inclusion of products designed in regional cultures and heritages. For the realization of such actions, it is of paramount importance to understand the impacts of universities on their surrounding spaces, that is, communities, positively and actively supporting the growth and economic development of local, regional, and national cultures, which in short describes the urgent need for the paradigm shift proposed by Morin, as a way to transform teaching into multidisciplinar. In this way, the term "fashion sustainability", seen peripherally to the disciplines and as an additional competence for future designers, becomes a result, integrated and primordial in multidisciplinary discourses [1, 26, 34, 36]. In practice, what is observed are desperate attempts to address sustainability in fashion, which Obadas et al. [39] describe as a certain difficulty on the part of the courses in adopting sustainable practices, and as a consequence, the difficulty of encouraging future designers to use sustainable practices, since there is a gradual disappearance and lack of interest in artisanal cultural techniques and artisanal productive techniques, as in the case of textiles.

Currently, changes can be observed in the context of European fashion design education, albeit punctual, with regard to the paradigmatic change of thought in teaching, with a focus on Morin's values and human understanding. We cite here two examples relevant to the subjects discussed.

The London College of Fashion, through the "Centre for Sustainable Fashion",[5] addresses a methodology centered on the pillars of academic research development, knowledge exchange and sustainable educational practices. Through this triad, they develop dialogue between society, culture, economy, and environment. Among the new approaches of the London College of Fashion are the approaches that contemplate the EU's 2030 agenda, in a platform called "Fashion Futures 2030"[6] highlighting the human and social relations pertinent to the future of design. In this context, they visualize different scenarios related to the future of the fashion industry and of a global nature: climate change, scarcity of resources and population growth.

Through initiatives such as the Institut des Métiers d'Excellence, founded in 2014, which aims to transmit knowledge of excellence from around the world to new generations through a "training program with a work-study format", the LVM[7] seeks to revitalize artisanal knowledge that were in danger of disappearing. Currently, the program has 27 handicraft métiers that, through a theoretical and practical methodology, teach young people ancestral craft practices from various countries.

In the article "The 7 Complex Lessons from Edgar Morin Applied in Fashion Design Education for Sustainability" [1], we argue that part of the change in the curricular model of fashion design education should encourage discussions, between institutions, and between education professionals and the institutions themselves, around the need for approaches that include society and cultural factors as a way of

[5] See https://www.sustainable-fashion.com/.

[6] See https://www.fashionfutures2030.com/scenarios/home.

[7] See https://www.lvmh.com/.

reconciling different approaches that go beyond the theoretical contents of the classroom, passing through practices with the local community in which the educational institution is inserted [1]. We believe that through a multidisciplinary action approach, it is possible to integrate disciplines, academia, society, and industry in the concrete resolution of problems associated with the sustainable future of fashion. Likewise, we discussed the need to train fashion professionals with multiple skills, endowed with characteristics implicit in creative leadership, having the ability to solve the multiple problems that involve the conception of new products, being a designer-facilitator, passing through the roles of designer educator and communicator, both in an academic and social environment, imbuing the environment in which they are inserted with human, ethical, collaborative and sustainable ideas, that is, also acting as an activist designer, since in this way they begin to influence and fight for social causes and policies that may contribute to the vision of a more sustainable world.

4 Discussion and Conclusions

In the fashion design education approach, understanding humanistic challenges and multiple cultural expressions refers to preparing future professionals to deal with global challenges and sustainable approaches, developing skills and abilities that go beyond technical knowledge, creating a human and intellectual awareness of craft techniques belonging to us and creative ways of dealing with global and future complexity.

Although challenging and aware of the need for a broad discussion around the theme of fashion design course curricula being rethought to better respond to the needs of the contemporary world and the challenges to be faced in the near future, we present a synthesis of what we believe translates the proposed links through existing approaches between Edgar Morin's discourse, specific to human understanding, fashion design, fashion design education, multidisciplinarity and sustainability (Fig. 1).

In the proposed vision, we understand that the areas of fashion design, education, sustainability, philosophy, anthropology, and sociology (these last three described through Morin's work), represent, in short, human communication, the need and ways to expand and strengthen these dialogues. The interaction between the languages of fashion, fashion design education and Morin's specific approaches to his sixth lesson, "Human Understanding: understanding each other", is evident, since they all seek to understand social and cultural factors. For Morin [4] understanding the other requires awareness of human complexity, since we are multicultural beings, coming from different peoples, origins, and cultural cores.

Through educational approaches derived from multidisciplinary methodologies, it is possible to connect local craft knowledge to global values and processes. For this, it is important for higher education institutions to modernize in order to open doors to traditional knowledge and cultures and that professors are also receptive to new methodologies and approaches, based on sustainability and local knowledge,

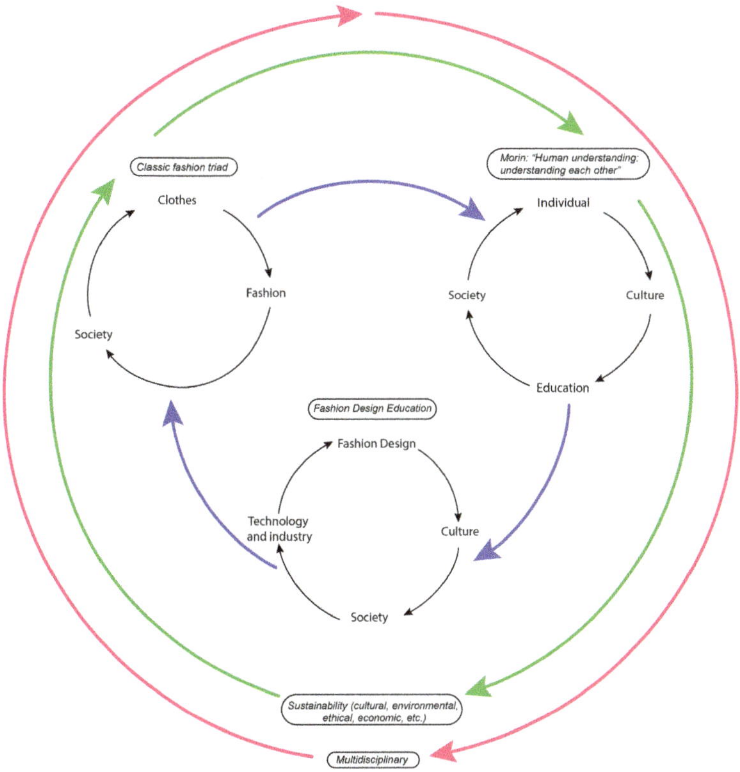

Fig. 1 Relational model of the concepts necessary for the sustainable education of fashion with a focus on human understanding

which Bertola [34] defines it as an education focused on a cultural model. It will be necessary, through this new approach, to focus the teaching of fashion design towards collective, collaborative, sustainable, social, cultural, and economic objectives, as well as to guide new designers in a perspective of a professional with multiple capacities, capable of responding to social, environmental, and economic demands.

The cases cited throughout the proposed dialogue bring light to a new approach in fashion design. Portugal, Italy, England, and France have been looking for alternatives to avoid erasing the multiple cultures that represent them, as well as adding human and local values in industrial contexts. These approaches allow the consumer to find identification and representation models, as designers, universities and industries develop an open, multicultural, and multidisciplinary dialogue.

Finally, recognizing individuals, particularities, details intrinsic to each culture is of paramount importance for the future of sustainable fashion, even though it is complex, it is necessary that we change our approaches, so that we can achieve an education model that responds to modern society, globalized and multicultural.

Acknowledgements This work is financed by Project UID/CTM/00264/2021 of 2C2T – Centro de Ciência e Tecnologia Têxtil, funded by National Funds through FCT/MCTES, and by Project "BE@T- Bioeconomia Sustentável - Iniciativa 6", reference - TC-C12-i01, funded by National Funds through Fundo Ambiental – Plano de Recuperação e Resiliência, and by European Funds through Program NEXT GENERATION EU.

References

1. Schulz FE, Freire LH, da Cunha JLFL (2022) The 7 complex lessons from Edgar Morin applied in fashion design education for sustainability. Springer Series in Design and Innovation 25:193–208. https://doi.org/10.1007/978-3-031-09659-4_15
2. Morin E, Da M, and De Assis Carvalho E (2007) Educação e complexidade : os sete saberes e outros ensaios. Cortez, São Paulo
3. Maura MAP (2021) El pensamiento moriniano en Educacíon. In: 100 años Edgar Morin. Humanista Planetario, 1st edn. [online] Universidad Mayor de San Andrés-La Paz, Bolivia. Available at: https://www.researchgate.net/publication/356145350_100_anos_Edgar_Morin_Humanista_Planetario. Accessed 15 May 2023
4. Morin E (2014b) La Tête bien faite. Repenser la réforme, réformer la pensée. Média Diffusion
5. Williams R, Baravalle G (1994) Cultura: sociología de la comunicación y del arte. Paidós, Barcelona
6. Campello LGB, Santiago MR, Andrade SL (2018) A valorização da identidade cultural como desafio à concretização do direito ao desenvolvimento. Rev Direito Bras 19(8). https://doi.org/10.26668/indexlawjournals/2358-1352/2018.v19i8.3220
7. Morin E (2001) Les sept savoirs nécessaires à l'éducation du futur. United Nations Educational, Scientific and Cultural Organization (UNESCO), Paris
8. Anon (2022) 17 objetivos • ODS - BCSD Portugal. [online] Available at: https://ods.pt/ods/
9. UNESCO (2022) Re | Shaping policies for creativity. UNESCO Publishing
10. Soini K, Birkeland I (2014) Exploring the scientific discourse on cultural sustainability. Geoforum 51:213–223. https://doi.org/10.1016/j.geoforum.2013.12.001
11. UNESCO (2001) UNESCO—Universal declaration on cultural diversity. In: Unesco.org. Accessed at: https://en.unesco.org/about-us/legal-affairs/unesco-universal-declaration-cultural-diversity. Accessed 10 Feb 2023
12. Kurin R (2007) Safeguarding intangible cultural heritage in the 2003 UNESCO convention: a critical appraisal. Museum Int 56:66–77. https://doi.org/10.1111/j.1350-0775.2004.00459.x
13. UNESCO (2022) Basic texts of the 2003 convention for the safeguarding of the intangible cultural heritage. In: Unesco.org. https://ich.unesco.org/en/basic-texts-00503 Available at: https://ich.unesco.org/doc/src/2003_Convention_Basic_Texts-_2022_version-EN_.pdf. Accessed 10 Feb 2023
14. Skrzypaszek J (2014) Cultural heritage: transformational and inspirational framework for future education. In: Amoeda R, Lira S, Pinheiro C (eds) Heritage 2014. Paper presented at the International Conference on Heritage and Sustainable Development, Guimaraes, 22–25 July. Greenlines Institute for Sustainable Development, Barcelos, Portugal, pp 761–768
15. Susan MP (2000) The making of cultural heritage. In: Values and heritage conservation research report. The Getty Conservation Institute, Los Angeles, pp 59–64. https://doi.org/10.1179/2159032x13z.00000000011
16. Mirrlees T (2020) Global culture. In: Reimagining communication: meaning. Routledge, pp 117–133
17. Raikhan S, Moldakhmet M, Ryskeldy M, Alua M (2014) The interaction of globalization and culture in the modern world. Procedia Soc Behav Sci 122(1877–0428):8–12. https://doi.org/10.1016/j.sbspro.2014.01.1294

18. Krucken L (2009) *Design e território: valorização de identidades e produtos locais*. Studio Nobel, São Paulo
19. Tung F-W (2021) An entrepreneurial process to build a sustainable business for indigenous craft revitalization. Des J 24(3):363–383. https://doi.org/10.1080/14606925.2021.1883790
20. Vencatachellum I (2005) Foreword. In: Sethi R, Duque C, Vencatachellum I (eds) (2005) Designers meet artisans: a practical guide. Published jointly by Craft Revival Trust, Artesanías de Colombia S.A. and UNESCO. Available at: https://unesdoc.unesco.org/ark:/48223/pf0000147132. Accessed 10 Feb 2023
21. Strand EA, Harlow M (2018) Introduction. In: Andersson Strand E, Ebert CES, Frisch S, Harlow M, Bjerregaard L (eds), Traditional textile craft—an intangible cultural heritage, 2nd edn. Grafisk - University of Copenhagen, Copenhagen
22. Marinucci S (2022) Artisan voices: dialogues for sustainable practices. [online] e-space.mmu.ac.uk. Available at: https://e-space.mmu.ac.uk/630519/. Accessed 18 June 2023
23. Filho ER (2013) Design and craftsmanship: The Brazilian experience. Des Issues 29(3):64–74. https://doi.org/10.1162/desi_a_00221
24. Sethi R, Duque C, Vencatachellum I (eds) (2005) Designers meet artisans: a practical guide. Published jointly by Craft Revival Trust, Artesanías de Colombia S.A. and UNESCO. Available at: https://unesdoc.unesco.org/ark:/48223/pf0000147132. Accessed 10 Feb 2023.
25. Niedderer K, Imani Y, Overton MG (2011) *Craft as a tool for multidisciplinary collaboration and design practice*. [online] Semantic Scholar. Available at: https://www.semanticscholar.org/paper/Craft-as-a-Tool-for-Multidisciplinary-Collaboration-Niedderer-Imani/719ee1f87c54ff0159e1937e14407bca56e28043. Accessed 17 June 2023
26. Schulz FE (2021) Do crochê artesanato para o crochê design: contribuições possíveis das ferramentas de comunicação de moda no ensino do design de moda com foco no futuro da moda sustentável. Handle.net. [online] https://hdl.handle.net/1822/83029
27. Arizpe L (2000) Cultural heritage and globalization. In: Values and heritage conservation. The Getty Conversation Institute, Los Angeles, pp 32–37. https://doi.org/10.1179/2159032x13z.00000000011
28. Moura M (2018) O design que o design não vê. 1° edn. Orfeu Negro, Lisboa
29. Giusto RM, Buono M (2021) Kalokagathìa, made in Italy and cultural heritage in Campania region. In: Advances in human dynamics for the development of contemporary societies: proceedings of the AHFE 2021 virtual conference on human dynamics for the development of contemporary societies, July 25–29, 2021, USA. Springer International Publishing, pp 150–157
30. Tarquini A, Mühlbacher H, Kreuzer M (2022) The experience of luxury craftsmanship—a strategic asset for luxury experience management. J Mark Manag 38(13–14):1307–1338
31. Dallabona A, Giani S (2020) The good, the bad, and the ugly: Dolce & Gabbana and narratives of heritage and national identity. In: Storytelling in luxury fashion. Routledge, pp 38–50
32. Leitch L (2020) In Florence, a new renaissance takes hold as Dolce & Gabbana celebrates artistry in Alta Moda. [online] Vogue. Available at: https://www.vogue.com/slideshow/dolce-gabbana-alta-moda-florence-2020. Accessed 6 May 2022
33. Skrzypaszek J (2016) Intangible and tangible heritage in a cross-cultural setting: integrity versus profit. In: Amoeda R, Lira S, Pinheiro C (eds) Heritage 2016. Paper presented at the international conference on heritage and sustainable development, University of Lisbon, Lisbon, 12–15 July. Green Lines Institute for Sustainable Development, Barcelos, Portugal, pp 1003–1012. [online] Available at: https://research.avondale.edu.au/theo_conferences/12/. Accessed 10 Feb 2023
34. Bertola P (2018) Reshaping fashion education for the 21st century world. In: Soft landing. Helsinki Aalto University of Arts, Design and Architecture, Helsinki, Finland, pp 7–14 [online]. Available at: https://cumulusassociation.org/wp-content/uploads/2021/09/PDF_SINGLE_cumulus_soft_landing.pdf. Accessed 2 June 2023
35. Morin E (2014) Introduction à la pensée complexe. Seuil, Paris
36. Murzyn-Kupisz M, Hołuj D (2021) Fashion design education and sustainability: towards an equilibrium between craftsmanship and artistic and business skills? Educ Sci [online] 11(9):531. https://doi.org/10.3390/educsci11090531

37. Cunha J, Providência B, Costa MC (2013) Alma: design, corpo: bijouteria ... Anais do 9º Colóquio Moda 6ª edição Internacional, 9 a 12 Setembro 2013, Fortaleza, Brasil [online]. http://coloquiomoda.com.br/anais/ColoquiodeModa-2013/COMUNICACAO-ORAL/EIXO-1-DESIGN_COMUNICACAO-ORAL/AlmaDesign,corpoBijouteria.pdf
38. Providência B, Cunha J (2014) Corpo e alma do design emocional. Atas do Iº Seminário Iberoamericano de Estudos e Pesquisas em Comunicação e Moda: Estéticas contemporâneas. Universidade do Minho, Centro de Estudos de Comunicação e Sociedade (CECS), 11–12 abril, Braga, Portugal. http://hdl.handle.net/1822/37355
39. Odabasi S, von Busch O, Moon C, Sansone L, Rissanen T (2022) Transition design and fashion. Fash Pract, 1–19. https://doi.org/10.1080/17569370.2022.2133183

Weaving the Gap: Giving a Place to Textile Design in Portuguese Higher Education

Sónia Seixas, Gianni Montagna, and Maria João Félix

Abstract This preliminary research is part of a design investigation and seeks to examine the Portuguese higher education landscape in textile design and the challenges faced by the sector. The world is undergoing transformation, with an increase in problem complexity. Emerging challenges in sustainability, circular economy, decarbonization, and digital economy are impacting the textile industry. Textile designers must adapt their thinking and approach to address these challenges, making it crucial for higher education in textile design to keep pace with these changes. To determine the key competencies required by textile designers in their profession, a literature review and data collection were conducted, linking various research topics to stimulate reflection and open new perspectives in the field of research. The research concludes that there are essential skills for textile designers to effectively respond to these challenges. However, the availability of Portuguese higher education programs in textile design is limited. Bringing together textile design-focused education in a close partnership between academia and industry is imperative to prepare textile designers who will actively contribute to a circular economy and shape a promising future for the textile industry.

Keywords Textile design · Higher Design Education · Designer skills · Portugal

1 Introduction

The textile and clothing industry is part of the Portuguese culture, has a long history and remains an important industry that contributes significantly to wealth and job creation and is one of the main pillars of the national economy [1]. It is an inseparable

S. Seixas (✉) · G. Montagna · M. J. Félix
Research Centre for Architecture, Urbanism and Design, CIAUD, Lisbon School of Architecture, Universidade de Lisboa, Rua Sá Nogueira, Polo Universitário Do Alto da Ajuda, 1349-063 Lisboa, Portugal
e-mail: sonia.seixas@gmail.com

M. J. Félix
e-mail: mfelix@ipca.pt

D. Raposo et al. (eds.), *Perspectives on Design III*, Springer Series in Design and Innovation 34, https://doi.org/10.1007/978-3-031-43516-4_16

cog in the engine of the national industry. In 2021, despite the pandemic COVID-19, this sector recorded a remarkable growth in export volume, with an increase of 16% compared to the previous year, corresponding to an export value of 5.4 million euros, showing the importance of this sector for the Portuguese economy and society [2].

However, the textile industry is currently in a transitional phase and is actively seeking further advances and opportunities for more environmentally friendly solutions, as the amount of waste generated has less positive impact on the environment. Climate issues are in the spotlight, particularly in relation to the textile industry, as it has a significant impact on the environment, energy consumption, water consumption and resource depletion [3–6]. It is worth noting that in 2018, the fashion industry alone was responsible for generating approximately 2.1 million tons of greenhouse gas emissions [7]. In light of this, there is an urgent necessity to implement sustainable practices throughout the production chain, from fiber production to product disposal [8–10], focusing on the circular economy, decarbonization, and the digital economy [4, 6, 11], with the various actors being accountable for the choices made and adopting more circular and sustainable practices.

There is a necessity to promote a sustainable circular system for textiles by calling for indispensable and systemic changes across the entire value chain. According to the Ellen Mac Arthur Foundation, this must be a reparative and regenerative system that, through its design, brings benefits not only to the economy but also to society and the environment. Within this process, the role of the textile designer becomes increasingly crucial, as the choices made in developing textile products at the process and material levels have a significant influence on the environmental and climate impacts throughout their life cycle [4, 11, 12]. The integration of circular thinking concerns is essential to establish a new strategic positioning that fosters a fresh mindset and attitude throughout the value chain [6], in which the textile designer plays a key role in developing textile products for more durable use, focusing on reuse, repair, recycling or disassembly. These skills and ways of thinking [13–15] are described as a set of competencies that enable circular solutions to be found and that the academia must teach future textile designers in order to support the textile industry in this much-needed process of change.

The world is constantly changing and the complexity of problems is increasing. New challenges are emerging, including environmental, social, ethical, cultural, and economic. Therefore, it is crucial to contemplate the mission of design and the role of academia in adequately preparing and educating professionals in the field, as well as fostering responsible citizenship. The field of design is interdisciplinary and multifaceted, designers do not work in isolation when creating solutions, and it is important to note that solutions are not always tangible in nature [16], responses to problems have changed significantly as they have become more complex. The analysis and revision of textile design higher education curricula should lead textile designers to also acquire competencies in sustainability, circular economy, decarbonization and digital economy. Active participation in a circular economy is essential for textile designers as they contribute to shaping a textile economy of the future [6, 17].

Of the seven Portuguese textile and fashion design undergraduate programmes, only two include the title "textile" in their didactic offerings. The "Fashion and

Textile Design" undergraduate programme at the Higher School of Applied Arts from Castelo Branco Polytechnic Institute, and, the "Fashion and Textile Design and Production" undergraduate programme at the Higher School Manuel Teixeira Gomes [18]. However, it is understood that the other undergraduate programmes cover contents related to textile design, but they are not part of the "core" of the programmes. Since Portugal has a long history of textile industry, dating back to 1836, it is difficult to see the reduced offer of specialized training in textile design. Analyzing the relevance of specialized training in the field of textile design is crucial, as it can enable the industry to effectively confront new challenges and maintain its position as a wealth and employment generator.

The purpose of this research is to explore and understand why there are no higher education undergraduate programmes specialized in textile design, when the textile industry generates wealth and provide sustainable employment opportunities. While education in textile engineering can certainly address certain aspects of the industry, it may not fully encompass the creative elements inherited from the Bauhaus and its unique workshop approach. The Bauhaus workshop, known for its emphasis on creativity, experimentation, and interdisciplinary collaboration, has a distinct legacy in the field of textiles, the only workshop that has survived during the school's existence. To shape the future while drawing inspiration and wisdom from the past, designers must remain cognizant that they are, in a way, reimagining the world with each design endeavor they undertake [19]. Designers must integrate economic, social, environmental, cultural and ethical values into the creative process without compromising the ecosystem [14, 20]. An attitude centered on the circular economy necessitates a shift towards seeking sustainable solutions through a harmonious relationship between production and consumption. Design can serve as a powerful ally in addressing the pressing concerns for the future imposed by the endangered state of our planet [21]. By creating new products that promote equity in the distribution of resources, designers can contribute to a more sustainable and balanced world [22].

Through the literature review and data collection that connected the themes of this research, it was possible to enumerate a set of competencies for textile designers and define some strategies for higher education in textile design so that the textile industry can continue to weave a promising future.

2 The Thread of History

2.1 Unwind the Skein of the Portuguese Textile Industry

The textile industry, founded in 1836, is considered one of the most traditional and oldest national industries [1]. There were numerous phases of development and difficulties, but they were overcome and still exist today as an industry that drives the national economy. It continues to prove its importance in the economic and social weave of Portugal, with a 19% share of employment, 10% of national exports and 8%

of manufacturing turnover, according to the latest data from the Portuguese Textile Association for 2019 [23].

The need of the human being to dress, a basic need, has accelerated the emergence of the production of fabrics and clothing, thus accompanying the history of humankind. The transition from nomadism to sedentarism allowed the domestication of animals, the development of agriculture and the invention of the loom [24].

The mechanization of the textile industry, originating in England during the Industrial Revolution, reached Portugal towards the end of the eighteenth century. Until then, the Portuguese textile industry was essentially artisanal, domestic and manual, focusing on the production of woolen, linen and hemp fabrics for local consumption. It was during this period that the Portuguese factory system emerged, representing a crucial turning point in the industrial development of the country. The changes brought about by the factory system also had a profound impact on family dynamics and social life in Portugal. With the introduction of mechanized looms and spinning machines, cotton production changed as it became easier to process and could be imported from Portuguese, African and Brazilian colonies. As technology advanced, so did weaving techniques. Industrial schools emerged in the nineteenth century and played an important role in teaching the art of textiles. At the same time, the textile industry had already transformed into an industrial system [24]. At the beginning of the twentieth century, the cotton textile industry took the lead, followed by the wool textile industry, which contributed significantly to the national economy [24, 25]. Vertical factories emerge with the aim of industrial reorganization, driven by government strategies under the influence of the political period of the Portuguese Estado Novo (1933–1974). State intervention, both at the level of economic and political protection, as well as funding, directly or indirectly, allowed the process of industrialization of the textile industry [25].

The opening to European markets in the 1960s marked a new industrial cycle. The country's reputation for providing excellent value for money has made it one of the world's largest exporters of textiles and clothing. As a result, the textile industry has played a pivotal role in the growth of the Portuguese economy and has secured a prominent position within it. National and European support programs enabled the modernization of the sector in the 1980s. Portugal's accession to the European Union in 1986 provided access to new public financing instruments, new markets and new technologies that were important for the development of the industrial fabric, especially in the textile and clothing sector [26], having diversified the production of textiles including silk, wool, synthetic fibers concentrating production in high quality products [24, 25]. The globalization of markets in the 1990s meant that companies had to become more competitive at all levels, national, community and international [25].

Against all odds, the Portuguese textile industry remains resilient and an engine of Portugal's social and economic weave [1, 2, 6]. Sustainability, circular economy, decarbonization and circular economy are the buzzwords for the textile sector, both in a current and future vision [1, 6, 25]. Problems that are becoming increasingly complex, with the textile designer playing a key role in finding solutions to these challenges. For this reason, it is also important that academia provide training programs in textile design. This will allow the education and development of professionals who can contribute to the textile industry, aiding in its progression and ensure the continuity of the historical heritage of the national industry [27–29].

2.2 Unwind the Skein of the Portuguese Education in Textile Design

In the first decades of the nineteenth century, industrial training was considered important for Portugal to overcome its backwardness with respect to other European countries and to promote the country's industrial development. In 1844, two industrial schools were founded, the Marquez de Pombal Industrial School in Lisbon and the Industrial and Commercial School of Campos Mello in Covilhã, where the textile arts were taught and foreign technicians were hired, but it was not until 1852 that industrial training was made official [24].

Industrial-technical education is restructured between 1916 and 1918, creating three types of schools: Industrial Schools, Applied Arts Schools and Arts and Crafts Schools [30]. António Arroio (1856–1934), a notable figure in Portuguese industrial education, advocated the division of technical training into two distinct areas: industrial and artistic. António Arroio emphasized the importance of limiting industrial training to two specialized schools that focus on this particular area of training. Consequently, in 1914, the creation of technical and vocational schools came into effect, namely António Arroio in Lisbon and Soares dos Reis in Porto. From the 1940s onwards, technical-professional education expanded to include vocational training in various areas such as industrial, commercial, and decorative arts [31].

Portugal in the first decade of the twentieth century was still a little industrialized and essentially rural country with a high illiteracy rate, which made it difficult for design to spread [26]. Design education in Lisbon and Porto emerges tentatively in the António Arroio and Soares dos Reis technical and vocational schools and is complemented by informal learning in professional practice in the studio. Frederico George (1915–1944) began to gain his first experience of teaching design in the 1950s at the António Arroio school, with the ideals received from the Bauhaus. Officially, however, teaching in the field was introduced only after 1974, to accompany the strong international current that used design as a contemporary economic lever, with the autonomous formulation of design as a discipline and as an economic, professional and cultural activity. In 1969, the first Portuguese school dedicated exclusively to the continuous teaching of design was established. This was an important milestone when the discipline of design began to assert its unique identity and demand recognition in the educational system: the IADE Faculty of Design, Technology and Communication [30].

It was not until 1980 that design education was officially introduced, since at the European level there was already an inseparable relationship between design, production and consumption [32]. At that time, the textile and clothing sector held a pivotal position as the central axis of the Portuguese economy, which led to the emergence of vocational training centers that had the task of developing vocational training courses to meet the needs of the sector, creating the first vocational training courses in this field [33].

The University of Minho creates the first course of Textile Engineering in 1975 and the Lisbon School of Architecture from University of Lisbon creates the first course of Fashion Design in 1991, which is taught from 1992 [34, 35], so that in the last decade of the twentieth century, there were more and more schools throughout the country specializing in textile and fashion design. This expansion reflected the growing recognition of the importance of these fields and the demand for education and training in the textile and fashion industries.

Presently, existing proposals for higher education in textile design are proving to be limiting. They are mostly related to the fashion and clothing industry and only a few to the field of textile design. To fill this gap, it is considered important to introduce specialized textile design education in higher education. This curriculum should encompass areas such as decarbonization, circular economy, sustainability, and the digital economy. By incorporating these subjects into the education system, we can provide support to the industry in tackling pressing environmental and economic concerns.

2.3 Unwind the Skein of the Design Education

One cannot talk about teaching in the field of design without mentioning the Bauhaus, founded in 1919, which is considered the first design school in Europe and the strength of higher education in design. Bauhaus driven on linking the gap between art and industry by combining design education with art education. It was formed from the merger of two institutions, the Academy of Art and the School of Arts and Crafts, based in Weimar, Germany. It was initially headed by Walter Gropius (1883–1969), who defined as a guiding principle that design was neither an intellectual study nor a material matter, but an integral part of a civilized society [36, 37]. At the heart of the lesson structure was a pedagogy of "learning by doing". This approach aimed to prepare students for hands-on education by actively engaging them in the design process of objects that serve functional purposes in everyday life. Students were encouraged to create designs that met the necessity and requirements of practical use, integrating interdisciplinary work in the workshops [38].

The workshops held a central and valued position within the Bauhaus programme. Among these workshops, the weaving workshop stood out as the only one that persisted throughout the duration of the Bauhaus and was highly valued for its valuable contributions to the school. The weaving mill attracted women of great talent, such as Anni Albers (1889–1994), Margarete Willers (1883–1977), Gunta Stölzl (1897–1983), and others who became artists and textile designers [39, 40]. Stölzl became a teacher in weaving and appropriated different systems of looms that oriented learning towards an industrial character, which led to a jump towards industrial design, a systematization of the creative process [39].

This is how the industrial designer comes into being. The professional who masters not only the technical language, but also, the formal language, leading to a transformation in the professional practice of the traditional craftsman [41].

The Bauhaus initiated the pedagogy of design, which was consolidated in the postwar period with the Ulm School (1955–1968) [37]. The statement emphasized the significant societal impact of design and its influence on design theory, practice, and education. It proposed the integration of a framework that acknowledged the importance of technical and scientific disciplines and includes a special department of industrial design dedicated to the study and improvement of creative methods [36]. These schools emphasized the importance of art and design in daily life.

In Portugal, the influence of the Bauhaus on design education was not felt until the 1950s, due to the late development of the industry, which was late to address the issue of design, in spite of the triumphs of the textile sector since the Industrial Revolution, which allowed the development of technology and machinery.

3 Data Collection and Analysis

The author of this research hosted an OpenTalk in the form of a seminar in May 2019 [42] to discuss the future of higher education in fashion and textile design in Portugal. This event brought collectively industry experts who pointed out gaps, especially the weakness of textile designers.

Building upon the literature review, we gained insight into the emerging challenges confronted by the textile industry and the potential role of academia in equipping textile designers to address these challenges, a survey and an analysis of the higher education offer of the existing Portuguese textile and fashion design undergraduate programmes were carried out, interviews were conducted to understand what essential competencies a textile designer must have in order to practice their profession, and finally a focus group was held to understand how an undergraduate programme in textile design can be designed.

3.1 Analysis of Portuguese Undergraduates Programmes in Textile and Fashion Design

Higher education in textile and fashion design is still quite recent in Portugal. There are currently seven undergraduate programmes, four of which are offered by public institutions and three by private institutions. Two integrate the term "textile" into their training, the undergraduate programme in "Fashion and Textile Design" from Higher School of Applied Arts from Castelo Branco in public education and the

Table 1 Portuguese Undergraduate Programmes in Textile and Fashion Design (Author, 2023)

Higher Education Institution	Acronyms	Establishment	Undergraduate Programmes	Year of implementation
Higher School of Applied Arts, Castelo Branco Polytechnic Institute	ESART	Public	Fashion and Textile Design	1999
University of Minho	UMINHO	Public	Fashion Design and Marketing	2005
University of Beira Interior	UBI	Public	Fashion Design	2000
Higher School Manuel Teixeira Gomes	ISMAT	Private	Fashion and Textile Design and Production	2022
School of Communication, Architecture, Arts and Information Technologies—University Lusófona	ECATI	Private	Fashion Design and Production	2021
Lisbon School of Architecture, Universidade de Lisboa	FAUL	Public	Fashion Design	1992
School of Art and Design	ESAD	Private	Design with a specialization in Fashion	2004

undergraduate programme in "Fashion and Textile Design and Production" from the Higher School Manuel Teixeira Gomes in private education (Table 1) [18].

The analysis of the curricula has shown us that all the institutions integrate in curricular units that deal with the field of textile design, whether in the field of laboratory, project or materials (Table 2) [34, 35, 43–46].

In a percentage analysis, ESART is the Higher Education Institution that incorporates a bigger significance of curricular units that address the field of textile design with 21.11%, followed by UMINHO with 16.67%, UBI with 16.11%, ISMAT with 10.00%, ECATI with 5.56%, FAUL with 3.89%, and finally, ESAD with 3.33% (Fig. 1). It is important to note, however, that none of the current programmes are specifically focused on "Textile Design". Instead, all existing offerings encompass both, fashion design and textile design simultaneously.

3.2 OpenTalk

The OpenTalk, which took place as a seminar in May 2019, gathered a panel of eight industry experts to deliberate on the future of higher education in textile and fashion design in Portugal. In attendance were representatives from industry, academia and designers (Table 3).

Table 2 Curricular Units in Textile Design Field from Portuguese Undergraduate Programmes in Textile and Fashion Design (Author, 2023)

Higher Education Institution	Curricular Unit in Textile Design Field	ECTS	TOTAL ECTS
ESART	Textile Design I and II	9	38
	Knitwear Design	4	
	Textile Materials and Technologies	4	
	Studio and Textile Production	5	
	Studio Materials	4	
	Computer Aided Textile Design	3	
	Project	9	
UMINHO	Textile Materials and Processes I, II, III and IV	20	30
	Textile Design—Fabrics and Knits	5	
	Textile Design—Printing	5	
UBI	Fabric Design Lab	6	29
	Knitwear Design Lab	6	
	Color and Ennoblement Lab	5	
	Creative Textiles Lab	6	
	Fashion Materials	6	
ISMAT	Fashion Materials and Technology	5	18
	Printing	4	
	Interior Textile Design	5	
	Textile Art Lab	4	
ECATI	Textile Materials and Processes	5	10
	Printing	5	
FAUL	Fashion Materials I and II	7	7
ESAD	Materials Lab	6	6

The speakers pointed out the importance of strengthening the connection between academia and industry. The aim of these discussions was to explore opportunities for establishing specialized profiles within the sector, with a particular focus on training textile designers who can effectively tackle the challenges of the industry. When asked about the fundamental competencies that textile designer should have, they referred to the thorough knowledge of materials, processes, production, marketing and management, as well as the scientific field of design. They emphasized that textile design teaching should include a robust practical component, "learning by doing," "knowing how to do it," involving learning in a work context to enable students to understand the realities of the industrial world [42].

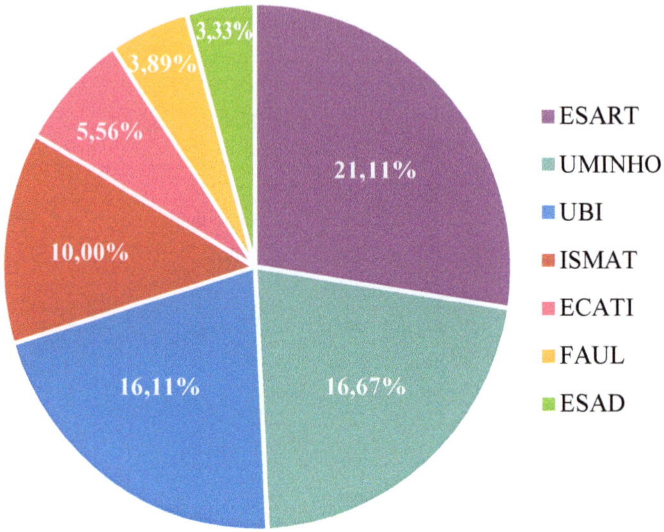

Fig. 1 Ratio of Curricular Units in Textile Design Field from Portuguese Undergraduate Programmes in Textile and Fashion Design (Author, 2023)

Table 3 Characterization of the Speakers (Author, 2019)

Type of Business	Function
Textile Industry	Head of the Innovation and Development Department
Textile Industry	Company Manager
Fashion and Textile Industry	Consultant and Fashion Creative Director
Training Company	Company Manager
Academia	Teacher
Academia	Teacher
Fashion Brand	Fashion Designer
Fashion Accessories Brand	Fashion Designer

3.3 *Interviews*

In May 2021, semi-structured interviews were conducted with twelve industry experts (Table 4) to comprehend what essential competencies the textile designer must own in order to perform his profession.

The results suggest that the textile designer must combine a range of multidisciplinary knowledge. He must have technical knowledge such as materials and textile processes, combined with knowledge in the field of design. In addition, it was emphasized that a textile designer should possess an understanding of management and planning aspects in the textile industry. This broad knowledge enables professionals

Table 4 Characterization of the Interviewed (Author, 2021)

Type of Business	Function
Textile Design	Individual Textile Designer and Teacher
Textile Design	Individual Textile Designer
Textile Design	Industrial Textile Designer
Textile Craftsman	Textile Craftsman and Teacher
Textile Craftsman	Textile Craftsman and Teacher
Technological Center of the Textile and Clothing Industries	General Director
Centre for Nanotechnology and Smart Materials	General Director
Portuguese Textile Cluster	Executive director
Portuguese Textile Association	President
Portuguese Business Association	Executive Administrator
Selectiva Moda Association	Director
ModaLisboa Association	President and Teacher

to practice their profession effectively by addressing the demands of the market and society. Transversal skills are fundamental, since the designer does not perform an isolated activity, but must work in a team with other professionals such as textile engineers, merchants, marketers, among others, it is a collaborative activity, so communication skills, responsibility, interrelationships and listening skills should be promoted in the academic training. The interviewees reiterated the need for this profession to know how to execute textiles, that is, in addition to the creative component, it must know how to conceptualize, and it must have practical knowledge, "learning by doing". It was acknowledged that application of acquired knowledge in a real-world setting with tangible challenges is critical to a comprehensive understanding of how concepts are implemented in an industrial setting. This hands-on experience allows students to grasp the practical application of their acquired knowledge and to navigate real-world scenarios.

3.4 Focus Group

To better understand how to design an undergraduate programme in textile design, a focus group of eight industry experts (Table 5) was formed in May 2022. During this meeting, in addition to the main objective, it was possible to identify that there is a lack of workers with knowledge of the textile sector in several areas, but also that there is a need to change the image of the sector in front of young people and show them that this industry has changed, that it has modernized and has many innovations.

Table 5 Characterization of the Focus Group Participants (Author, 2022)

Type of Business	Function
Textile Industry	Team Leader Textiles for Automotive
Textile Industry	Development Director
Home Textile Industry	Innovation Director
Fashion Industry	Innovation and Sustainability Director
Training Textile Academy	Director
Portuguese Textile Cluster	Executive director
	Facilitator of the Special Interest Group
	Project Manager

The group pointed out that a textile design course should include an important practical component, i.e., the acquisition of practical knowledge based on experience so that students learn how to deconstruct textiles through experimentation. They stressed the importance of textile designers having a sound knowledge of raw materials and production processes, considering the premises of the circular economy and combining design with performance. They pointed out the importance of establishing protocols for collaboration between the university, knowledge centers and industry to provide students with experience in a real environment that allows them to gain a deeper understanding of industrial dynamics, through the realization of concrete projects so that students understand technological boundaries through a collaborative dialogue between creativity and production. Finally, they mentioned that a programme of this type should consider a faculty with not only theoretical but also practical knowledge.

3.5 *Reflections*

From the analysis of the curricula of the two national programmes that encompass the field of textile design, the percentage of curricular units related to more specific content of the field of textile design is 21.11% in ESART and 10.00% in ISMAT. It is also true that both include in parallel the universe of fashion design and production, which are not specific to the field of textile design. In the OpenTalk and in the interviews conducted, the absence of textile designers to meet the demands of the industry was highlighted, raising the question of how the textile industry can effectively identify and recruit these professionals when the supply from national academia is limited.

This scenario prompts us to recognize the significance of integrating a degree in textile design into the Portuguese higher education system to prepare and train textile designers capable of further promoting the textile industry and contributing to overcoming the tasks it faces. Such training, as mentioned in the focus group, should focus on collaboration in discovering solutions to complex problems, and this is an emerging concern of the twenty-first century. To effectively respond to emerging challenges and achieve strategic positioning of the textile industry, it is crucial to adopt a multidisciplinary, interdisciplinary, and transdisciplinary approach that incorporates diverse knowledge and perspectives. This approach encourages the integration of different disciplines and fosters innovation and problem-solving in a holistic way.

4 The Thread of the Future

4.1 Weave the Role of the Textile Designer

According to the World Design Organization, the primary focus of industrial designers should be on placing the human being at the core of the process. Their aim is to gain a profound comprehension of user requirements by involving them in the problem-solving procedure. Through empathy, designers create user-centered products, systems, services, and experiences. By strategically integrating various professional fields and business concerns, designers employ creativity to drive innovation and find solutions. Therefore, this profession is inherently transdisciplinary. It is crucial for designers to consider environmental, social, and economic implications during the development phase to collaboratively create solutions that enhance the overall quality of life [47].

The role of the textile designer is crucial in the selection of materials and production methods while seeking solutions to environmental and social issues [48]. Their responsibility encompasses all aspects of the product, from aesthetics to technological considerations, with the objective of creating textile objects that fulfill the requirements of industry, society, users, and the planet. Consequently, it is essential for textile designers to broaden their knowledge, including technical training in the textile industry, and to incorporate aspects of sustainability, circular economy, decarbonization, and digital economy into their current paradigm [49]. The designer also assumes the responsibility of participating to changes in society, taking a more active role, being an agent of change, proposing innovative solutions and even reshape our perspectives of the world [13, 20], focusing his practices not only on the appearance but also on the interaction of objects with the user and society [50]. Act as a social innovator with tools that allow you to make informed decisions aimed at a more socially just and better developed future [51–53].

The design process is a bridge between the identification of a problem and the proposal of a possible solution, but for this it must consider the context in which the problem is embedded and understand the social and symbolic aspects and must coexist in a set of values and not just in a single objective. Concerned with the context and the natural environment coexisting in harmony with the environment and society where the human dimension must be included to contribute to the global balance between humanity and the natural world. The designer must maintain a constant awareness that they are, in a way, actively reshaping the world in some way when he undertakes a design project [19]. He must consider and integrate social, ethical, and cultural values while also ensuring the preservation of the ecosystem [14]. Design is a complex process involving several phases; it is not an isolated activity, rather, it is a collaborative and interconnected process.

The practice of textile design requires an understanding of the technical limitations, methods, and complexities of the marketplace and should strive to balance innovation, creativity, and commercial viability [54] working collaboratively with the different actors in the search for solutions to the problems that are increasingly complex [55]. Textile designers ought to engage in collaborative efforts within multidisciplinary, interdisciplinary, and transdisciplinary teams, leveraging their diverse expertise, to contribute towards a more sustainable textile industry and reduce environmental impacts through responsible consumption practices to ensure the planet and human sustainability.

4.2 Weave the Skills of the Textile Designer

Knowledge related to the problems of sustainability, the circular economy, decarbonization and the digital economy is inherent in the profession of textile design, which must ponder the origin of materials throughout the creative process. In the search for solutions to the current and future problems already mentioned, which are becoming increasingly complex, it is necessary to promote an interdisciplinary and multidisciplinary mentality in support of the preservation of the planet and the well-being of humanity, textile designers should actively consider the environmental, economic, social, ethical, and cultural implications [4, 6, 11].

A collaborative mindset allows you to respect diverse perspectives, critique, and constructively analyze complex real-world problems. Actively collaborate across the entire value chain working together to develop innovative solutions and promote a sustainable textile system. This system aims to regenerate and repair natural systems while minimizing pollution and waste. By embracing this approach, the textile designer contributes to the improvement of society, the environment, the planet and the economy as a whole [4, 6, 11].

The creation of a textile product involves multiple intricate phases that demand continuous deliberation. It is a complex process in which textile designers should contemplate not only aesthetic, functional, and material aspects but also socio-cultural factors. By placing design at the core of the socio-ethical dimensions of sustainability, designers can effectively address the broader implications of their work and contribute to a more socially responsible and sustainable textile industry [56, 57].

The establishment of collaboration strategies between academia, knowledge centers, and industry [58] is crucial. These partnerships aim to equip future textile designers with knowledge that aligns with the emerging challenges of the sector and the needs of users. Moreover, such collaborations foster a deep respect for the well-being of humanity and the preservation of the planet. By cultivating a new mindset that emphasizes the interplay between production and circular consumption, we can pave the way for sustainable practices and a more harmonious relationship between human activities and the environment [59].

To cultivate the skills necessary for interdisciplinary [60] and transdisciplinary collaboration among textile designers, it is imperative for academia to demonstrate a stronger commitment. This commitment involves fostering interactions and relationships with diverse disciplinary fields. One approach to facilitating knowledge transfer is to integrate industrial and academic practices within the same educational context through collaborative teaching initiatives. Aligning educational systems to the evolving landscape of the textile industry is crucial, as it enables academia to be a proactive part of the solution. By adapting and evolving as the industry changes, academia can play a pivotal role in preparing designers to address the complex challenges of the industry.

4.3 Weave the Challenges and Opportunities for Portuguese Higher Education in Textile Design

Throughout this article, a number of skills required to become a textile designer have been listed, and the problems facing the textile industry have been highlighted. Education in the twenty-first century is in a process of change. Recognizing the significance of a comprehensive approach, it is essential to integrate pedagogical practices that span different knowledge domains and incorporate cross-cutting themes such as sustainability, circular economy, decarbonization, and the digital economy. By doing so, educators can cultivate a multidisciplinary, interdisciplinary, and transdisciplinary vision that prepares textile designers to address the industry's diverse challenges. This integrated approach not only equips designers with a broader perspective but also enables them to develop innovative solutions that are mindful of the environmental, economic, and technological aspects that will shape the future of textiles.

Creativity, critical thinking, mastery of information and communication technologies, collaboration, communication, and intercultural understanding must be incorporated into education to meet the challenges of this century, according to the Organisation for Economic Co-operation and Development report (2018) [61]. In design activity, problems are often seen as undefined [62], with the space of the solution and the problem co-evolving [63]. Therefore, a collaborative attitude is necessary in the search for different solutions that adapt to different contexts.

By assuming a more proactive and interventionist role, designers have the potential to drive substantial societal transformations. They can accomplish this by actively participating in the creative evolution of objects and also by educating consumers about their consumption patterns [20]. He must therefore also be prepared for the interconnected complexity of social and human behavior, behavioral science, social and political issues [13].

Moving from a problem-solving design model to a complexity-based model requires a change in approach [64]. A dynamic system that constantly adapts to circumstances and context through an ongoing process and active dialogue [65]. Incorporating the experiences of other professionals when resilience and adaptability are important in a transdisciplinary approach. A sustainable design culture is fostered through a pluralistic approach that challenges while envisioning an intentional future. This approach explores new ways design can be used to address these issues and serves as a crucial catalyst for positive environmental, economic, and social change. As interactive and holistic knowledge education becomes the norm, integrating thought and action, and fostering complex and multidisciplinary collaboration and communication, a new model of design curriculum is required to meet these evolving conditions.

Education-oriented strategies for the Sustainable Development Goals (ESD) promotes a transdisciplinary approach to social, environmental, and economic issues by encouraging critical and creative thinking, long-term thinking, dealing with uncertainty, and finding solutions to complex problems. It emphasizes the interconnectedness of the environment, economy, society, and cultural diversity, spanning from local to global scales. It is necessary to understand that current actions and attitudes will have implications for the future for human life and the planet, and that we must act responsibly [51, 52]. The ESD allows the concepts of sustainability and sustainable development to be integrated into the classroom, preparing students to change their behavior and make more conscious and sustainable decisions. Fostering the ability to think about future scenarios, promoting critical and creative thinking, encouraging collaborative decision making, with the vision of improving the planet and society [66].

Textile designers possess the ability to exercise control (either full or partial) over the choice of materials and production techniques used in textile products, and work closely with the various stakeholders involved in the process. Consequently, it is imperative for them to comprehend the existential, cultural and social requirements of their environment and actively contribute to the substitution of harmful processes and materials. This commitment serves the well-being of humanity and the planet. Gain a new perspective of knowledge and a new way of thinking through differentiated learning experiences. Encourage textile designers to think in complex, critical, and deep ways to ensure that a range of social and ethical obligations are met [13, 15, 19]. To provide them with a toolkit that will enable them to make forward-looking decisions in a more socially just and developed world, to continuously adapt to change, to become agents of change, and to act as social innovators [51–53]. Academic and practical knowledge that focuses on the creative process and integrates research, theory and practice in a real-world context in a more holistic way should be taught in textile design education.

In Portugal, there is an opportunity to explore specialized training in textile design in higher education, as the industry is looking for professionals with this profile to help find solutions to the problems mentioned, and existing national offerings have proven to be reduced.

5 Conclusion and Further Research

The primary aim of this research was to examine and analyze the absence of higher education opportunities in textile design in Portugal. Through a comprehensive review of existing literature and data collection, the research triangulated and interrelated different themes to reveal that the textile industry is undergoing a transitional phase. Among the immediate challenges it faces are sustainability, circular economy, decarbonization and adaptation to the digital economy [4, 6, 11]. It was found that the restructuring of production processes and the practices of textile product development are changing, with the need to consider the entire production chain from its beginning, that is, from the production of the fiber to the disposal of the product [8, 10], taking into account the protection of the human being, society and the planet.

The historical background has reinforced the importance of the textile industry in the economic and social landscape of Portugal. Being one of the oldest industries in Portugal, the textile sector has gone through many phases of development throughout its history and has faced various challenges, but its adaptability and resilience have overcome them, so that it currently continues to prove itself as an industry that drives the national economy [1, 2]. With regard to teaching in the field of design, there were several attempts at officialization that emerged only in the second half of the twentieth century [32]. Simultaneously, vocational training centers were established to facilitate the advancement of vocational education, particularly in the textile and clothing sector. This industry played a pivotal role in the Portuguese economy in the 1980s and led to the introduction of the first vocational training programs in this field [33].

Analysis of undergraduate programmes in textile and fashion design revealed that higher education in textile design is reduced. Of the seven existing, only two integrate the nomenclature "textile", namely the undergraduate programme in "Fashion and Textile Design" of ESART and the undergraduate programme in "Fashion and Textile Design and Production" of ISMAT, and even these are created in parallel with the fashion field [18]. Against this background, it can be said that the existing offerings meet the needs of the fashion and clothing industries, but with regard to the textile industry, the response of academia in preparing and training textile designers is proving to be reductive. The textile industry is facing problems that are proving to be increasingly complex, considering that higher education institutions should play a more intervening role in the training of textile designers to help this industry remain competitive, but this will be difficult since there is no specific higher education for textile design.

Textile designers have the potential to make substantial contributions to societal transformations by assuming a more active role and acting as change agents [13, 20]. In the development of textile products, the selection of materials and production processes plays a crucial role in determining the environmental and climate impacts throughout their lifecycle. As such, textile designers hold an important position in the decision-making process, where their choices can have a significant influence on the overall sustainability of the products [4, 11, 12, 48]. Collaboration among multidisciplinary, interdisciplinary, and transdisciplinary teams is essential to effectively addressing the challenges faced by the sector, society, and the planet. By bringing together individuals with diverse knowledge and expertise, these teams can combine their perspectives and skills to generate innovative and holistic solutions. This approach fosters a comprehensive understanding of complex issues and enables the development of effective strategies that transcend disciplinary boundaries for the betterment of the sector, society, and the planet.

It is believed that the most important contribution to design with this research is that it has been possible to recognize that there is a shortage of textile designers working with the national textile industry to remain competitive. It was possible to list a series of technical and cross-cutting skills that are fundamental to the practice of this profession. Finally, it was also possible to identify that a higher education specialized in textile design, covering sustainability, circular economy, decarbonization and digital economy, can help the textile sector to face the pressing challenges and continue to weave a promising future. Designing a degree program in textile design fills an existing gap. The textile designer must be trained to work as a team, a collaboration with the various professionals in the value chain in finding solutions to complex problems that are an emerging concern of the twenty-first century. To effectively address new challenges and establish a strategic positioning for the industry, it is crucial to integrate diverse knowledge through a multidisciplinary, interdisciplinary, and transdisciplinary approach. By bringing together individuals from various fields and disciplines, this collaborative effort can leverage different perspectives, expertise, and insights [6]. Provide academic and practical knowledge that is centered around the creative process. This knowledge should integrate research, theory, and practice in a real-world context in a holistic way. By doing so, a comprehensive understanding of complex contexts is fostered, and complex, critical, and deep thinking is stimulated. Furthermore, this approach ensures that a range of social and ethical commitments are addressed [13, 15, 19]. By awakening such thinking and incorporating these commitments, textile design education can effectively respond to the demands and challenges of the industry, society, and the planet.

For future studies, a continuation of this research is foreseen to understand what kind of curriculum should be developed and proposed to train textile designers to face the challenges of the sector and use the knowledge to build a textile economy of the future that guarantees the socio-environmental well-being of the planet and the human being.

To do this, starting from the looms of knowledge, it is necessary to begin to delicately weave a curriculum for textile design. A challenge that the author of this research proposes to contribute to the promotion of knowledge in this field in Portugal.

Acknowledgements This work is financed by national funds through FCT—Fundação para a Ciência e a Tecnologia, I.P., under the Strategic Project with the reference UIDB/04008/2020 and UIDP/04008/2020, and through the individual research grant 2020.04735.BD.

References

1. DGAE (2018) Indústria Têxtil e Vestuário (Sinopse). Direção Geral das Atividades Económicas, Lisboa, Portugal
2. ATP (2022) Press Release: exportações de têxteis e vestuário ultrapassarão os 5,3 mil milhoes de euros em 2021. https://atp.pt/wp-content/uploads/2022/01/PressRelease-Exportacoes-da-ITV-Novembro21_10.1.22.pdf
3. UNECE Traceability of sustainable value chains. Enhancing transparency in the garment and footwear sector for informed and responsible choices. https://unece.org/trade/traceability-sustainable-garment-and-footwear. Last accessed 5 May 2021
4. Ellen MacArthur Foundation (2020) Vision of a circular economy for fashion. London, UK
5. Duhoux T, Blévennec K. Le, Manshoven S, Grossi F, Arnold M (2022) Textiles and the environment: the role of design in Europes circular economy. European Environment Agency (EEA)
6. ATP (2021) Visão Prospetiva e Estratégias ITV 2030. Contributo para um Plano Estratégico para o Sector Têxtil e Vestuário Português até 2030. ATP—Associação Têxtil e Vestuário de Portugal, Vila Nova de Famalicão, Portugal
7. Berg A, Magnus KH, Kappelmark S, Granskog A, Lee L, Sawers C, Polgampola P, Lehmann M, Syrett H, Arici G (2020) Fashion on climate: how the fashion industry can urgently act to reduce its greenhouse gas emissions. McKinsey & Company; Global Fashion Agenda
8. Fletcher K, Grose L (2012) Fashion & sustainability. Design for change. Laurence King Publishing Ltd, London, UK
9. Gwilt A (2020) [2014] A practical guide to sustainable fashion. Bloomsbury Publishing Plc, London, UK
10. Seixas S, Montagna G, Félix MJ (2021) Materials matters in textile and fashion design education. In: Shin CS, Bucchianico G Di, Fukuda S, Ghim YG, Montagna G, Carvalho C (ed) Advances in industrial design. AHFE 2021. Lecture notes in networks and systems. Springer, Cham, New York, USA, pp 681–688. https://doi.org/10.1007/978-3-030-80829-7_84.
11. Ellen MacArthur Foundation (2017) A new textiles economy: redesigning fashion's future. London, UK
12. European Commission (n.d.) Sustainable product policy. https://ec.europa.eu/jrc/en/research-topic/sustainable-product-policy. Last accessed 23 Jun 2021
13. Meyer MW, Norman D (2020) Changing design education for the 21st century. She Ji 6:13–49. https://doi.org/10.1016/j.sheji.2019.12.002
14. Manzini E (2009) Viewpoint. New design knowledge. Des Stud 30:4–12. https://doi.org/10.1016/j.destud.2008.10.001
15. Swanson G (2020) Educating the designer of 2025. She Ji 6:101–105. https://doi.org/10.1016/j.sheji.2020.01.001
16. Davis M (2017) Teaching design: a guide to curriculum and pedagogy for college design faculty and teachers who use design in their classrooms. Allworth, New York, USA
17. Sterling S (2004) Higher education, sustainability, and the role of systemic learning. In: Corcoran PB, Wals AEJ (ed) Higher education and the challenge of sustainability. Problematics, promise, and practice. Kluwer Academic Publishers, Dordrecht, Netherlands, pp 49–70
18. DGES (n.d.) Direção Geral de Ensino Superior. https://www.dges.gov.pt/pt/pagina/licenciatura. Last accessed 1 Jan 2023

19. Findeli A (2001) Rethinking design education for the 21st century: theoretical, methodological, and ethical discussion. Des Issues 17:5–17. https://doi.org/10.1162/07479360152103796
20. Manzini E (2011) Design schools as agents of (sustainable) change. International Symposium CUMULUS//DRS for Design 1:9–16
21. Félix MJ, Santos G, Barroso A, Silva P (2018) The transformation of wasted space in urban vertical gardens with the contribution of design to improving the quality of life. Int J Qual Res 12:803–822. https://doi.org/10.18421/IJQR12.04-02
22. Chiaradia LD, Pazmino AV (2015) Save the Bio: o design como ferramenta contra a perda da biodiversidade. MIX Sustentável 1:77–85
23. ATP (2019) Fashion from Portugal 4.0. Diretório 2019. ATP—Associação Têxtil e Vestuário de Portugal, Vila Nova de Famalicão, Portugal
24. Pereira A dos S (2017) A Indústria Têxtil Portuguesa. Clube do Colecionador, Lisboa, Portugal
25. ATP (2015) ATP 50 anos. ATP—Associação Têxtil e Vestuário de Portugal, Vila Nova de Famalicão, Portugal
26. Quintela P (2019) Design e políticas públicas em Portugal: transformações, avanços e impasses. Oficina do Centro de Estudos Sociais
27. Seixas S, Montagna G, Félix MJ (2023) Where is textile design in Portugal? Interlace the past to weave the future. In: Raposo D, Neves J, Silva R, Correia Castilho L, Dias R (ed) Advances in design, music and arts II. EIMAD 2022. Springer Series in Design and Innovation. Springer, Cham, Castelo Branco, Portugal, pp 220–237. https://doi.org/10.1007/978-3-031-09659-4_17
28. Seixas S, Montagna G, Félix MJ (2023) Weaving the skills of the textile designer as a contribution to the construction of a textile ecosystem of the future. In: Broega AC, Cunha J, Carvalho H, Providência B (ed) Advances in fashion and design research. Springer International Publishing, Cham, Portugal, pp 505–517. https://doi.org/10.1007/978-3-031-16773-7_43
29. Seixas S, Montagna G, Félix MJ (2022) The textile designer skills to face the emerging challenges of textile industry and the role of academia. In: Montagna G, Carvalho C (ed) Human factors for apparel and textile engineering. AHFE (2022) International Conference, pp 23–30. AHFE Open Access, New York, USA. https://doi.org/10.54941/ahfe1001534
30. Santos RA (1995) O Design e a Decoração em Portugal, 1900–1994. In: Pereira P (ed) História da Arte Portuguesa, do Barroco à Contemporaneidade. Círculo de Leitores, pp 437–503
31. Almeida VMM de (2009) O Design em Portugal, um Tempo e um Modo. A Institucionalização do Design Português entre 1959 e 1974
32. Lopes NL (2000) Os anos 80/90. O novo design e a transformação dos modos de habitar. In: Anuário 2000. Ano oito. n.21/22—O Tempo do Design. Centro Português de Design, Lisboa, Portugal, pp 80–87
33. Lopes NL (2000) O pós 74 e as instituições de design. In: Anuário 2000. Ano oito. n.21/22—O Tempo do Design. pp. 86–87. Centro Português de Design, Lisboa, Portugal
34. FAUL (n.d.) Faculdade de Arquitetura de Lisboa. https://www.fa.ulisboa.pt/index.php/pt/cursos. Last accessed 1 Mar 2023
35. UMINHO (n.d.) Universidade do Minho. https://www.uminho.pt/PT/ensino/oferta-educativa. Last accessed 1 Mar 2023
36. Maldonado T (1999) Design industrial. Edições 70 Lda, Lisboa, Portugal
37. Souza PLP de (2008) [2000] Notas para uma história do design. 2AB, Rio de Janeiro, Brasil
38. Lupton E, Miller JA (2008) ABC da Bauhaus: a Bauhaus e a teoria do design. Cosac Naify, São Paulo, Brasil
39. Weltge-Wortmann S (1993) Women's work: textile art from the Bauhaus. Chronicle Books, San Francisco
40. Bauhaus Kooperation (n.d.) Knowledge. The Bauhaus. Tarining. Workshops. https://www.bauhauskooperation.com/knowledge/the-bauhaus/training/workshops/. Last accessed 2 Oct 2021
41. Cardoso R (2004) [2000] Uma introdução à história do design. Edgard Blucher, São Paulo, Brasil
42. Seixas S (2019) Contributos para o Desenvolvimento de Processos Criativos e Pedagógicos, para os Cursos de Design de Moda e Têxtil em Portugal

43. ESART (n.d.) Escola Superior de Artes Aplicadas, https://www.ipcb.pt/esart/escola-superior-de-artes-aplicadas. Last accessed 1 Mar 2023
44. UBI (n.d.) Universidade da Beira Interior. http://www.ubi.pt/. Last accessed 1 Mar 2023
45. ULHT (n.d.) Universidade Lusófona de Humanidades e Tecnologias. https://www.ulusofona.pt/. Last accessed 1 Mar 2023
46. ESAD (n.d.) Escola Superior de Artes e Design. https://esad.pt/pt/cursos. Last accessed 1 Mar 2023
47. WDO (n.d.) World Design Organization. https://wdo.org/about/definition/. Last accessed 1 Oct 2021
48. Papanek V (1995) Green imperative: ecology and ethics in design and architecture. Thames & Hudson Ltd, New York, USA
49. Studd R (2002) The textile design process. Des J 5:35–49. https://doi.org/10.2752/146069202790718567
50. Norman D (n.d.) Design education: brilliance without substance. https://www.core77.com/posts/20364/Design-Education-Brilliance-Without-Substance. Last accessed 2 Sep 2021
51. UNESCO (2017) Education for sustainable development goals learning objectives. UNESCO, Paris, France
52. UNESCO (ed) (n.d.) UNESCO. https://en.unesco.org/themes/education-sustainable-development. Last accessed 27 Oct 2020
53. European Commission (2020) Press statement by President von der Leyen on the New European Bauhaus
54. Gale C, Kaur J (2002) The textile book. Berg, Oxford, UK
55. Seixas S, Montagna G, Félix MJ (2022) Textile design: a transdisciplinary approach in higher education in Portugal. In: Proceedings of the 2nd International Conference on Research and Education in Design (REDES 2022), 19–20 May, 2022, Lisboa, Portugal, p 10. Lisbon Shcool of Architecture, Lisbon, Lisboa, Portugal
56. Fletcher K (2008) Sustainable fashion & textiles. design journeys. Earthscan, London, UK
57. Vezzoli C, Manzini E (2008) Design for environmental sustainability. Springer-Verlag, London Limited, London, UK
58. Muratovski G (2020) The making of an American design school: lessons learned. She Ji 6:67–82. https://doi.org/10.1016/j.sheji.2020.01.002
59. Sbordone MA, Pizzicato B, Montagna G, Seixas S (2021) An ideal triangulation in fashion and textile: industry, academia and users. In: Shin CS, Bucchianico G Di, Fukuda S, Ghim YG, Montagna G, Carvalho C (ed) Advances in industrial design. AHFE 2021. Lecture Notes in Networks and Systems. Springer, Cham, New York, USA, pp 698–706. https://doi.org/10.1007/978-3-030-80829-7_86
60. D'Itria E, Vacca F (2021) Fashion design for sustainability. A transformative challenge across the European fashion education system. In: 7th International Conference on Higher Education Advances (HEAd'21). Universitat Politècnica de València, pp 679–686. https://doi.org/10.4995/head21.2021.13029
61. OECD (2018) The future of education and skills. Education 2030. OECD
62. Simon HA (1973) The structure of ill structured problems. Artif Intell 4:181–201. https://doi.org/10.1016/0004-3702(73)90011-8
63. Dorst K, Cross N (2001) Creativity in the design process: co-evolution of problem-solution. Des Stud 22:425–437
64. Dorst K (2019) Design beyond design. She Ji. 5:117–127. https://doi.org/10.1016/j.sheji.2019.05.001
65. Buchanan R (2019) Surroundings and environments in fourth order design. Des Issues 35:4–22. https://doi.org/10.1162/desi_a_00517
66. Seixas S (2021) The emergence of sustainability and the textile and fashion design education. In: PAD 20. Fashion and textile design reconstruction. Aiap Edizioni, pp 19–38

Textile Waste Is the Raw Material for New Fashion Products

Regina Aparecida Sanches, Francisca Dantas Mendes, Maurício de Campos Araújo, and Maria Goreti Issac

Abstract The industrialization of fashion and the consolidation of the Fast Fashion System result in the sale of fashionable clothing products at more affordable prices. The globalized media and fashion communication that disseminate in real time the novelties of fashion clothing causing a programmed obsolescence of the clothes that have already been acquired, stimulating production and consumption. The result is: a lot of waste generated, and many pieces of clothing are no longer purchased, and many clothes are discarded by consumers. Improper disposal of textile waste and post-consumer clothing results in a negative impact on the environment. Currently the city of São Paulo—Brazil is destined to landfills 55 tons/day. Some possible solutions to minimize the impact and to collaborate with SDG 12 which aims to substantially reduce the generation of waste through the Circular Economy and its actions of prevention, reduction, recycling, and reuse of waste are the use of Upcycling technique using discarded textiles as raw material and stimulating the Circular Economy. These solutions are presented by the Research Support Center of the University of São Paulo—Brazil conducting the upcycling contest and socio-environmental projects.

Keywords Post-consumer clothing · Textile waste · Upcycling technique

1 Introduction

This article aims to present part of the research carried out by researchers from NAP SUSTEXMODA—Research Support Center of the University of São Paulo—Brazil.

The fashion chain is considered as one of the industrial chains that cause the greatest impact on the planet. It is important to study it and understand the reasons

R. A. Sanches (✉) · F. D. Mendes · M. de Campos Araújo
University of São Paulo, São Paulo, Brazil
e-mail: regina.sanches@usp.br

M. G. Issac
Research Support Center of the University of São Paulo, NAP SUSTEXMODA, São Paulo, Brazil

D. Raposo et al. (eds.), *Perspectives on Design III*, Springer Series in Design and Innovation 34, https://doi.org/10.1007/978-3-031-43516-4_17

for these impacts and seek solutions to minimize them, remedy them and even as much as possible avoid them.

The history of humanity tells the evolution of inputs, raw materials, to produce clothing, in addition to the evolution of its visual aesthetics resulting in the Universe of Fashion. In this universe, with the advancement of economic globalization, the acceleration of clothing production and social media promoting the dissemination of new fashion garments, there has been an increase in consumption, production and generation of waste and disposal of post-consumer pieces.

The objective of this article is to present solutions to minimize these impacts from the Upcycling technique giving a new design to the pieces using textile waste and post-consumer parts, stimulating the circular economy.

The scientific research methodology used is exploratory, bibliographical, documentary, experimental and case study described by Lakatos et al. [1] and Gil [2], on the socio-environmental impacts caused by the Brazilian fashion chain and reverse logistics and upcycling and study of a socio-environmental project.

It is important to study the universe of fashion and the impacts caused by the importance of the numbers it presents in Brazil. According to ABIT [3], the Brazilian textile and clothing chain, the largest chain in the West, is the 2nd largest employer in the manufacturing industry, employing 16.7% of the jobs in this industry. It has 25.5 thousand formal companies that generate 1.5 million direct jobs and 8 million indirect ones, the female workforce represents 75% of the jobs generated. The average production of textile companies in 2020 was 2.4 million tons (2.4% of world textile production) and of garments is 9.4 billion pieces (2.6% of world garment production). These numbers make Brazil one of the main markets of the global fashion industry. In 2020, about 9.4 billion pieces were made, which is equivalent to an average of 43 pieces/inhabitant/year. IEMI and ABIT [3] point out that the Brazilian industrial park has 25.2 thousand clothing companies, 96.8% of which are micro and small companies.

2 Theoretical Framework

The fashion chain is considered the second most polluting and harmful to the environment, given its accelerated production and consumption speed. In this way, it is a matter of social responsibility, to seek the reuse of products discarded post-consumption, because the greater the consumption of new products, the greater the production of the entire chain and the disposal by the consumer of the products after their use [4].

The Fashion Chain comprises a network of industries and companies resulting in the Fashion Universe. This universe comprises the textile production chain, which is attended by a large industry producing the raw materials that supply each subsequent link starting with the agriculture and chemical industries with the production of fibers, followed by the production of yarns, fabrics, trimmings, and cloths. All these products are benefited by many processing industries that carry out the transformation processes conferring new visual and comfort characteristics: washing, dyeing, embroidery, cleaning, and ironing. In parallel the Fashion Industry with the participation of the bureaux of trends collaborated with the evolution of clothing with the visual changes in shapes, volumes, colors, embroidery throughout our history. Currently in partnership with new marketing companies, new marketing models and the intense participation of social media stimulates the consumption of clothing with fashion characteristics, launched every weekly [5].

The model of production and consumption adopted by supply chains, since the industrial revolution, is carried out in a linear way that is, raw materials are extracted from nature, transformed into products and after their use are discarded. It has been a successful model over the years, but it is reaching its limit, as it assumes that resources are abundant, available and do not recover the waste generated during the manufacturing process and after the useful life of the product [6].

2.1 *Impacts*

The negative impacts caused by the Fashion Universe affect both the environment and the social sphere. Motta [7] highlights two important impacts: the negative social impacts are: intensive labor, exhaustive routines, low remuneration, absence of labor contracts, child labor, insecurity of manufacturing facilities, poor ventilation, respiratory problems (cotton dust and synthetic particles), muscle problems (due to repetitive exertion), spinal diseases and visual fatigue, among others. The main negative environmental impacts are intensive use of pesticides, use of animal leather, use of synthetic fibers (non-renewable), intensive use of energy and water, liquid effluents (chemical dyes), gaseous effluents (CO_2 emission in transportation), solid waste (leftovers and manufacturing shavings), among others.

By analyzing the production process of the fashion chain, it is verified that in all stages, from the obtaining of raw materials to the confection, it is possible to identify the socio-environmental impacts caused by these companies and industries that make up the Fashion Universe [8].

The production of clothing companies is the most fragmented, has many suppliers to produce parts, resulting in a greater difficulty to track the socio-environmental impacts of their production process [9].

The production process of this chain uses large amounts of chemicals and natural resources, such as land and water, generating a high environmental impact. The negative impacts caused by the fashion chain affect both the environment and the social sphere. Figure 1 highlights and illustrates the negative results of each of the stages of this Fashion chain, demonstrating its main socio-environmental problems.

The negative impacts of the fashion chain extend to the consumption and post-consumption phases. Even before disposal of the piece by consumers, during the maintenance of textile articles, in washing and ironing, consuming water and energy.

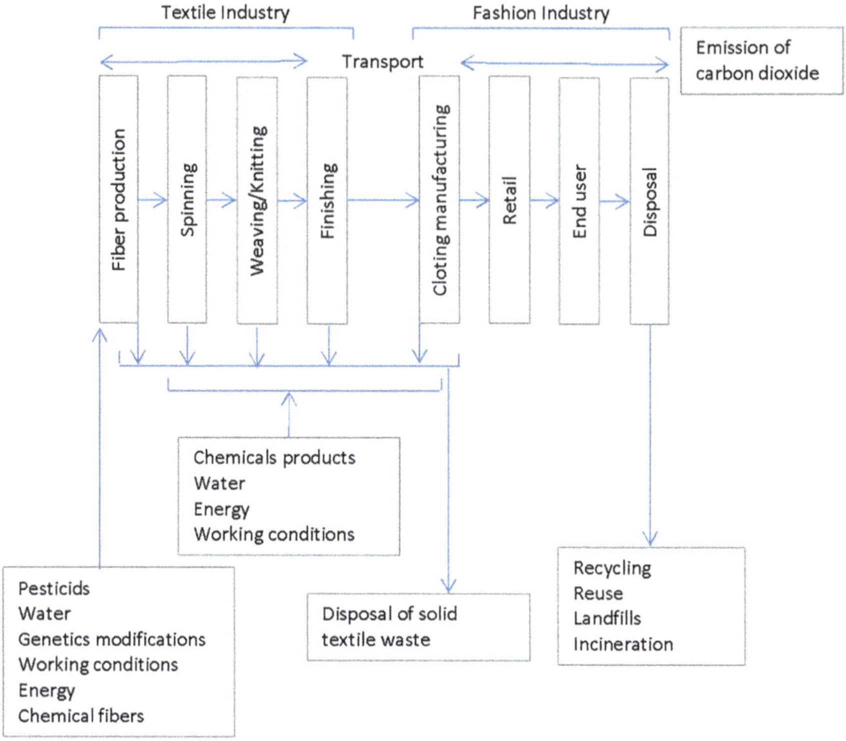

Fig. 1 Brazilian fashion chain: main negative socio-environmental impacts (*Source* Adapted from Farias[9])

Main raw materials, production, and impacts. Main raw materials used by the textile fiber fashion chain). According to the Textile Exchange [10], world fiber production in 2018 was approximately 107 million tons, of which 62.3% were synthetic fibers, 31.5% natural fibers and 6.2% artificial fibers. The most used fiber in the Brazilian fashion industry, according to MODEFICA [11] is cotton. About 40% of women's fashion products and 70% of men's fashion are produced with this fiber.

According to ABRAFAS [12], in 2018, polyester represented 68% of the total produced among synthetic fibers. Viscose, according to TEXTILE EXCHANGE [10], although not produced in Brazil, is the third most consumed fiber by national industries.

Cotton fibers. It is a vegetable fiber. During its cultivation it consumes about 24% of insecticides and 11% of pesticides, in addition to causing pulmonary dysfunction caused by the aspiration of cotton fibrils. The production of cotton fibers uses a large amount of irrigation water and fossil fuels in agricultural machines for: irrigation, ginning and baling [13].

Polyester Fibers (PET). In the production of PET volatile organic compounds are emitted, releasing toxic pollutants into groundwater. When compared to the production of natural fibers, it consumes more energy and less water [14].

Viscose fibers. Viscose is an artificial fiber produced from cellulose. The most questioned aspect of its production process is the use of chemicals that harm human health and the environment. Both caustic soda and sulfuric acid are highly corrosive chemicals that are hazardous to the work environment and can cause damage to the environment, and carbon disulfide is highly toxic to humans and can lead to serious health problems, including parkinsonism, heart attack and stroke [15].

Impacts of the Production of yarns, fabrics, processing. During yarn production, there is a high volume of disposal of solid textile waste, energy consumption by the equipment used in the spinning process, generation of dust and suspended fibers that are highly toxic, pollute the air and endanger human health [16].

The greatest environmental impacts observed, according to Pereira et al. [13], during the transformation processes of textile fibers into a made-up product are in spinning and textile processing (dyeing and finishing). Weaving, knitting, confection and transport operations generate less impact on the environment.

2.2 *Fast Fashion*

In the late 1990s, the media created the expression "fast fashion" to identify the increased consumption of fashion clothing products. In this system, retail stores supply new collections almost daily, to force the consumer to buy more and to make collections rotate quickly. Globalization and quick access to any type of information, product, and services influence consumer behavior [17].

According to the Ellen MacArthur Foundation [18], about 100 billion clothes were produced in the year 2015, approximately 70% of these clothes produced went to landfill or incineration at the end of their useful life.

Attracted by the success of retail sales, the Fast Fashion system appears. Previously fashion apparel collections were released at the start of the 2 main weather seasons of the year: winter and summer. In the Fast Fashion system. The proposal is to launch mini collections every 15 days throughout the year. For the targets to be achieved, production needs to be accelerated.

Therefore, there is an increase in the generation of waste and discarded post-consumer clothing [19].

Fast fashion is not solely responsible for the excess of articles produced. Excessive consumption causes the need for increased production throughout the fashion chain, increasing the demand for natural resources, consumption of raw materials, use of water, of energy, the disposal of solid waste, the disposal of post-consumer articles, among other negative impacts of this chain [20].

Rampant consumption causes the daily disposal of many products by consumers. Materials such as paper, glass, plastic, metal, and electronic waste have several selective collection points in the city of São Paulo and are sent for recycling. However, fabrics and textile materials, rubber, ceramics, and wood still do not have a correct destination in Brazil.

2.3 *Textile Waste and Post-Consumer Discarded in the City of São Paulo*

Post-consumer textile waste is clothing and other textile articles that are discarded by the population after use. About 80% of this material can be reused or recycled, but they are usually discarded in the common trash and sent to landfills, as many consumers are unaware of the environmental impacts caused by its incorrect disposal [21].

According to the website www.sustexmoda.org, and a survey carried out by NAP SUSTEXMODA, together with the company LOGA, which performs household collection in São Paulo, the largest metropolis in Brazil, 55 tons of textile waste are discarded daily. Of this total, 20 tons of post-consumer clothing, in the of Vila Maria neighborhood, in the North Zone of the city of São Paulo.

In this region of the North Zone, the Community Promorar Vila Maria III is located it works as a local economic center, generating jobs and income for a good part of the community. It houses several sets of sheds that sell, wholesale, lots of used clothing for bazaars (thrift stores). Garments are discarded by consumers for many reasons: outdated style, inappropriate size, boredom, among others, resulting in end of life. The most common disposal routes are donations to charities, transfers to family or friends, resale to online stores, disposal in household waste. Some people reuse or recycle their clothes instead of discarding them [22].

2.4 *The Sustainable Development Goals (SDGs)*

The ONU, in 2015, launches the 2030 Agenda for Sustainable Development, based on 17 specific goals for sustainable development aimed at meeting the aspirations to transform the world.

These objectives are goals that must be met by countries in each period, to reduce inequality and the threat of depletion of Planet Earth.

The SDGs, according to ABIT [23], as called by the UN, are objectives outlined by the organization so that agreements on the environment and development made by member countries are fulfilled.

According to Fashion Revolution [24], the SDGs that are among the top topics for the fashion sector are: gender equality (SDG 5); decent employment and economic growth (SDG 8); responsible consumption and production (SDG 12) and combating climate change (SDG 13).

According to the 2030 agenda, objective number twelve (SDG 12) aims to ensure sustainable production and consumption patterns. In the fashion sector, SDG 12 seeks to reduce environmental impacts through the sustainable management of the entire chain and the efficient use of natural resources [24].

Among the 17 ODS, the objectives for this article, we worked on the goals of SDG 12 whose mission is: "Ensure sustainable production and consumption standards."

The III SUSTEXMODA Congress held in November 2023, in its WORKING GROUP on Economics, proposed "SDG 12: Economy" as a theme, which aims, in addition to presenting research related to the negative and positive impacts caused to the Economy, to disseminate best practices carried out by the Textile Chain and Fashion Industry and emphasizes the research that promotes the precepts of SDG 12 highlighted: substantially reduce waste generation through the Circular Economy and its actions of prevention, reduction, recycling and reuse of waste; encourage companies to adopt sustainable practices and integrate sustainability information; promote relevant information and awareness about sustainable development and lifestyles in harmony with nature; support developing countries to strengthen their scientific and technological capacities aiming at more sustainable production and consumption.

It is important to produce research that highlights quantitative data regarding national recycling rate, tons of recycled materials; global citizenship education and education for sustainable development, including gender equality and human rights; support given to developing countries for research and advances in sustainable technology, production, and consumption.

2.5 *Circularity in the Apparel Industry*

According to Morelli and Ender [25], apparel, trimmings, household items, tires, machining, bearings, furniture, electronic waste, industrial waste, among others, when disposed of in landfills and dumps, take hundreds of years to decompose. However, these objects can be recycled or recovered and transformed into a new product generating a Circular Economy.

As opposed to the linear model, the circular model can be defined as an economic model aimed at the efficient use of resources by minimizing waste, reducing the exploitation of primary resources and closed product cycles [26].

In the circular economy model, there are no discards of materials or products produced. The destination and recycling of waste are defined at all stages of the production process—from product design to post-consumer disposal [27]. Leitão [28] adds that the model is based on nature itself, it is implemented through innovation, design and processes that aim to reduce the consumption of raw materials, energy, and water.

According to the MacArthur Foundation [29], one of the biggest challenges of the circular economy in the fashion chain is the increase in the volume of textile waste discarded by consumers after use. The consumer's choice of disposal route for their post-consumer apparel will determine the degree of impact the discarded garment will have on the environment.

According to the MacArthur Foundation [29] circular garments must have the following characteristics: be recyclable, be available for a recycling system and be made from recyclable materials. In this context, a sustainable alternative for post-consumer products is the use of garment reuse techniques, such as upcycling technique.

2.6 The Upcycling Process

There are no limitations in the application of the upcycling technique. It consists of having materials available at the end of their useful life and associating them with a creative application involving some adaptations. The greatest difficulty in working with this technique is that the materials discarded by consumers are different and require a study for product development.

Upcycling transforms discarded pre- and post-consumer waste, generally without commercial value, into new products of equal or greater added value. The technique consists of reusing materials, in their original state, without performing chemical transformations, preserving all the original properties of the materials, in something totally new [30].

According to Morelli and Ender [25], two requirements must be respected for the part to be considered genuinely upcycling: (i) the raw material must be a used part, it cannot be a new part (not used) and it must be at the end of of its useful life; (ii) the upcycling technique requires that the part must change its function, that is, it must have a different function from the one assigned at the beginning of its production.

The upcycling process is divided into 8 stages: (i) Cleaning; (ii) Analysis; (iii) Screening; (iv) Design definition (model); (v) Disassembly; (vi) Reassembly; (vii) Complementary techniques and (viii) Quality control [31].

3 Case Studies

SUSTEXMODA (https://www.sustexmoda.org) started in 2014 motivated by the concerns of a group of people, society, academia, and public authorities concerned about the causes of the negative impacts caused by the Universe of Fashion, in the economy, society and environment. The researchers from the University of São Paulo, coordinated by Prof. Associate Dr. Francisca Dantas Mendes has, over time, carried out studies and publications, developed socio-environmental projects, academic events and other similar events aimed at disseminating positive information and seeking effective solutions for the impacts caused on the economy, society, environment by the Textile Chain and the Fashion Industry.

The Research Support Center of the University of São Paulo Brazil—NAP SUSTEXMODA, approved by the dean of research at the University of São Paulo in 2017, with the purpose of carrying out research and offering viable solutions to negative impacts and, when possible, presenting improvements the positive impacts on the three pillars of Sustainability: Economy, Society and Environment involving the Textile Chain and the Fashion Industry.

As of 2017, NAP SUSTEXMODA researchers have developed a textile residue meter, based on information provided by the company LOGA, which shows that 55 tons of Textile Waste are discarded daily. LOGA is responsible for home collection in the city of São Paulo—Brazil. The textile residueometer is updated weekly, computing the sum of the 5 days of the week of textiles collected by the company, which discards them in sanitary landfills in the municipality of São Paulo. On day 2023/6/28 the Residuometer presented the total of 66.860 tons (www.sustexmoda.org).

In 2018, socio-environmental projects began in partnership with the public authorities of the municipality of São Paulo. The projects with the purpose of empowering and increasing the self-esteem of people in high social vulnerability, carry out training courses using textile waste and post-consumer clothing as raw material to enhance effective actions based on experiments and research aimed at reducing the discard and empower people. www.sustexmoda.org.

3.1 International Congress on Textile and Fashion Sustainability—SUSTEXMODA

The International Congress on Textile and Fashion Sustainability was a proposal by students of a postgraduate course taught to students in the second half of 2018 with the proposal to offer a space for the exchange of experiences and research between researchers, professors, students, professionals, and entrepreneurs of the Fashion Universe. It is an inclusive international congress, free of charge, with simultaneous translation, with presentation in a single auditorium, allowing interaction between all participants. With oral and banner presentation of peer-reviewed and blind research. It has three working groups linked to the three pillars of sustainability Economy, Society and Environment. During the days of the event, there will be round tables with national and international participants, exhibitions and the Upcyclin contest, with online transmission of this first event.

The first congress—I SUSTEXMODA took place in May 2019 in person, in the main auditorium of the School of Arts, Sciences and Humanities of the University of São Paulo—EACH USP. The II SUSTEXMODA, in November 2020, took place completely remotely at the Institute of Advanced Studies of the University of São Paulo—IEA USP. The III SUSTEXMODA took place in November 2023 in the EACH-USP auditorium, returning to the original format.

Fig. 2 The Community Promorar Vila Maria III (São Paulo-Brazil) *Source* www.sustexmoda.org

Fig. 3 The Community Promorar Vila Maria III (São Paulo-Brazil) *Source* www.sustexmoda.org

The object of study is the research project that results in the realization of upcycling products carried out by undergraduate students under the guidance of NAP SUSTEXMODA research professors and presented at the III SUSTEXMODA.

The project begins with an immersion in the streets of the Vila Maria neighborhood, where students find discarded clothes on the sidewalks. 10 pairs of students participate in this research. Each pair collects an amount of clothing that they believe is enough to carry out their research. Figures 2 and 3 present this moment of collection and choice.

From the selected pieces, each pair of students develops their creations. Subsequently, the development of the modeling and sewing processes takes place in the sewing laboratory, under the guidance of NAP SUSTEXMODA research professors. All materials used are removed from the collected parts.

After completion of the execution, the pieces are photographed. For the exhibition, banners are created that present images of the processes. These banners are displayed next to each mannequin that presents the clothing. The Figs. 4 and 5, show 2 banners and the image of the exhibition during the III SUSTEXMODA. www.sustexmoda.org.

The Flower Button socio-environmental project proposes training transsexual people in extreme social vulnerability, homeless, to use post-consumer clothing and textile waste as raw material for their creations. In this case, the raw material is offered and each participant in the project selects the piece and the residues he wants to work with. www.sustexmoda.org.

During the III SUSTEXMODA, the Upcycling pieces 6 and 7 figures created and executed during the previous semester in the Flower Button project were also presented on display (Fig. 6 and 7).

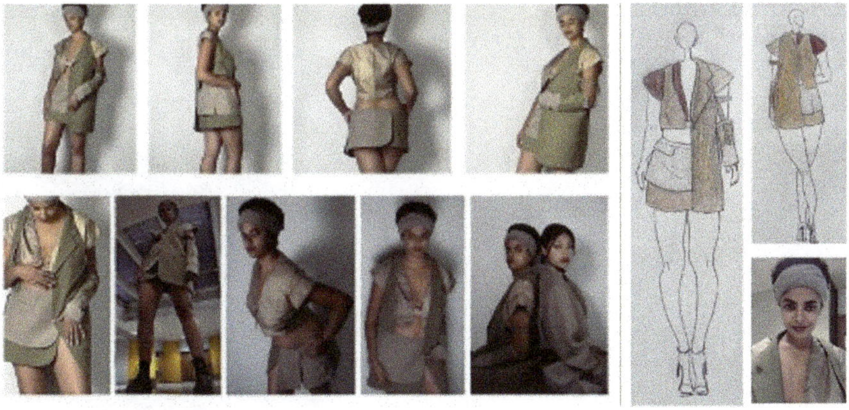

Fig. 4 Final product and drawing (creative process) *Source* www.sustexmoda.org

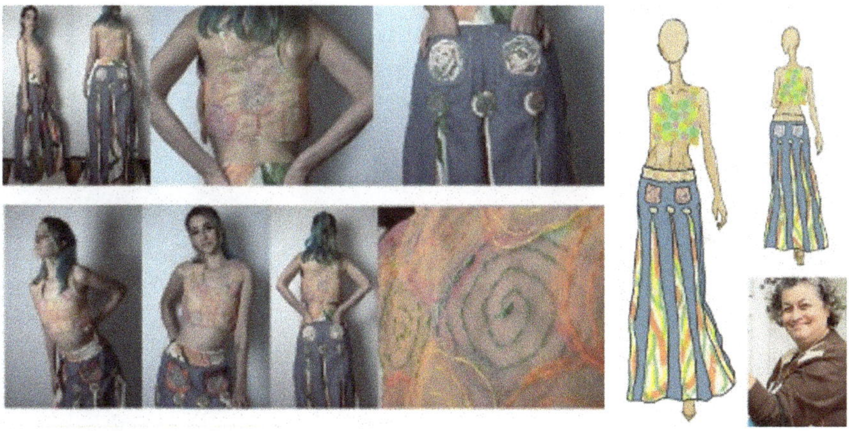

Fig. 5 Final product and drawing (creative process) *Source* www.sustexmoda.org

4 Final Considerations

The importance of the brasilein Fashion Universe is perceived by the number of pieces, 9.4 billion pieces (2.6% of world garment production) produced during the year and its complexity by the number of companies involved in each productive link. The negative impacts caused by each production stage demonstrate the importance of added values in garments, demonstrating the urgency of research and solutions. We highlight the number of 33,000 people in extreme social vulnerability and the volume of 55 tons of parts discarded daily, demonstrating the need for research and innovation so that these numbers are reduced to the minimum possible.

The Upcycling pieces presented by the case study demonstrate the importance of using this technique to meet SDG 12, boosting the Circular Economy, and resulting

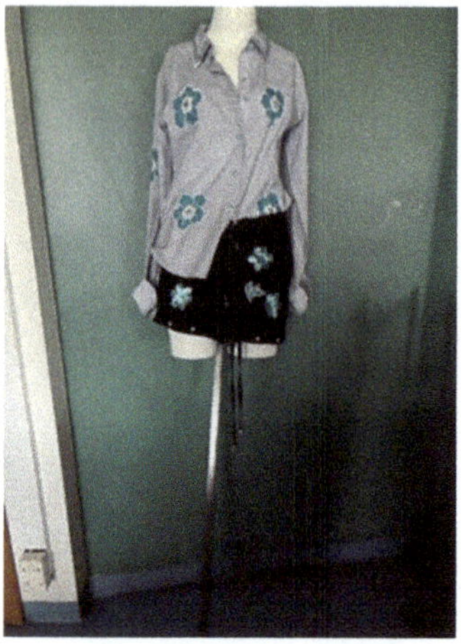

Fig. 6 The Flower Button project *Source* www.sustexmoda.org

Fig. 7 The Flower Button project *Source* www.sustexmoda.org

in a reduction in the number of garments destined for landfills in the city of São Paulo, in addition to the possibility of using of this material as raw material in the creation of new products by the homeless population, resulting in empowerment and income generation.

References

1. Lakatos EM, Marconi MA (2003) Fundamentos da Metodologia Científica. Atlas, São Paulo
2. Gil AC (2002) Como elaborar projetos de pesquisa, 4th edn. Atlas, São Paulo
3. ASSOCIAÇÃO BRASILEIRA DA INDÚSTRIA TÊXTIL E DE CONFECÇÃO – ABIT (2020) Cartilha Indústria Têxtil e de Confecção Brasileira—Cenários, Desafios, Perspectivas e

Demandas. 2020. Brasília/DF: [s.n.], http://abit-files.abit.org.br/site/publicacoes/cartilha.pdf. Last accessed 15 Apr 2021
4. Boström M, Micheletti M (2016) Introducing the sustainability challenge of textiles and clothing. J Consum Policy 39(1):367–375
5. Mendes FD (2010) Um Estudo Comparativo entre as Manufaturas do Vestuário de Moda do Brasil e da Índia. Tese de Doutorado em Engenharia de Produção. Universidade Paulista, São Paulo
6. Andrews D (2015) The circular economy, design thinking and education for sustainability. Local Econ 30:305–315
7. Motta JA (2021) A incorporação dos Objetivos de Desenvolvimento Sustentável em empresas gaúchas de moda. Dissertação de Mestrado. Universidade Federal do Pampa, Santana do Livramento (RS)
8. Sanches RA, Rocha R, Duarte AYS (2022) Proposal for producing new fabric through the use of fabric scraps discarded by Ibitinga clothing manufacturers: a Brazilian example of circular economy. In: Raposo D, Neves J, Silva R, Castilho LC, Dias R (org) Series in design and innovation, 1st edn. Londres: series in design and innovation, vol. 1, pp 328–341
9. Farias MM (2016) Consumo consciente de moda e o metabolismo futuro do guarda-roupa: uma abordagem quantitativa com público feminino, residente do interior de São Paulo (SP). Dissertação de Mestrado. Universidade Metodista de Piracicaba, Piracicaba
10. TEXTILE EXCHANGE (2021) Guide to recycled inputs, https://textileexchange.org/wp-content/uploads/2021/09/GRS-202-V1.0-Textile-Exchange-Guide-to-Recycled-Inputs.pdf. Last accessed 20 Dec 2021
11. MODEFICA, FGVces, REGENERATE (2021) Fios da Moda: Perspectiva Sistêmica Para Circularidade. MODEFICA, São Paulo
12. ASSOCIAÇÃO BRASILEIRA DOS PRODUTORES DE FIBRAS ARTIFICIAIS E SINTÉTICA – ABRAFAS (2020) Fibras manufaturadas. http://www.abrafas.org.br/site/vitrinenoticias/index/materia/fibras-Manufaturadas/c/b6f. Last accessed 10 Jan 2022
13. Pereira GS, Berretta-Hurtado AL, Futami AH, Gouvêa CAK, Recouvreux DOS (2016) Estudo comparativo entre o impacto ambiental resultante da fabricação de malha 100% algodão e com fios reciclados. Espacios. 37:26–32
14. Stone C, Windsor FM, Munday M, Durance I (2019) Science of the total environment natural or synthetic—how global trends in textile usage threaten freshwater environments. Sci Total Environ. https://doi.org/10.1016/j.scitotenv.2019.134689. Last accessed 10 Apr 2022s
15. CHANGING MARKETS FOUNDATION (2017) Dirty fashion. https://www.changingmarkets.org/portfolio/dirtyfashion. Last accessed 16 Jan 2023
16. Periyasamy AP, Wiener J, Militky J (2017) Life-cycle assessment of denim. Sustainability in Denim. The Textile Institute Book Series, pp 83–110
17. Pinto A, Sousa CSM (2015) Roupas Feitas de Roupas. São Paulo
18. ELLEN MACARTHUR FOUNDATION (2017) A new textiles economy: Redesigning fashion's future. http://www.ellenmacarthurfoundation.org/publications. Last accessed 25 Nov 2022
19. Mendes FD, Santos MCL (2017) Cradle-to-Cradle na Manufatura do Vestuário de Moda: o Design como ferramenta de gestão de geração e descarte de resíduos têxteis, Edicação de Moda para o futuro: desenvolvimento social nas dimensões, social, econômica, ambiental, cultural e geográfica/organizadora, 1 edição. EACHUSP, São Paulo
20. Lucietti TJ, Trierweiller AC, Soratto RB, Silva SMO (2017) uso do upcycling: um estudo de caso no segmento da moda. Anais do ENSUS – Encontro de Sustentabilidade em Projeto. Universidade Federal de Santa Catarina, Florianópolis
21. Sandes F, Leandro J (2016) Exploring the motivations and barriers for second hand product consumption. https://www.researchgate.net/publication/334399322_EXPLORING_THE_MOTIVATIONS_AND_BARRIERS_FOR_SECOND_HAND_PRODUCT_CONSUMPTION. Last accessed 10 Mar 2023
22. Bianchi C, Birtwistle G (2010) Sell, give away, or donate: an exploratory study of fashion clothing disposal behavior in two countries. Int Rev Retail Distribt Consum Res 20(3):353–368

23. CONFEDERAÇÃO NACIONAL DA INDÚSTRIA (CNS) (2017) O setor têxtil e de confecção e os desafios da sustentabilidade. Confederação Nacional da Indústria, Associação Brasileira da Indústria Têxtil e de Confecção—Brasília. https://static.portaldaindustria.com.br/media/filer_public/bb/6f/bb6fdd8d-8201-41ca-981d-deef4f58461f/abit.pdf. Last accessed 12 June 2023
24. FASHION REVOLUTION (2019) Relatório. Índice de transparência da moda Brasil 2019. London, Inglaterra. https://www.fashionrevolution.org/brazil-blog/transparencia-e-tendencia-indice-de-transparencia-da-moda-brasil. Last accessed 6 May 2023
25. Morelli G, Ender J (2017) Upcycling: um novo caminho para a moda sustentável. 6º GAMPI Plural, Joinville (SC). https://pdf.blucher.com.br/designproceedings/gampi2017/12.pdf. Last accessed 28 Feb 2023
26. Morseletto P (2020) Targets for a circular economy. Resources, Conservation and Recycling, vol. 153, p 104553
27. Pearce DW, Turner RK (1990) Economics of natural resources and environment. Harvester Wheashealf, Londres
28. Leitão A (2015) Economia circular: Uma nova filosofia de Gestão Para o séc. XXI. Jornal Português de Finanças, Gestão e Contabilidade 1(2)
29. ELLEN MACARTHUR FOUNDATION (2015) Towards the circular economy: economic and business rationale for an accelerated transition. Ellen MacArthur Foundation [s.l: s.n.]. https://www.ellenmacarthurfoundation.org/assets/downloads/publications/Ellen-MacArthur-Foundation-Towards-the-Circular-Economy-vol.1.pdf. Last accessed 10 June 2021
30. Moreira RN, Marinho LFL, Barbosa FLS (2015) O Modelo de Produção Sustentável Upcycling: o caso da empresa Terra Cycle. XVII Encontro Internacional sobre Gestão Empresarial e Meio Ambiente, 2015, São Paulo. Anais [...]. São Paulo: FEA/USP.
31. Gwilt A (2014) Moda sustentável: Um guia prático. Gustavo Gili, São Paulo
32. Amutha K (2017) Environmental impacts of denim. In: Muthu SS (ed) Sustainability in Denim. Woodhead Publishing, Cambridge, pp 27–48
33. CHANGING MARKETS FUNDATION (n.d.) Annual report 2017, http://changingmarkets.org/wp-content/uploads/2018/06/CMF_Annual-report_2017.pdf. Last accessed 10 June 2023
34. Choudhury AKR (2018) Environmental impacts of denim washing. In: Muthu SS (ed) Sustainability in Denim. Woodhead Publishing, Cambridge, pp 49–81
35. INSTITUTO DE ESTUDOS E MARKETING INDUSTRIAL (IEMI) (2020) Brasil têxtil: relatório setorial da indústria têxtil brasileira. Free Press, São Paulo
36. ORGANIZAÇÃO DAS NAÇÕES UNIDAS (2015) Transformando nosso mundo: a agenda 2030 para o desenvolvimento sustentável. Nova York, Estados Unidos, ONU 2015. Traduzido pelo Centro de Informação das Nações Unidas para o Brasil (UNIC Rio)
37. RECICLA SAMPA (2020) Saiba tudo sobre a reciclagem de resíduos têxteis no Brasil. Reciclagem de tecidos. https://www.reciclasampa.com.br/artigo/saiba-tudo-sobre-a-reciclagem-de-residuos-texteis-no-brasil. Last accessed 4 Apr 2023
38. SUSTEXMODA (n.d.) https://www.sustexmoda.org. Last accessed 25 June 2023

Principles and Values of Prospective Ergonomics and Its Approach to Creative Economy

Sandra Regina Rech

Abstract Considering the complexity of the Fashion Industry's Productive Chain and the socioeconomic and cultural panorama of Brazil, this work, the result of a literature review, aims to investigate whether the use of the fundamentals of Prospective Ergonomics, coupled with the prospection of scenarios, guided by the 17 UN Sustainable Development Goals, allows to scrutinize scenarios for the future of work in companies in the Creative Economy. Furthermore, it intends to understand how the Fashion Industry's Productive Chain will be affected by the transformations in technological development in the future, contributing to a process of innovation and sustainable change in the organizational project. As a result, we expect to provide conditions for innovative projects with added value to products and services within the area of Prospective Ergonomics, aiming at competitive sustainability, productivity, effectiveness, and efficiency of organizations, through problem solving, generation and application of innovation processes. We emphasize that this work is configured as an initial reflection of the research. Therefore, it disseminates an embryonic academic provocation about the problem, considering the multiple challenges of researching Prospective Ergonomics and Creative Economy in a complex and polarized society. The methodological design adopted comprised exploratory research of a qualitative nature and the method chosen was Grounded Theory.

Keywords Prospective Ergonomics · Creative Economy · Sustainable Development Goals

1 Introduction

The digital transformation of the last decades, especially from 2020 onwards, during the pandemic has changed the creation, production, communication, distribution, and consumption of fashion products. It is notorious that new technological trends directly impact the organization of work, labor market, work environment, and policy

S. R. Rech (✉)
Santa Catarina State University, Florianópolis, Brazil
e-mail: sandra.rech@udesc.br

D. Raposo et al. (eds.), *Perspectives on Design III*, Springer Series in Design and Innovation 34, https://doi.org/10.1007/978-3-031-43516-4_18

formulation of work. Due to artificial intelligence, blockchain technology, organizational innovations, and automation in manufacturing and service companies, the current composition of the work environment is being shaped, directly affecting the entire work structure. Some jobs are disappearing, and perhaps soon others will cease to exist.

Notably, in the context of the Creative Economy, an incessant search for differentiated products can be observed as a way to distinguish them from commodities, which only generate profitability in companies with high production scale, is still the main component for the survival of these businesses. In this context, design, as a proactive and interface element between people and markets, continues to be an essential resource to induct and improve sustainable competitive strategies, besides being a basic element of the innovation process. It is well-known that internationally recognized companies adopt sustainable competitiveness strategic parameters. However, these parameters are not always adopted by businesses located in the so-called Global South.

Thus, we have been reflecting on some points that must be considered for the induction of sustainable competitive strategies in the Creative Economy of Brazil, considering the new work paradigms, Prospective Ergonomics, and the 17 UN Sustainable Development Goals (SDG). It is fundamental to highlight the questions that guided the elaboration of this work: (a) Can prioritizing research and continuous product innovation help reconfigure the fashion supply chain in current markets of fierce competition? (b) What can the various links in the fashion supply chain do to accelerate responsible innovation? (c) How can companies in the Creative Economy deal with current challenges and opportunities in a sustainable way? (d) How can we organize new work configurations, according to technological trends, without affecting the entire production system? (e) How do technologies catalyze current changes? (f) Is there a labor regulation that protects the fundamental rights of workers, such as adequate wages, limits on working hours, safe and healthy workplaces that allow for the development of competencies and skills? (g) Can Prospective Ergonomics foresee scenarios to reorient organizational, production, technological and communication processes in the current global context? (h) How can the fulfillment of the 17 SDG help the organizational system of Creative Economy enterprises?

These are such difficult questions to answer, but which provide thoughts for (re)thinking and prospecting possibilities, opportunities, gaps, and obstacles to current business models in the field of Creative Economy. Perhaps the starting point can be given by the meaning of Sustainability. In this text, the word takes on a new meaning, it does not only refer to the environment, economics, and the responsible use of natural and economic resources, but also regards respect for the health and rights of workers and consumers; the simplification of creative project and production processes; in addition to fostering research and innovation.

Hence, by researching, attending congresses, and reading thematic reports led us to analyze particularities of work organization that may contribute to establish feasible and sustainable competitive strategies for the Brazilian Creative Economy. In other words, this work aims to investigate whether "the principles and values of Prospective Ergonomics, as well as the generation of scenarios based on the 17 UN SDG can contribute to sustainable changes in organizational design in Creative Economy industries in Brazil?".

This text is the result of a literature review and is part of a broader research on scenarios for the future of work and Prospective Ergonomics, developed, since 2021, in the Futuro do Presente Laboratório (Future of the Present Laboratory) [1] at the Santa Catarina State University (UDESC, Brazil). The methodological design adopted here comprised exploratory qualitative research [2, 3] and the method chosen was Grounded Theory [4]. In addition to this introduction and the final considerations, the text is organized in three subsections that addressed the main concepts and theoretical frameworks, namely: (a) Macroergonomics: The Prospective Ergonomics as an Approach; (b) Brazilian Fashion Industry's Productive Chain: Data, and Facts; (c) Creative Economy and the 17 Sustainable Development Goals.

2 Theoretical Framework

2.1 Macroergonomics: The Prospective Ergonomics as an Approach

Organizational Ergonomics, called Macroergonomics and known by the acronym ODAM—Organizational Design and Management, is concerned with the optimization of sociotechnical systems, including their organizational structures, policies, and processes, in a top-down approach [5]. Thus, it aims to evaluate the systemic interactions between humans and work devices, to optimize productivity; to increase the company's efficiency and effectiveness and to identify shortcomings in the workplace. The scope is to investigate work from an organizational perspective, prioritizing people, and their relationship with each other or with other elements that surround them in the work environment, thus ensuring a fully harmonized system. It is based on three subsystems as pillars: (a) Technological; (b) Personal; (c) The design of the work system.

It consists of the interface among human being, machine, organization, and environment, at a macro level [6], and can be analyzed according to three paradigms: (a) Science—investigation of human performance and the limitations when developing interfaces; (b) Perspective—global view of the system, enhancing the effectiveness of ergonomic interventions; (c) Method—work system with intervention in job design, work design, hardware, software, and environment. Interventions in Organizational Ergonomics are characterized by: (a) Reach (e.g., micro, macro); (b) Purpose (e.g., adaptive, corrective, prospective); (c) Area (e.g., psychology, engineering, medicine, fashion). Likewise, it can be seen as a multidisciplinary science that integrates Human, Biological and Exact Sciences.

The literature points out that Prospective Ergonomics is associated with a European line of research in Ergonomics, particularly French studies. It focuses on anticipating and preventing future problems and is considered an approach within the sphere of Macroergonomics. The main characteristic of Prospective Ergonomics is its ability to identify current needs and prevent future ones, to build something new to meet those needs [7]. The first authors to mention Prospective Ergonomics in their works were Laurig (1986) and Laurig and Vedder (1992) [7]. Following this, Norman (2007), in his book The Design of Future Things, stated that the ergonomic community should pay attention to the future and Van der Veer (2008), when analyzing the history and development of Cognitive Ergonomics, presented his own methodology, called Envisioning Design, clearly related to the design of future objects [7]. There are also many works in this area associated with Canadian research centers.

Prospective Ergonomic is multidisciplinary and has developed from Macroergonomics through "forward-looking in time" [8]. It is human-centered, emphasizing the user's background through individual, social, cultural, political, economic analysis of scientifical, technological and environmental factors. The emphasis on the selected elements will depend on how they will influence the strategic management of companies, in relation to the anticipation of user needs and the development of new products and services; whether they will be useful and whether they will provide a positive user experience. In practical terms, Prospective Ergonomics creates awareness among stakeholders that anticipating user needs and imagination regarding radically new products and services are essential for the survival of organizations and their business ecosystems. Considering the intricate relationship between the collaborators of a production chain and their plural objectives, prospective interventions support innovative activities, with emphasis on deliberative processes, using prospective methods and tools.

Ergonomics has been concerned with two main activities [7]: (a) Correction; (b) Prevention. Corrective Ergonomics is related to the past and has a relation to the demand of a client, prioritizing the correction of situations and aiming to reduce or eliminate problems. The proposal is to find the best solution to the problem. Preventive Ergonomics is related to the present, to a demand, and to a client. The challenge is to make the best design project, after defining the scope of the project and the functional requirements of the product. On the other hand, Prospective Ergonomics (Fig. 1) is explicitly associated with innovation and relates to the future, not having a direct relationship with customer demands. Liem and Brangier [8] assert that Prospective Ergonomics conceives that the actors involved should be aware that anticipation of user needs, and new services are paramount to the survival of the business ecosystem. They advocate the revision of Ergonomics from the theories and frameworks of Design, Strategic Management, and the field of Innovation.

Therefore, the "retrospective analysis" [9] corresponds to the activities orientated to the past, such as identification of root cause; and the "prospective analysis" is related to actions focused on the future, for example, creative thinking, evaluation of consequences, scenarios, etc. Although Corrective and Preventive Ergonomics can lead to innovation, they differ from Prospective Ergonomics, since innovation is not the main objective, and the solution is limited to the problem presented. However, it

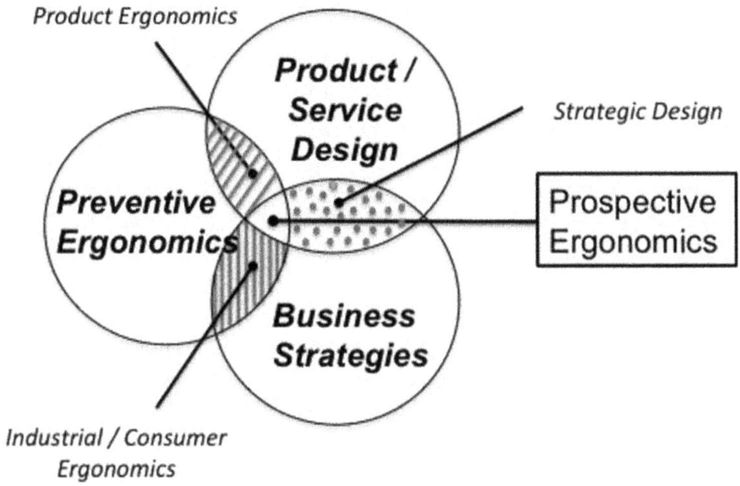

Fig. 1 Prospective ergonomics and the point of interaction between design, strategies and preventive ergonomics [11]

is important to note that the three categories of activities overlap in the ergonomic process.

The four characteristics of Prospective Ergonomics [7] are: (a) Focus oriented towards the human being and future technologies; (b) Comprehension of the needs, motivations, interests, and experiences of users through the investigation of the activities of potential users and their products in their contexts; (c) Ability to prospect the future, based on different prospective methods; (d) Generation of innovation, through the promotion of creativity.

There are two directives for Prospective Ergonomics [10]: (a) Market-pull; (b) Technology push. In the first directive, the driving force behind innovation is inadequate customer satisfaction. In other words, when the individual needs to stimulate and lead the development of technology, articulating their subjective demands. In the Technology push directive, the stimulus for new products and processes derives from the results of external research, with the purpose being the commercial use of a new know-how. It is essential to ratify that the distinctions between the two guidelines are not rigid and that ergonomics specialists cannot, when starting new projects, neither completely ignore the market, nor abandon pre-project approaches.

Prospective is a tool that allows the company, through a collective reflection of future challenges, to structure and evaluate its strategic and market options, to clarify its actions. Like that, the prospective attitude consists of controlling the change, acting in proactivity, preparing for the transformations, as well as causing desired changes in the present scenario. The generation of scenarios, according to the Prospective Ergonomics angle, allows the decision making in three main stages of a Project [12]: (a) Analysis of problem-situations at the beginning of the process; (b) Generation of design solutions at various levels of complexity; (c) Evaluation of these project decisions according to the criteria of user-centered design. In this context, the scenarios in the early stages of the design project aim to consolidate the current knowledge of designers and their assumptions about future activities and not solely provide a specific view of the future activity of the user. In the same way, scenarios are seen as an administrative tool, since they are an approach of strategic thinking that recognizes the unpredictability of the future, outlining possible paths of improvement in the present. Consequently, the use of scenarios for the future, and of Prospective Ergonomics, is not only limited to materials for analysis, but also to a creative product of design and advances in the organizational system.

Likewise, there is ample potential for the implementation of Prospective Ergonomics at the meta-project stage, i.e., from a strategic concept, which can be introduced into a Fuzzy Front-End or Innovation Front-End process [13], when the future product and/or service proposals are researched. This allows the adoption of innovation practices with the purpose of obtaining competitive differentials in the market. Consequently, the value of Prospective Ergonomics is generated through the development of radically new products, systems, and services, in a strategic way, focused on human needs and the design of new products and services.

In fragmented systems, the scenarios are used for the development of the system, however there is no unique process since the scenarios can be a detailed textual narrative of the practices and interactions observed in the workplace; a case analysis of the use of a model of domain; a daily video viewing of a future product or instructions in an experiment for evaluation. Therefore, scenarios have a potential advantage for the strengthening of the design and Prospective Ergonomics should not be limited to the mining of ideas for projects that have already been decided, and that exist somehow, almost always due to the initiative of others. This corresponds to the so-called defined future. In fact, the scope is much larger than that. Prospective Ergonomics should include the search for projects that have not yet been decided and do not even exist. This can become a reality due to the initiative of ergonomists and corresponds to the so-called indefinite future. The objective of the restructuration of the system, with the addition of Prospective Ergonomics, is to invest in the challenge of dealing with the future and innovation.

2.2 *Brazilian Fashion Industry's Productive Chain: Data, and Facts*

Analyzing the current conjuncture of the Fashion Industry's Productive Chain (Fig. 2) in Brazil, we verify that, in the wake of a dynamic and globalized market, of persistent competitive increase, the strategic motto for sustainable growth remains the differentiation of products, and the public policies promoted by the State reflect in changes occurred in the organizations. Thus, innovation and the introduction of new concepts

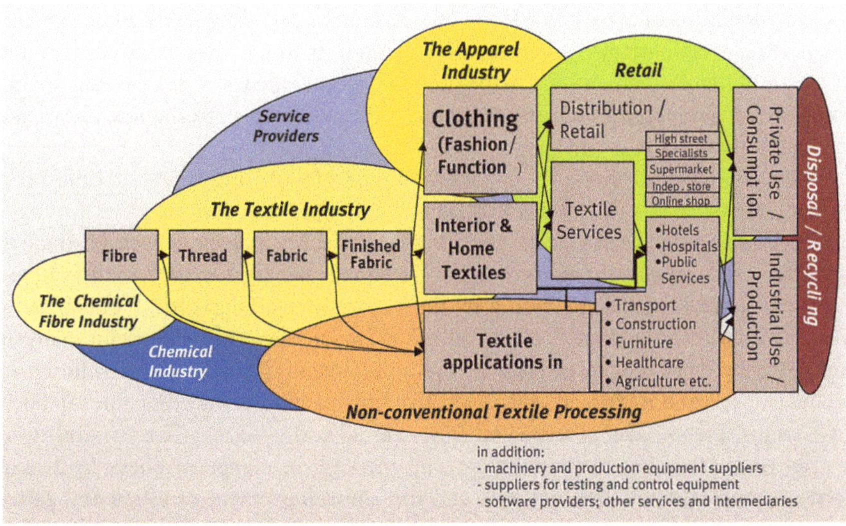

Fig. 2 An overview of the complexity and variety of actors in the textile clothing business [15]

are important factors in the evolutionary scale of companies, given that the development of this productive chain, in its entirety, comes not only from individual business commitment, but, above all, from the interrelationship between the company and their external interlocutors (suppliers, clients, intermediaries, consultants, government).

According to data from the Program for Internationalization of the Brazilian Textile and Fashion Industry [14], Brazil is a world reference in swimwear, jeans wear and home wear design, having also grown in the fitness and lingerie segments, besides having the largest complete textile chain in the West. Brazil is also among the five largest producers and consumers of denim and among the four largest producers of knitwear in the world, besides São Paulo Fashion Week being among the five largest fashion weeks in the world.

The textile and apparel industry are present throughout the national territory, concentrating 22.5 thousand formal companies throughout the country, being the second largest employer in the transformation industry, second only to the food and beverage sectors. It represents 19.5% of the jobs and 6% of the transformation industry's revenues, with a total of 1.34 million direct employees and 8 million, if we add the indirect ones and the income effect, of which 60% are women. In 2021, the Brazilian textile production was 2.16 million tons/year and the clothing industry, which includes clothing, socks, accessories and bed, table, and bath linen, was approximately 8.1 billion pieces/year. This means a turnover of R$190 billion. The investments, in 2021, were R$4.9 billion, especially in technology and production structure [14].

Despite the significant numbers of the sector, the Brazilian market presents many shortcomings and difficulties, especially for micro and small businesses. The fragility and fragmentation of these companies, characteristics prevailing in the main productive poles of Brazil inevitably influences the level of productivity and the competitive insertion of these organizations in the different market niches, since the sustainable competitive advantage is the foundation of the industrial performance above the medium to long term.

There are several terms, in the literature, to identify the types of Enterprise Arrangements, such as Clusters, Industrial Complexes, Local Productive Arrangements, Business Networks, Industrial Districts, and Locally Innovative Productive Systems, used, frequently, as synonyms. In Brazil, the term widely used is Local Productive Arrangement, including by the Federal Government itself, constituting itself as a productive cluster, either due to political causes or superficial analysis supported by empirical research with multiple meanings [16]. The constitution of productive poles in Brazil, and the respective organization of the companies in business arrangements, was accentuated from the 80's, due to: (a) The possibility of restrictive overcoming to growth; (b) The increase in competitiveness in distant domestic and international markets; and (c) The achievement of efficiency gains. In the field of fashion, we can point out some cases of successful productive poles, outlining the aspects and experiences of sustaining competitiveness, especially of micro and small companies: (a) Rio de Janeiro—garment manufacturing, underwear, knitwear and swimwear; (b) Minas Gerais—garment manufacturing, knitwear; (c) São Paulo—retail, spinning, weaving, dyeing, garment manufacturing; (d) Ceará—garment manufacturing, jeanswear, swimwear, underwear; (e) Santa Catarina—spinning, weaving, dyeing, garment manufacturing, jeanswear, knitwear; (f) Rio Grande do Sul—knitwear.

To improve the current scenario, it is first necessary to recognize the problems that exist in the Fashion Industry's Productive Chain, such as: (a) Managerial behavior, which does not adopt organizational and business strategies; (b) Lack of investments in the qualification (entrepreneurial, managerial and creative) of human resources; (c) Insufficient investment capacity of companies; (d) Failure to review product positioning in the market; (e) Little associative capacity; (f) Incipient knowledge to transform intangible product characteristics into value for the final consumer. Then, understand that innovation is seen as a common denominator in design activities today, since intangible characteristics result from organizational learning processes, in which the organization develops or obtains knowledge about its operations.

According to data from the Global Innovation Index [17], which evaluates the ability of a country to convert efforts into innovation and new products in the market, in 2022, Brazil ranked 54th in the world, appearing for the first time among the three most innovative economies in Latin America and the Caribbean, alongside Chile and Mexico. In the same report, "Brazil makes marked improvements in innovation outputs, notably in Creative outputs, including in Intangible assets and Online creativity, as well as in the indicators Trademarks (19th) and Mobile app creation (34th)" [17].

Thus, aiming at the continuous improvement of this reality, the document "2035 Vision: Brazil, developed country—sectorial agendas for achieving the goal" [18] presents a development agenda for the country on the 2018–2035 horizon and addresses, in one of the chapters, the Creative Economy, recognizing it as a significant field for the national Gross Domestic Product (GDP), as it stimulates innovation and knowledge transfer in all sectors of the economy. According to internationally established estimates, the Creative Economy should follow this positive trajectory and expand by 4.2% per year until 2021. In this context, Brazil stands as a country with high development potential, as it counts with a vast and diverse culture. However, for the full realization of its potential, there are several challenges that still must be overcome.

2.3 *Creative Economy and the 17 Sustainable Development Goals*

Creative Economy is a broad and evolving concept and has been dominating discussions on new economic thinking. Although it is a polysemic term, depending on the approach of the authors, Creative Economy in general can be understood as a set of cultural activities, goods or services that are both economic and cultural in nature, encompassing sectors linked to artistic-cultural production, new media, content industry, architecture, design, and fashion. Cooperation and sharing of knowledge constitute its core, being also intangible and symbolic. In the context of fashion, it is essential to intertwine some considerations on the inventive role intrinsic to project activities, the viability of innovation through ideas (projects), the applicability, development and execution in spaces and products, since "fashion" is formally and constructively exteriorized by materiality. Consequently, it is not of our interest to romantically exalt the figure of the "fashion creator" as, due to his ability to combine culture and creativity, is apart from the fashion designer, traditionally linked to the market and that, in an "artistic" view, would not be free to exercise his creative capacity.

Thus, we conceive Creative Economy as a holistic and multidisciplinary approach, that deals with the interface among economy, culture, and technology, centered on the predominance of products and services with creative content, cultural value and market aims, resulting from a gradual change of paradigm [19], in which the conventional boundaries between services and manufacturing disappear and there is the incorporation of services with high value added in all production processes. Consequently, there must be an explicit shift away from conventional development strategies centered on terms of trade focusing on primary commodities and industrial manufacturing [19]. Thus, we realize that the structuring of consensual foundations and institutional articulation for the development of dynamic sectors in this new industrial model are decisive for the effectiveness of actions and public policies.

The concept of sustainable development is also constantly evolving and, since the last three decades, has required a systemic and interdisciplinary approach at different levels in the international arena. Sustainable development today means improving people's quality of life by combining economic growth, social development, and environmental protection for present and future generations. This process requires different actions depending on the continent, region, or country, and demands a global commitment that is collective and individual with regard to governments, institutions, and individuals.

The 2030 Agenda for Sustainable Development was approved in 2015 by the United Nations as a mutual commitment to global development for the preservation of the environment and human well-being. It is composed of 17 Sustainable Development Goals (SDGs) [20], which are crucial for its realization until 2030. It covers a wide range of interconnected issues such as poverty eradication, climate action, quality education, building sustainable cities, and promoting gender equality, among others. Progress regarding each of the goals is monitored regularly and requires the collaboration of governments, the private sector, civil society, organizations, and individuals to implement the necessary actions.

It is essential to note that the 17 goals of the 2030 Agenda are listed in relation to the characteristics of the three dimensions of sustainable development [20], namely: (a) Environmental dimension: not to exceed the "resilience" of the biosphere-geosphere, i.e., its ability to absorb anthropogenic disturbances without causing irreversible degradation phenomena, such as climate change, acidification and land use; (b) Socio-ethical dimension: the ability of future generations to meet their own needs and the achievement of equity and social cohesion, in which a key issue is the egalitarian redistribution of resources, following the principle that everyone should have the same access to global natural resources; and (c) Economic dimension: promoting inclusive and sustainable economic growth, employment and decent work for all.

Thus, the 17 SDG [20] are as follows (Fig. 3).

No Poverty: Reducing extreme poverty has been a central goal since the creation of the Millennium Development Goals (MDGs) in 2000. SDG 1 seeks to end poverty in all its forms everywhere.

Zero Hunger: SDG 2 aims to ensure universal access to safe and nutritious food by promoting sustainable agriculture and increased agricultural productivity.

Good Health and Well-being: SDG 3 focuses on ensuring healthy lives and promoting well-being for all people at all ages, addressing issues such as maternal and child health, infectious diseases, and access to health services.

Quality Education: SDG 4 seeks to ensure inclusive, equitable and quality education, promoting lifelong learning opportunities for all.

Gender Equality: SDG 5 seeks to achieve gender equality and empower all women and girls by eliminating gender-based discrimination and violence.

Clean Water and Sanitation: SDG 6 seeks to ensure the availability and sustainable management of water and sanitation for all, with a focus on water quality, water use efficiency and sanitation.

Affordable and Clean Energy: SDG 7 seeks to ensure access to affordable, reliable, sustainable, and modern energy for all by promoting the transition to renewable energy sources.

Decent Work and Economic Growth: SDG 8 addresses the need to promote sustained, inclusive, and sustainable economic growth, full and productive employment, and decent work for all and combating child labor.

Fig. 3 Sustainable development goals infographic [21]

Industry, Innovation, and Infrastructure: SDG 9 focuses on building resilient infrastructure, promoting sustainable industrialization, innovation, and technology development.

Reducing Inequality: SDG 10 seeks to reduce inequalities within and among countries by promoting social, economic, and political inclusion of all, regardless of age, gender, disability, race, ethnicity, origin, religion, or economic status.

Sustainable Cities and Communities: SDG 11 aims to make cities and human settlements inclusive, safe, resilient, and sustainable by promoting adequate urban planning, access to adequate housing and sustainable transport.

Responsible Consumption and Production: SDG 12 focuses on promoting sustainable consumption and production patterns, responsibly managing natural resources, and reducing waste.

Climate Action: SDG 13 aims to take urgent action to combat climate change and its impacts by promoting education, awareness raising and climate resilience.

Life Below Water: SDG 14 focuses on the conservation and sustainable use of oceans, seas, and marine resources, combating pollution and protecting marine biodiversity.

Life on Land: SDG 15 aims to protect, restore and promote the sustainable use of terrestrial ecosystems, sustainably manage forests, combat desertification and halt biodiversity loss.

Peace, Justice, and Strong Institutions: SDG 16 seeks to promote peaceful, just and inclusive societies by strengthening institutions and ensuring access to justice for all.

Partnerships to achieve the Goals: SDG 17 addresses the need to strengthen the implementation of the SDGs through global partnerships, resource mobilization, and promoting cooperation among governments, the private sector, and civil society.

It is essential to underline that promoting economic sustainability means fostering inclusive and sustainable economic growth, ensuring employment and decent work for all. In other words, the economic dimension of sustainability commits us to promoting models of production, environmental and social consumption that are ethically sustainable, but also economically profitable.

The fundamental role of decent work for all in achieving sustainable development is highlighted by SDG 8, which aims to "promote sustained, inclusive and sustainable economic growth, full and productive employment and decent work for all" [20]. By an intentional choice and considering the question of this research, "can the principles and values of Prospective Ergonomics, as well as scenario generation, guided by the UN Sustainable Development Goals, contribute to sustainable changes in organizational design in the Creative Economy industries in Brazil?", we will focus on 8th SDG.

At this point, it is appropriate to emphasize that the crucial aspects of decent work, job creation, social protection, rights at work and social dialogue are integral elements of the 2030 Agenda for Sustainable Development and are widely rooted in the goals of many of the other 16 goals. Moreover, the same agenda also reiterates in different sections the need to generate employment for vulnerable groups, specifically women, urban poor, unemployed rural workers, as well as low-income urban residents.

From three categories (orientation, processes, and value), we can trace the main points of intertwining between Prospective Ergonomics and Creative Economy, aligned to the 8th SDG of the UN, aiming to contribute to sustainable changes in the organizational project of Brazilian industries.

As for the orientation, we can seek responsible sustainability in the balance between performance and productivity, between human and social well-being in a collective way. By placing the needs and desires of human beings at the center of the design process and encouraging the diversity of cultural and creative expressions, Creative Economy companies can intensify the growth of their sustainable competitiveness in relation to other industrial sectors. And to be innovative, it is necessary to apply Prospective Ergonomics, which takes a proactive role with a focus on future products and services, using a global multidisciplinary approach guided by a STEEP analysis. This also opens up the possibility of heterogeneous products and services, strengthening social cohesion and eliminating barriers that supposedly would interfere with mutual perception and communication among people. The idea is to provide products designed by people for people [8].

As for the processes, in Prospective Ergonomics, the designer acts as a facilitator to constructively extract stakeholder views and competencies to anticipate and create future user needs [8]. The designer must then orchestrate a compilation of design methods and tools to be applied in a participatory manner. The fundamentals of Prospective Ergonomics and the Creative Economy can drive the incorporation of sustainability and social responsibility into organizational practices. By considering the product life cycle, reducing the consumption of natural resources, minimizing waste, and promoting recycling, more sustainable production can be achieved. In addition, they can promote socially responsible actions, such as support for local communities and respect for workers' rights, thinking especially about minorities, a weak part of the labor pyramid. This provides an opportunity to strengthen the organizational structures of Creative Economy businesses in relation to all the dimensions of sustainability, focusing on the social side, promoting inclusive and responsible economic growth.

As for the creation of value, the collaborative approach among designers, ergonomists and Creative Economy businesses enables the exchange of knowledge, experiences, and perspectives, providing the opportunity to generate innovative and sustainable solutions. This is directly related to business competitiveness, which must impact social sustainability. To generate value, we must map supply chains and develop training programs for teams, aiming to improve the quality of life, expectations, and performance of people at work. Similarly, we must value the intangible aspects and aesthetic narratives of products. In short, value creation in the Creative Economy, based on the principles of Prospective Ergonomics and the 8th SDGs, encompass the generation of social, cultural, and economic benefits through innovation, cultural preservation, social impact, sustainable and responsible economic growth, and intangible value provided by creative and cultural activities and products.

3 Final Considerations

As a final consideration, we can say that by incorporating Prospective Ergonomics into processes of creation, production, and commercialization of the Creative Economy, combined with the 8th SDG, Brazil can boost its fashion business by promoting innovation, improving the quality of products and services, increasing user satisfaction, and providing a healthy and productive work environment for creative professionals.

In the last 25 years, the value of Ergonomics has expanded beyond legislation related to occupational health and safety. While it continues to address such issues for consumers and workers, there has been a paradigm shift, and currently the value of ergonomics lies in supporting companies' sustainable competitive strategies.

Understanding the use of Organizational Ergonomics fundamentals, in particular the Prospective Ergonomics approach, allied with scenario forecasting, made it possible to scrutinize the future of work in companies of the Brazilian Creative Economy. Furthermore, it allows us to understand how the Fashion Industry's Productive Chain will be affected by technological development in the future and how it contributes to the process of innovation and sustainable change in organizational design.

In addition, Prospective Ergonomics directly impacts education and practice, since ergonomists also act as strategists and project managers pondering on the future, since a "competitive intelligence analysis" is required, with data and expert opinions, as well as insight, intuition, creativity, motivation, and initiative. Brazil has innovation potential in the area of Design, and the path to this achievement is through the articulation between industry, university, and creative professionals.

Therefore, we hope that the diffusion of the information resulting from this study provide conditions for innovative projects with value added to products and services within the area of Prospective Ergonomics. This aims at the competitive sustainability, productivity, effectiveness, and efficiency of organizations, through problem solution, generation, and application of innovation processes. We highlight that this article is an initial reflection of this research. Thus, neither the concepts nor the conclusions here are exhaustive or definitive, but rather we disseminate an embryonic academic provocation on the theme, considering the multiple challenges of researching Prospective Ergonomics and Creative Economy in a complex and polarized society.

Organizations need to follow the maxim that proactively invites them to design the future instead of just reacting to it. Creating sustainable value in a moment of crisis, require new skill sets and forecasting capabilities in the face of managing and generating resilience in complex contexts. De Masi [22] states that "Brazil is already the largest of the Neolatine nations in number of inhabitants and creativity; now it is necessary to be so also at the technological and economic level" in a competitive and sustainable way.

In conclusion, it is not a matter of doing more, but of doing differently.

References

1. Rech SR, Chinchilla GS (2011) Research project future of the present: The process and the importance of signs observation into fashion. In: Silva A, Simões, R (eds) Handbook of research on trends in product design and development: Technological and organizational perspectives, 1st edn. IGI Global, Hershey, Pennsylvania, USA, pp 312–327
2. Bauer MW, Gaskell G (eds) (2013) Pesquisa Qualitativa com Texto, Imagem e Som—um manual prático. Vozes, Petrópolis, Rio de Janeiro, Brasil
3. Rech SR (2020) Trends management: The qualitative approach as a methodology. In: Raposo D, Neves J, Silva, J (eds). Springer series in design and innovation, 1st edn. Springer International Publishing, Cham, Switzerland, pp 283–292
4. Glaser BG, Strauss AL (2017) The discovery of grounded theory: Strategies for qualitative research. Routledge Taylor & Francis Group, New York, USA.

5. Hendrick HW, Kleiner BM (2002) Macroergonomics: Theory, methods, and applications. Lawrence Erlbaum Associates Inc., Publishers, Mahwah, New Jersey, USA
6. Iida I (2016) Ergonomia: projeto e produção. Editora Edgard Blücher, São Paulo, Brasil
7. Robert JM, Brangier, E (2012) Prospective ergonomics: Origin, goal, and prospects. Work: J Prev, Assess Rehabil 41: 5235–5242
8. Liem A, Brangier E (2015) Strategic design and prospective ergonomics: Differences, similarities, and relationships. In The value of design research—11th international European academy of design conference proceedings, European Academy of Design, Paris, France
9. Karwowski W, Marras WS (1999) Occupational ergonomics: Design and management of work systems. CRC Press LLC, Boca Raton, Florida, USA
10. Brem A, Voigt K (2009) Integration of market pull and technology push in the corporate: Front end and innovation management-insights from the German software industry. Technovation 29(5):351–367
11. Liem A (2017) Prospective ergonomics. ISTE, London, England
12. Rosson MB, Carroll JM (2002) Scenario-based design. In: Jacko J, Sears A (eds) The human-computer interaction handbook: Fundamentals, evolving technologies, and emerging applications. Lawrence Erlbaum Associates, Nova Jersey, EUA, pp 1032–1050
13. Smith PG, Reinertsen DG (1991) Developing products in half the time. Van Nostrand Reinhold, New York, USA
14. Texbrasil Homepage. https://texbrasil.com.br/pt/imprensa/dados-da-industria-textil-e-de-confeccao/. Last accessed 18 June 2023
15. Euratex (2004) European Technology Platform: for the future of textiles and clothing—A vision for 2020. European Apparel and Textile Organization, Brussels, Belgium, p. 4
16. Teixeira RMM (2018) Os Processos de Internacionalização no Cluster do Vestuário (Tese de Doutoramento). Mestrado em Economia e Gestão Internacional, Universidade do Porto, Porto, Portugal.
17. Dutta S, Lanvin B, Léon LR, Wunsch-Vincent, S (eds) (2022) Global innovation index 2022: What is the future of innovation-driven growth? World Intellectual Property Organization, Geneva, Switzerland
18. Puga F, Castro LB de (2018) Visão 2035: Brasil, país desenvolvido—agendas setoriais para alcance da meta. BNDES, Rio de Janeiro, Brasil
19. Reis, ACF (ed) (2008) Economia Criativa como Estratégia de Desenvolvimento: uma visão dos países em desenvolvimento. Itaú Cultural, São Paulo, Brasil
20. United Nations Homepage. https://sdgs.un.org/2030agenda. Last accessed 18 June 2023
21. Sustainable Development Goals. https://br.freepik.com/vetores-gratis/infografico-sdg-gradiente_26411362.htm. Last accessed 18 June 2023.
22. De Masi D (2014) O Futuro Chegou. Casa da Palavra, Rio de Janeiro, Brasil

Trade Fairs from 2016 to 2022: Trends of Flexible and Modular Furniture for Hybrid Working Sceneries

Rita Cruz and **Fátima Pombo**

Abstract The lifestyle changed and the evolution of mobile technology made it possible to introduce new nomadic ways of working. The future of work lies in a hybrid model between remote and on-site work. Covid-19 accelerated the change to more flexible working models. Trade fairs dedicated to workplace furniture show the trends of collaborative and modular furniture for these new working sceneries. As well workplaces express the need to acquire versatile furniture to create more collaborative work environments and creative experiences that we cannot have at home. This research intends to recognize furniture design as a modular and flexible feature that contributes to the creation of atmospheres compatible with these new forms of cooperative and agile work. The research was carried out by studying five visited trade fairs dedicated to workplace furniture and a sample of workplaces, considering the premises: function/comfort, materials/sustainability and flexibility/form. The principal output of this study is evidencing the relevance of furniture design in the creation of more collaborative and sharing scenarios in new dynamic working models, to improve the wellbeing and sustainability of work communities.

Keywords Furniture Design · Hybrid workplaces · Trade Fairs · Lifestyle

1 Introduction

The ways of working are changing considerably for a more collaborative and sharing model. From globalization to the technological and digital evolution, that facilitates the nomadism and the flexibility of lifestyles and has an impact in the way people interact and their working routine, there are many factors that influenced the change to a new model. The covid-19 pandemic evidenced and accelerated, the already

R. Cruz (✉) · F. Pombo
Department of Communication and Art, Aveiro University, Aveiro, Portugal
e-mail: ritamccruz@ua.pt

F. Pombo
e-mail: fpombo@ua.pt

D. Raposo et al. (eds.), *Perspectives on Design III*, Springer Series in Design and Innovation 34, https://doi.org/10.1007/978-3-031-43516-4_19

foreseen, change to a more hybrid and flexible work model. From one day to the next it generated a massive experiment in remote working that validated the availability and effectiveness of technology, leading to the emergence of new requirements to the workplaces. The trade fairs dedicated to workplace furniture show how designers pay attention and can contribute to fulfill the needs of the work routine and provide scenarios that are more appropriate to new ways of working.

Considering the relevance of furniture design to humanization and to the creation of a pleasant experience in the workplace and recognizing the impact of trade fairs for the sector of office furniture, this study intends to answer the following research questions: To what extent do trade fair trends anticipate and fulfill the needs of workplaces? How can furniture design contribute to the creation of scenarios compatible with the new forms of hybrid and agile working? How will we be working in future?

In this perspective, a special emphasis is given to the study of five visited trade fairs dedicated to workplace furniture and a sample of workplaces that were also visited. Following a literature review, careful visits to trade fairs were carried out and a standard interview template was created and used in the visits to the workplaces, which were relevant to compile information and understand the real requirements of people to the workplace.

This article aims to reflect on the importance of furniture design to create scenarios compatible with the new working models, considering and analyzing the following premises: function/comfort, materials/sustainability and flexibility/form.

2 New Landscape of Workplaces

Industry 4.0 was driven by the innovative technological and digital evolution that are already part of our everyday life. With the dominance of that digital phenomenon, we enter into the post-digital era [4]. Digital nomadism is completely integrated into contemporary society [8], becoming a new normal. The post-digital era stands out for the acceptance of digitization as inevitable, so intrinsic to our life that it is reflected in society's behaviors and routines including in new ways of working. The Covid-19 global pandemic evidenced and accelerated not only the transition for this post-digital era, but also forced organizations and companies to introduce remote work overnight, and consequently to make rapid transitions to hybrid working models [3]. The recent study [15], about workplace harmony and balance also indicates that the Covid-19 pandemic has driven the transition to a post-digital era, which made this topic more relevant and urgent. Thus, it boosted the change to a new working model that incorporates the spirituality concept, based on the idea of bringing personal life closer to professional life in order to motivate employees. These changes are particularly visible in organizations and companies "in the emerging post-digital era where collaboration, sharing, mutual nurturing and co-evolution are the norms of business operation [15].

With technological and digital evolution, the workplaces are also adapting, as the social behaviour changed and also the ways of working. Spaces and products are constantly reinventing themselves in order to becoming a new normal. The post-digital era stands out for the acceptance of digitization as inevitable, so intrinsic to our life that it is reflected in society's behaviors and routines including in new ways of working. The Covid-19 global pandemic evidenced and accelerated not only the transition for this post-digital era, but also forced organizations and companies to introduce remote work overnight, and consequently to make rapid transitions to hybrid working models respond to the needs and requirements of society. An exhibition that was on display at Orgatec 2016 (trade fair dedicated to workplace furniture) in Cologne posed the following question: "What does your desk say about you?" (Fig. 1).

In fact, the desk says a lot about the user's needs for working. Workplaces have been adapting over time, mainly to technological and digital advances that in addition to leading to a reduction of the number of necessary objects to work activities, made them more portable, which has consequently affected the ways of working. The contrast of a 1940s office with a contemporary one shows this evolution (Fig. 2).

Fig. 1 "What does your desk say about you?" in Orgatec 2016, Köln. © Rita Cruz

Fig. 2 The contrast of a 1940s with a 2020s office. (a) Source: Pile, J., & Gura, J. (2014). A History of Interior Design (Fourth Edition). John Wiley & Sons, p. 328. (b) Source: accessed May 20, 2023, https://www.vitra.com/en-lp/office/projects/clients/details/wl-gore-and-associates-gmbh

In 1940s, each worker with his workstation (desk and chair) and their work objects. Nowadays technology and digital devices allows for greater mobility, more nomadic ways of working and more collaborative activities, which makes work increasingly less formal. In fact, today it is possible to work from anywhere and not just in the office, but also at home, in the cafe, in travel situations like on the plane, train, airport, hotel and even in the garden or in the beach.

The covid-19 pandemic came to accelerate the change of the work paradigm, to more hybrid and nomadic ways of working, as it was already foreseen. The pandemic context had consequences in the personal and professional life and in our routines which changed the way we work and interact with others. The general lockdown emerged, physical distance and mobility restrictions were required to prevent contamination, which suddenly had an impact in the exponential increase of people working remotely from home. While in the past organizations and companies limited themselves to theorizing and doing something related to new models of hybrid working, with the pandemic they were forced to accelerate the process of changing for a more flexible work paradigm. A study considers that the break with past is the first step to achieve a new more flexible and less formal workplace model compatible with the new ways of working [5]. In fact, in this post-pandemic period it's important to reflect not only about the impact of pandemics in the way we work and interact, but also in what was learned with that experience and with the sudden necessity to work remotely. And to thereby also take the opportunity to improve the work requirements and shift to a more flexible work model based on a healthier and comfortable work environment, in a work-life balance, travel time and costs and other commodities that were evident with the pandemic and still are priorities for people [1].

In the Vitra Summit 2020, a digital forum organised by Vitra (a reference company in the furniture sector) about the future of work and home realized in October 2020, one of the topics discussed revolved around the question: "We will miss the office if it disappears?" A mural from an exhibition in the halls of Orgatec 2016 anticipates the answer: "the office will never die!" (Fig. 3).

In fact, we will not miss it because the office will not disappear, it will change and adapt and will be a complementary workplace to our home. People will go to the office increasingly less, but they will always have that need, and therefore

Fig. 3 Orgatec 2016, Köln. © Rita Cruz

the workplace will be for moments of collaboration and socialization, sharing and interaction between teams and people. And there should be spaces that offer a level of comfort as close as possible to home. In this way, the hybrid work model that is already a reality, stands out as a new working pattern and a new trend for the working sceneries.

Considering that a hybrid and more flexible work model requires changes to the workplace allowing it to be in different locations, we are facing a new concept of workplace. Taking into account that the hybrid model of work enables work activities both alone and in teams, Mikael Krogerus & Roman Tschäppeler created a table that represents four different work possibilities, as shown in Fig. 4. The authors organized the table in such a way as to demonstrate that it is possible to work alone in space and time (alone in home-office or another location when teams work distributed and everyone can be engaged in concentration work activities without being disturbed), alone in space but together in time (alone in home-office or another location but working in team remotely by a video call meeting), alone in time although together in space (teams are in the same workplace at the same time but everyone works alone in individual activities) and together in space and time (face-to-face team work which includes diverse activities of collaboration, socialization and interaction) [13].

With this hybrid model of work, trips to the offices will be smaller, but important and fruitful for moments of collaboration and socialization between work teams [7] To facilitate these moments and make them more rewarding and productive, it is necessary to rethink workplaces and orient them more to moments of collaboration, not forgetting the need to adapt and maintain some spaces for work activities alone. To support hybrid collaboration is increasingly evident the need to create more flexible and agile workplaces, considering the importance of technology and employee

Fig. 4 How to hybrid work? by Mikael Krogerus & Roman Tschäppeler, accessed March 3, 2023, file:///C:/Users/ritam/Downloads/DynamicSpaces_digital%20EN%20(1).pdf

wellbeing [6]. Hybrid collaboration meetings have become a daily reality, and therefore it is important to create conditions and spaces to connect people in person and remotely at the same time. In fact, this change in the work paradigm to a hybrid model is a big change, which, in addition to boosting the technological advance of companies, makes work more human, improving the work life balance [9]. Equity, engagement and ease are three key concepts essential to be considered to create workplaces for a better hybrid collaboration that promote equitable and inclusive work experiences [10].

Furniture design should approach versatility as a sustainable solution, as modularity is essential to create more efficient and dynamic multifunctional workplaces that ensure stable workflows, allow working collaboratively and that are able to respond to the needs of different users. Flexibility is an important concept and one to consider in the hybrid work model, as it allows the people to work wherever they want without limitations and offers comfort to the body and mind [11]. Like the modularity of the furniture allows to create different configurations easily and quickly throughout the day and working in different spots, which makes the workday healthier.

Considering that the work routine is increasingly dynamic, leading to the need to create varied layouts and work situations, Vitra and the designer Stephan Hürlemann have developed the solution Dancing Wall [12] as can be seen in Fig. 5.

This solution is perfect for agile work environments and can be spontaneously adapted to different requirements of users. These metal frames are easy to move and can be assembled in different configurations: as a room divider, as a bookshelf, as shelving for potted plants and with diverse accessories like TV unit or with removable magnetic whiteboards and other technology products integrated. With the relevance that covid-19 pandemic gave to the necessity to create agile workplaces easily adaptable to changing situations, Vitra also developed a Comma office system [14] as it is displayed in Fig. 6.

This modular system consists of a few elements that can be easily assembled and configured into diverse structures that can be changed to adapt work environments

Fig. 5 *Dancing Wall* by Vitra, 2018. Accessed May 23, 2023, https://www.vitra.com/en-lp/product/dancing-wall

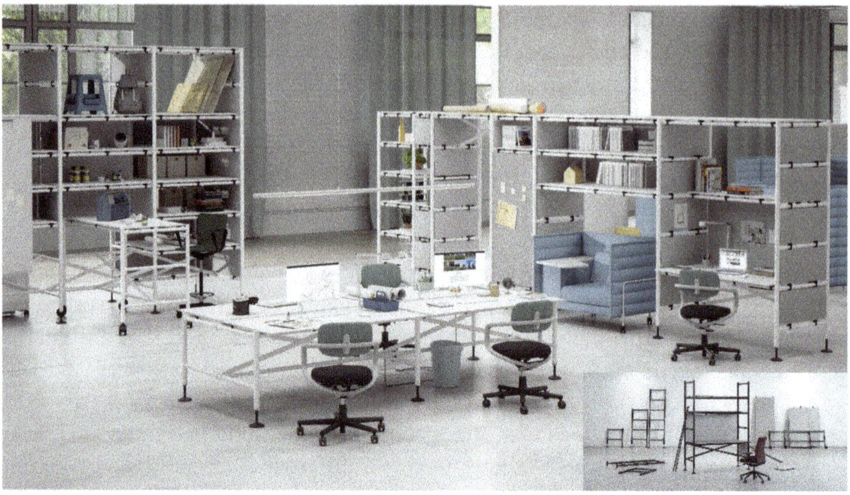

Fig. 6 Comma office by Vitra, 2022. Accessed May 23, 2023, https://www.vitra.com/en-lp/product/comma

Fig. 7 *Flex Collection* by Steelcase. Accessed May 25, 2023, https://www.steelcase.com/products/desk-systems/steelcase-flex-collection/#flex-neighborhoods_collaborate

and their functions to user's needs. The Steelcase Flex Collection (Fig. 7) is also designed for hybrid workplaces, allowing to create a diversity of spaces to support collaborative work, brainstorming meetings, social connections but also focus zones for individual work activities.

The flexibility of these collections, in addition to facilitating the change between different work modes, offers technology and interconnected tools which are essential for hybrid work. Acoustics, materials and comfort were considered to bring the most diverse work environments closer to the coziness of home.

The relevance of materials and their choice is essential to ensure an adequate level of lightness, acoustics, comfort and wellbeing, which are fundamental to the relationship and experience of users. Since the idea of sustainability and circular economy is to reduce the negative impact on the environment and health, the characteristics and origin of materials, shapes, production processes, are essential to the design process. process.

To celebrate the 60th anniversary of the Milan International Furniture Fair (Salone del Mobile), in the 2022 edition, the Bolognese architect Mario Cucinella created an installation entitled "Design with Nature - A design experience narrating the potential reconciliation between man and nature" (Fig. 8). Taking into account the events of recent years, the architect focused on social connections and sharing, highlighting the new lifestyles, increasingly nomadic and flexible, supporting a new way of experiencing the city and considering that "coexistence/collaboration with technology and awareness to social dynamics" are fundamental.

In this installation, the concepts of sustainability and ecological transition are approached taking into account nature and the ways of the past, calling for the available resources to be used respecting their regeneration times and placing the environment as a priority for the future.

The new working concepts, more agile, collaborative and sharing, go in line with the sustainable development goals defined by the Unesco 2030. Of the 17 proposed goals (Fig. 9), we can highlight 4 goals: n°8 Decent work and economic growth; n°11 Sustainable cities and communities; n°12 Responsible consumption and production; n°17 Partnerships for the goals.

The concern with the working conditions of employees, regarding physical and mental wellbeing, comfort, motivation, work life balance, are crucial in the design of new workplaces to improve productivity and consequently promote an inclusive and sustainable economic growth. In addition it contributes to the sustainable, inclusive and safety growth of the communities and cities. About ensuring sustainable consumption and production patterns, trends show an increase in concern about the circular economy of products as well as using sustainable materials and production techniques. It is also increasingly evident the need to create partnerships that support research and knowledge creation for the sustainable development of products and their value chain. The New European Bauhaus initiative aims to bring communities together and link the European Green Deal to our routines, living spaces and experiences. Based on three inseparable values: beautiful and together, it aims to encourage all Europeans to build a better future. This artistic and multidisciplinary movement launched by the European Commission is also a sign of the necessity to create partnerships to encourage new creative projects aimed at the wellbeing and sustainability of communities. Therefore, it is important to consider the relevance of furniture design in the creation of scenarios compatible with the new hybrid working models, and thus generate creative and comprehensive experiences to ensure the quality of life and sustainability of communities.

Fig. 8 *Design with Nature*, by Mario Cucinella. Salone del Mobile. Milano, 2022. © Rita Cruz

Fig. 9 Sustainable Development Goals by Unesco. Accessed May 26, 2023, https://en.unesco.org/sustainabledevelopmentgoals

The new ways of working require a new landscape of workplaces with more flexible and modular furniture, in line with sustainable issues, to create more collaborative and hybrid working sceneries. In the study that follows, a qualitative reflection about the trade fairs trends and the requirements of collaborative workplaces was considered demonstrating the importance of furniture design to create hybrid working sceneries.

3 Methodology

This research is based on a qualitative study consisting of the analysis of two groups of visits related to the theme: (1) visit and analysis of collaborative workplaces (coworking's, companies and business incubators); (2) visit and analysis of trade fairs dedicated to workplace furniture. In order to analyze these visits and the importance of workplace furniture design in hybrid working scenarios, the following parameters were considered: function/comfort, materials/sustainability and flexibility/ (Fig. 10).

The parameter function/ comfort related with ergonomic issues of furniture design is relevant to the wellbeing and health of workers. Materials/ sustainability are linked to the careful choice of materials of the furniture but also the circular economy of the products, are fundamental concerns to ensure sustainability of consumption. The flexibility/ form correlated to the modularity and versatility of the furniture is crucial to the new working dynamics that requires quick and easy changes layouts to support different work activities. These pairs of parameters are a fundamental tool to this qualitative study.

3.1 Analyses and Interpretation of Collaborative Workplaces

For this study, data was collected between April 2020 and April 2023, through a visit to collaborative workplaces and an informal interview with its founders, managers or other person responsible. Some of those interviews were carried out via videoconference. Due to the covid-19 pandemic and the consequent lockdowns combined with the restrictions created, there was some difficulty to concentrate in timing of the visits, which were carried out in several stages, and also in conducting the visits and therefore some interviews were made virtually. The outcome of the informal interviews was analyzed in a qualitative way by crossing the data of the interview with the information collected while observing and feeling the workplaces through the visits.

The study is carried out by analyzing 18 coworking spaces, 3 business incubators and 5 companies that were selected by web research about the most interesting collaborative workplaces in the cities selected by their location and convenience. Many of the workplaces which were contacted refused to receive visits due to the pandemic, others did not even respond and some in other cities had to given up due

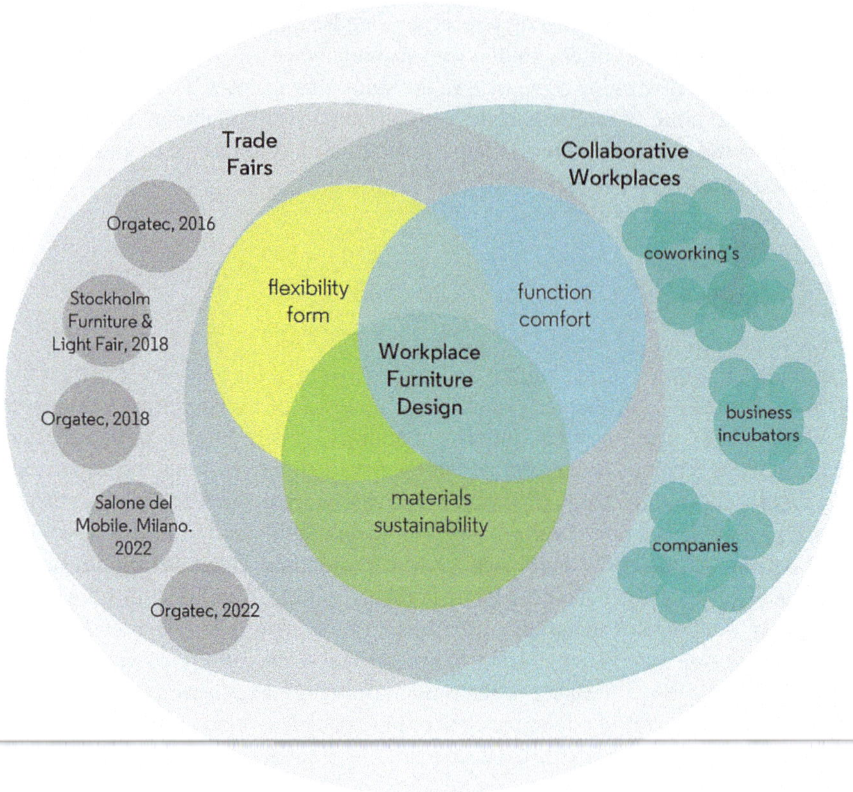

Fig. 10 Mind Map of the research methodology. © Rita Cruz

to some travel restrictions. The first set of visits, which was already the subject of a study [2], was carried in Oporto city.

From the data collected in the interview and the observation during the visits, tables were created in order to systematize the data and other information acquired.

3.1.1 Coworking Workplaces

Table 1 displays the general data of each coworking workplace.

Table 2 shows the analysis of the available furniture considering as main parameters the pairs: function/comfort, materials/sustainability and flexibility/form.

Table 3 showcases the available furniture in the workplaces.

Table 1 General data of each coworking workplace © Rita Cruz

Coworking	Foundation Year	Location	Founders/ Managers	Occupation/ Capacity	Visit Date	Keywords
Circus	2015	Porto, Portugal	André Carvalho Ana Muska (founders)	capacity for around 12 people	June, 2020	Creativity Synergies Spontaneity Collaborative Art gallery
Facts	2010	Porto, Portugal	Leo Lopes (community mananger	capacity for around 40 people	July, 2020	Community Collaborative Tech ambience Networking
Land	2018	Porto, Portugal	Mário Gomes (founder)	capacity for around 20 people	June, 2020	Identity Nature Networking Design Art gallery
Marechal 1551	2017	Porto, Portugal	Miguel Campos (founder)	capacity for around 30-35 people	July, 2020	Sophistication Comfort Cooperation Sharing Economy Prestige
Oficina 2	2013	Porto, Portugal	Vítor Rocha Catarina Casanova David Revez	capacity for around 20 people	June, 2020	Charismatic Memory Sharing Identity Architecture
Selina Navis	2018	Porto, Portugal	Hugo Neves (manager)	capacity for around 90 people	June, 2020	Iconic building Networking Digital nomads Community Dynamic
Synergy	2019	Porto, Portugal	Hugo Neves (manager)	capacity for around 20 people	June, 2020	Synergy Flexibility Proactivity Creativity Collaboration
Temporada	2018	Porto, Portugal	Vítor Miller (founder)	Variable. No fixed coworkers	June, 2020	Flexibility Identity Modularity Community Coffee bar
Typographia	2016	Porto, Portugal	Beatriz Silva (commodity manager)	capacity for around 22 people	June, 2020	Identity Memory Community History Collaboration

(continued)

Table 1 (continued)

Coworking	Foundation Year	Location	Founders/ Managers	Occupation/ Capacity	Visit Date	Keywords
WOW Finsa	2018	Porto, Portugal	FINSA company	capacity for around 40-45 people	June, 2020	Material gallery Didactic Flexibility Dynamic Networking
Fluxo	2021	Coimbra, Portugal	Rodrigo Alves (founder) Mondego Group	capacity for around 60 people	November, 2021	Comfort Dynamic Networking Sophistication
Pátio	2019	Coimbra, Portugal	Coimbra City Council	capacity for around 30 people	October, 2021	Identity Memory History Sharing Creativity
Casa da Bicicleta	2020	Aveiro, Portugal	Ciclaveiro (Association)	capacity for around 6 people	February, 2022	Community Mobility Identity Flexibility Sustainability
Fusion	2011	Aveiro, Portugal	Hugo Cavaleiro (founder)	capacity for around 80 people	October, 2021	Community Cooperation Identity Sharing
Sitio Work	2023	Aveiro, Portugal	Grupo Himo	capacity for around 170 people. Occupancy variable from day to day.	April, 2023	Flexibility Identity Community Dynamic Comfort
CREC Coworking Eixample	2016	Barcelona, Spain	Roman Calavera (founder and CEO)	capacity for around 32 people.	May, 2021	Community Synergy Collaboration Connect
NewWork	2021	Barcelona, Spain	Group of investors and friends	capacity for around 300 people.	May, 2021	Identity Memory Comfort Dynamic Sophistication
Spaces	2018	Barcelona, Spain	Martijn Roordink (founder)	capacity for around 150 people.	May, 2021	Flexibility Collaboration Comfort Community Sophistication

Table 2 Analysis of the available furniture in the workplaces considering as main parameters the pairs: function/comfort, materials/sustainability and flexibility/form © Rita Cruz

Analysis parameters			
Coworking	Flexibility/ Form	Materials/ Sustainability	Function/ Comfort
Circus	• Stackable chairs • Easy desmountable desks (legs + plates) • Simplicity	• Cheap materialso • Laminated mdf plates	• Balanced layout • Connection with the art gallery • Gallery and shop
Facts	• Easy desmountable desks • Neutral furniture	• Arquitectural details	• Ergonomic chairs
Land	• Work tables with wheels • Easy desmountable desks • Folding chairs with Land logo • Strong identity/ personality	• In some details and furniture pieces	• Ergonomic chairs • Natural light • Balanced layout with plants and connection with the art gallery
Marechal 1551	• Flexible lighters • Sophisticated design	• Some recyclable materials	• Ergonomic chairs • Comfortable sofas • Phone booth • Cozy atmosphere
Oficina 2	• Original furniture created thinking about the proposition use of space • Strong identity	• Furniture recovery • Acustic cork panels • material recovery	• Workbenches for various work positions (sitting and standing)
Selina Navis	• Some areas with furniture and flexible layout	• Recovered furniture: tables, sofas • Woods reused for structures and stairs • Energy efficiency	• Ergonomic chairs • Balanced layout
Synergy	• Stackable chairs • Easy desmountable desks • Collapsible furniture for a learning space (workshops, events, etc.)	• Some recyclable materials	• Lounge area for relax
Temporada	• Flexible and modular furniture • Tables with wheels	• Some recyclable materials	• Ergonomic chairs and lighting • Balanced layout, connection with the coffee shop • Skype hub and nap hub

(continued)

Table 2 (continued)

Analysis parameters			
Coworking	Flexibility/ Form	Materials/ Sustainability	Function/ Comfort
Typographia	• Flexible cafeteria tables	• Recovered work tables • Recovered old ceilings	• Chairs from fixed places • Balanced layout
WOW Finsa	• Furniture is very flexible, the assembly of the desks is done by inserts • Flexible layout	• The materials used are from Finsa that has this concern	• Ergonomic chairs • Balanced layout • Furniture created with this premise
Fluxo	• Diversity of work and conviviality areas	• Some recyclable materials • Arquitectural details	• Ergonomic chairs • Comfortable sofas • Balanced layout, connection with the kitchen, balcony and leisure areas • Cozy atmosphere
Pátio	• Stackable chairs • Simplicity	• Arquitectural details • Recovered building • Some recyclable materials	• Ergonomic chairs • Balanced layout • Comfortable sofas
Casa da Bicicleta	• Modular shelving • Simplicity	• Recovered furniture or offered second-hand furniture: tables, sofas • Material recovery • Some recyclable materials	• Balanced layout • Connection with the bike repair and workshop (cicloficina) and art gallery • Ergonomic chairs
Fusion	• Some furniture pieces are flexible • Diversity of work areas	• Some recyclable materials	• Ergonomic chairs • Phone call rooms • Relaxed atmosphere

(continued)

Table 2 (continued)

Analysis parameters			
Coworking	Flexibility/ Form	Materials/ Sustainability	Function/ Comfort
Sitio Work	• Diversity of work and conviviality areas • Flexible and modular furniture for workshops, events, conviviality	• In some details and furniture pieces • Some recyclable materials	• Ergonomic chairs and phone booth • Comfortable sofas and convivality areas • Balanced layout, connection with garden and kitchen • Cozy atmosphere with identity
CREC Coworking Eixample	• Some flexible spaces • Simplicity	• Some recyclable materials • Arquitectural details	• Ergonomic chairs • Balanced layout
NewWork	• Diversity of work and conviviality areas • Sophisticated design	• Arquitectural details • Recovered building • Some recyclable materials	• Ergonomic chairs and phone booths • Natural light • Balanced layout with plants • Cozy and comfortable areas
Spaces	• Diversity of work and conviviality areas • Some flexible spaces • Sophisticated design furniture	• Some recyclable materials	• Ergonomic chairs, phone booths, sofas with acustic properties • Balanced layout with natural light and plants, connection with a diversity of areas • Cozy atmosphere

3.1.2 Companies

Table 4 identifies the general data of each company.

Table 5 presents the analysis of the available furniture in the companies, considering as main parameters the pairs: function/comfort, materials/sustainability and flexibility/form.

Table 6 shows the available furniture in the companies.

3.1.3 Business Incubators

Table 7 displays the general data of each business incubator.

Table 3 Available furniture in the workplaces. © Rita Cruz

Coworking	Photos
Circus	
Facts	
Land	
Marechal 1551	
Oficina 2	
Selina Navis	
Synergy	
Temporada	

(continued)

Table 3 (continued)

Typographia	
WOW Finsa	
Fluxo	
Pátio	
Casa da Bicicleta	
Fusion	
Sitio Work	
CREC Coworking Eixample	
NewWork	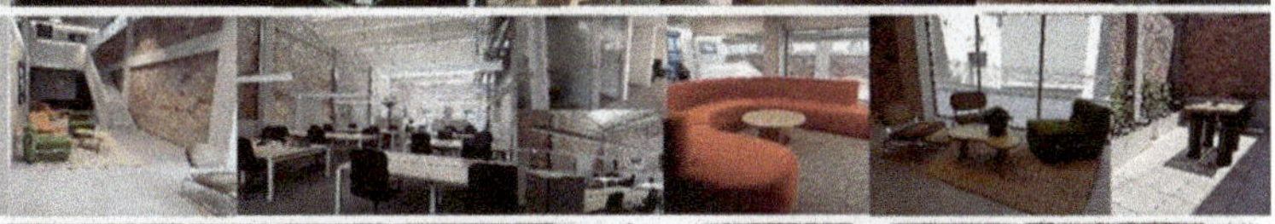
Spaces	

Table 4 General data of each company. © Rita Cruz

Companies		Foundation Year	Location	Founders/ Managers	Occupation/ Capacity	Visit Date	Keywords
Basecone	basecone Wolters Kluwer	2017	Porto, Portugal	Grupo Wolters Kluwer	capacity for around 60 people	October, 2021	Innovation Wellbeing Comfort Enjoyable
Blip	BLIP	2009 2012 (purchased by Paddy Power Betfair)	Porto, Portugal	José Fonseca e André Moniz (founders) Paddy Power Betfair (since 2012)	capacity for around 440 people (220 with the pandemic restrictions)	March, 2022	Colaboration Transparency Innovation Wellbeing Agility
Critical Software Coimbra Headquarters	Critical software	1998 (Coimbra Headquarters)	Coimbra, Portugal	Gonçalo Quadros (President) João Carreira (CEO) (founders)	1000 employees in total I 480 employees at the headquarters in Coimbra	October, 2021	Innovation Collaborative Dynamic Wellbeing Community
Loba	LOBA	2000 (Oliveira de Azeméis Headquarters)	Oliveira de Azeméis, Portugal	Adelino Silva João Gaspar (founders)	115 employees in total I 4 offices: Oliveira de Azeméis (headquarters), Aveiro, Lisbon and Guarda	September, 2020	Sharing Innovation Experience Wellbeing Community
HBK - Spectris Innovation Centre	HBK HOTTINGER BRÜEL & KJÆR spectris	2019 (Spectris Innovation Centre - Porto)	Porto, Portugal	HBK from Spectris Group	capacity for around 60 people	November, 2021	Experience Sustainability Flexibility Dynamic Innovation

Table 8 shows the analysis of the available furniture in the business incubators considering as main parameters the pairs: function/comfort, materials/sustainability and flexibility/form.

Table 9 showcases the available furniture in the business incubators.

Table 5 Analysis of the available furniture in the companies considering as main parameters the pairs: function/comfort, materials/sustainability and flexibility/form. © Rita Cruz

	Analysis Parameters		
Companies	Flexibility/ Form	Materials/ Sustainability	Function/ Comfort
Basecone	• Some areas with furniture and flexible layout • Diversity of work and leisure areas	• In some details and furniture pieces	• Ergonomic chairs and desks • Balanced layout with natural light and plants, connection with a diversity of areas • Relaxed atmosphere
Blip	• Diversity of work and conviviality areas • Flexible and modular furniture for workshops, events, conviviality	• In some details and furniture pieces • Some recyclable materials	• Ergonomic chairs, phone booth, leisure areas • Balanced layout, connection with a diversity of areas • Relaxed and cozy atmosphere
Critical Software Coimbra Headquarters	• Flexible and modular furniture • Tables with wheels • Diversity of work and conviviality areas	• Some green activities • Some recyclable materials • Energy efficiency	• Ergonomic chairs and phone booth • Comfortable sofas and convivality areas • Balanced layout, versatile and collaborative areas • Cozy atmosphere
Loba	• Some furniture pieces are flexible • Diversity of work areas	• Some recyclable materials	• Ergonomic chairs and sofas with acustic properties • Meeting and phone call rooms • Relaxed and cozy atmosphere
HBK - Spectris Innovation Centre	• Flexible and modular furniture • Innovative and simplicity areas • Diversity of work and conviviality areas	• In some details and furniture pieces • Some recyclable materials	• Sofas with acustic properties • Phone booths and ergonomic chairs • Relaxed and cozy atmosphere • Balanced layout, connection with a diversity of areas

Table 6 Available furniture in the companies. © Rita Cruz

Companies	Photos
Basecone	
Blip	
Critical Software Coimbra Headquarters	
Loba	
HBK - Spectris Innovation Centre	

Table 7 General data of each business incubator. © Rita Cruz

Business incubators		Foundation year	Location	Founders/ Managers	Occupation/ Capacity	Visit date	Keywords
Nest Collective Downtown/ Uptown	NEST {•} COLLECTIVE	2015	Coimbra, Portugal	Miguel Antunes	Around 12 companies	October, 2021	Identity Flexibility Creativity Networking Collaboration
Oliva Creative Factory	OLIVA CREATIVE FACTORY	2012	São João da, Madeira, Portugal	São João da Madeira City Council	Around 22 companies	September, 2020	Identity Creativity Memory Networking Community
District Offices and Lifestyle Regus Batalha	DISTRICT OFFICES AND LIFESTYLE Regus	2018	Porto, Portugal	Regus Group	Around 80 companies	November, 2021	Simplicity Comfort Memory Sharing Dynamic

Table 8 Analysis of the available furniture in the business incubators, considering as main parameters the pairs: function/comfort, materials/sustainability and flexibility/form. © Rita Cruz

Analysis Parameters			
Business Incubators	Flexibility/ Form	Materials/ Sustainability	Function/ Comfort
Nest Collective Downtownl Uptown	• Stackable chairs • Simplicity • Easy desmountable desks • Collapsible furniture for a learning space (workshops, events, etc.)	• In some details and furniture pieces	• Ergonomic chairs • Balanced layout, connection with balcony with a nice landscape • Diversity of work areas
Oliva Creative Factory	• Some furniture pieces are flexible • Diversity of work and conviviality areas	• Arquitectural details • Recovered building • Some recyclable materials • Some pieces of furniture recovered	• Diversity and comfortable areas • Balanced layout with identity
District Offices and Lifestyle Regus Batalha	• Diversityn of work areas • Simplicity and sophisticated design	• Arquitectural details • Recovered building • Some recyclable materials	• Ergonomic chairs and a diversity of meeting and phone call rooms • Natural light • Balanced layout • Cozy and pleasant areas

Table 9 Available furniture in the business incubators. © Rita Cruz

3.1.4 Interpretation

The coworking workplaces visited are quite diverse, both in size and typology. However, in all interviews with coworking founders or managers, all share the idea that coworking is the future of collaborative workplaces. Even with the pandemic, which was a challenge for almost all coworking spaces both in terms of survival and the restructuring, how we learned to work in a decentralized way also became a growth opportunity. Some of the visited coworking spaces, even emerged in the post-pandemic. The same happened with the 3 visited business incubators, which in the post-pandemic were once again looked for by small companies in search of doing networking and sharing the workplace to reduce costs. This kind of spaces which will increasingly be workplaces directed for versatile demands of hybrid and collaborative work.

Of the 5 companies that were visited, all considered that the pandemic ended up having a positive impact on acceleration of the transition to work models that are more hybrid. Companies took advantage of the moment and began to make the transition to more flexible work regimes, letting employees alternate between remote and presential work. In this regime, presential collaboration meetings and social activities are the focus of the workplace. So, companies also began to create shared workstations, which are not fixed, depending on the daily occupation, the employee is allocated to a workstation or can choose a free one.

In the analysis of the interviews, for all collaborative workplaces, the flexibility and modularity of furniture are highlighted as essential to facilitate the spontaneous and dynamic working routine and the functionality of workflows. Not all spaces have this typology of furniture, either because they haven't purchased it yet or because costs are an obstacle to the acquisition, but everyone understands that it is the most effective solution.

Regarding the flexibility/ form parameter it was the most relevant for all and it was pointed as a parameter with improvement potential. Especially, for shared working areas and common spaces, informal meetings, workshops, spontaneous and scheduled events, which often lead to sudden layout changes. Since one of the great advantages of coworking spaces and business incubators is networking and creating cooperation partnerships it is essential to have a balanced and dynamic layout that creates efficient workflows to allow people to cross each other in the right place and time to interact and collaborate. But companies are also increasingly investing in versatile work layouts to promote teamwork and improve wellbeing. The materials/sustainability parameter is a concern in most cases, especially when choosing materials with acoustic properties that provide comfort and functionality to the work atmosphere. About the sustainability of furniture materials, there is not always a rigorous choice, just in some details. Regarding function/ comfort parameter, it is noticeable that the ergonomics and comfort of the chairs are considered essential especially for people that spend a long time sitting. For agile working activities, the mobility and flexibility of workstations are more important, considering that the dynamics are usually different. The comfort and pleasantness of the space are also considered essential for wellbeing and motivation.

3.2 *Analyses and Interpretation of Trade Fairs Dedicated to Workplace Furniture*

For the purpose of this analysis, 5 trade fairs were visited between October 2016 and October 2022. The fairs were selected by their importance in the workplace furniture area and the convenience of their location. Due to the covid-19 between the years 2020 and 2021 pandemic there was a period when fairs were not performed. The data collected is qualitative, that results from experience and observation during the visit to the fairs, and it is represented and organized in tables.

Table 10 shows the general data of each trade fair.

Table 11 shows the analysis of the available furniture exhibited considering as main parameters the pairs: function/comfort, materials/sustainability and flexibility/form.

Table 12 showcases the presented furniture in the trade fairs.

Table 10 general data of each trade fair. © Rita Cruz

Trade Fair		Date	Location	Keywords
Orgatec—New Visions of Work		October, 2016	Köln, Germany	New Materials Acoustics Integrated Technology Color and Texture
Stockholm Furniture & Light Fair		February, 2018	Stockholm, Sweden	Acoustics Materials Confort Flexibility Harmony
Orgatec—New Visions of Work		October, 2018	Köln, Germany	Ergonomy Confort Acoustics Integrated Technology Color and Texture

(continued)

Table 10 (continued)

Trade Fair		Date	Location	Keywords
Salone del Mobile. Milano	Salone del Mobile. Milano	June, 2022	Milan, Italy	Nature and Sustentability Flexibility New Materials Tecnology Ergonomy
Orgatec—New Visions of Work	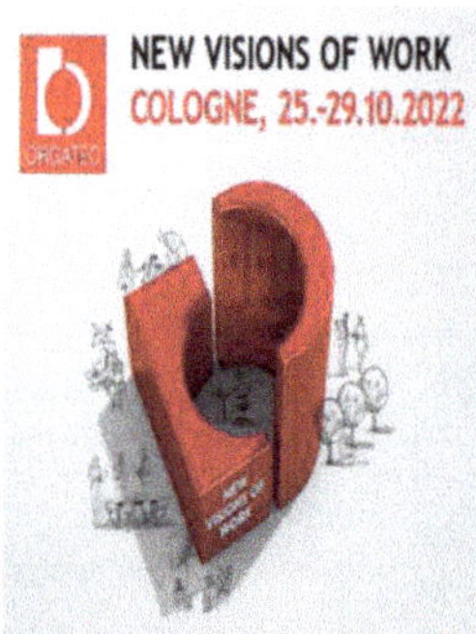	October 2022	Köln, Germany	Sustentability New Recycled Materials Flexibility Hybrid work Acoustics Collaboration

3.2.1 Interpretation

Of the 5 visited fairs, 3 were the Orgatec in Cologne, in 3 different editions: 2016, 2018 and 2022. Orgatec is Europe's most emblematic international trade fair of office furniture in Europe and one of the world's leading fair, which has been held since 1953. This fair is dedicated exclusively to furniture design, equipment and technology for offices and workplaces and for that reason is the most oriented to this research. This biennial fair in Cologne, with the slogan "New visions of work", stands out for its success as a platform for presenting and sharing innovative ideas for the market sector. The Stockholm Furniture & Light Fair was first held in 1951, it was a local furniture fair with only Swedish furniture manufacturers and dealers. Over time, it has evolved and today it features not only Scandinavian exhibitors but also exhibitors from all over the world. This is the largest trade fair for Scandinavian furniture and lighting design for domestic and public office and catering environments and it is also part of the Stockholm design week, which also counts with many installations, events and exhibitions throughout the city. The Salone del Mobile was held for the first time in Milan in 1961. Today, it is a world reference event for the furniture and design sector, especially covering living and domestic furniture, but also bathroom, kitchen, lighting, catering, outdoor, wellness and workplace. The first editions were dedicated to Italian furniture, but over time it was extended to other countries and

Table 11 Analysis of the available furniture exhibited in the trade fairs, considering as main parameters the pairs: function/comfort, materials/sustainability and flexibility/form © Rita Cruz

	Analysis Parameters		
Trade Fair	flexibility/form	materials/ sustainability	function/comfort
Orgatec—New Visions of Work, 2016	• Modular sofas • Screens • Integrated technology in the furniture • Desks with height adjustment	• New materials with acoustic characteristics • Fabrics—greater use of color and textures	• Screens, sofas with acoustic properties • Desks with height adjustment • Colors and textures that bring the workplace closer to the comfort of home
Stockholm Furniture & Light Fair, 2018	• Modular sofas, work and meeting stations, Screens • Acoustic and phone booths • Technology Integrated into the furniture • Desks with height adjustment • High and mobile tables (casters) for quick and informal meetings • Mobile solutions that improve acoustics	• Materials with acoustic properties • Warm and colorful colors in harmony with different wood finishes • Fabric combinations	• All kinds of solutions to improve the acoustic: partitions, screens, lamps, sofas, wall coverings, phone booths, open and closed booths. • Integrated technology • Desks with height adjustment • Colors and textures • Furniture dedicated to leisure
Orgatec—New Visions of Work, 2018	• Modular sofas, work and meeting stations, Screens • Acoustic and phone booths • Technology Integrated into the furniture • Desks with height adjustment • High tables for quick and informal meetings	• Materials with acoustic properties • Warm and colorful colors • Fabric combinations	• Phone booths, partitions, screens, sofas with acoustic properties and integrated technology • Desks with height adjustment • Colors and textures that bring the workplace closer to the comfort of home • furniture dedicated to leisure

(continued)

markets, and today it is the largest fair in this area worldwide. In addition to the fair, several events, installations, exhibitions and animations are held throughout the city of Milan, in particular in the areas of Brera and Tortona.

Table 11 (continued)

	Analysis Parameters		
Trade Fair	flexibility/form	materials/ sustainability	function/comfort
Salone del Mobile. Milano. 2022	• Modular sofas, work and meeting stations, screens, partitions, flexible and easily mobile acoustic solutions • Acoustic and phone booths • Integrated technology in furniture, less and less visible but present • High and mobile tables (casters) for quick and informal meetings • Mobile solutions that improve acoustics	• Recyclable and recycled materials • Materials with acoustic properties • Environments closer to nature • Colors with textures, whether in fabrics or other materials, patterns, marbles or recycled materials that create patterns and the mix of these different finishes	• Acoustic and phone booths, screens, sofas with acoustic properties • Desks with height adjustment • Colors and textures that bring the workplace closer to the comfort of home • Furniture dedicated to leisure • Environments closer to nature and increasingly flexible
Orgatec—New Visions of Work, 2022	• Modular sofas, poufs, flexible and easily mobile benches for informal meetings/ collaboration and socializing • Acoustic booths (individual/group) • Mobile high tables (casters) for meeting/ collaboration/ socializing • Mobile small tables • Solutions that improve acoustics: screens, lighting, vases, wall applications • Partitions with applications: magnetic frames, whiteboard, potted plants, tv screens, etc	• New recyclable and recycled materials • Materials with acoustic properties • Environments closer to nature: vases with plants • Colors with textures, whether in fabrics or other materials, patterns, marbles or recycled materials that create patterns and the mix of these different finishes	• Individual and group acoustic and phone booths • Partitions and sofas with acoustic properties • Desks with height adjustment • Colors and textures that bring the workplace closer to the comfort of home • Furniture dedicated to leisure/ collaboration and socialization and allowing greater mobility during the working day • Environments closer to nature and increasingly flexible

Table 12 Presented furniture in the trade fairs. © Rita Cruz

Trade Fair	Photos
Orgatec - New Visions of Work, 2016	
Stockholm Furniture & Light Fair, 2018	
Orgatec - New Visions of Work, 2018	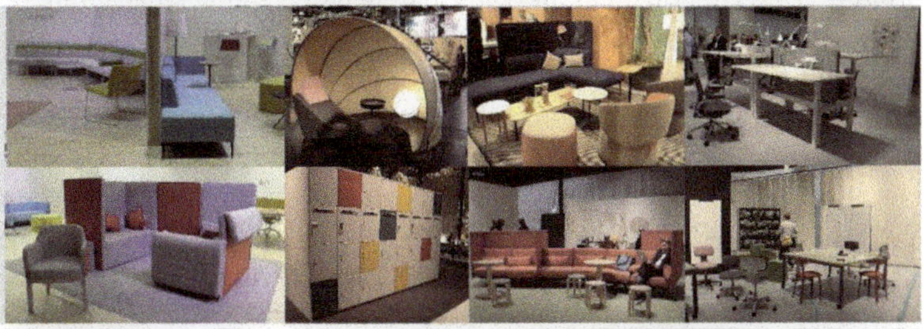
Salone del Mobile. Milano, 2022	
Orgatec - New Visions of Work, 2022	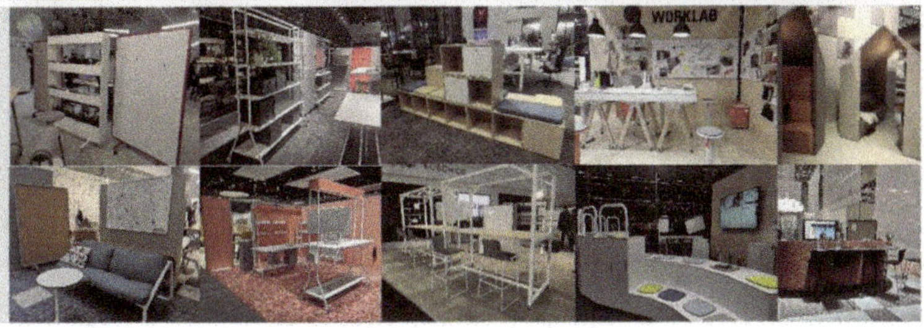

The furniture shown at fairs demonstrates the growing trend and concern to create flexible products for hybrid and collaborative workplaces. As we can understand at fairs before the Covid-19 pandemic, Orgatec 2016 and 2018 and Stockholm Furniture Fair 2018, there was already a trend towards more modular furniture solutions thinking about more agile working models. After the pandemic, the acceleration of this trend is evident. If previously there were only a few stands that had just a few pieces of flexible furniture, after the pandemic almost all of them started to bet on this trend and were almost exclusively dedicated to dynamic and cooperative environments.

Orgatec 2016

At Orgatec 2016, with the theme "New Visions of Work" and the sub-theme "Creativity works", the highlight was office furniture with integrated technology, new materials where color and texture stood out, and concern for the acoustics of environments.

A great focus was given on furniture in the contract area, such as sofas and other furniture for reception areas and informal meetings, but also furniture related to the acoustic quality of the workplaces. New materials that were more in line with the comfort of the home, more fabrics and warm colors that make the workplaces more harmonious and cozier. Regarding furniture with acoustic capacity, from screens, partitions, wall accessories, screens, cupboards, they were covered with new materials, from fabrics to agglomerates with high acoustic performance. There were also many soundproof cabinets to create partitions and environments with better acoustics and modular sofas with the flexibility to create informal meeting modules with screens that allow them to isolate and create a better acoustic environment, were also a trend at this fair. The technology associated with furniture was also a focal point: in lockers with opening and closing systems by card or mobile phone, in desks with height adjustment, in chargers and plugs integrated into sofas, in adjustable screens with lighting, among other accessories.

One of the exhibitions in the halls of the fair, took the visitor to reflect on what the desk/workstation tells about us, because the objects and work tools and their change and reduction in the face of technological and digital development, as already reported in Chapter 2 and represented in Fig. 1. The digital evolution that allows working anywhere is also addressed in this exhibition, launching the idea that even so the office will not disappear, it will only change.

The Vitra Stand with the theme "Work" highlighted not only for its size but also for its commitment to a new concept of more flexible and agile work. Vitra brought together other partners and suppliers to the stand, which created interesting synergies. The big focus on modular sofas and flexible and informal workstations point to a clear tendency to allow a more relaxed work environment, more adapted to the increasingly nomadic lifestyle. Technology, in partnership with its partners, allowed the creation of workstations with adjustable screens and height adjustment that surprised and made the difference at the fair.

Stockholm Furniture 2018

At Stockholm Furniture Fair 2018, the focus was on acoustics and new materials to provide comfort and pleasant sound in the interiors of workplaces, considering the new dynamic ways of working. In this edition, sustainability and "green" production methods and business practices to preserve resources were an obvious concern, which went from concept to reality for many companies. Tendencies for increasingly flexible workplaces and changes in postures and work positions were presented, as well as the approximation of these office environments to the comfort of home.

Flexible solutions for meeting places were a clear focus, with some original solutions such as mobile meeting tables (with casters) that simultaneously carry all the necessary infrastructure and allow for informal meetings, conviviality, workshops, among other group activities. It is also possible to find many modular sofa solutions, most with integrated or optional acoustic and technology solutions, such as mobile phone charging and other accessories. The concern with acoustics is effectively one of the strongest points of this fair and of Scandinavian furniture trends. With all kinds of solutions to improve the acoustic quality of workplaces such as partitions, screens, lamps, wall coverings, phone booths, open and closed booths. There are also solutions for screens that improve not only the acoustics but also isolate the workstation in some way and hide all the technology and mechanisms for adjusting the height of the desk. The care with comfort, ergonomics and health and wellbeing was also evident with leisure solutions such as swings, lounge, conviviality areas. And also, adjustable furniture that allows and forces a constant change of the posture, like ball poufs for desks, tables with height adjustment and among others. The warm colors, textures of the different materials and fabrics, the beautiful and impeccable wood finishes that provide harmony and comfort to environments, feature and distinguish Scandinavian furniture. The integration of nature, plants and a harmonious environment with the outside was also reflected in this fair.

Orgatec 2018

At Orgatec 2018 with the theme "New Visions of Work" and the sub-theme "Culture@work", with emphasis on the future of culture in the workplace. The ergonomics and comfort stand out as key factors for the motivation and consequent optimization of work processes. In addition to the obvious commitment to acoustics and integrated technology that was already felt in the previous edition in 2016, the human being is the focus. Comfort and ergonomics centered on the health and wellbeing of the people and the improvement of their quality of life. Thus, the sector's priority areas are the attractiveness of the workplace, with the support of more collaborative activities establishing conditions for balance and wellbeing associated to the concern with materials and sustainability. Modular sofas, benches, poufs and screens are a trend and are available in the most diverse configurations: from workstations, meeting areas, lounge environments, training rooms and workshops, among others. Warm

Fig. 11 *Meeting Culture – Garden lodge.* Orgatec 2018, Köln. © Rita Cruz

colors and textures, fabrics and integrated technology highlight these more collaborative and informal work scenarios in almost all stands. The height adjustable desks with integrated technology also make a strong presence, to improve the ergonomics of the workstation. As well as completely closed acoustic cabins or with openings are also an evident trend. Regarding to individual workstations, only a small investment is seen in management workstations, mainly in wood and with luxury finishes. Workstations are increasingly hybrid and meetings more informal, thus the trend on high tables for quick standing meetings and more collaborative meeting tables. Solutions more dedicated to leisure and wellbeing were also shown, such as swings, furniture for resting, bicycles and treadmills to place next to the workstation, standing work solutions that imply balance. These are trends that show the growing concern with ergonomics and physical and mental health.

One of the exhibitions in the lobby entitled "Meeting Culture – Garden lodge" (Fig. 11) a rest area with live music, demonstrated the importance of pause, conviviality, the experience of space and time for reflection to motivate and stimulate creativity, improve networking and sharing, as well as productivity.

Figure 12 presents another installation with a table made of plastic waste taken from Amsterdam channels, showing the importance and possibility of designing new recycled and recyclable materials, placing the sustainability of the furniture as a priority.

Vitra's stand which stands out at the fair, makes a clear highlight and displays with a clear focus displays a convergence of workplace and public spaces, under the title 'WORK' (as in the previous edition), the installation highlighted how the flexibility and agility are important in today's working world. Thus, Vitra presents three

Fig. 12 *Meeting Culture – Table made from Amsterdam Canal Plastic.* Orgatec 2018, Köln. © Rita Cruz

concepts of workplaces: "shared office" designed by Barber & Osgerby, "company home" by Sevil Peach and "super flexible office" by Konstantin Grcic. In the first, a clear commitment to modular sofas and common spaces for socializing and informal work, responding to the comfort and versatility of new work models and reducing the number of desks. In the second, the emphasis on the need for the wellbeing and ergonomics of the employee based on regulated and more comfortable furniture that enables a new work dynamic in companies. In the third, the flexibility and agility of the space designed for more collaborative and interactive work activities throughout the working day and changes in the companies' human resources.

Salone Del Mobile 2022

The Salone del Mobile in Milano its 60th anniversary in this 2022 edition and featured all the events: from the International Furniture Fair and the International Exhibition of Furniture Accessories and Workplace 3.0 to the biennial events, Euro Cucina with the parallel event FTK, Technology for the Kitchen and the International Bath Exhibition. It also featured S. Project, the transversal space dedicated to different areas of design, with the Salone Satellite a showcase of talented young designers. The highlight of this post-pandemic edition is the sustainability and consideration of nature together with the flexibility and modularity required by the new hybrid model of work and the relevance of quality of life and wellbeing.

Fig. 13 *Designing for our future selves. Sustainability*, by Christophe Guberan. Salone del Mobile. Milano, 2022. © Rita Cruz

Flexible and modular furniture solutions define this edition of the fair, with more and more models that can have different configurations and are easily changed during the same working day. Collections of sofas with screens and workstations that can be arranged in different configurations, mobile screens and shelves (with casters), poufs, high tables for quick and informal meetings and other accessories to support more collaborative forms of work. Furniture finishes for workplaces tend to be closer to those at home, which provides greater comfort. Colors with textures, whether in fabrics or other materials, patterns, marble or recycled materials that create patterns are also an obvious trend. Bringing environments closer to nature is also relevant to the experience of workplaces. Integrated technology and lighting are less and less visible, but they are present.

Christophe Guberan responsible for the Salone Satellite exhibition with the theme "Designing for our future selves. Sustainability" highlights the importance of exploring new materials in the creative design process and presents an installation that invites visitors to escape the hustle and bustle of everyday life, slow down and connect with other essential experiences (Fig. 13). The installation by Mario Cucinella "Design with Nature - A design experience narrating the potential reconciliation between man and nature" described in Chapter 2 (Fig. 8), pointed the 60th anniversary celebration, which taking into account the events of recent years, also giving great relevance to the issue of sustainability considering the increasingly nomadic lifestyles.

Orgatec 2022

The Orgatec 2022 with the theme "New Visions of Work", highlighted for its post-pandemic return and an acceleration of the changes and work routines. It presented visionary solutions aimed at mobile and agile work concepts. The return was positive for a post-pandemic, although some companies have not yet attended. This edition marks the transition to the new hybrid and flexible work models, already foreseen, which are now the future of the work culture, as could be seen in almost all the stands at the fair.

Modular solutions such as sofas, poufs, mobile partitions and shelves and also easily mobile benches and tables for informal meetings, collaboration activities and convivial moments, was presented in almost every stands. The acoustic booths and other solutions that improve acoustics: screens, lighting, vases, wall applications were also relevance. The partitions and screens also offered diverse possibilities with applications: whiteboards, magnetic frames, potted plants, tv screens, shelves, hangers and other options. These solutions are almost always associated with agile work environments, as a fundamental support for the wellbeing and diverse working routine activities.

In addition to the obvious commitment to furniture for collaborative work to workplaces, there was also a concern to relate this commitment to the home office, investing in some scenarios for home office. In fact, it is possible to see at this fair how the boundaries between home and office furniture are becoming increasingly blurred. The colors and textures in fabrics or other cozy materials, the typologies of furniture, plants in vases and in other furnishing accessories, bring the workplace environment closer to the comfort of home and also to the nature.

As an example, the Guialmi stand (Fig. 14) which exhibited as their focus diverse working informal environments with flexible and collaborative furniture and acoustic solutions, but also presented more formal spaces and individual workstation orientated to management cabinets or home office.

Furthermore, to the investment in furniture to flexible working with smart technologies conjugated, the focal points of the trade show this edition also included the issue of sustainability. Since new recyclable and recycled materials that create patterns, to the materials with acoustic properties, to the concern with circular economy and waste in production, there are several manifestos that show how sustainability is a focus in this area.

A special event was organized in collaboration with zgoll:GmbH to this edition to show #InspiredHybridOffice project. This exhibition (Fig. 15) in addition to hosting a few talk shows around the theme, presented some insights and working spaces dedicated to hybrid and collaborative working to inspire people. It shows a diversity of spaces to work like coworking space, home, collaboration, break out area, socializing area, reception, workshop, openspace, conference room, garden and even a think tank area.

So, this trade fair show working environments closer to nature and increasingly flexible, with furniture dedicated to leisure, collaboration and socialization and allowing greater mobility during the working day.

Fig. 14 Guialmi stand. Orgatec 2022, Köln. © Rita Cruz

Fig. 15 *#InspiredHybridOffice project*. Orgatec 2022, Köln. © Rita Cruz

4 Final Remarks

This research offered new insights into the relevance of flexible furniture design to create scenarios and atmospheres compatible with hybrid working models and shows how trends of trade fairs, dedicated to workplace furniture, fulfill the needs of collaborative workplaces.

From the previous qualitative analysis, we can conclude that trade fairs anticipate the trends by meeting the requirements of people with the workplace. The companies that exhibit at fairs are attentive to the trends and their furniture and office accessories are suited to the needs of their customers. At trade fairs they end up launching new work concepts and products that meet the present and future requirements. The trends of flexible and modular furniture are the focus of the latest editions of trade fairs dedicated to workplace furniture. Both the literature review and the workplaces visited show evidence of the same trend to resolve the issues of the new models of work. The connection between the three pairs of parameters analyzed in this study reflect how this trend is essential to create agile work environments and to balance workflows between the diverse work activities during the day. The three parameters end up being interconnected with the concern about flexibility and versatility of the furniture.

The future of workplaces will increasingly focus on group activities and collaboration, considering that people can be presentially and remotely in the same meeting at the same time. Therefore, furniture design has the challenge of associating the necessary digital technology to mobile and flexible furniture.

Acknowledgements This work is financed by national funds through the FCT – Fundação para a Ciência e a Tecnologia, I.P., under the scope of the project SFRH/BD/146306/2019.

References

1. Caramelo Gomes C (2023) On site or remote? A time to reimagine the workplace. Springer Series in Design and Innovation 25:424–440. https://doi.org/10.1007/978-3-031-09659-4_32/COVER
2. Cruz R, Franqueira T, Pombo, F (2021) Furniture as feature in coworking spaces. Spots in Oporto city as case study. In A. Garcia and R. Santos (Eds). Res Mobilis. Revista Internacional de Investigación En Mobiliario y Objetos Decorativos. Conexiones. III Congreso Iberoamericano de Historia Del Mueble, 10(13–3), 316–338. https://doi.org/10.17811/RM.10.13-3.2021.316-338
3. Cruz R, Pombo, F (2023) Designing Furniture for Versatile Spaces of Collaborative Work. Covid-19 Accelerating the Change. In: Raposo, D., Neves, J., Silva, R., Correia Castilho, L., Dias, R. (Eds) Advances in Design, Music and Arts II. EIMAD 2022. Springer Ser. Des. Innovation 25: 456–471. https://doi.org/10.1007/978-3-031-09659-4_34
4. Daugherty P, Carrell-Billiard M, Biltz, M. (2019). The post-digital era is upon us: are you ready for what's next? Accenture Technology Vision 2019: Full Report.

5. de Lucas Ancillo A, del Val Núñez MT, Gavrila SG (2020) Workplace change within the COVID-19 context: a grounded theory approach 34(1): 2297–2316. http://www.Tandfonline.Com/Action/AuthorSubmission?JournalCode=rero20&page=instructions. https://doi.org/10.1080/1331677X.2020.1862689
6. Eltringham, M. (2023). Hybrid working and the other legacies of lockdown, three years on. Sedus. https://whats-up.sedus.com/en/hybrid-working-and-the-other-legacies-of-lockdown-three-years-on/
7. Gillen N (2019) Future office: Next generation workplace design, Riba Publishing., Ed, London.
8. Pereira S, Fernandes-Marcos A (2020) O PROCESSO CRIATIVO NA ERA PÓS-DIGITAL Uma reflexão crítica baseada na prática artística. In: Silva B. (Ed.), Proceedings of 2nd international conference on transdisciplinary studies in arts, technology and society, ARTeFACTo2020, Faro, Portugal, Centro de Investigação e Comunicação (CIAC), November 26–27, pp 127–135.
9. Steelcase (2023a) Hybrid realities what the research says. Work Better Magazine https://www.steelcase.com/content/uploads/2023/05/2023_Spring-Work-Better-Magazine_Beyond-Hybrid.pdf
10. Steelcase (2023b) Ideas for designing inclusive workplaces https://www.steelcase.com/research/articles/topics/design/ideas-designing-inclusive-workplaces/
11. Tuncel DB, Kayan HZ (2018) The design of flexible furniture for the new generation offices. Civil Eng Architect 6(2), 78–87. https://doi.org/10.13189/CEA.2018.060205
12. Vitra. (2018). Vitra | Dancing Wall | Official Vitra®. https://www.vitra.com/en-pt/product/dancing-wall
13. Vitra (2022a) Dynamic Spaces. E-Paper Issue 08, (2022). file:///C:/Users/ritam/Downloads/DynamicSpaces_digital%20EN%20(1).pdf
14. Vitra (2022b) Vitra | Comma | Official Vitra®. https://www.vitra.com/en-lp/product/comma
15. Yin, E., & Mahrous, A. (2022). Covid-19 global pandemic, workplace spirituality and the rise of spirituality-driven organisations in the post-digital era. J Humanit Appli Soc Sci 4(2) https://doi.org/10.1108/jhass-11-2021-0177

MUSAE: A Creative Process in Three Acts

Liliana Soares, Ermanno Aparo, Rita Almendra, and Fernando da Moreira da Silva

Abstract With this paper the authors wonder to know if the introduction of a creative processes between the design research, the business sector and the music and performing arts domain can be a sustainable and innovative solution. Methodologically the study is exploratory and generative. The authors will study what exists and has been done to produce new information and knowledge. The paper is focus on the process of creating a documentary film as an artistic and experimental typology. The documentary film describes the productive development that brought together participants from the three areas already identified. Together, they designed a streaming show on the stage of a theater in the North of Portugal, during the pandemic period. With this philosophy in mind, the authors want to prove that it is possible to create alternative models of education programmes to ensure quality education. In addition, partnership with local organizations can be an occasion to create sustainability, stimulating business competitiveness and effective improvement on the shows produced.

Keywords Creativity in Design · Design Methods · Documentary film

---

L. Soares (✉) · E. Aparo
CIAUD, Research Centre for Architecture, Urbanism and Design, Lisbon School of Architecture, Universidade de Lisboa, Rua Sá Nogueira, Polo Universitário do Alto da Ajuda, 1349-063 Lisboa, Portugal
e-mail: lsoares@estg.ipvc.pt

IPVC Instituto Politécnico de Viana Do Castelo, Rua Escola Industrial E Comercial Nun'Álvares, 34, 4900-347 Viana Do Castelo, Portugal

R. Almendra · F. da Moreira da Silva
CIAUD, Research Centre for Architecture, Urbanism and Design, Lisbon School of Architecture, Universidade de Lisboa, Rua Sá Nogueira, Polo Universitário do Alto da Ajuda, 1349-063 Lisboa, Portugal

D. Raposo et al. (eds.), *Perspectives on Design III*, Springer Series in Design and Innovation 34, https://doi.org/10.1007/978-3-031-43516-4_20

1 Introduction

Etymologically, the word creativity refers to the quality of giving rise to something, through imagination or thought evident by the power to create [1]. A probability to have the courage to act based on being and not on a divine reason. As Friedrich Nietzsche states [2] it demands a proactive force for motivations, the courage to the forbidden and the choose for a process-oriented process. "*(...) And the will to economize in the grand manner - to hold together his strength, his enthusiasm... Reference for self; love of self; absolute freedom of self...*" [2]. Nowadays, perhaps it means that to will is to generate new values in the sense that will to power is something that works when many different forces come together to develop a relationship with each other, a relationship that produces strength with quality. Gilles Deleuze defended this idea explaining that "*will to power must be interpreted in a completely different way: power is the one that wills in the will. Power is the genetic and differential element in the will. This is why the will is essentially creative.*" [3] A creative idea that is unique, appropriate, non-obvious, unexpected, and adds value [4]. It is something abstract determined by those that can be influenced by society's judgments and values, who imagined and communicated an idea, storytelling with words, images and sounds together, and therefore, involving more creativity [5] to produce an idea. Thus, storytelling methodology is a moment of reflection to creative process and can be seen as a form of simplification, complementing information with an engaging and innovative narrative [6]. It means, if the cognitive capacities of memory are limited, they hand out to oblivion, distortion, but also innovation [7]. Plus, the use of a creative process in design research is not only an innovative solution for society, but also to the 17th sustainable development goals defined by the UNESCO 2030 (partnership for the goals, it means, working in partnership with local organizations) [8].

Today, as individuals are new types of beings, hybrids of nature and culture [9], creativity becomes a complex, contradictory, and diffuse process. As if there was a need to inquire about new languages with the competence to provide experiences in people's lives. Therefore, in this study, it means the need to use a dialectical and experimental process [10] between research, profession, and education, namely, using documentary as storytelling.

As we live in a period in which the discussion on the relationship between education and democracy is once again part of the agenda, it seems particularly relevant to resume this issue from the perspective of documentary film education in the first half of the twentieth century. In the sense that, as now, in that period Europe lived through two world wars and, in some countries, democracy was threatened.

2 Methodology

The study is exploratory and generative. The authors study what exists and has been done to produce new knowledge and experimentation.

The exploratory phase contextualizes and studies what exists and has been done in documentary film as an artistic and experimental typology to achieve an analysis about the process of producing a documentary film and to cause new knowledge.

The generative phase focuses on the process of creating a participatory documentary film. The documentary describes the productive development of a show performed in a theater, that brought together researchers, lighting prototypes, musicians, light, image and sound technicians, and a filmmaker. This phase includes the verification and validation of recorded material before and during the show. This means that the documentary film develops the creative process and the results in three different acts: (1) the production of the prototypes in a lighting factory, (2) the rehearsals with the musicians in a music school and (3) the recordings in the theater with all the participants and the filmmaker.

3 Documentary Film as an Artistic and Experimental Typology

3.1 Definition

Although, documentary film has never had a precise definition it coincides with the introduction of sound technology and as a different form of cinema like an ever-changing story that contributes to continuing discussion [11]. As John Grierson stated it is the "capacity for getting around in a new and vital form" [12] and there are at least the filmmaker's, the film's, and the audience's [11]. Documentary film offers the esthetic experience of sounds and images to stand for qualities and concepts of a more abstract nature. It is the connection between precise time and space and the articulation of these specific parts in a whole that is greater than the sum of the parts [11]. To reach the public, the documentary film refers to rhetoric and persuasion, a communication strategy that uses symbolic, emotional, and social consciousness resources to communicate a particular message about the world [11]. Additionally, the documentary film is classified in the three class divisions of rhetoric (see Table 1).

Moreover, the documentary film is as a process of cooperation, integration and articulation of the results described with metaphors that help us to comprehend the world in terms of our empirical encounter with the situation [11].

The documentary movement get started in 1920s with the implementation of poetic experimentation and the creative process between cinema and the various modernist avant-gardes of that reality, narrative storytelling, and rhetorical oratory [11]. A category emerged on the 1930s and writing by individuals which contributed towards social equality, highlighting working-class experience, autobiographies,

Table 1 The topics that documentary film is about. *Source* Adapted from Nichols, 2001

Topic	Content	Examples
Legislative or Deliberative	Deliberations are forward-looking and pose questions about **what should be done**	War, welfare, conservation, abortion, artificial reproduction, national identity, and international relations
Judicial or Historical	Public issues of morality and tradition, **value and belief are put to the test**	Holocaust, The Fall of the Romanov Dynasty, the history of the civil rights movement in the United States
Ceremonial or Panegyric	This is the domain of praising or blaming others. The orator draws on the past **to prove worthiness or unworthiness**	Worthy hunter and father, respectful description of the lives of individuals within a black and Latino urban gay subculture

collections of interviews material [13]. During the 1970s appeared a group connected with semiotic and aesthetic theories [13]. The superb age of documentary began in the 1980s. In Europe there have been significant transformations to documentary culture, while in the USA the limits have been the extension of outstanding qualities [14]. The independent documentary brought a new look to world events and narrated stories, with imagination, broadening horizons and awakening new possibilities [11]. The competence for a documentary film become popular is on the mixture of storytelling, directing ability and the presentation of an universal theme in the public. Today the dissemination of documentaries, also, happens through internet [11].

In fact, the production of a documentary film is still deliberated a border area and nominated as a marginalized zone [15]. So, this study can, also, become an opportunity to promote discussion and dialectic between the notions of truth and beauty, science and art, fiction and non-fiction, the business world, and the artistic world, teaching and profession.

3.2 Brief History of Documentary Film in the First Half of the Twentieth Century Age of Documentaries

In the western context, after the First World War, the United States of America (USA), Italy, Germany, France, and England invested heavily in the production and distribution of films that exalted national issues [16].

In 1922, the north American filmmaker Robert Flaherty directed and produced the first documentary 'Nanook of the North'. His work influenced Britain and European directors, such as, John Griersons (Scottish) or Manoel de Oliveira (Portuguese) [11].

In 1928, the International Institute of Educational Cinematograph (IECI) appeared in Rome. Under the aegis of Mussolini, it had famous names, as Louis Lumiere (French), Hans Cürlis (German), Carl Milliken (American), G.T. Hankin (British) influencing nations no fascists, like Britain. The IECI, also, included reformist women's factions and religious groups [17]. Between 1929 and 1934, the IECI supported a monthly multilingual cinema journal, expanded studies of the effects of films on children, empirical surveys of film and education, studies about connection between literateness and film comprehension, reports about Africa and colonial invasions [17]. In 1932 the first Venice Film Festival was created and in 1933, Rudolph Arnheim took up a position at the IECI. It is possible to highlight, for instance, the role of Laszlo Maholy-Nagy while he wrote articles on film painting. During the 1930s, Rudolph Arnheim edited an encyclopedia about cinema that ended up in the English edition in 1957 [17]. While Rudolf Arnheim saw the arrival of the sound as a threat, in Britain John Grierson defended the cinematic uses of sound in cinema [13]. There were other theorists, such as Béla Belâzs (Hungarian), Sergei Eisenstein (Soviet) and Vsevolod Pudovkin (Russian and Soviet) that sustained documentary beyond the photographic representation of external reality and investigate the formal properties of cinematography and editing [18].

Between 1927 and 1939 the documentary film movement was created in Britain by John Griersons, influenced by the IECI, producing propaganda for the war effort, making films for different institutions, and starting to service a campaign for political and cultural change [13]. This documentary film movement intended to be an independent entity and played a very important role in the role of educating the mass media, influencing contemporary television documentary production and educational institutions. [17].

In Portugal, the first documentary film was 'Nazaré, Praia de Pescadores' (1929), by Leitão de Barros. Other Portuguese directors who stand out in this period were João de Almeida e Sá and Manoel de Oliveira [19]. However, the production and realization of documentaries films were linked to economic and legal constraints, namely, with the change of financing policies. These new laws contributed, decisively, to an impoverishment of the documentary film in Portugal and the public began to see merely documents of Portuguese life. Only in 1948 the National Cinema Fund (FCN) allowed an improvement in the quality of the documentary [20]. And later, after 1974, a large production of documentaries appears on national television (RTP).

3.3 *Types of Documentary Film*

In the western context, documentary films were developed according to time, place causalities and circumstances. Bill Nichols states [11] there are six types of documentaries (see Table 2).

Considering the above, this study presents and develops a mixed expository and reflexive documentary film, entitled MUSAE. This artistic production registers the link between the music, performing and visual arts, the business circumstance and design field as an opportunity for all to renew themselves. This documentary film is hybrid. MUSAE is expository as it portrays an event, emphasizing facts and arguments for what the film is narrating. It is reflective because it is rhetorical and presents the idea of what the creative process between entities of different nature would be like if all the arguments and evidence presented in the documentary were taken as

Table 2 Types of documentary film. *Source* Adapted from Nichols, 2001

Topic	Content	Time
Poetic	Too Abstract. Lack of specificity. Alternative forms of knowledge. Shares a common territory with the modernism avant-garde	Since 1920s
Expository	Too Didactic. More rhetorical or argumentative frame than an aesthetic or poetic one	Since 1920s
Participatory	Being there. The filmmaker goes into the field and participates with the others and reflects on this experience. Excessive faith in witnesses	Since 1960s
Observational	Being here. The filmmaker observes what happens in front of the camera without overt intervention. Lack of history	Since 1960s
Reflexive	Too abstract. The focus is the processes of negotiation between filmmaker and the viewer	Since 1980s
Performative	The filmmaker raises questions about knowledge and meaning is a subjective phenomenon. Loss of emphasis on objectivity	Since 1980s

true and feasible. The documentary film MUSAE intends to register if the process of partnership between local organizations contributes to the effective improvement of the shows produced. On the other hand, it is expected to demonstrate that the entertainment industry can be transformed into an experimental laboratory for design education and for the business environment.

4 MUSAE, A Mixed Expository and Reflexive Documentary Film

This study refers to 17th sustainable development goal defined by the UNESCO 2030 as it revitalizes the global partnership for sustainable development. In addition, the research states to 4th sustainable development goal defined by the UNESCO 2030 as it proposes alternative models of teaching to provide quality education for all. The research developed a new perspective on the rapport between the academic world, the business world and the performing and visual arts. The introduction of new creative processes—involving design, teaching, industry, music, a municipality and theater—intended to improve the world of entertainment and the business universe, privileging the environment and society as a whole.

4.1 Concept and Interpretation

The study expresses to universal concept of MUSAE, the three sister divinities in Greek mythology and according to Greek traveler and geographer Pausanias (AD 143–176) heading over music, art, and science [21]. In Pausanias' description, the three deities were clearly perceived as forming a triad, communicating, and meaning the virtue of intelligence, the creative power, and beauty [22]. Pausanias emphasizes that the three goddesses—Aglaíā, Euphrosúnā Thalíā—were the first graces ever to be worshipped by humans and referring to the beauty and the pleasure that derive from social integration [23]. Aglaíā (Aglaea) symbolized the clarity and lighting, Euphrosúnā (Euphrosyne) personified the sense of joy and beauty of men and gods, and Thalíā (Thalia) represented nature, fertility, and bloom. The three goddesses were represented by artists over time as a fresco from Pompeii, in the T. Dentatus Phanthera house present in the Museo Archeologico Nazionale in Naples, in paintings by Sandro Botticelli (1445–1510), Giovanni Antonio Pellegrini (1675–1741), Peter Paul Rubens (1630–1635), William Etty (1787–1849) or Edward Burne-Jones (1833–1898) in sculptures like Antonio Canova (1757–1822) or in poetry like John Milton (1608–1674).

As a verb, MUSAE is, also, to think about something cautiously and thoroughly [24], something that requires continuous reflection. On the need to be cautious in our actions Bruno Latour stated that to design could mean equally any of those adverbs and as matters of concern [25]. Bruno Latour examines in detail the five advantages of the design concept: modesty, attention to detail, semiotic competence, a process in which designing is always redesigning, and the dimension ethics, to conclude that design today calls for prudence and significance [26].

These references support the objectives and relevance of this study as collaboration, integration and articulation with local organizations can be an opportunity to generate sustainability. Aglaia (Brightness), Euphrosyne (Joyfulness), and Thalia (Bloom) represented design research, a light company and music and performing arts domains. This interpretation allows us to think of design as a wise and responsible action like a muse that draw and develop things and, calculating the impact of the product lifecycle, safeguarding all living beings and the environment [27].

4.2 *Aims*

The study intends to prove that the stage can become a place of testing solutions, sharing knowledge, cooperating, integrating and articulating all factors that may enter in the creative process. Factors, such as, cultural aspects, social and political factors, and validating a creative process, through an experimental and diffused action between different fields. Plus, to contribute so that cooperation between different areas of knowledge helps to reflect and test new ways of using and enjoying innovative products in the field of lighting. Finally, to legitimize the action of design in the construction of systemic solutions for the entertainment sector and for the business environment.

4.3 The Documentary Film Process

The documentary metaphorizes the three muses of Pausanias, namely, the scope of design—includes researchers and designers—the business sector—includes a lighting company—and music, performance, and visual arts entities—includes musicians and lighting, image and sound technicians, and a filmmaker. The process consisted on an open briefing for all participants. To trigger creativity, the documentary film includes all the actors that define the reality that is being experienced, so that the creative process is an opportunity for everyone to transform themselves.

The production of the MUSAE documentary includes recording interviews and manufacturing processes, recording artistic performances (multi-camera video recording, audio recording, mixing and mastering), video editing of the documentary and documentary photographic recording of the entire process. The director of the documentary film, Flávio Cruz, began by witnessing the designers' ideation process, namely, in recording the choice of a universal theme understandable by everyone, including the public.

This part was characterized by the analysis of six musical pieces created by six different composers. The works were chosen with the music professors, who presented a musical program with four pieces for a wind quintet and two pieces for a string quartet. The six pieces were analyzed by the designers, who selected four composers based on the connection that the pieces could have with the muse theme. The three musical pieces chosen for the wind quintet were: 'Early Hungarian dances from the seventeenth century' (1959) by Ferenc Farkas; 'A-flat Op. 14' (1903) by Gustav Holst and 'Rêverie' (1890) by Claude Debussy. In the string group it was chosen the piece 'F major, Op. 96, the American Quartet' (1893) by Antonín Dvořák. As we were in 2020, the pandemic prevented face-to-face meetings and the ideation phase of lighting objects was filmed, individually, by each designer in their homes and not by the director who later included the videos in the documentary (Fig. 1).

In a second part, with the lack of definition, the filming took place in a contemporary way, but in two different spaces. On the one hand, in the lighting company with the presence of the director and two of the designers, documenting and substantiating the production process of the prototypes of two of the lamps. This phase had the testimony of different professionals from the company, from the CEO to the worker who cuts the brass tubes. On the other hand, at the music school and with the presence of the designers, the rehearsals that music students had with their teachers were validating. This phase included statements by music teachers not only about the importance of the project as a total work, but also about the possibility for music students to complete their portfolio with a recording. This phase included statements by music teachers not only about the importance of the project as a total work, but also about the possibility for music students to complete their portfolio with a recording.

The third part consisted on the footage from the show, with all the performers. Due to lack of funding, the show was supported by the participants During the

Fig. 1 Photographic record of the recording of interviews and artistic performances (*Source* the authors)

investigation, a teaser [28] and, a pilot installation [29] of a show recorded and filmed by director Flávio Cruz.

The production took place at the Sá de Miranda theater in Viana do Castelo on July 22, 2021. After considering two different situations—a live show with an audience and a show recorded and filmed without an audience—the circumstances of the pandemic period were evaluated and the option was chosen, i.e., filmed without audience. The project was disseminated on social media and featured in the digital press and on national television.

The fourth phase of the documentary film began in February 2023, once the project had secured funding. Between February and May, the testimonies of different stakeholders were gathered, in a fieldwork carried out between the cities of Viana do Castelo, Vila Nova de Famalicão and Lisbon (Portugal). The MUSAE project ends with a video made in collaboration with a video maker, a sound engineer and a first violin of the 'Casa da Música do Porto' Evandra Gonçalves, to join together in the lighting company's setting, where the project was born and developed. At the moment, the documentary film process is in the video editing phase.

5 Results

For the Academic world, this paper was an opportunity to design involving professors and researchers in R&D projects. The academy may take advantages from the experiences carried out with case studies to use it in future educational plans as a diffused learning and, for this reason, transdisciplinary. Methodologically, the paper was based on an open briefing and in constant change, developed in cooperation, articulation and integration. The working approach was based on cooperation, creativity, resilience and survival as a responsible and sustainable process of productive and cultural development of society. The school can benefit from this methodological action, constructing potential teaching models.

For Society, the theatre stage became an experimental laboratory able to translate creativity as a consequence of the synergy between different players, driving it to expose on the current reality, and assuming the impacts of the pandemic as events that fit to the process. For instance, the Internet wired the dissemination of knowledge in cooperation with design methodologies. This was also an opportunity to create moments of debate, rhetoric and critical analysis.

As a result, this project was an opportunity to design creative and sustainable strategies from the stage. At a historic moment when companies have difficulties in promoting their creations, the implementation of the project has made it possible to rethink new promotion and dissemination strategies.

For the lighting industry this was an event to test new methodologies, developing new partners, technologies, new materials, and to estimate the product's impact on the market.

On behalf of the music area and the visual and performing arts sector, this was a chance to review their programs, in order to solve issues of funding and non-attendance of public.

6 Conclusions

The production of a documentary film to report a creative process is a fundamental tool to offer an exhaustive overview of procedures and methods. On the other hand, a documentary film is an opportunity to identify useful strategies for future professionals and researchers. In particular, in a project marked by the presence of an anomalous situation such as the pandemic, it becomes important and courageous to share these experiences for the benefit of other projects or other activities that involve different areas of culture.

The pandemic situation provided the possibility of disclosing part of the process on social media, following a current trend of expose and making available the result of the process. This choice allows the use of current media to disseminate culture abroad as a right for all. The diffusion of the experience, through a documentary film that is liberated on social networks, is also an important contribution, in the sense that it increases the critical dimension and transforms the research process into something more comprehensive for the public. This is an occasion not only to raise public awareness, but also to bring together different opinions in a broad and inclusive light on the project.

Finally, it seems possible to consider that the documentary film is an important tool for design process, considering that it interacts with the available media channels, informs and instructs. Something that serves as an intuition to have the courage to act based on the human being and on the choice for the unknown, something creative, unique, unexpected and that adds value. In the case of a complex and articulated project like MUSAE, the choice of documentary film happens as an ideal narrative structure to announce a project that celebrates diversities as characteristics that portray the multi-directional culture of our time.

References

1. https://www.merriam-webster.com/dictionary/creative. Last accessed 20 June 2023
2. Nietzsche F (2009) O Anticristo. Edições 70, Lisboa.
3. Deleuze G (2006) Nietzsche and philosophy. Columbia University Press, New York
4. Crilly N (2015) Fixation and creativity in concept development: The attitudes and practices of expert designers. Des Stud 38:54–91
5. Berger A (2021) The creative process: An ethnographic analysis. Cambridge Scholars Publisher, Cambridge
6. Fontana A (2012) Manuale di Storytelling. Rizzoli ETAS, Parma
7. Simay P (2005) Tradition as injunction: Benjamin and the critique of historicism. In: Andrew B (ed) Walter Benjamin and history. The tower building, London, pp 137–155
8. LNCS Homepage. https://www.un.org. Last accessed 20 June 2023
9. Latour B (1993) We have never been modern. Harvard University Press, Harvard
10. Cross N (2006) Designerly ways of knowing. Springer-Verlag AG, London
11. Nichols B (2001) Introduction to documentary. Indiana University Press, Bloomington
12. Grierson J (1946) First principles of documentary. Grierson on Documentary, London
13. Aitken I (2013) Film and reform: John Grierson and the documentary film movement. Routledge, London
14. Rosenthal A, Corner J (2005) New challenges for documentary. Manchester University Press, Manchester
15. Renov M (2012) Theorizing documentary. Routledge, London
16. Trevisan AR (2022) Cinema, educação e democracia em John Grierson: uma análise sociológica do filme Drifters (1929). Sociologia & Antropologia 12(3):1–21
17. Druick Z (2007) The international educational cinematograph institute, reactionary modernism, and the formation of film studies. Canadian Journal of Film Studies 16(1):80–97
18. Chapman J (2015) A new history of British documentary. Palgrave Macmillan, London
19. Pina L (1977) Documentarismo português. Instituto Português de Cinema, Lisboa
20. Penafria M (2013) Problemáticas do cinema português: os documentários dos realizadores de ficção. In Baptista T, Martins A (eds) Atas do II Encontro Anual da AIM. AIM, Lisboa, pp 450–463

21. Frazer J (2012) Pausanias's description of Greece. V.5: Cambridge University Press, Cambridge.
22. Champion-Smith V (1998) Pausanias in athens: An archaeological commentary on the agora of athens. University College London, London
23. Nagy G (2021) Pausanias tries to visualize the three 'Graces' of Orkhomenos in Boeotia. Classical Inquiries, Harvard
24. https://www.merriam-webster.com/dictionary/muse. Last accessed 20 June 2023
25. Latour B (2008) A cautious prometheus? A few steps toward a philosophy of design (with special attention to Peter Sloterdijk). In Hackne F, Glynne J, Minto V (eds) Proceedings of the 2008 annual international conference of the design history society—Falmouth. e-books, Universal Publishers, pp 2–10
26. Soares L (2012) O designer como intérprete de cenários de equipamentos. UA Editora, Aveiro
27. Soares L, Aparo E, Almendra r, Da Silva FM (2023) Design for systemic lighting products. In Raposo D, Neves J, Silva R, Correia Castilho L, Dias R (eds) Advances in design, music and arts II. EIMAD 2022. Springer Series in Design and Innovation, vol 25. Springer, Cham, pp 490–501
28. URL: https://www.youtube.com/watch?v=A7Y1DDPEmTI
29. URL: https://www.youtube.com/watch?v=dpPVRPvPToI&t=1s

www.ingramcontent.com/pod-product-compliance
Ingram Content Group UK Ltd.
Pitfield, Milton Keynes, MK11 3LW, UK
UKHW022215051026
15624UKWH00001B/175
9783031435157